UNITED TASTES

UNITED TASTES

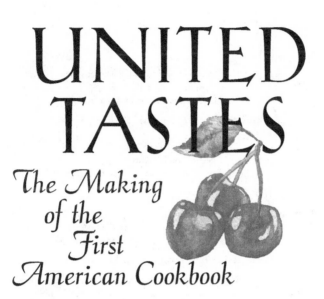

The Making of the First American Cookbook

KEITH STAVELY

AND

KATHLEEN FITZGERALD

UNIVERSITY OF MASSACHUSETTS PRESS

Amherst and Boston

ISBN 978-1-62534-322-2 (paper) 321-5 (hardcover)

Designed by Sally Nichols
Set in Goudy Oldstyle
Printed and bound by Maple Press, Inc.

Cover design by Sally Nichols
Cover art: (Foreground) *Hand Painted Cherries* by Yunaco/Shutterstock.
(Background) title page and "Bread Pudding" recipe in *American Cookery*, Albany edition, 1796.
Courtesy, American Antiquarian Society.

Library of Congress Cataloging-in-Publication Data

Names: Stavely, Keith W. F., 1942– author. | Fitzgerald, Kathleen, 1952– author.
Title: United tastes : the making of the first American cookbook / Keith Stavely and
Kathleen Fitzgerald.
Description: Amherst : University of Massachusetts Press, [2017] | Includes
bibliographical references and index.
Identifiers: LCCN 2017020928| ISBN 9781625343222 (pbk.) | ISBN 9781625343215
(hardcover)
Subjects: LCSH: Cookbooks–United States–History–18th century. |
Cooking–United States–History–18th century–Sources. | Cooking,
American–Early works to 1800. | Simmons, Amelia. American cookery. |
United States–Social life and customs.
Classification: LCC TX703.S53 S73 2017 | DDC 641.50973–dc23
LC record available at https://lccn.loc.gov/2017020928

British Library Cataloguing-in-Publication Data
A catalog record for this book is available from the British Library.

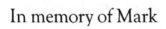
In memory of Mark

CONTENTS

PREFACE

O ur recent book, *Northern Hospitality*, an anthology of historic New England recipes, includes a generous selection of recipes from a 1796 cookbook entitled *American Cookery*. As *Northern Hospitality* neared publication, we decided to promote it with a presentation featuring descriptions of how we had cooked several of the dishes it contained. We soon found that we were choosing to cook a disproportionate number of dishes from *American Cookery*. Here was something worth pondering, we thought. *American Cookery*, even though extremely short, is a source of excellent food, at once acceptable to our present-day palates and yet different from a great deal of what we're used to.

To our historical sensibilities, this looked like a perfect "recipe" for a subject worth exploring. Like many historians, perhaps, we are drawn to material that is distant and alien from the present yet not so distant and alien as to seem inaccessible. The topic was only made more alluring by the riddle of *American Cookery*'s authorship. According to its title page, it was written by "an American Orphan." This was a familiar enough trope in American culture to be sure, but it wasn't usually thought of as having made an appearance this early in American history. Nor had it commonly taken female form. Plus this particular American orphan, one Amelia Simmons, left no other traces of herself in the record. Who was she? These were tantalizing mysteries indeed. This was more than enough to lure us into taking the plunge. The result, five years later, is this book.

We are once again indebted to New England's diverse array of public, academic, and historical society libraries: in Rhode Island, the Ocean State Libraries Network, Robert L. Carothers Library of the University of Rhode Island Libraries, and the Rhode Island Historical Society; in Massachusetts, the Minuteman Library Network, Boston Public Library, Needham Public Library's Interlibrary Loan Department, Schlesinger Library, Radcliffe Institute, Harvard University, Houghton Library, Harvard University, and the American Antiquarian Society; in Connecticut, the Connecticut Historical Society; and in Vermont, the Bailey/Howe Library of the University of Vermont Libraries. We thank the Connecticut Historical Society for permission to quote from three manuscript cookbooks in its collection: two anonymous works dating from 1789 and 1813–21 respectively, and one kept by Zeloda Barrett, probably in the 1820s. We also thank Houghton Library, Harvard University, for permission to quote from the Ruth Haskins Emerson manuscript cookbook in its collection.

We're also grateful for the ongoing support and encouragement for our work from members of the Culinary Historians of Boston, especially Joseph Carlin, Jeri Quinzio, Barbara Wheaton, James O'Connell, Marylène Altieri, and Agni Thurner. Others whose kind words have assisted us in persevering include Blake Perkins of the online magazine *British Food in America*, and the appreciative auditors of our presentations at a great many libraries and historical organizations around New England.

This project has benefited immensely from the interventions of Andrew F. Smith and Robert S. Cox, who scrutinized the manuscript with great care for the University of Massachusetts Press and offered comments that were unfailingly constructive. Nor would it exist in its present form without the patient ministrations of our editor, Matt Becker, which included steering us toward cartographer extraordinaire Kate Blackmer. Once again we are grateful for the expert assistance of the entire staff of the press, especially managing editor Carol Betsch and designer Sally Nichols. Our thanks also to copy editor Margaret A. Hogan for her thoughtful engagement with our prose. We of course retain sole responsibility for any shortcomings that remain.

Members of our family—Maryanne Fitzgerald, Elliot Berusch, Tony Stavely, Mary Mayshark-Stavely, Jary Stavely, and Patricia Marien—have paid good-humored heed to our long-winded disquisitions on work in progress, as have our friends Susan Smolinsky, Kathy Caple, Sandy Mack, and Elaine Mack. The last named also generously proofread the manuscript before it was submitted for publication. Special thanks to our son, Jonathan, a kindred spirit in seeking after historical enlightenment. And, somewhere, the person to whom this book is dedicated, our late brother, Mark Fitzgerald, is smiling and raising an eyebrow at the whole spectacle.

A brief word about money. At various points, we have occasion to consider the price of *American Cookery*, at others the levels of income or wealth of individuals or groups under discussion. In an effort to make these portions of our argument more comprehensible to readers, we have converted the figures found in the late eighteenth- and early nineteenth-century sources into twenty-first-century terms. Our calculations are based on John J. McCusker, *How Much Is That in Real Money?* 49–60 (table A-1, column 6), 84 (fig. C-2), and the more recent information in Lawrence H. Officer and Samuel H. Williamson, "Annual Consumer Price Index."

UNITED TASTES

AMERICAN COOKERY,

OR THE ART OF DRESSING

VIANDS, FISH, POULTRY and VEGETABLES,

AND THE BEST MODES OF MAKING

PASTES, PUFFS, PIES, TARTS, PUDDINGS, CUSTARDS AND PRESERVES,

AND ALL KINDS OF

CAKES,

FROM THE IMPERIAL PLUMB TO PLAIN CAKE.

ADAPTED TO THIS COUNTRY,

AND ALL GRADES OF LIFE.

By Amelia Simmons,

AN AMERICAN ORPHAN.

PUBLISHED ACCORDING TO ACT OF CONGRESS.

HARTFORD:

PRINTED BY HUDSON & GOODWIN.

FOR THE AUTHOR.

1796.

Title page from *American Cookery,* Hartford edition, 1796.

Introduction

American Cookery lends itself to being read through a romantic lens. When the book first appeared in print it was a clear underdog, small in dimensions and cheap in price, a minor contender in the marketplace, struggling among an array of far more elaborate and expensive British cooking manuals. It was written by an obscure, first-time American author, a woman, and if her title-page proclamation is to be believed, an orphan. Here are many of the elements of a sensational story. The book and the circumstances of its creation fit the image of the upstart embarking on an unlikely quest for fame and fortune. Powerhouses of British publishing and cookery were being put on notice—American publishers and American authors were now on the scene.

Some aspect of this recounting turns up in almost all modern popular references to American Cookery. The cookbook has gained public exposure over the last few decades, becoming an emblem of historic American cuisine for journalists, food bloggers, and cookbook writers. Its prominence can be attributed to its designation as "the first cookbook of American authorship to be printed in the United States." On this basis, the Library of Congress lists it among eighty-eight "Books That Shaped America." But its broad appeal derives from something more visceral—its seeming close fit with one of our most cherished national myths. Over 200 years after American Cookery's first publication in 1796, and almost 250 years after we declared our independence from Britain, we Americans still like to see ourselves as parvenus. We love to repeat tales about how, despite the odds, we bested the best. American Cookery is thought to fit the narrative perfectly. This little book has also begun to attract attention in the scholarly world. Historians cite it when discussing an array of topics in early national history, including political attitudes, regional differences, anti-British sentiment, and gender. American Cookery, slight though it is, lends itself to a multitude of purposes.[1]

Few would disagree that present-day efforts to resurrect our first national cooking treatise and celebrate its low-status female author are well spent. But should we characterize the book in what amounts to stereotypical

1

ways before we have properly understood it? And should we create such conveniently modern myths about it and its author based on partial understanding? For many decades of the nineteenth and early twentieth centuries, American Cookery suffered from neglect—it was consigned to the shelf, considered antiquated and certainly never read as a historic resource. Now it seems threatened from the opposite direction, a newfound enthusiasm for it turning it into the modern equivalent of what Nathaniel Philbrick has called, speaking of the myth-making surrounding the Pilgrims and their Thanksgiving, "nostalgic and reassuring legends." But surely American Cookery will no more benefit from a descent into caricature than have the Pilgrims and an idealized feast they never ate.[2]

For one thing, flattening the work to fit a comfortable but ungrounded narrative of American aspiration and success obscures its more complex features. Its irregularities, as compared to more staid British cookbooks, and its author's rough edges, revealed in the prefaces and errata page in her two editions, are the very things that make the entire enterprise worth a second look. Remove those quirky features and we are left with a cookery knockoff derived from well-known British sources. With them, we have a window into a society struggling to become "American" twenty years after the first exchange of bullets at Lexington and Concord began the process.

Perhaps the most egregious fault to which modern writers have fallen prey in considering American Cookery is a failure to apply rigorous historical standards in reading the work. The book's relationship to its time and place, and questions concerning what can be known or fairly deduced about its author, are too often neglected in favor of broad statements about patriotism and other American themes. To rescue American Cookery for our time, we must understand, or attempt to understand, its meaning in its own time. By contextualizing the work in culinary, publishing, social, and geographic terms; by providing a deep analysis of its parts, both its recipes and front- and backmatter; and by exploring the modes of authorship that had at the time of its publication begun to develop for American writers and publishers, we have aimed to construct a new, more nuanced and historically grounded narrative in support of a small but important work from the first American era.

Readers who follow the path we have set out will perhaps be struck, as we were when we first undertook our researches, by the range of topics necessary to consider in order to put into perspective a work of forty-seven pages in its first edition and sixty-four in its second. Yet without some familiarity with the origins of the English cuisine upon which American cuisine was largely based, and without an equivalent understanding of the types of cooking manuals available to eighteenth-century consumers, the aesthetic and gastronomic choices that underlay the recipes included in *American Cookery* are apt to go unnoticed. Likewise, to discern how conditions influenced the cuisine found in the book, we must become acquainted with the social trends, especially the rise of refinement, that most influenced Federalist Connecticut and its hinterlands; we must dissect the dynamics of the region's social structure. And we must become acquainted with the interplay that occurred at the end of the eighteenth century between agricultural interests and those allied with the market revolution.

The question of the identity of Amelia Simmons, the author of *American Cookery*, was among the most vexing but also the most intriguing we encountered in studying the first American cookbook. We hope the aspects of the discussion devoted to her convey some of the excitement we felt as we attempted to unravel the perplexities of her identity and social status in the early republic. In discussing what we can and cannot know about her, it is, again, the connection the text gives us to issues of the day that opens up the most fruitful lines of inquiry. For instance, placing Simmons's identification of herself as an orphan and her remarks about female virtue and self-determination in the context of popular novels of the period featuring female orphans allows us to align her with what the literary critic Cheryl L. Nixon calls "the emerging discourse of individualism."[3]

However, the eighteenth century offers a far different orphan trope as well, one that we also bring to bear on Simmons's orphan status. In the second decade of the century, an unknown printer's apprentice named Benjamin Franklin came to the aid of his brother's faltering printing enterprise by creating a lucrative publishing controversy in letters written under the pseudonym Silence Dogood, identified as an orphaned apprentice with "no Relation on Earth within my knowledge."[4]

Who, then, is Amelia Simmons—an exemplar of the emerging self-determination of women or an imaginary construct devised by publishers? Or some amalgamation of the two? Or perhaps she is Amelia Simons, a young Connecticut woman who may have been known to *American Cookery*'s publishers? There is not enough evidence to answer such questions definitively. But we can get to know the elusive Amelia Simmons better by getting to know the eighteenth-century company she keeps in fellow cookbook authors, literary devices, and actual persons.

Up and down the Connecticut and Hudson River Valleys, and as far west as the new settlements in Ohio, *American Cookery* made its way between 1796 and 1831. In small towns and newly settled farming regions, the presence of this inexpensive collection of moderately refined, mainly British recipes, interspersed with a few American favorites, heralded the establishment of a Connecticut-inspired social structure. It was this social structure that the book was published to promote, the one deemed by those who composed and published it to be the most fitting model for an emerging national identity. For those behind the project, the ideal for the new nation's social identity—what it meant to be American—resided in the golden mean between rustic and ritzy. Americans, they hoped, would embrace a rational and moderate gentility, be modestly convivial and polite in discourse, manners, and modes of living. The ethos of refinement, when it was restrained and modulated far more than it was in England and on the European continent, could thus be enjoyed by a majority of American citizens. And wasn't that, after all, the point of establishing a new republican political order?

But *American Cookery*, for all that, remained a provincial product. It began life, we contend, as a Connecticut Federalist enterprise. A nationwide transportation system and an equally extensive network of printers necessary for nationwide publishing did not yet exist. So the first American cookbook was American in name only. But the choice of the title, even if only aspirational, introduced the possibility of a national cuisine. It is the story of that cookbook and the cuisine it presented, along with the story of its creator, its publishers, and its social setting, that we invite you to pursue with us.[5]

PART I
Cooks and Books

American Cookery in its first and second editions, both brought out in 1796, begins with a recipe for roast beef and proceeds to offer up roast mutton, veal, and lamb. For at least a century before this, roast beef had been celebrated as the English national dish, not only by cookbook authors but also by such cultural luminaries as Joseph Addison, Henry Fielding, and William Hogarth. The art of roasting had been perfected in early modern England and had come to symbolize Englishness. In 1617, the traveler Fynes Moryson testified that "the English Cookes, in comparison with other Nations are most commended for roasted meates." So commencing a volume on American cookery with English roasting instructions and English preferences in meat amounts to an emphatic proclamation of continuity with the cookery of the mother country.[1]

This sense of an ongoing adherence to English national preferences and methods persists throughout the cookbook. The most prominent categories of recipe other than meat and poultry are pies and tarts, puddings, and cakes. These were all dishes to which "the English Cookes" had also devoted themselves and in the execution of which they were thought to have excelled. According to culinary historian Gilly Lehmann, "By the middle of the seventeenth century pies had become a peculiarly English specialty; even the French were prepared to concede superiority." As for puddings, one particular seventeenth-century Frenchman, Henri Misson, conceded superiority to the English here as well: "BLESSED BE HE THAT INVENTED PUDDING, for it is a manna that hits the palates of all sorts of people; . . . Ah, what an excellent thing is an English pudding!"[2]

There are more cakes in American Cookery than any other type of food. The English fondness for cake, reflected in a proliferation of varieties in eighteenth-century English cookbooks, had behind it the long and ultimately successful struggle that took place in a cold and stony northern land to grow enough wheat to satisfy the longings of its people for this most esteemed of all European grains.[3]

Roast meats, pies, puddings, and cakes. Clearly the single most important influence on the culinary content of the first American cookbook was the English cooking tradition. In our initial survey of *American Cookery* in chapter 1, we therefore stress the derivative nature of the majority of the book's recipes. In this respect the work was entirely typical of its time and place. American culture as a whole remained as yet a minor offshoot of English culture. The principal materials available for the construction of an American "national imaginary" were English.[4]

But what specifically were the tools provided to a fledgling American cuisine by the English culinary tradition? In our first detailed contextual reconstruction in chapter 2, we explore this question and identify what, in the final quarter of the eighteenth century, this tradition stood ready to bequeath to its transatlantic offspring.

There is more to *American Cookery* than its strictly culinary content. In *Empire of Liberty*, Gordon S. Wood states that "printed matter, with its republican capacity to reach the greatest numbers of people, . . . came to be valued" in the early republic above all other forms of communication. Intensity of demand for print, particularly in New England with its Puritan-inspired tradition of reverence for the Bible and associated works, called forth unprecedented levels of supply. Cookbooks such as *American Cookery* were a small part, but a part nonetheless, of the flood of such material circulating in the country's first decades. "Three-quarters of all the books and pamphlets published in America between 1637 and 1800," writes Wood, "appeared in the last thirty-five years of the eighteenth century."[5]

In our world of instant access to print and readerly jadedness, it is difficult to imagine the depth of engagement on the part of the early national reading public and the difficulties that public faced in fulfilling its desire for information and instruction. In chapter 3, we address the complex nature of the print and publication system that predated independence and the ways in which that system expanded in the early decades of the new nation, even as the physical conditions for the dissemination of print continued to hinder growth.

Along with these conditions, there are additional features of eighteenth-century print culture that distinguish it from our own. We show in chapter 1 that the ties between *American Cookery* and English culinary tradition are so close that quite a few of the recipes were copied verbatim from English cookbooks. But Amelia Simmons was far from the only author of the day who took material from other authors. Indeed, plagiarists were relatively unabashed, even about extensive "borrowings." This suggests that the model of the individual writer producing an "original" work was not yet fully established. In the eighteenth century, the need for acknowledgment of individual ownership was more often than not outweighed by acquiescence in the acknowledgment of discursive material as community property.

Such perspectives found answering views and inclinations among printers and publishers. Rather than regarding the enterprise as an individual venture competing with others of the same sort, a typical eighteenth-century printer thought of him- or herself as engaged cooperatively with other printers in mobilizing scarce printing and publishing resources in order to supply a massive demand that would otherwise have become overwhelming.

As we see in chapter 3, the flexible forms of resource-sharing and cooperation developed during the colonial period were not discarded after political independence but rather were adapted and altered to meet abruptly increasing levels of public demand for material that only printers could supply. A grasp of the intricate and intriguing publication history of *American Cookery* is impossible without an understanding of these configurations and dynamics.

CHAPTER 1

Adapted to This Country

On Monday, May 9, 1796, a notice from the Federal Court for the "District of Connecticut" appeared on page 3 of the *Connecticut Courant*, Hartford's leading newspaper. (Founded in 1764, the *Courant* is still going strong—its masthead today boasts of its status as "America's Oldest Continuously Published Newspaper.") "BE IT REMEMBERED," the notice began, "that on the twenty eighth day of April, in the twentieth year of the Independence of the United States of America, Amelia Simmons of the said district hath deposited the title of a book the right whereof she claims as Author."

The notice went on to include the lengthy full title of the book, along with the author's title-page self-identification:

American Cookery, or the art of dressing Viands, Fish, Poultry and Vegetables, and the best modes of making Pastes, Puffs, Pies, Tarts, Puddings, Custards and Preserves, and all kinds of Cakes, from the imperial plumb, to plain Cake: adapted to this country, and all grades of life. By Amelia Simmons, an American Orphan.

After a formal statement that it had been issued "in conformity to" the federal copyright law that had been enacted just a few years before in 1790, the notice concluded with the imprimatur of "SIMEON BALDWIN, Clerk of the District of Connecticut." As required by the Copyright Act, the notice was printed in the *Courant* for the next three weeks in succession.[1]

The choice of the *Courant* for the appearance of this notice was no accident. The law required only that formal copyright notice "be published in one or more of the newspapers printed in the United States." But as was true of almost all New England newspapers in the eighteenth century, the owners and printers of the *Courant*, Barzillai Hudson and George Goodwin, also printed books, and *American Cookery* was being printed by them "For the Author" under their firm name of Hudson & Goodwin. It was to be an unassuming paperbound volume of only forty-seven pages.[2]

That the author for whom the work was being printed, Amelia Simmons, was a resident of "said district" of Connecticut was also in keeping with the way the world of printing and publishing remained set up at the end of the eighteenth century. Historian of print James N. Green notes that printers in most places besides Boston, New York, or Philadelphia, when they brought out anything other than "the old colonial staples of newspapers, almanacs, government printing, and pamphlets relating to current events," tended to issue locally written works.[3]

By June 8 if not before, *American Cookery* was available for sale, for on that date an advertisement appeared in the *Connecticut Journal* in New Haven that the book was "just published and to be sold by Isaac Beers, Price 2/3." The ad also ran for the following two weeks. Then for three weeks in late July and early August, "S. Green" offered *American Cookery* for sale to read-ers of New London's *Connecticut Gazette* at the lower price of one shilling, six pence. Immediately thereafter, the *Middlesex Gazette* of Middletown, Connecticut, had it "For Sale at this Office." Additional advertisements appeared in late August in both the Bennington *Vermont Gazette* ("Just Pub-lished, and for sale at the Printing Office, Price 2s") and the *Albany Gazette* ("This Day Received at Webster's Bookstore . . . Price 2s 8d."). In today's money, the prices range from about $4.50–7.00.[4]

So this little cookbook by "an American Orphan" was being distributed right away to the south, east, north, and west of its place of publication—in other words, in an area corresponding roughly to that in which the *Courant* itself had circulated for three decades. In most of these instances, the owner of the newspaper printing the advertisement was also the owner of the premises where the book was for sale. This again was the standard arrangement in New England in the eighteenth century and well into the nineteenth—that in any given town or district, the printing of newspapers, books, and pamphlets, and the vending of these various types of printed matter, were carried on by a single concern. Curiously, even though Hudson & Goodwin was, in accordance with this model, a bookseller as well as a newspaper printer and book publisher, it did not advertise *American Cookery* in the *Courant*.[5]

Toward the end of the year, the *Albany Gazette* again announced that *American Cookery* was to be had "at Webster's Bookstore." That would be the store owned by Charles R. and George Webster, also the proprietors of the *Gazette*. This ad differed from the ones the *Gazette* had run back in August, however, for it deployed the pointing hand icon so often found in

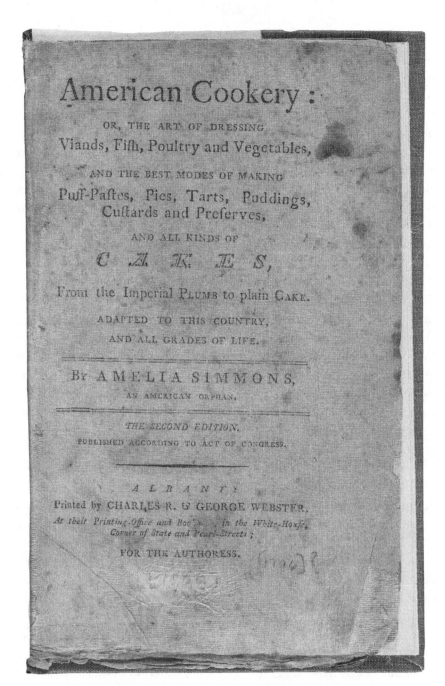

FIGURE 1.1. Title page from *American Cookery*, Albany edition, 1796.

newspapers of the day to alert readers that "This Edition has been considerably enlarged and carefully corrected. Price 3s." The higher price was perhaps justified by an enlargement from the forty-seven pages of the first edition to the sixty-four pages of this new one. The printer of this second edition of *American Cookery* was no longer Hudson & Goodwin of Hartford but rather its Albany purveyors, Charles R. & George Webster.[6]

Advertisements for this new edition were forthcoming the following winter and spring—just down the river in Hudson, New York; in Newark, New Jersey; and in New York City. The most expansive spread was placed in *Greenleaf's New York Journal and Patriotic Register* on May 3, 1797: "This Day is Published, And for sale at Greenleaf's Book-store, No. 54, Wall-street, and several other stores in this city, The Second Edition" of *American Cookery*. A pointing hand drew the eyes of readers to the price, "1/6," and to a claim that the book "has been highly recommended, and we shall only remark, that the knowledge of HOUSEWIFERY and COOKERY is absolutely necessary to EVERY FEMALE. The foreign essays on Cookery come high charged; this is compressed into a small compass, and is cheap." Later in the year, an ad in another New York paper referred to the author as "Miss Simmons" and listed, in the dollars and cents currency that had been established in 1786 and reaffirmed in 1792 but was not yet everywhere in use, a price of eighteen cents. Both of the New York City prices for *American Cookery*'s second edition would translate in today's money to about $3.50.[7]

Simmons stated in the preface to this second, or Albany, edition that she had been placed "under a necessity of publishing" it by the "rapid" sale of the first, or Hartford, edition, and indeed this claim is given credence by the subsequent publishing history of the work. The Hartford edition was reprinted twice, in Northampton, Massachusetts, in 1798, and in Troy, New York, in 1808. The Albany edition was reissued in Salem, New York (1804); in an unknown location (1808); then in Walpole, New Hampshire (1812); Brattleboro, Vermont (1814, 1819); Poughkeepsie, New York (1815); Windsor, Vermont (1816); Zanesville, Ohio (1816); New York City (1822); and Woodstock, Vermont (1831).[8]

In addition to being frequently reprinted, *American Cookery* was paid the tribute of extensive and repeated plagiarism—by "An American Lady" in *New American Cookery* (New York, 1805), by Lucy Emerson in *The New-England Cookery* (Montpelier, Vt., 1808), by Harriet Whiting in *Domestic Cookery* (Boston, 1819), and by the author of *The Cook Not Mad* (Watertown, N.Y., 1831). The book's impact was further registered in the fact that American

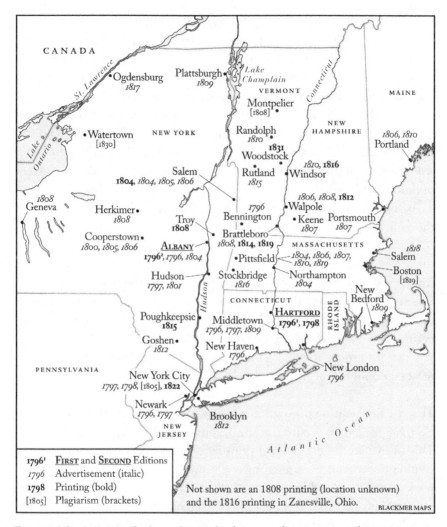

FIGURE 1.2. *American Cookery*: Original editions, advertisements, later printings, and plagiarisms, 1796–1831.

—Drawn by Kate Blackmer, Blackmer Maps

editions of English cookbooks that were brought out in the first two decades of the nineteenth century featured sections "Containing Several New Receipts Adapted to the American Mode of Cooking."[9]

So for more than three decades, this "first American cookbook," as the culinary historian Mary Tolford Wilson dubbed *American Cookery*, held sway in the northeastern portion of the young republic. These later reprints were advertised for sale throughout New England and upstate New York.[10]

An 1807 advertisement in the *New Hampshire Gazette* of Portsmouth tells us something about the basis of *American Cookery*'s appeal. This ad featured several other cookbooks as well and gave prices. The most expensive of the books, at about $27.50 in today's money, was *The English Art of Cookery* by Richard Briggs. Hannah Glasse's *The Art of Cookery Made Plain and Easy* (probably the 1805 American edition) was offered for about three-fourths the price of the Briggs volume. Susannah Carter's *The Frugal Housewife* (probably the 1803 American edition) could be had "bound" for just over half the price of the Briggs. A "half bound" copy was just under 50 percent of the cost of Briggs.[11]

As for *American Cookery*, it was, in accordance with the claim made in the earlier *Greenleaf's* advertisement, far and away the cheapest of these four cookbooks. *American Cookery* was selling for five dollars, less than one-fifth the price of the most expensive book, the Briggs *English Art of Cookery*, and still far less compared to the next cheapest option, the half-bound Carter. The very need to make the Carter title available in a less expensive version (unbound, as it were, from full refinement) underscores the uniqueness of—perhaps the uniquely American nature of—*American Cookery*. It and it alone was sent into the marketplace fully adapted not only "to this country" but most especially to "all grades of life."[12]

That the final edition of *American Cookery* and the final pirating of it, in *The Cook Not Mad*, both occurred at the beginning of the 1830s was no accident. This was when the era of local printing of the works of local authors was coming to an end. Emerging in its place was the era of consolidation of book printing and publishing, in which the trade was dominated by metropolitan firms such as Carey, Lea of Philadelphia and Harper & Brothers of New York. Books started circulating more widely, and their authors, backed by the ampler resources of these larger publishing enterprises, started to become more widely known. Many of the authors of the cookbooks published in the 1820s and 1830s were, like Lydia Maria Child and Sarah Josepha Hale, already celebrated by virtue of previous writings on other subjects. Others, such as Eliza Leslie, were made famous by their cookbooks.[13]

In this world of mass production, mass promotion, and mass distribution, of spotlights on and megaphones in the hands of a selected few, an unassuming, somewhat slapdash, primarily provincial little book such as *American Cookery* fell rapidly into oblivion. We have found only two considerations of it between 1831 and the middle of the twentieth century. An article on

"Centennial Cookery" in *Scribner's Monthly* in the spring of 1876 commences by referring to *American Cookery*, in the form of the Hartford edition, as something utterly unknown: "a volume entitled 'American Cookery.'" "For the assistance of anxious caterers [of] 'Centennial tea parties' and 'Lady Washington suppers,'" the *Scribner's* author provides excerpts from the preface, the Hartford edition's marketing advice, and several of the recipes.

Comments on how antiquated it all seems are interspersed throughout the article: "Some of [the] instructions [on how to choose meats and vegetables in the market] are indicative of the changes which eighty years have made in ways of locomotion. . . . Bear in mind that there were then no patent eggbeaters. . . . Of receipts for sweet cakes . . . each of them demands an unconscionable number of eggs. It is no wonder that our notable great-grandmothers were obliged to pay strict attention to their poultry yards."[14]

Several decades later, in 1909, a writer in the *Atlantic Monthly* saw fit to inform readers of the existence of *American Cookery*, having been given a copy of the Albany edition by a friend "who found it in her attic, where it had doubtless lain for years." This time around, what historian E. P. Thompson so aptly called "the enormous condescension of posterity" is laid on with a trowel. Simmons is derisively labeled "Amelia" or "the Orphan." Anything in the book of which the writer of the article is ignorant immediately serves to render the book even more ridiculous: "And what, oh, what, are emptins? I was in despair till I discovered a little foot-note on the very last page which tells us how to make them, or it. . . . I can imagine no more agreeable pastime than taking my plumbs and codling them in many waters till they are as green as grass, if I but knew what it meant." Misreadings of recipes, careless or deliberate, add to the merriment: "Now, here are directions [for election cake], but they appear to involve an entry into the oven on the cook's part; she is not however to do this idly, she is to 'work in the plumbs when going into the oven.' I do wish some one would try it."[15]

So after the 1830s, when *American Cookery* was no longer a living presence in American society, it was remembered, if at all, only as an amusing curiosity. Serious historical recollection of the book did not begin until 1957, when a prestigious scholarly journal, the *William and Mary Quarterly*, published an article by Mary Tolford Wilson on how "Amelia Simmons Fills a Need: American Cookery, 1796." The following year Wilson's article served as the introduction to a facsimile reprint of the first edition, brought out under the auspices of Oxford University Press. This edition was itself reprinted in 1984 by Dover Books.[16]

The key pronouncement in Wilson's groundbreaking essay was that *American Cookery* was "in its minor sphere, another declaration of American independence." Wilson based this characterization on the fact that this "first cookbook of American authorship to be published in the United States" includes a number of recipes for distinctively American dishes, such as "Johny Cake" and custardized "Pompkin" pie, and includes as well a good deal of distinctively American terminology, such as "molasses" (instead of "treacle") and "shortning" (for the fats used in baking).[17]

The next significant contribution to *American Cookery* scholarship was made in 1996, in food historian Karen Hess's introduction to a facsimile reprint edition of the second edition. Ironically, given that this edition was in effect a celebration of the bicentennial of this supposed declaration of American culinary independence, Hess disputed just about all of Wilson's assertions about the uniquely American nature of the cuisine made available in *American Cookery*. Where Wilson had stressed the fact that several recipes such as Johnny cake and Indian pudding were based on a New World grain, maize, Hess retorted that maize had already been featured in earlier European cookbooks and that, in any case, the maize or corn recipes included in *American Cookery* were actually English or Scottish recipes in which the maize readily available in North America had simply been substituted for oats or other traditional British Isles grains. So it was as well, Hess continued, with other "American" elements in the book, such as pumpkin pie and "the use of cranberries with turkey." In every case, there were English or European precedents for the procedures, and sometimes the ingredients, recommended in *American Cookery*.[18]

Recently, we ourselves weighed in on the discussion of the place of *American Cookery* in the Western culinary tradition. We argued, essentially, that Wilson and Hess were both right. While *American Cookery* is indeed heavily dependent on English sources and traditions, in many instances it adapts those sources and traditions to such a degree that the results deserve to be regarded as creatively and distinctively American. In this respect, "American cookery" at its founding moment, as well as subsequently, is no different from the English cuisine from which it is derived and adapted. For much of English cuisine as expressed in cookbooks had itself developed from French cuisine, producing through its particular panoply of altered emphases something uniquely English. By the same token and through the same process, French cuisine had emerged from Italian cuisine. And so on.[19]

There have been some efforts to situate *American Cookery* within not just a culinary but also a broader cultural, social, and political context. In 1999, Glynis Ridley took Wilson's stress on the distinctively American nature of the book and ran with it, claiming that the book's title page and suite of recipes together constitute "an overt political statement (of anti-British sentiment)." Ridley links the authorial identity of "an American Orphan" to the strain in revolutionary propaganda that portrayed the "parent-child relationship" between Britain and America "as having soured so much that America is effectively an orphan, or would be better off being so." She interprets some of the language on the title page, such as "from the imperial plumb to the plain cake" and "adapted to this country and all grades of life," as reinforcing the suggestions of equal opportunity, upward mobility, and democratic inclusiveness that are discernible in the fact of an orphan's having become a published author.

According to Ridley, the culinary content of *American Cookery* is equally patriotic. The recipes for Indian pudding and other maize-based dishes are to be understood "against the background of English contempt for Indian corn." Such recipes don't merely acknowledge American distinctiveness and independence. They defiantly insist on it. The same assertive nationalism is conveyed by the recipes for pumpkin pie and by the use of pearl ash instead of yeast as a "raising agent" in many of the cake recipes. And these features of the book "are entirely representative" of its agenda of fostering "national pride" and supporting "the viability and self-sufficiency of the American economy."[20]

Another feature of *American Cookery* that Ridley mentions in support of her political approach to the book is the addition in the Albany edition of recipes for "Election Cake, Federal Pan Cake, and Independence Cake." Nancy Siegel expanded on this point in an article published in 2008. With their names, mammoth proportions designed for festive occasions, and "lavish and expensive" ingredients, these cakes, Siegel states, represent "within the domestic sphere" an "approval of the democratic process," a "commitment to the ideals of independence so necessary for the new nation to prosper."[21]

The two most recent scholarly discussions of *American Cookery* essentially continue in the same vein. In a book about the pumpkin published in 2012, Cindy Ott focuses on the two recipes for pumpkin pie in *American Cookery*. According to Ott, the presence of the pumpkin in the American diet symbolized that the United States was a land of democratic self-sufficiency:

"Eating pumpkins signified a family's taking care of itself on its own piece of land, no matter how humble the size, and depending on no one but itself. . . . The pumpkin . . . embodied the Jeffersonian agrarian ideal of a nation of self-sufficient farmers." The pumpkin pie recipes in *American Cookery* evoke all these meanings: "Making the lowly pumpkin—a vegetable Europeans stigmatized as primitive and rustic—a delicacy and publishing a recipe for it in the first American cookbook was a powerful expression of American pride and independence." Finally, in Katharina Vester's *A Taste of Power* (2015), these various formulations of the idea that *American Cookery* was an assertion of American culinary independence are revisited. Vester mentions a point that we explore in depth, that the food presented in *American Cookery* is that of the Northeast. The book thus asserts "New England's hegemony over other regions."[22]

The work done on *American Cookery* by Wilson and those who have followed after her has fully established the idea that serious attention should be paid to this first American cookbook. Thanks to all these scholars, it has been rescued from the status of a laughable antique to which it had been consigned. On the other hand, whereas the few treatments of the late nineteenth and early twentieth centuries disregarded context, those of the second half of the twentieth century and the first decades of the twenty-first century have contextualized the work but in a way that is incomplete. Of course we want to know first and foremost about what Wilson and Hess debated—where *American Cookery* stands in relation to other Western cuisines.

But we also want to know where it stands in relation to its own time and place—a desire Wilson acknowledged with her remark that the book was "in its minor sphere, another declaration of American independence." That remark, while true to a degree, essentially sent the writers of the past two decades off on a false scent. Certainly much time, energy, and effort was devoted in the early years of the American nation to various types of reiterated declarations of independence. But a lot more was going on in those years as well. For example, people began to ask, "What now? Now that we are independent, what type of society are we, among ourselves, going to be?" In relation to the broad range of such additional questions and concerns, interpretations of *American Cookery* that see assertions of "national pride" or "democratic values" as the sum and substance of the book's social and cultural resonance begin to seem at best thin and one-dimensional and at worst positively misleading. Is it really adequate, for example, to say that

American Cookery, brought out by publishers whose political allegiances were entirely Federalist, conveys a "Jeffersonian agrarian ideal"?

To situate *American Cookery* accurately within the story of American national development requires that we first restore it as far as we possibly can to its time—before, during, and after "the twentieth year of the Independence of the United States of America"—and its place—the Connecticut and Hudson River watersheds. Such an approach is intended to correct and enrich the recent emphasis on the book's patriotic and democratic dimensions.

In her 1957 essay, Mary Tolford Wilson acknowledged that many of the recipes in *American Cookery* "were outright borrowings from British cookery books of the period, particularly Susannah Carter's." But neither Wilson nor Karen Hess forty years later described the extent of this "borrowing." We have found that the plagiarisms, some of them corrupted, begin right on the title page. The opening phrase of the subtitle closely follows that of Carter's *The Frugal Housewife*, first published in London in 1765 and later published in North America in Boston (1772), New York (1792), and Philadelphia (1796). *American Cookery* is announced to be about "the art of dressing viands, fish, poultry, and vegetables." In *The Frugal Housewife* this announcement had been correctly given as "the art of dressing all sorts of viands." Misunderstanding the term "viands" (articles of food), *American Cookery* makes a linguistic blunder right at the outset by using the term as though it meant just another category of food, like fish or vegetables.[23]

The misuse of Carter's subtitle is of course only the beginning. Examining the recipes within *American Cookery*'s two editions, we find that they can be divided into four categories: those that are copied verbatim from Carter or other British sources, those that are taken from such sources with some alteration, those that have no clear source but are of a type also found in earlier British cookbooks, and finally those without distinct analogues in earlier cookbooks.

There are 192 recipes in all. Twenty percent of them (38) are flat-out plagiarized from British sources. Fifteen percent (29) are mostly plagiarized, though somewhat altered in word choice or ingredients. Forty-two percent (81) are not quoted from any source verbatim, as far as we can tell, but are types of dishes regularly found in British cooking. And a mere twenty-three percent (44) are recipes with no obvious line of print descent.[24]

But percentages can be deceiving. Limited though they may be in number, the recipes that made their print debut in *American Cookery* are distinctive. They have come to define American cooking, at least the northern variety, in its first flush. These include five recipes using cornmeal (three Indian puddings, as well as a "Johny Cake or Hoe Cake" and an "Indian Slapjack"), two custard-style "Pompkin" puddings (puddings in pastes, that is, which we would call pies), another vegetable pie called by the borrowed American Indian word "squash" ("A Crookneck, or Winter Squash Pudding"), and the pairing of roast turkey with "cramberry-sauce." In *American Cookery* we also find, in addition to molasses and "shortning," the first instance in print of the term "cookie" (derived from the Dutch), replacing the British small cakes or biscuits. And here is the first appearance of the American chemical leavening agent, pearl ash, the precursor of baking soda, as well as the first recipe for brewing "Spruce Beer."[25]

The culinary and linguistic originals found in *American Cookery* have been much remarked upon since Wilson first broached the subject. But this list of firsts has tended to obscure the predominantly derivative nature of a work three-fourths of which depends on British dishes and culinary practices.

Let's return to the title page: "American Cookery . . . by an American Orphan." It begins and ends in American-ness. In between, the framing language is taken from the primary British source, and the specific preparations listed in the remainder of the subtitle are all distinctly British as well. One is even monarchical: "Pastes, Puffs, Pies, Tarts, Puddings, Custards and Preserves, and all kinds of Cakes, from the imperial Plumb, to plain Cake." So there's a slightly strident insistence, perhaps, in the recurrence of "American" in the authorial identity statement. The book would like to be American and not something else, but it cannot really achieve that identity in a convincing way.

In this respect—proclaimed American distinctiveness combined with ongoing cultural dependence on rather than independence from Great Britain—*American Cookery* is typical of American culture as a whole at this time. Sometimes the dependence was absolute. For example, we learn from historian Kariann Akemi Yokota that there was a definite demand among many of the people of the new nation for tableware ornamented with patriotic insignia. But this demand could not be supplied by domestic manufacturers. Being mostly local potters, they did not have the capability to make anything but "simple red earthenware." It was Josiah Wedgwood and other English manufacturers who supplied this demand. They exported "jugs, plates, and mugs" on which were depicted "rousing scenes of the defeat of the mighty [British] empire" by the American rebels. American customers happily purchased them.[26]

In almost exactly the same way, postwar American textile manufacture, insofar as it succeeded at all, concentrated on producing "a rough material." Those higher on the social ladder who wished to cover their bodies with finer fabrics still had to get them, as always, from Britain. And here again declarations of American "independence" in apparel form were supplied ready-made by English artisans and entrepreneurs: "With a few passes of an engraving tool, [English] printed textile manufacturers scratched out all references to Britain, and a redcoat was instantly transformed into George Washington."[27]

Within this pattern, there is to be observed a continuum from productions that were utterly derivative to those that varied sufficiently from the original British theme to amount to truly American variations on that theme. For example, as Laurel Thatcher Ulrich has shown in *The Age of Homespun*, some American textile objects became more authentically Americanized by the early decades of the nineteenth century. Women weavers and needleworkers all over New England "played freely with the forms and motifs of English models, until innovation rather than imitation became the dominant value" manifested in the blankets and counterpanes they produced.[28]

In the realm of books, at the completely derivative end of the scale was the notion on the part of printers and booksellers that, as James N. Green writes, any English book they reprinted was "an American book." After all, it was "printed in America, employing American laborers, preferably on paper from American mills and with American-made type. If the author was American, so much the better, but it was not essential." A bit less cultural subordination to the former mother country is to be seen in the practice of hiring a writer to substitute manifestly American for manifestly English content in selected passages in these English reprints. As compared to these examples, *American Cookery*, with its dimension of indigenous American ingredients and uniquely American turns of phrase, looks like an exemplar of patriotic creativity.[29]

The impulse to assert American identity utilizing English materials and forms was especially strong in the place where *American Cookery* probably was written and certainly was initially published—Connecticut. In the summer of 1776, Timothy Dwight was in the fifth of a six-year term as a tutor at Yale

College in New Haven. A native of Northampton, Massachusetts, Dwight had graduated from Yale in 1769. His family had played a leading role in various Connecticut River Valley towns since the seventeenth century. His maternal grandfather, Jonathan Edwards, was particularly distinguished, having been a major figure in the midcentury Great Awakening and unquestionably the most significant theologian and intellectual that New England had yet produced.[30]

Now in 1776, just weeks after the signing of the Declaration of Independence, it fell to Dwight to address the class graduating from Yale in that eventful year. He urged his "young gentlemen" listeners to consider themselves "as being concerned in laying the foundations of American greatness." Apparently others besides the graduating class were in attendance, for a sophomore from West Hartford by the name of Noah Webster appears to have been present and been deeply moved by what Dwight had to say.[31]

Webster was descended from a seventeenth-century governor of Connecticut, but the fortunes of his family had become pinched to such an extent that his father had had to mortgage the family farm to pay for Noah's Yale education. By 1783, Webster was back in the Hartford area, overseeing the publication of the first of the three parts of his *Grammatical Institute of the English Language*. This work was destined to become the bestselling book ever written by an American and to be popularly known as "Webster's Blue Back Speller." The purpose of the speller, Webster stated, was to provide the United States with an Americanized language that would be based on "the same republican principles as American civil and ecclesiastical institutions."[32]

Here was an effort to follow through on Dwight's injunction to lay "the foundations of American greatness," and it would have a major impact. As we explore more deeply in later chapters, Webster moved steadily toward realizing his goal of representing and instructing readers in the use of a truly Americanized version of the English language. But the early editions conformed to the pattern of reproducing existing English precedent and practice. As historian Joseph J. Ellis has observed, the "first edition of the speller made very few revisions in standard English spelling and pronunciation." Likewise, in its initial form the second part of Webster's work, the grammar, "made no major revisions" of the English grammatical textbook it was seeking to displace as the standard work on the subject in the United States. "Webster proposed no new rules based on American ways of speaking or writing."[33]

Another sophomore who may have heard Dwight's address directly or had a report of it from his friend Webster was a western Connecticut farm boy by the name of Joel Barlow. Within a few years, in the mid-1780s, Barlow, Dwight, Dwight's fellow tutor John Trumbull, and David Humphreys, another Yale friend, had constituted themselves as a set of "Gentlemen of taste," residing in or frequently visiting Hartford, who were striving through literary projects to form and define American culture and life at the outset of the new nation's existence. These young men formed the group that subsequently became known to American literary history as the "Connecticut Wits."[34]

Most of the work of the Connecticut Wits was poetry. In 1782, Trumbull's *M'Fingal*, a mock-heroic satirical retrospective of the American Revolution, was published. The year 1785 saw the appearance of *The Conquest of Canaan* by Dwight, an attempt at an American epic in which, according to an anonymous English reviewer, the new nation and its "late war" are "allegorized under the name of Canaan." A year later, Humphreys's *Poem on the Happiness of America* made it into print in the United States. In 1787, Barlow's *The Vision of Columbus* was published.[35]

Both of these last two works are "prospect" poems, panoramic visions of the present felicity and/or future greatness of the United States, along the lines articulated by Dwight in his 1776 address. In the words of Humphreys's *Poem on the Happiness of America*, "Then wake, Columbians! fav'rites of the skies / Awake to glory and to rapture rise! / Behold the dawn of your ascending fame / Illume the nations with a purer flame." In Barlow's *Vision of Columbus* such sentiments appear as "Each orient realm, the former pride of earth, / Where men and science drew their ancient birth, / Shall soon behold, on this enlightened coast, / Their fame transcended and their glory lost."[36]

Trumbull's *M'Fingal* and Dwight's *The Conquest of Canaan* are not exclusively devoted to ecstatic visions of the American future, but they do conclude with them. In *M'Fingal*, Trumbull asserts that "Th' American empire" shall "To glory, wealth and fame ascend / Her commerce rise, her realms extend." In *The Conquest of Canaan*, Dwight muses, "beneath auspicious skies, / To nobler bliss yon western world shall rise, . . . / Here Empire's last, and brightest throne shall rise; / And Peace, and Right, and Freedom, greet the skies."[37]

As with the reassertion of American-ness in the authorial attribution on the title page of *American Cookery*, the stridency of these proclamations of a unique American identity and destiny by a group of literary young men indicates a defensive acknowledgment on their part that in all sorts of crucial ways these works are not American at all. Rather, they are deeply dependent on precedents and conventions in the English literary tradition—the visions of the future granted to Adam at the close of John Milton's *Paradise Lost*; Samuel Butler's ridicule of Puritans in his mock-epic *Hudibras*; and, most pervasively, the rhymed couplet in iambic pentameter. The last had been made the norm for English poetry by John Dryden and Alexander Pope. In the course of the eighteenth century it had gotten encumbered with the sort of stilted diction (e.g., the ocean is the "azure main") that is fully on display in these poems and that William Wordsworth would shortly dispatch into an extended interval of disfavor.[38]

The highly derivative nature of these various declarations of cultural independence does not mean that they should be dismissed as being of no lasting significance. Rather, constructed from English materials and traditions—the primary influences on their creators—these works should be seen as early drafts of the American story, initial sketches of the American panorama. Some of them would be discarded altogether. Others, such as Ulrich's needlework specimens, would be reworked and revised until they emerged into creatively finished autonomy. And still others may have remained half-formed in and of themselves but gained ongoing interest and importance from the circumstances of their creation—from their proximity, for example, to activities and projects of a similar sort. In our view, such is the case with the postrevolutionary Hartford initiatives.

Not only were the works of the Connecticut Wits and Noah Webster all sent forth into the nation from Hartford; all of them but one were also published by the same publisher, and that publisher in the next decade would also publish *American Cookery*. The only one of these works that was not published by Hudson & Goodwin, Dwight's *Conquest of Canaan*, was published by Joel Barlow and his partner of the moment, Elisha Babcock. And Babcock was a former employee of Hudson & Goodwin.[39]

Such a convergence is intriguing to say the least. The five authors of these Hartford Americanizing projects all lived lives of prominence and influence, although the form this took in Joel Barlow's case—participation in the French Revolution followed by adherence to Jeffersonian Republicanism—was viewed by his onetime Hartford associates with extreme disfavor. John Trumbull became a Connecticut state legislator and a judge of the state superior court. David Humphreys served as aide-de-camp to George Washington during the war and represented the new nation on diplomatic missions right after it. He would continue in this latter role until he retired to the life of a Connecticut gentleman farmer. By the mid-1780s, Timothy Dwight had already become an important Connecticut clergyman. Ten years later he would be chosen president of Yale, and in this position he would exert influence well beyond Yale itself. As for Noah Webster, it was his continuing success as an author that earned him a place at the table of those who mattered.[40]

As we see in subsequent chapters, Barzillai Hudson and George Goodwin—proprietors of the *Connecticut Courant* and partners in the printing and bookselling firm of Hudson & Goodwin—were already by the 1780s operating on the same level of social potency as their stable of illustrious authors. For now, we present just a single piece of evidence bearing on this point: when Hartford was municipally incorporated in 1784, one of the members of its first City Council was Barzillai Hudson, serving alongside the man whose poem, *M'Fingal*, he had published two years before, John Trumbull.[41]

So the words and actions of the Connecticut Wits, of Noah Webster, and of Barzillai Hudson and George Goodwin counted for something. It was through the print medium provided by Hudson & Goodwin that, immediately upon the achievement of American political independence, the visions and plans of a set of "young gentlemen" from Yale for "laying the foundations of American greatness" were disseminated. Ten years later there issued from the same press another project of national definition whose social provenance could not have been more antithetical—the ideas of a young female "American Orphan" about what Americans should be eating and how they should be cooking it.

Was this a mere coincidence? We think not. Historian Christopher P. Bickford reminds us that Timothy Dwight, Noah Webster, and just about all of Connecticut's movers and shakers "shared a profound sense of Connecticut exceptionalism—a belief in the coherent identity and the uniquely special qualities of the State." The people of Connecticut were viewed by their social superiors and leaders as being "more virtuous, better educated, and politically wiser than everyone else, including the citizens of other New England States."[42]

Other historians have explored this exceptionalist outlook more fully. The Connecticut Wits, writes Sam Haselby, "gave a full range of self-conscious symbolic expression to a vision of the American nation," describing "a whole society: family life, the arts, education, labor, politics, social hierarchy, recreation, gender roles, religion and more." In their writings is to be found "the first fully articulated vision of American nationality."[43]

If this set of convictions was at least part of the reason that Hartford became the venue for the Americanizing projects of the 1780s, then it may also have had something to do with the appearance of *American Cookery* in the same place and from the same publisher in the 1790s. By bringing forward a cookbook written by a woman, and an orphan to boot, a collection of recipes claiming to be "adapted to this country and all grades of life," the elite that had moved swiftly and energetically to assert cultural leadership was, we believe, endeavoring to make its projection of American identity more socially comprehensive and more heedful of everyday life.

To present as fully as possible the world from which *American Cookery* emerged, we have striven to make accessible to our readers the social and cultural developments that lay behind the creation of this *particular* book at this *particular* time in this *particular* place. In *American Cookery* we find a convergence of culinary tradition, print culture, a Connecticut poised between an agrarian past and a commercial and capitalist future, the popular assertiveness unleashed by the Revolution that would allow an orphan to claim the status of an author, and a national identity in the making. In the pages that follow, we describe this world, tracing its contours and recreating as far as possible what it felt like to live in it.

We believe, along with anthropologist Clifford Geertz, that it is only within its context, in this case that of 1790s Connecticut and its offshoots, that a particular artifact, in this case *American Cookery*, "can be intelligibly—that is, thickly—described." The result of our investigations, we trust, will be to reveal for the first time the full significance of the first American cookbook.[44]

CHAPTER 2

Culinary Tradition

W hen *American Cookery*'s first two editions appeared in 1796, most American cooks who relied on recipes at all were accustomed to using handwritten ones they or their kitchen predecessors had copied into the pages of manuscript recipe collections. This was an old custom. Often, a housewife inherited a collection from a relation then added her own favorite dishes to the volume. Recipes were collected from cookbooks that circulated informally among friends and relations. Some were original to the cook. Just such an album combining original recipes and copies of printed ones—and including notes and amendments added by the cook—was kept by Anne Gibbons Gardiner, a wealthy Boston merchant's wife, in the 1760s and 1770s. Her choice of dishes from print sources reveals a great deal about the culinary inclinations of the New England colonial elite. Many are taken from Hannah Glasse's *The Art of Cookery Made Plain and Easy* (1747) and Elizabeth Raffald's *The Experienced English Housekeeper* (1769), two of the British cookbooks best known in the colonies. The intertwining of manuscripts and printed books was so close that women sometimes ordered blank leaves to be bound into the cookbooks they purchased to allow room for handwritten recipes. Neither printed nor written sources took precedence.[1]

In America after the Revolution, when British goods were once again sold in American markets and the public commenced buying books again, booksellers began to increase their inventories of cookery titles. The demand was such that both British imports and American reprints of British cookbooks sold well. Yet the practice of copying recipes into manuscript collections continued among literate American women.

Keeping manuscript recipe collections began as a favorite pastime among the English upper classes. The fashion took hold in the middle of the sixteenth century, with collected recipes falling into three general categories: cookery, confectionery, and remedies. The cosseted women of the aristocratic and gentry classes took particular interest in copying into their private collections recipes for fancy confections and homemade cures. These, rather than cookery, were the areas of domestic life in which they were apt to become involved. The kitchen was not a place where the women who led large estates or substantial households were likely to be found. The heavy, hot, and dangerous work that took place there to roast massive joints of meat and produce baked goods of gargantuan proportions was better left to servants and cooks. When highborn women did copy out cookery recipes, it was often because a new culinary fashion had caught their attention, as when herbs began to replace spices to flavor sauces.[2]

Confectionery recipes made up the majority of entries in the early modern English manuscript collections. The more elaborate and expensive the sweetmeat the better. Sugar molded in the shapes of animals, ships, bridges, and other novelties, an art much loved by the Tudors, adorned festive tables. These sculpted forms, along with sugar-coated fruits, seeds, and nuts, called comfits; jams, jellies, compotes, and marmalades made of exotic fruits and sugar; hard sugar candies known as suckets; and sweetened biscuits and creams—all became known collectively as "banquetting stuffe." They were the delights set out during the "banquett" course of a feast. This initial incarnation of the dessert course often took place in a separate room; small buildings set in garden enclosures were sometimes designed for the purpose. The banquet course provided an opportunity to display wealth and entertain guests in an atmosphere more relaxed than that of the formal part of the meal. When produced by ladies' soft hands, the value of this sweet "stuffe" was further enhanced.[3]

Sugar also played a significant part in the remedies collected by those who kept handwritten recipes. English food historian C. Anne Wilson notes that sugar's "medical reputation" was especially high in the early modern world. It was offered to the sick in many forms. It might be combined with powdered licorice, aniseed, or coriander to make cough cures, or melted into a syrup and mixed with violets and rose petals to reduce "burning agues" and "purge choler and melancholy."[4]

Despite the delights and benefits that sugarwork provided to wealthy households, by the end of the seventeenth century working directly with it, or indeed with any kind of food or medicine, was no longer considered a fashionable pursuit for English women of high social standing. Those who set the trends abandoned all culinary pursuits. They retreated to their drawing rooms, and instead of making fanciful "stuffe" became themselves the centerpieces on display.[5]

The upper classes may have tired of recipe collecting and the making of confectioneries and curatives, but women of somewhat lesser means took up where aristocrats left off. Gentry women began to master a modified version of the high art of sugarwork and to learn other recipes and remedies, both to furnish their own tables and to teach their servants. Women at this level of society, who wished to produce elegant sweets and stock their cellars and storerooms with cordials, salves, and syrups, found that developing their domestic skills and increasing their culinary knowledge helped them to advance socially. It wasn't until the nineteenth century that English women who aspired to gentility completely relinquished their domestic roles and adopted the aristocratic model of the lady of leisure.[6]

Recipe collecting and direct management of household activities held their allure even longer in colonial society, where the wealthiest lived in a manner far below that of English lords and ladies, and the example they set was more restrained. Prosperous American women could be found working side by side with their kitchen maids and other servants, or at the very least providing them with guidance and instruction in their domestic duties. The manuscript recipe collection was a means of preserving and disseminating the culinary tips and fashions these women gathered, often over the course of a lifetime. Historian Kevin J. Hayes writes of colonial women that they "took advantage of both folk and literary traditions to create their own personal works." This pattern continued for American women of all classes after independence. They were unashamed to keep house, to keep handwritten collections of their favorite dishes, and to be known to keep both.[7]

Along with their role in spreading domestic knowledge and stylish practices such as sugarwork both laterally and down the social scale, manuscript recipe collections contributed to the development of the genre of the cookbook. British food historian Gilly Lehmann considers them "the principal source of English cookery books." Before the seventeenth century, as another British historian, Elizabeth Spiller, notes, there was "no distinct or fully established category of cookbooks." But as influential as the manuscript recipe collection was in the making of the cookbook, other factors also came into play.[8]

Printed books containing cooking instruction emerged as a part of the culture of print that transformed early modern Europe. Like all instructional writing, these works were considered examples of new "knowledge practices," on a par with topics like surgery and chemistry. The distinction we tend to maintain in print today between practical and theoretical approaches was not then so clear. Recipes, formulas, directions, advice, and ethical guidance were intermixed in early printed treatises. Printing had altered the medieval equation in which "philosophical sciences" had been "written knowledge," while mechanical and technical arts were part of the oral culture of "guild practices." All types of knowledge were now committed to print. So "improving" discourses might be interspersed with useful recipes, and health advice offered in the midst of a moral exhortation.[9]

Many literary genres, some still with us today, originated in the imaginative and technological renaissance that accompanied the rise of printing. For our purposes, three in the English tradition are most important as they most influenced the form of the modern cookbook. These are books of "secrets," which combined alchemical experimentation with recipes and other domestic tutelage; books on health and nutrition known as dietaries; and books on husbandry and the management of estates in both farm and household aspects.[10]

Like the manuscript recipe collections upon which they often drew, secrets books included directions for making confectioneries and remedies. Besides that will-o'-the-wisp, alchemy, the earliest works in the genre focused on the "mechanical arts" of printing, dyeing, mining, optics, and even husbandry. But in time cookery, especially the making of sweet foods, became the secrets books' main topic. Although "hidden behind the men who presented the books," as Lehmann notes, the authors of these domestic secrets books were often women. Even more extraordinarily, the audience for them was primarily women.[11]

The logic of combining in one printed source recipes for fancy sweet dishes and potions for ailments may seem elusive. But to early moderns these subjects were united in an important respect: they involved new insights into the properties of matter and its manipulation. The practices that created this often startling new knowledge were compelling enough to be classified as the "secrets" of the social and scientific elites. An example of the kind of secrets these books contained is the chemical changes that occur when heat or cold is applied to certain foodstuffs. The ices or syrups that result could be viewed in either culinary or medicinal terms. The making of confections and the making of "medeson" were thus both thought to be within the domain of the secrets book.[12]

Many secrets books also purported to reveal the inner workings of the English court and the concoctions for health and pleasure favored by the nobility. One such work was The Queens Closet Opened, published in 1655.

Its compiler, known only by the initials W.M., may have been Walter Montagu, formerly private secretary to Queen Henrietta Maria, wife of Charles I. The book was first published six years after the trial and execution of the king, when the queen was in exile. The look back it offered on a vanished royal court may have been its most appealing "secret." Whatever the reason, it was a great success, going into multiple editions and spawning imitations such as Hannah Woolley's *The Queen-Like Closet* (1670). By the 1680s, *The Queens Closet Opened* was for sale in the colonies.[13]

The recipes found in the secrets books are often vague and imprecise. Spiller argues that the books are "neither fully medieval nor fully modern in their assumptions about the relationships among art, nature and knowledge." Permeating them is the "residual medieval sense" that knowledge is most valuable when "curious," that exceptional "jewels" and "delightes" are to be most highly prized. While the modern perspective to see knowledge as most useful when replicable is present in these books, arcane information that is unprovable and not illustrative of general processes is equally valued. The proof of a recipe's effectiveness, whether as a food, a medicine, a cleaner, or for some other use, often relies on nothing more than the name of the reputable person for whom it is said to have "worked." For example, in later editions of *The Queens Closet Opened*, "The Prescribers, and Approvers of most of these rare Receipts" are named; recipes are tagged simply "prooved" or "*probatum est.*"[14]

Hugh Plat, who wrote *Jewel House of Art and Nature* (1594) and *Delightes for Ladies* (1600), was perhaps the most famous author of books in the secrets vein. Yet he was renowned, too, as a scholar of natural science. One admirer deemed him "the most curious man of his time." But curious is a curious word—it can be taken to mean inquisitiveness as well as something or someone singular. As both a collector of marvels and an early scientist, Plat straddled the medieval and modern worlds that the secrets books themselves exemplify.[15]

The next precursor of the cookbook, the dietary, reveals "a sophisticated awareness of the interconnection between food and health," according to British historian Lynette Hunter. Some dietaries, such as Andrew Boorde's *The Breviary of Healthe* (1552), offer cures based on plant and food remedies. These forerunners of more specialized books on medicine and pharmaceuticals provide dietary regimens and cooking techniques that promote health or offer therapies that address illness and injury. They were particularly useful to those for whom the services of a physician, surgeon, or apothecary, all guild members since the sixteenth century, were out of reach.[16]

The Galenic theory of the "humors," in which, put simply, sickness was seen as an imbalance of bodily fluids, is often associated with the dietaries. For instance, in *The Haven of Health* (1584), Thomas Cogan explains that eating cold, moist foods such as melons produces different effects depending on the constitution of the person eating them: "If they do finde flewme in the stomacke, they be turned into flewme, if they finde choler, they be turned into choler." Along with culinary and medical wisdom, dietaries provided their early modern readers with guidance in matters of conduct and morality. The connection between moral rectitude and physical well-being, as between health and diet, was considered self-evident. Hannah Woolley's *The Gentlewomans Companion* (1673) is a late example of the dietary. In it, Woolley gives advice on conduct to women in all stages and walks of life, while offering medicines and foods to counter various physical ailments. "Diet as preventive" is the overarching theme of the dietaries.[17]

Books of husbandry combining cooking with estate management can also be considered antecedents of the cookbook, and like the secrets books, their cooking sections were sometimes based on women's recipe collections. The husbandry books are extensive, often multivolume works, with sections or separate volumes devoted to the preparation of food and drink. Lehmann argues that books combining cookery and household management tended to be "less ambitious about their readers" than the secrets books, which emphasized confectionery. In the most famous work in this style, Gervase Markham's *The English Hus-wife*, first published in 1615 (with subsequent editions using various spellings of "Housewife"), a housewife is advised to serve food that is "rather esteemed for the familiar acquaintance she hath with it, then for the strangenesse and raritie it bringeth from other Countries." These estate management manuals were aimed primarily at a gentry audience, those whom Lehmann characterizes as "running a country household living off its own production."[18]

The directions for baking bread given in *The English Hus-wife* provide an illustration of the kinds of practical instruction readers might encounter in works of this nature. It is one of the earliest printed recipes for baking bread. In the brown bread section of the recipe, a rustic bread to be made for the estate's farmhands calls for two bushels of barley, two pecks of peas, and a peck of wheat or rye, to be mixed with a peck of malt. The recipe illustrates the scale on which country estate kitchens and bake houses ran. Yet even such works as Markham's did not eschew sumptuous dishes. His advice to the housewife to serve food with which she had a "familiar acquaintance" is belied by his inclusion of foreign recipes such as "olla podrida," an elegant Spanish spiced meat dish, along with a section devoted to "Banquetting stuffe and conceited dishes."[19]

All of the types of printed works we have been surveying influenced the formation of the modern English cookbook. For American colonists, the secrets books and the husbandry books, rather than the dietaries, held the most interest. *The Queens Closet Opened*, Woolley's *The Queen-Like Closet*, and *The English Hus-wife* appeared on seventeenth-century colonial booksellers' lists and were found in probate inventories. The first and second are in the secrets tradition, the third an example of a husbandry manual. Both of these approaches to cuisine came to the fore in the eighteenth century, although in slightly different forms than they had taken in the sixteenth and seventeenth centuries.[20]

The first and more refined of the two styles was favored by English royalty and the nobility. It was a cuisine based on innovations originating in France. The earliest practitioners were the French court cooks, led by François Pierre de La Varenne, author of the bestselling *Le cuisinier françois* (1651; translated into English in 1653 as *The French Cook*). La Varenne developed entirely new methods of cooking that relied on concentrated meat stocks and reductions known as *bouillons* and *jus*, and used *liaisons*, cooked mixtures of flour and fat, to thicken and enrich sauces. One *liaison*, the *roux*, continues to serve as the basis of such classic French sauces as *béchamel* and *velouté*. La Varenne also introduced the *ragoût*, a seasoned stew of meat, fowl, or vegetables. His novel methods inaugurated a new gastronomic era that finally dethroned the sweet and sour flavor combinations and generous use of spices that had dominated high cuisine during the Middle Ages.[21]

Other French cookbook authors built on the groundwork laid by La Varenne, among them Nicolas de Bonnefons, with his *Les delices de la campagne* ("The Pleasures of the Countryside," 1654); Pierre de Lune, author of *Le cuisinier* (1656) and *Le nouveau cuisinier* (1659); and the anonymous author of *Le pastissier françois* (1653). The bestselling and most influential French court cook, however, came to the fore at century's end. François Massialot's best-known work was *Le cuisinier roïal et bourgeois* (1691), translated into English in 1702 as *The Court and Country Cook*. Like La Varenne, Massialot wrote primarily for other cooks, the cadre of professionals who served the nobility and wealthy patrons wishing, as historian of the French table Barbara Ketcham Wheaton observes, to "advance their social ambitions by offering meals that were too good to refuse." Also like La Varenne, Massialot's contributions to the art of cooking had a profound impact on continental and English gastronomy. He seems to have been a peripatetic, freelance cook, "operating independently of a specialized food guild or of a great household," and, along with other master cooks, catering wedding feasts and banquets for the likes of the duc d'Orléans, brother to Louis XIV, and others of high rank. He developed two versatile preparations in particular upon which he based his exquisite dishes. These are the *coulis* (cullis in English), a strained and thickened meat, fruit, or vegetable broth, and ham essence, a highly flavored meat juice. He was also a great innovator in the realm of desserts. The meringue is one of his sweet creations.[22]

French cooks of the eighteenth century published books that amplified and in some instances modified the classic French approach. Vincent La Chapelle's *The Modern Cook*, first published in English in 1733, and in French in 1735, was a massive compendium of 1,500 complete recipes. Food historian and chef Anne Willan describes it as "a treasury of eighteenth-century French cooking." But La Chapelle's work succumbs to what Wheaton laments as "a permanent and disagreeable feature of the craft of cooking"—plagiarism. Many of La Chapelle's recipes were taken from Massialot and other predecessors. The French method, at least one hundred years old by the middle of the eighteenth century, was modernized by the foremost eighteenth-century French cookbook author, François Menon. His works include the highly successful *Nouveau traité de la cuisine* (1739; translated as *New Treatise on Cooking*, 1742) and the midcentury *Les soupers de la cour* (1755; translated as *The Professed Cook*, 1767). Although he promoted a simplified style, Menon did not neglect classic French kitchen disciplines, such as knife skills, and the sauces, reductions, and blanching and braising techniques upon which French haute cuisine had been built.[23]

While they served the upper echelons and wrote for other professionals, the French court cooks and authors had an effect on broader culinary developments. For example, a standard of bourgeois English cooking, the "made dish," a preparation of various ingredients cooked together, which was considered "a more elaborate mode of cookery than plain *frying, broiling,* or *roasting,*" can be said to descend, if rather distantly, from the tradition of the court cooks.[24]

In Britain through the first decades of the eighteenth century, the foods served at the tables of the great were invariably in the French mode. English lords, who presided over the greatest houses in Britain, preferred, whenever possible, to staff their kitchens with French cooks. Vincent La Chapelle, for example, worked in London for Philip Stanhope, 4th Earl of Chesterfield, from about 1728 to 1735, when he left to serve William IV, Prince of Orange.[25]

But French chefs (the term *chef de cuisine* was first used by Menon) were rather thin on the English ground. A crop of English proponents of the continental high style took up the French court cooks' mantle. Many of them published cookbooks to promote themselves and their cooking style. The cuisine portrayed in Henry Howard's *England's Newest Way* (1703), Patrick Lamb's *Royal Cookery* (1710), John Nott's *Cook's and Confectioner's Dictionary* (1723), Richard Smith's *Court Cookery* (1723), and Charles Carter's *Complete Practical Cook* (1730) follows the French model.[26]

Despite the enduring influence of these French and English high-style cooks, the gastronomic excesses they championed (for instance, requiring "six Pounds of Butter to fry twelve Eggs," as Hannah Glasse complained) began to lose their appeal at the pinnacle of British society after about 1730. English royalty had begun to head in the direction of *primus inter pares*, and the food found at court, as well as on the tables of the aristocracy and the rising professional classes, began to shift toward plainer English fare. A new wave of cookbooks celebrated this turn toward what historian Stephen Mennell calls "English country notions in food." These were written by English women who learned and practiced their craft as cooks, often as cooks and housekeepers both, in less exalted households. As Gilly Lehmann explains, these housewife-style cooks were well received in the expanding market for cookbooks, where buyers "preferred the traditional mix of culinary receipts and remedies to the grandiose dishes of the ambitious court-cooks." The French chefs and their lavish menus did not completely disappear. They continued to be "the particular prerogative of the grandest of the Whig grandees." But English society had begun to associate patriotism with the consumption of simpler, native foods and preparations, such as roast beef. The combination of two ideas—that food choices were a matter of national identity and that foreignness and urbanity (especially of the French variety) were marks of dissipation—led to the broad acceptance of "country notions" in dining.[27]

The imperial rivalry between Britain and France, and one political event in particular, the Hanoverian accession, played a part in giving food a patriotic significance. When George I, the solidly Protestant first monarch of the House of Hanover, ascended the throne on the death of Queen Anne in 1714, the English nation was in turmoil. Factions more and less hostile to Catholicism contended for control. For those fighting to purge Britain of Catholic belief and culture, anything associated with France and its Catholic, absolutist monarchy was tainted.[28]

Antipathy toward French food and ambivalence about French sophistication in general are attitudes that have persisted into our own day. Nevertheless, it has proved impossible to rid English cuisine of all traces of French gastronomy. French modes of cooking became so ingrained in British foodways that French recipes graced British cookbooks even during fervently anti-French periods, and even in those books most in the patriotic and democratizing vein. Food historians have noted (indeed we ourselves have noted in an earlier work) that an English cookbook author's condemnation of expensive ingredients and rarified cooking styles, especially those associated with France, often went hand in hand with rampant plagiarism from the same disparaged sources. Despite this disingenuousness, a distinctly simpler English mode did emerge that was in conflict with French extravagance.[29]

It can reasonably be argued that the history of British cookbook publishing in the eighteenth century followed a downward social trajectory, from the court cooks' high style that spared no expense and celebrated the arcane skills of kitchen cognoscenti to an approach advanced by mistresses of more moderate means and their cooks. This latter approach, while producing a less lavish and complex cuisine, was the more modern one. It adapted fashionable dishes in a manner that pared away excessive expense and it emphasized the virtues of traditional country cooking. In purely commercial terms, as Lehmann writes, "the woman's product was much better adapted to the requirements of the cookery-book-buying public than the chef's magnum opus." As far as sales went, "the women win hands down." Refocusing culinary artistry to the lesser gentry increased the distance between English and continental norms. English cookbook authors such as Elizabeth Raffald believed that they could "join Oeconomy with Neatness and Elegance," and that their cutting of culinary corners would not affect the taste of a dish, a notion French epicures found laughable. For the English, the desire to rise in status, which prompted many a cookbook purchase, was ever at war with the desire to run the household economically. These competing goals not only formed the new English cuisine but also set up one of the most enduring dynamics within the bourgeois ethos.[30]

Of particular interest to us as we trace the influence of English cuisine on American cooking is that this innovative mode of cooking, developed primarily by women, was disseminated mainly through the modern means of print and its marketplace forces. For the court cooks, cookbooks were far less important than kitchen practice. The professional French cooks believed that knowledge of haute cuisine was best transmitted through networks of skilled practitioners, in a manner that dated back to the medieval guilds. The women cookbook authors, on the other hand, turned their outsider status (women were not permitted to apprentice in the all-male professional kitchens) to their benefit. It turned out that they, rather than the French chefs and their English acolytes, were more in tune with the rising middle classes. The women cooks were aligned with a public ever more influenced by print.[31]

Although they met with publishing success, many of the women culinary writers did not receive credit on their title pages. Often their works were signed simply, "By a Lady," a convention that continued to be used by women writers into the nineteenth century. (Jane Austen's *Sense and Sensibility* first appeared as "By a Lady" and *Pride and Prejudice* as "By the Author of 'Sense and Sensibility.'") This tactic concealed the writer's identity while establishing her gender and vaguely claiming a high social position. Women writers of cookbooks may have chosen anonymity in order to be shielded from the inevitable criticism their works received from their male counterparts. Gilly Lehmann tells us that women "were not easily accepted, either professionally or socially" as experts on cooking, and "men were quick to criticize women's lack of training or 'profession.'" Samuel Johnson thought that "women can spin very well; but they cannot make a good book of Cookery." His pronouncement coincided with the beginning of a two-hundred-year period during which women writers dominated the English cookbook market.[32]

Even Hannah Glasse's remarkably enduring *The Art of Cookery Made Plain and Easy*, first published in 1747, entered the world as "By a Lady," although Glasse formally registered her work with Stationers' Hall on August 16, 1746. Nonetheless, Dr. Johnson and other pundits of the day disputed her authorship and created the impression that a man had written the defining British culinary work of the eighteenth century. As late as 1929, *The Art of Cookery* was being misattributed. In 1938, an antiquarian named Madeleine Hope Dodds finally put the matter to rest with research that proved Glasse was the author. Yet as early as the fourth edition of 1751, Glasse's signature had been included on the title page, and her trade card had been inserted in the book.[33]

For other women cookbook writers of the eighteenth century, initials served to disguise identity. The first four editions of E. Smith's *The Compleat Housewife* (1727), the bestselling cookbook of the early part of the century, are attributed to E– S–. The author's surname appears for the first time only in posthumous editions; her first name remains unknown.[34]

In some cases, the female cookbook author's identity was revealed, and even played up. The gender and relatively modest circumstances of Elizabeth Raffald, author of *The Experienced English Housekeeper*, certainly didn't hurt sales of her book, which Anne Willan calls "the ultimate English manual for domestics." Raffald cleverly exploited her experience as housekeeper at Arley Hall, Cheshire, and later as owner of a successful fine food and confectionery shop. Female servants who wished to advance as cooks or housekeepers, or women who simply wanted to keep their homes with some grace, were eager to purchase works such as Raffald's.[35]

The eighteenth-century English bourgeois desire to enjoy fashionable but unostentatious dining and a new propensity to elevate the more rustic aspects of English cooking were not without precedent. There was a country inflection to the interests and preferences of the English aristocracy in the sixteenth and seventeenth centuries. *The Closet of the Eminently Learned Sir Kenelme Digbie Kt. Opened* (1669) is an exemplar of the uniquely English aristocratic predilection for the foods of its own countryside. Although "larded with French terms" in the manner of all secrets books, Kenelm Digby's work is, as Stephen Mennell asserts, a reflection of the concerns "arising directly out of practical housekeeping on modest country estates."[36]

The basis of this preference for the rural lay in the structure of English life, in which landed classes, comprising peers, gentry, and freehold farmers, dominated the social order. Distinctions among various levels of these closely associated groups were minimized by the anomaly of what has been described as overlapping incomes, whereby some prosperous non-nobles were wealthier than some peers, as well as by the fact that primogeniture required many younger sons of the peerage, those not in line to inherit titles or estates, to become in essence part of the gentry. In short, English landowners, from great to small, constituted a large, influential, and fairly close-knit segment of society, one that lived both on and by their estates, and took pride in the quality of nourishment obtained from their holdings. And just as the courtly influence on social norms was more subdued in

England than in France, so too the country influence exerted by this class on the English court was more acutely felt. Country life, then, held high prestige in England, much higher than it held in France.

The point is nicely illustrated in an offhand remark of Digby's: "My Lady of Portland told me since, that she finds Neats-tongues to be the best flesh for Pies." In other words, the high-born "My Lady of Portland" concerned herself with such mundane matters as the type of meat in her household's pies, pies that we can assume were made under her guidance, if not by her hand, and in which "Neats-tongues" (beef tongues) came from her own herds. Mennell concludes that "urban and rural life interlocked far more in England than in France, and this was valued." As we alluded to earlier, even the royal diet (grand occasions excepted) varied little from the substantial country fare enjoyed by minor gentry.[37]

In the eighteenth century, the Lady of Portland's great-granddaughters turned their noses up at making neat's tongues and mince pies with their own hands, but her descendants' tenants and servants certainly did not. The expanding English market for cookbooks included many whose rising status required them to learn not only more and better modes of cooking but also etiquette, the finer points of morality, and instruction in handwriting. The servants, who once were expected only to be able to read, were increasingly expected to master writing as well.[38]

From the 1740s, adding to these liberalizing social trends, London lost its place at the center of cookbook publishing, as provincial printers began to develop their own notable lists. *The Young Woman's Companion; or, The Servant-Maid's Assistant* (1753), by former York housekeeper Mary Johnson, provides an example. The work sold well enough to be reissued the year after publication. But this time its publisher, and perhaps its author, found the original title lacking. For a cookbook and confectionery guide that also instructed in grammar, spelling, arithmetic, and the moral duties of a servant, the title *Madam Johnson's Present; or, The Best Instructions for Young Women in Useful and Universal Knowledge* seemed a better fit. With this change, the work openly acknowledges that the mistress of the household is not the book's intended reader. Rather, she is expected to purchase it for her servant.[39]

Several other provincial British titles were published under circumstances that seem to presage those of *American Cookery*. Elizabeth Moxon's 1741 *English Housewifry* was printed by John Lister, publisher of the local

newspaper the *Leeds Mercury*. (Under similar arrangements, the first and
second editions of *American Cookery* would in 1796 be printed by newspaper
publishers in Hartford and Albany.) Upon Lister's death in 1753, his successor, Griffith Wright, continued to issue Moxon's domestic manual, thirteen
editions in all, into the 1790s. The influence of Moxon's work was such
that Sarah Jackson's 1754 *The Director; or, Young Woman's Best Companion*
is, with the exception of two recipes, a copy of the fourth edition. Jackson's
Director was made accessible to a wider audience by being brought out in
affordable weekly installments. This goal of attracting readers of limited
means is echoed in the pricing of *American Cookery*, a topic we return to in
chapter 9.[40]

Provincial newspaper publishers saw the expanding cookbook market as a
commercial opportunity. And provincial would-be cookbook authors found
with their local newspaper publishers an opportunity to promote themselves despite their cultural and geographic distance from London. Along
with Moxon's successful work, Wright brought out Ann Peckham's *The
Complete English Cook* (1767). Thomas Slack, who published a newspaper
in Newcastle, entered the cookery field with Ann Cook's *Professed Cookery*
(1754) and continued in it with Mary Smith's *Complete Housekeeper* (1772).
The market for such works was not limited to the middle classes. Even aristocratic women who had long relied on their trove of hand-copied recipes
as the basis of their households' diets occasionally bought one of the new
printed cookbooks by women authors, if only to give them as gifts to their
cooks and servants.[41]

By the last third of the century, native English foods, paired for special
occasions with vaguely French prestige dishes, were those favored by British
society. The two women authors who played the greatest role in shaping
this emerging cuisine, Hannah Glasse and Elizabeth Raffald, also had deep
personal ties to the provinces.[42]

Although her works were published in London, where she lived as an
adult, Glasse spent much of her youth far from the capital city in Northumberland. Her roots in a provincial family of professionals and clerics on her
father's side may have contributed to a cooking style with a stated bias toward
"good *English*" food. She was the illegitimate daughter of Isaac Allgood of
Hexham and an Irish widow named Hannah Reynolds, with whom Allgood
also had two other children. When Allgood's relationship with Reynolds
ended, daughter Hannah, calling her mother a "wicked wretch," chose to
remain with her father and was accepted into the Allgood household. At

sixteen, on the death of her stepmother and with her father in poor health, Hannah moved to London to live with her grandmother. Shortly afterward, she made a disastrous marriage with a poorly paid subaltern named John Glasse. Within several years, with young children in tow, both Hannah and her husband found employment in service to Arthur Chichester, 4th Earl of Donegall, in Essex. Other employers and business schemes followed, though it is likely that John Glasse was never gainfully employed after his time with Lord Donegall. As circumstances changed (and not for the better), the Glasses moved several times. They left Broomfield in Essex and lived in various parts of London, ending up in the very house in which Hannah had been born in Greville Street near Hatton Garden. Here the family remained for nine years, from 1738 to 1747, and here Hannah struggled to support herself and her family. She worked as a servant, sold patent medicines, and with the help of a daughter operated a "habit warehouse," or clothes shop. *The Art of Cookery Made Plain and Easy* was her one great success, with more than twenty editions in the eighteenth century. Two less successful books followed—*The Servant's Directory* in 1760 and *The Compleat Confectioner* in 1760 or 1761.[43]

Elizabeth Raffald, second only to Glasse in popularity, spent her life in and around Manchester. Before her marriage, she had been housekeeper to Sir Peter and Lady Elizabeth Warburton of Arley Hall, Cheshire. Based on original recipes, some developed during her time in service and others created later when she ran her shop in Manchester, Raffald's *Experienced English Housekeeper* was an immediate and immense success. Its section on dessert dishes in particular, based on those sold at her shop, found an avid following. The woman cook's focus on sweets, first exhibited by sixteenth-century ladies in their partiality to sugarwork, had found expression two centuries later in a woman of lower social standing but great industry and business acumen. Although provincial in origin, Raffald's cuisine was carefully crafted to meet the needs and aspirations of an expanding national middle class. She collected over eight hundred prepublication subscriptions but perhaps need not have been so diligent: her work went into more than thirty-three editions.[44]

Raffald's book is another example of a work by an untested author being printed by the publisher of her local paper. In Raffald's case, Joseph Harrop was not only the owner of the weekly *Manchester Mercury* but also her neighbor. The connection between the two deepened when Raffald "assisted in the continuance" of Harrop's paper. She was also involved with the startup of another local newspaper, *Prescott's Journal*.[45]

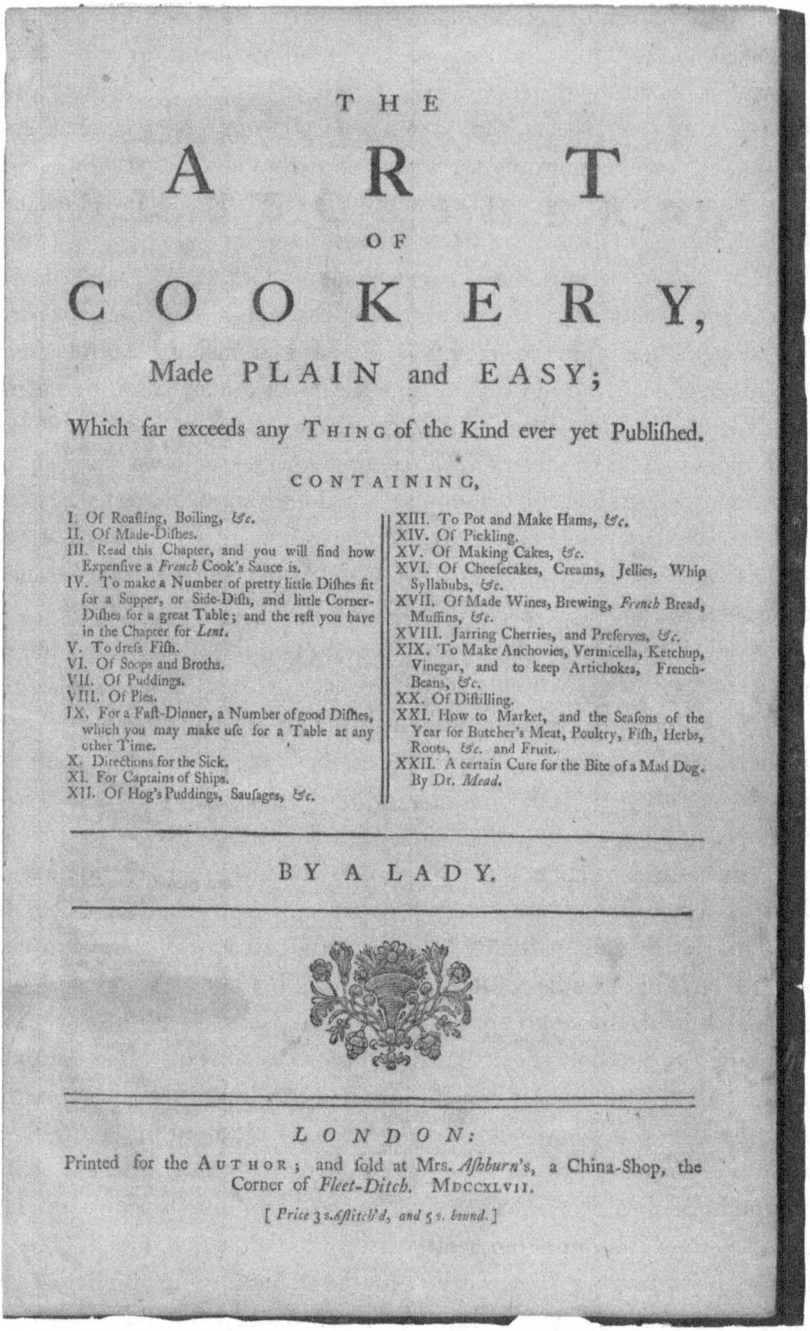

THE

ART

OF

COOKERY,

Made PLAIN and EASY;

Which far exceeds any THING of the Kind ever yet Publiſhed.

CONTAINING,

I. Of Roaſting, Boiling, *&c.*
II. Of Made-Diſhes.
III. Read this Chapter, and you will find how Expenſive a *French* Cook's Sauce is.
IV. To make a Number of pretty little Diſhes fit for a Supper, or Side-Diſh, and little Corner-Diſhes for a great Table; and the reſt you have in the Chapter for *Lent.*
V. To dreſs Fiſh.
VI. Of Soops and Broths.
VII. Of Puddings.
VIII. Of Pies.
IX. For a Faſt-Dinner, a Number of good Diſhes, which you may make uſe for a Table at any other Time.
X. Directions for the Sick.
XI. For Captains of Ships.
XII. Of Hog's Puddings, Sauſages, *&c.*
XIII. To Pot and Make Hams, *&c.*
XIV. Of Pickling.
XV. Of Making Cakes, *&c.*
XVI. Of Cheeſecakes, Creams, Jellies, Whip Syllabubs, *&c.*
XVII. Of Made Wines, Brewing, *French* Bread, Muffins, *&c.*
XVIII. Jarring Cherries, and Preſerves, *&c.*
XIX. To Make Anchovies, Vermicella, Ketchup, Vinegar, and to keep Artichokes, French-Beans, *&c.*
XX. Of Diſtilling.
XXI. How to Market, and the Seaſons of the Year for Butcher's Meat, Poultry, Fiſh, Herbs, Roots, *&c.* and Fruit.
XXII. A certain Cure for the Bite of a Mad Dog. By Dr. *Mead.*

BY A LADY.

LONDON:
Printed for the AUTHOR; and ſold at Mrs. *Aſhburn's*, a China-Shop, the Corner of *Fleet-Ditch.* MDCCXLVII.

[*Price* 3 s. 6 *ſtitch'd, and* 5 s. *bound.*]

FIGURE 2.1. Title page from *The Art of Cookery* (London, 1747).
–Lowell 4334.5. Houghton Library, Harvard University

The elevated tastes of the earlier eighteenth-century elites had now been either completely "assimilated into the English repertoire," as Lehmann tells us was the case with "raggoos" and "fricassees," or had been eclipsed by the new English style presented by Glasse, Raffald, and other, mainly women writers of domestic cookbooks. But this "more socially homogeneous style of cookery" could also be found outside the home, in the foods prepared by a new class of British male chefs, the tavern cooks. Tavern dining was on the rise in a society ever more socially and physically mobile, and the public had begun to demand better fare in these embryonic restaurants. The tavern cooks specialized in roast meats, and it was in their establishments that notions of the "copiously carnivorous diet of the English" and its link to "self-proclaimed manliness, courage, fierceness of character, and freedom of spirit" were perhaps best expressed. This "ideology of food chauvinism," as food historian Aaron Landau calls it, distinguished English cuisine yet further from the urbanity of the French. English food, and the democratic setting of the tavern in which to partake of it, thus played a part in the construction of the British national identity that had begun to assert itself in the new consumer society. To make it palatable politically, this new cuisine was marketed as traditional; to make it palatable to the pocketbooks of the emerging entrepreneurial and professional middle classes, it drew its inspiration from the economizing elegance of the housewifely cookbooks.[46]

From newspaper advertisements, booksellers' lists, and the catalogues of subscription and circulating libraries, we can identify the British cookery titles that were imported into the American colonies in the seventeenth and eighteenth centuries. Some early Virginia colonists wrote their associates in London to request books on husbandry and housewifery, and in 1620 they received in answer Gervase Markham's *The English Hus-wife*, the farm and household management treatise discussed earlier. It is likely that *The English Hus-wife* also found its way to Plymouth Colony. It is certain that multiple copies of Markham's work arrived in Boston in 1684.[47]

Additionally, in the 1680s in Boston, a book buyer could obtain a copy of W. M.'s *The Queens Closet Opened* and Hannah Woolley's *The Queen-Like Closet*. In at least one private library in Virginia, Robert May's *The Accomplisht Cook* (1660) and John Evelyn's *Acetaria: A Discourse of Sallets* (1699) could be found on the shelves. A copy of William Rabisha's *The Whole Body of Cookery* (1661) appears in the 1701 estate inventory of a Virginia planter who had a reputation for keeping a particularly good table and well-stocked wine cellar.[48]

Benjamin Franklin owned "a well-thumbed copy" of François Menon's *La cuisinière bourgeoise*, which is an early instance of a French work that, uncharacteristically, emphasizes country or regional cooking. In a 1748 reprint of this Menon title, a recipe for "Turkey Wings Many Ways," which could be taken from any of the English housewifely cookbooks, is on offer. Throughout Europe by this time, the New World bird had become commonplace. In France its culinary versatility was especially appreciated.[49]

Franklin's possession of this bourgeois-style cookbook (an anomaly for Menon, a chef known for his sophistication) reveals something about the kinds of cookery works likely to find a colonial audience. Those that drew the most attention in eighteenth-century America, both before and after the Revolution, were the same economical ones, usually written by women, that were most popular in Britain: Richard Bradley's *Country Housewife and Lady's Director* (1727; though written by a male chef, it is considered "closer in style to the women's books than to the court-cooks'"), E. Smith's *The Compleat Housewife*, Glasse's *The Art of Cookery Made Plain and Easy* and *The Compleat Confectioner*, and Raffald's *The Experienced English Housekeeper*.[50]

Bradley and Smith were known throughout the colonies. Glasse's *Art of Cookery* fared as well with colonial cookbook readers as it did with those in Britain. In the words of historian Kevin J. Hayes, it was "the most popular cookery book during the last three decades of the colonial period." Glasse's work on confectionery was somewhat less well known, though still widely used. Raffald's work appears in colonial recipe collections such as the one kept by Bostonian Anne Gibbons Gardiner, even though, as Anne Willan points out, "there is no record for advertisements of its sale by [American] booksellers." Its reputation may have spread by word of mouth among colonial gentry, some of whom might have encountered it on trips to Britain.[51]

Also in circulation, especially in more cosmopolitan places like Williamsburg and Boston, were Sarah Harrison's *The House-Keeper's Pocket-Book* (1733), aimed at thrifty yet upwardly mobile households; Mary Johnson's *Madam Johnson's Present*; Martha Bradley's *The British Housewife* (1756), a monumental and highly useful work directed at all levels of the household from the master and mistress to the lowliest servant, written by a former cook; and Richard Briggs's *The English Art of Cookery* (1788), published in Philadelphia in 1791 as *The New Art of Cookery*, a title perhaps considered more apt to appeal to Americans. This was another work aimed at women cooks of modest means.[52]

Susannah Carter's *The Frugal Housewife* (1765) was first printed on this side of the Atlantic in Boston in 1772. Its engraved copper plates illustrate such practical matters as the proper way to truss fowl and were etched by none other than soon-to-be Revolutionary War patriot Paul Revere. Much of *American Cookery* is taken from *The Frugal Housewife*, as we explore later in our story. For now, it is enough to note that Carter's was clearly an important work for the American market. Willan lists it among the "English cookbooks [that] had become spectacularly popular New World imports."[53]

Boston booksellers Edward Cox and Edward Berry featured the Boston edition of *The Frugal Housewife* in a full-page advertisement in their 1772 catalogue. Their sales pitch emphasized that the book was directed to the untrained cook. They also noted that it contained lots of recipes at a bargain price: "Any Person by attending to the Instructions given in this Book, may soon attain to a competent Knowledge in the Art of Cookery, &c.–And it likewise contains more in Quantity than most other Books of a much higher Price." However, *The Frugal Housewife*'s large number of recipes was achieved by plagiarizing earlier works, such as Glasse, Smith, and the massive compendium known as *The Whole Duty of a Woman* (1737).[54]

Before we judge Susannah Carter harshly, though, we might note that Hannah Glasse plagiarized extensively from the same source, as well as from Smith, La Chapelle, and others. The first edition of *The Whole Duty* itself took recipes from Smith, Richard Bradley, Charles Carter, and La Chapelle. And many recipes in *American Cookery* were taken from Susannah Carter. In the world of early cookbooks, the rights of authors and publishers were far from secure. But sometimes recipe theft had a positive outcome. The practice allowed recipes from expensive volumes to circulate more widely than they might otherwise have done.[55]

Although there is no conclusive evidence, it is possible that *The Whole Duty of a Woman* (its second edition got the more up-to-date title *The Lady's Companion*) reached the colonies directly as well as when other authors copied its recipes. In the manuscript recipe collection she began in 1763, Anne Gibbons Gardiner included some recipes from it that are not found in her other sources, Hannah Glasse and Elizabeth Raffald. This implies that they came either from an unknown secondary source or from *The Whole Duty* itself. So while we have evidence from import lists and probate records

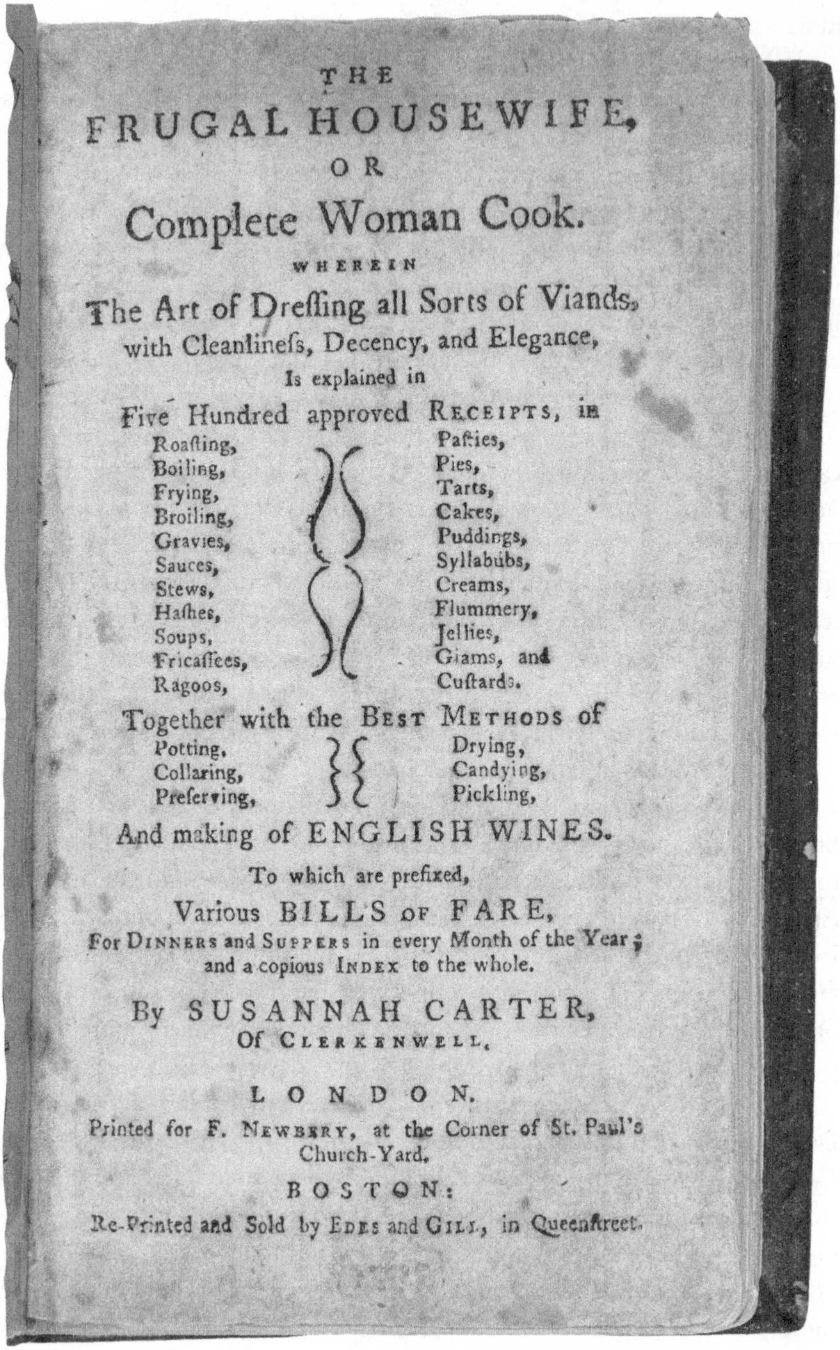

THE
FRUGAL HOUSEWIFE,
O R
Complete Woman Cook.

WHEREIN

The Art of Dreffing all Sorts of Viands,
with Cleanlinefs, Decency, and Elegance,

Is explained in

Five Hundred approved RECEIPTS, in

Roafting,	Pafties,
Boiling,	Pies,
Frying,	Tarts,
Broiling,	Cakes,
Gravies,	Puddings,
Sauces,	Syllabubs,
Stews,	Creams,
Hafhes,	Flummery,
Soups,	Jellies,
Fricaffees,	Giams, and
Ragoos,	Cuftards.

Together with the BEST METHODS of

Potting,	Drying,
Collaring,	Candying,
Preferving,	Pickling,

And making of ENGLISH WINES.

To which are prefixed,

Various BILL'S OF FARE,

For DINNERS and SUPPERS in every Month of the Year;
and a copious INDEX to the whole.

By SUSANNAH CARTER,
Of CLERKENWELL.

LONDON.

Printed for F. NEWBERY, at the Corner of St. Paul's
Church-Yard.

BOSTON:

Re-Printed and Sold by EDES and GILL, in Queenftreet.

FIGURE 2.2. Title page from *The Frugal Housewife* (Boston: Edes and Gill, 1772).
—Courtesy, American Antiquarian Society

about some imported cookbook titles, others might have made their way into wealthy colonial homes like Gardiner's.[56]

In 1742, printer William Parks of Williamsburg, Virginia, set into type the first colonial imprint of a British cookbook. He chose Smith's *The Compleat Housewife* for the purpose. It had taken a long time for a colonial printer to find it profitable to print a cookbook. To set the context for Parks's decision, we should recall that well into the eighteenth century, books of all sorts were luxury goods, reserved for those with ample financial and educational resources. Bibles and other religious texts continued to dominate the book market. It was only gradually that books on a range of subjects began to interest the reading public sufficiently to encourage printers and booksellers to expand their lists.[57]

But by the middle of the eighteenth century, the American gentry's attention had turned to cookery, just as it had to other secular pleasures such as singing, dancing, and fashion. Even before Parks presented *The Compleat Housewife* to the American book-buying public, recipes had begun to find their way into print in a colonial world hungry for the latest British fashions and entertainments. In 1737, the Philadelphia edition of William Bradford's *Young Secretary's Guide* included recipes. These were probably the first recipes to be printed in the colonies, although they did not constitute an entire work of cookery.[58]

As promised, lastly we turn our attention to the kinds of cookbooks that were *not* imported into the American colonies. The main types of work in this category are, not surprisingly, the English and French high-style works, those by Patrick Lamb, John Nott, Henry Howard, Charles Carter, François Pierre de La Varenne, François Massialot, Vincent La Chapelle, and François Menon. Although they had set the British gastronomic agenda in the late seventeenth and early eighteenth centuries, they had been superseded by the bourgeois manuals and their colonial audience was slim.

Of course, as we have mentioned, at least one work by Menon, *La cuisinière bourgeoise*, did make its way into at least one American library: Benjamin Franklin owned a "well-thumbed" copy of it. But this anomaly may be explained by Franklin's particular circumstances. During his years in France he might have developed an interest in French high cuisine. Then too, from among all of Menon's works, Franklin chose the book that the great chef wrote atypically in a country style. This was Menon's one flirtation with a rusticating fad, an attempt to join what Willan describes as "a countermovement against refinement . . . linked to the *cuisine bourgeoise* of towns . . . and to the countryside." It was a minor theme, a footnote, in French food history and in Menon's oeuvre. Yet it is the Menon Franklin owned. In all, the number of high-style French and French-inspired English cookbooks imported into America was exceedingly low. Only the ghosts of the French gastronomic legacy, found in modified techniques for à la mode, fricassee, ragout, and roux, made their way into American kitchens.[59]

Still, some books by male cooks did find an American audience. Willan reports that Richard Briggs's *English Art of Cookery* "brought him success in recently independent America, where his book was printed in three cities. His was the only cookbook by a male author to achieve such distinction at this time." Before independence, Richard Bradley's book also made the passage. He had written his work to show the lesser gentry and moderately wealthy farmers of Britain how to eat better but with little additional expense. According to Hayes, Bradley was known in Virginia and popular elsewhere in the colonies. But neither of these male cooks was in the court-cook tradition. Rather, they directed their instructions to women readers, and their culinary style was more in the housewifely tradition.[60]

A middle-class cuisine containing, in Gilly Lehmann's phrase, "adapted versions of grand court dishes" was to be found in colonial America, but the emphasis is on "adapted." Aspirations to culinary grandiosity were not completely absent from those in command of large colonial estates. But excess was tempered by the exigencies of colonial life. On the other side of the water, as the eighteenth century advanced, even highly successful court cook authors like Henry Harrison found it necessary to scale back their creations. They too were responding to necessity, but from a different source—the marketplace itself, where the power of the purse more and more in the hands of the middle class was shaping their gastronomy.[61]

Aristocratic sugarwork may have devolved into the pastry arts, practiced by servants or purchased from professional confectioners, but the English devotion to sweet foods persisted. And the English reputation for baking only grew. Cakes, biscuits or small cakes (cookies), pies, puddings, and creams were viewed as their specialties. The love of sweets found expression at all levels of society, giving dessert a prominence on the English table that it did not hold in France, where the fine art of French pastry-making was more circumscribed. For the French, dessert was important, but neither as exclusively sweet nor as dominant a part of the cuisine as it was for their British counterparts. The British sweet tooth influenced American tastes, as we see when we consider the number of confections to be found in *American Cookery*.

Until the eve of open hostilities between mother country and colonies, English cookbooks like Susannah Carter's *Frugal Housewife* continued to be imported for sale on the American market. They did well. The Boston printing of Carter's work in 1772 seems to have occurred within a brief window of opportunity for the sale of British goods that opened between the repeal of the Townsend duties in May 1770 and the beginning of the full-blown revolutionary crisis in the spring of 1773. The appeal of cookbooks that explained British practices and fashions to Americans was great, barely less so during these times of crisis. As soon as the dust of the Revolutionary War settled, British cookbooks were again imported into the new and independent nation. Independence notwithstanding, America's gastronomic agenda continued to be set by Britain.

CHAPTER 3

Print Culture

T he American appetite for British cookbooks, which was virtually unaffected by the revolutionary conflict, had as much to do with a taste for consuming print as it did with a taste for English food. Especially for New Englanders, the "book" part of "cookbook" had a long and revered history.

To appreciate the meaning of a printed work such as *American Cookery* as part of an effort to create national identity, it helps to understand the value placed on print in the young republic and in particular in the book's originating locale. The esteem in which reading was held and the extent to which literacy crossed gender and class barriers varied considerably from region to region in colonial and early national America. The legacy of Puritanism in Massachusetts and Connecticut assured that reading would be central to any New England conception of the new nation.

The Puritans were ardent readers of the Bible, sermons, theological treatises, and devotional writings. John Foxe, the sixteenth-century author of a book about the Protestant martyrs and one of the English Puritans' favorites, famously wrote that "the Lord began to work for His Church not with sword and target . . . but with printing, writing and reading." In the next century, printing, writing, and reading would be at the core of the Puritan vision of the godly society that some of their number hoped to establish on the shores of Massachusetts Bay.[1]

The emphasis on literacy in the colony can be contrasted with Virginia, where printing was not sanctioned by the authorities until the eighteenth century. It took Massachusetts only eleven years to establish its first press. A Puritan clergyman from Surrey, England, named Joseph Glover decided in 1638 to remove himself and his family to the more theologically congenial environment of Massachusetts. He also raised enough money to purchase a printing press, paper, and types to bring with him. As part of his arrangements, he contracted on June 7 of that year with fellow Englishman Stephen Daye, a locksmith, to operate his printing press in the New World in exchange for a loan to pay for Daye's passage and that of his household. Glover "fell sick of a feaver and dyed" before his plans could be carried out. But Daye emigrated, and along with three male servants set up the press in the town of Cambridge. He began printing in March 1639.[2]

In 1640, Daye printed the work for which he is most famous, the first book produced in British North America. This was a new metrical translation of the Hebrew psalms, collaborated on by New England's leading ministers. The *Bay Psalm Book* was eagerly adopted by the colony's churches. It was sometimes referred to as the New England version of the Psalms to distinguish it from an English translation by T. Sternhold and J. Hopkins that had provided the words and tunes first sung by Massachusetts colonists. For the sake of English meter, the Sternhold and Hopkins version took many liberties with the Hebrew text, leading some to call it, in jest, "Hopkins his Jigges" or "Genevah Jiggs" (referring to the Geneva Bible with which it was often paired).[3]

The pride taken in the *Bay Psalm Book* testifies to the Puritan passion for meticulous learning as the handmaiden of piety—and to printing as the handmaiden of learning. With an original edition of 1,700 copies, a revised 1651 edition of 2,000 copies, also printed in Cambridge, and many later editions, the *Bay Psalm Book* was used by English and American congregations well into the eighteenth century.[4]

Stephen Daye was succeeded at the Cambridge press by Samuel Green. In 1673, Green was approached by the colony of Connecticut to print its first book, a collection of general laws. The contract between Samuel Green and Connecticut began what would prove to be a long and fruitful association for the Green family.[5]

It wasn't until the early eighteenth century that Connecticut got around to appointing its own official printer. Historians have speculated that seventeenth-century authorities may have feared "the seditious potential of the press" more than they minded the inconvenience of sending important documents in manuscript form to Massachusetts or London to be printed. Even in keeping official papers, Connecticut colonists relied on handwritten records.

The next Connecticut printer, the first one officially appointed by the colony government, was not a direct member of the Green family, but he was related to the clan through marriage. Thomas Short of Boston unfortunately lived up to his surname, serving only from 1709 until his untimely death in 1712. His demise created a vacancy that was filled by another

Green, Timothy, grandson of Cambridge's second printer, Samuel Green. Timothy and his sons, working in New London, served as Connecticut's printers until Timothy retired from the trade in 1751.

As they consumed the English Bibles and other religious works that rolled off colonial presses or were imported from England, the English nonconformists who settled New England ("Puritans" as their disparagers called them) were more engaged and probing in their reading than most ordinary English people of the day. Put in its simplest terms, for these earnest seekers after religious truth, the sacred authority that had been wrested from the papacy and Catholic Church hierarchy during the Reformation was now situated within Christianity's sacred texts. These biblical writings and the exegesis provided by Puritan scholars could be made directly available to every Christian, without further clerical mediation, if that Christian could but read and had access to the printed word of God.

The reading engaged in by Puritans, often conducted alone and in private, was valued for its capacity to have a great effect on the reader. It was not pursued in the way most reading is done now, either for personal enjoyment or the disinterested pursuit of knowledge. Instead, Puritans read for very high stakes—to discern God's will and open themselves to the Holy Spirit. This emotionally charged intellection sometimes resulted in the Puritan laity drawing conclusions about the nature of divinity that differed from the interpretations of their own clergy. Although the society in which these contentions over orthodoxy took place disavowed the episcopal structure of the Church of England, it was nevertheless based on deference and hierarchy, controlled by an educated elite. Variant biblical interpretations, especially when they related to individual spiritual autonomy, met with firm official resistance. The response to open challenges to authority in this theocratic society might begin with stern reprimands but could end with expulsion from the community of believers.[6]

By encouraging the personal study of Holy Scripture but prohibiting dissent from Puritan doctrine, the established church of New England created an inherently untenable situation. The outcome was a series of bitter and protracted religious controversies that plagued Puritan communities throughout the seventeenth century. These disputes sometimes took dramatic form, as when the ministers and appointed magistrates of the infant Bay Colony, led by John Winthrop, were pitted against free-grace advocates, led by Anne Hutchinson and Reverend John Cotton. Trials, banishments, political victories, and defeats served only to mask the extent to which multiple interpretations of God's word existed within society and even within the established clergy. The unwillingness to sanction disagreement or to search for an acceptable means to carry on public debate on fundamental issues resulted in a society that appeared unified on its surface but often seethed underneath with resentment and antipathy.[7]

In the first half of the eighteenth century, two developments converged to dissipate, if not resolve, these tensions. First, the zeal of the founding generation, based on religious conviction and heightened by the ostracism many had experienced in England, cooled as colonials became wealthier and more established. With greater wealth, more leisure, and less religious intensity, interests broadened. Bibles and devotional manuals continued to be steady sellers—New England was still a highly religious society. But gradually these works were supplemented by reading matter of a decidedly secular nature. Newspapers, pamphlets, and books, among them imported cookbooks, found a ready audience.[8]

Second, the Great Awakening, an evangelical movement of the 1740s, upset New England's fragile religious and social equilibrium. The explosion of debate provoked by this movement loosened social restraints. The wrath of the powerful, fear of which had long restricted free thought and speech, was no match for revivalist fervor and the controversy it caused. The stage was set for a new eighteenth-century New England, one where religion had moved beyond the control of a conservative clergy and where secular interests and public debate increasingly found a place.

The old devotion to reading and literacy that was a bedrock of the New England character would be enlisted to serve the populace in new ways. As with their ancestors in the first decades of settlement, eighteenth-century New Englanders appreciated the connection between a robust infrastructure of printers, presses, book importers, and booksellers and the pursuit of learning as it was secularized and made a more public and social endeavor.

In Connecticut, the heightened demand for printed material was met by both old and new publishing alliances. In 1755, a printer who had been successful in New York and New Jersey, James Parker, took on a partner named John Holt with the intention of expanding their printing enterprise into Connecticut. They set up shop in New London and made their mark by publishing the colony's first newspaper, the *Connecticut Gazette*. Within a few years, positions within the firm were shuffled. In 1760, Holt left Connecticut to manage Parker's New York operation. The opening Holt's move created was filled by Thomas Green, one of Timothy Green's grandsons. Thomas Green had been working for Parker in New Haven since 1757. He became Parker's factotum in Connecticut, keeping New Haven as his base. We might have expected the Greens to be rivals of the interloping Parker & Company. Instead they joined forces. Yet as the generations of Green printers in Massachusetts and Connecticut illustrate, the trade was often a family affair. The skill required, along with the capital, equipment, and community ties needed to attract credit and business, were passed from one generation to the next.[9]

Although colonial printing tended to be concentrated in the hands of families like the Greens, who worked to perpetuate their business dynasties, there were times when sons were simply not available to be brought into the family line of work. In these cases, other close relations, friends, and at times even neighbors were tapped for the job. Some individuals entered the trade almost willy-nilly because of their blood or affective connections to printers. They included printers' wives, widows, and daughters, as well as unrelated children, whose impoverished parents indentured them as apprentices to serve printers perpetually in need of help.

Another shakeup of James Parker's company occurred in 1764, when the printer James Mecom bought out Parker's Connecticut interests. This change in bosses may have been the reason that Thomas Green finally left New Haven to set up shop on his own. He moved to Hartford, establishing that city's first press and founding its first newspaper, the *Connecticut Courant*, the country's oldest newspaper in continuous operation.

During his sojourn working for James Parker in New Haven, Thomas Green brought into apprenticeship a native of Bethlehem, Connecticut, named Ebenezer Watson. When Green subsequently headed to Hartford to open a printing operation there, he took Watson along. Green increased his workforce again in 1766 with the addition of a nine-year-old boy by the name of George Goodwin. Goodwin had been indentured to Green by his parents. He worked at first as Green's office boy. A year later (and a mere three years after setting up his business in Hartford), Green was back in New Haven. He was not dismantling his Hartford enterprise, however. Rather, he seems to have been exercising the peripatetic inclinations of members of his trade. His former apprentice, Watson, was made his new partner in Hartford. In 1769, the firm in its Hartford location took on an apprentice even younger than Goodwin had been when he went to work for Thomas Green. This was a seven-year-old named Charles Webster.[10]

The Green-Watson partnership lasted until 1770, when Watson took over both the Hartford press and the *Courant* newspaper. The young George Goodwin continued with the firm, now under Watson's sole proprietorship, and was probably promoted from the position of office boy to that of printer's apprentice.

It is likely that Ebenezer Watson's second wife, Hannah Bunce Watson, originally from nearby Lebanon, Connecticut, played a role in day-to-day operations of the firm. This experience may have helped her manage the business when her husband died in 1777. Along with another recently widowed woman whom we know only as Mrs. Ledyard, the widow Watson also took control of a paper mill in East Hartford, which she had inherited from her husband. Ebenezer Watson had opened the mill when the Revolutionary War caused a disruption in his paper supply and forced him to suspend publication of the *Courant* for a month in December 1775.[11]

To share responsibility for the Hartford printing business after her husband's death, Hannah Watson went into partnership with the now fully grown and full-fledged printer George Goodwin. According to renowned Massachusetts printer Isaiah Thomas, who drew on his own considerable knowledge and experience of the trade to write the first history of American printing, Goodwin was not merely competent to run the Watson business. He was a better printer than Ebenezer Watson had been. Certainly, the Watsons trusted Goodwin. It seems likely that at the onset of Watson's fatal illness the young apprentice, at the time only twenty, had taken complete responsibility for putting out the *Courant*.[12]

The active partnership between Hannah Watson and George Goodwin was not destined to survive for long. Within a couple of years, Watson remarried, again changing the ownership equation. In the year after Ebenezer Watson's death, a neighbor and perhaps occasional employee, a mason by trade named Barzillai Hudson, lost his wife, Margaret, to smallpox, leaving him with two small children. He appears to have been a respected member of the community, for he had been appointed in 1777 as a Revolutionary War commandant, assigned to oversee the militia that guarded British prisoners of war at Hartford's county jail.[13]

As we might now come to expect of those eighteenth-century New Englanders involved in the printing trade, the Hudsons were also related to the Watsons, if rather tangentially: Margaret Hudson had been a cousin of Ebenezer Watson's deceased first wife. In 1779, Hannah became Barzillai Hudson's second wife. The Watson-Hudson marriage occurred between two people who had been acquainted in their previous marriages, and the prior family connection of their deceased spouses may well have played a role in their union. With Hannah Watson's marriage to Barzillai Hudson, the Watson printing business remained loosely within the family circle.[14]

Upon her second marriage, Hannah Bunce Watson Hudson relinquished her active role in the business. Her new husband managed the printing shop and business interests. From what was now the Hudson & Goodwin shop, he sold the standard stationer's goods—ink, paper, and sealing wax, along with books, newspapers, and pamphlets. But like many a printer eager to make ends meet, he also traded in an array of goods. In his case these included "sugar, chocolate, spices, tea, coffee, pocketbooks, hats, pigtail tobacco," and "other items." George Goodwin, by this time a highly skilled printer, saw to that aspect of the business. *Courant* historian J. Eugene Smith wrote of Hudson's part in the enterprise: "In the new member of the company, who was then 37 years of age, the firm probably got what it most needed—a responsible person to manage and expand its business interests while Goodwin gave full time to the printing. . . . This was the beginning of the prominent firm of Hudson & Goodwin, book printers, and for many years to come, prosperous publishers of Hartford's *Connecticut Courant*."[15]

As a partnership between Barzillai Hudson and George Goodwin, the printing concern grew to publish the important early national works we have surveyed previously—Webster's speller, the writings of the Connecticut Wits, and, of course, *American Cookery*. In the mid-nineteenth century, children's author Samuel Goodrich ("Peter Parley") reminisced about Hudson & Goodwin as it was at the beginning of the century: "A firm then known all over this hemisphere, as publishers of the *Bible*, Webster's *Spelling-book*, and the *Connecticut Courant*. They were, in the popular mind, regarded as the bulwarks of religion, education, and federalism—three pretty staunch supporters of the New England platform, in that epoch of the world."[16]

Historians of the Connecticut print trade Christopher P. Bickford and Jeffrey H. Kaimowitz have pointed out regarding the earlier Green family printing empire that "it is natural that a printing family like the Greens, as long as they kept reproducing, would train their own children rather than encourage competition from outsiders. Barring this, they would look for individuals they knew in the community or through some other means." The principles by which the Greens lived were also put into practice by their associates and apprentices—as seen in the sequence of kinship and other pre-existing relations whereby the printing operation started by Thomas Green evolved into the firm of Hudson & Goodwin. This final incarnation would prove to be the most successful in a long line of profitable enterprises.[17]

The flourishing network of printers provided another kind of commercial connection between Hudson & Goodwin and the Green clan. The founder of the Hudson & Goodwin firm was Thomas Green, grandson of Connecticut's second official printer. Another member of the clan, "S. Green," *great*-grandson of Connecticut's first printer, advertised Hudson & Goodwin's newest production, *American Cookery*, in his New London newspaper in the summer of 1796.[18]

Several interesting trends emerge from this brief look at the history of printing in Connecticut, and of Hudson & Goodwin in particular. From the first years of settlement through the last decade of the eighteenth century, Connecticut printers relied on a strategy that involved building publishing houses based on kith and kin. This was a natural response to the uncertainties of the trade. But the small absolute number of those skilled in all aspects of the business meant that crossovers between and among firms and clans sometimes happened. At times, printers ignored the natural barriers between competing commercial interests to create dense webs of exchange among those in the trade.

While our focus is on New England printers and their influence in upstate New York and other areas populated by New Englanders, printers' networks existed elsewhere in colonial and early national society. The many geographic impediments to commerce in early America were determinedly overcome by a trade that lived by the exchange of information and that depended on extensive contacts. As a result, printers were among the most informed and connected artisans and tradespeople in America, although they were not considered part of the gentry class. Indeed, all acknowledged that theirs was, as historian Jeffrey L. Pasley writes, "a dirty, smelly, physically demanding job." But the prosperity of the most successful among them put them in close association with their well-heeled clients, who depended especially on the influence exerted by the printer-controlled newspapers. Even for small-town printers, professional ties often reached both up and down the social ladder and beyond the borders of their regions. Historian Karen A. Weyler, describing the scope of colonial printers' networks and partnerships, writes of the "intricate webs of relationships that stretched the length of the Atlantic seaboard."[19]

These associations extended as well to connections outside the printing trade and to locations beyond the Atlantic coast. Weyler provides an example in her discussion of the financial challenges faced by a Virginia printer who, like Hannah Watson, briefly ran the business she inherited from her husband. Clementina Rind mortgaged her "best bed" and other household goods, including a fish kettle, to raise money for her business, perhaps to finance the purchase of the new English-made typeface for which she was then negotiating. Rind's mortgage-holders were an influential lot: John Blair, a jurist and member of the Virginia House of Burgesses; Robert Miller, a merchant and revenue officer who served as treasurer of the College of William and Mary; James Southall, a wealthy tavern owner; and John Tazewell, a local attorney and official of a public hospital for the mentally ill. Although new to the world of business, Rind clearly already had the trust of members of the gentry class in her own community. And well beyond that community, she had commercial contacts that allowed her to make a costly overseas purchase to advance her business interests. On April 14, 1774, she proudly informed the readers of her newspaper, the *Virginia Gazette*, that she had ordered from London an "elegant" set of type fonts.[20]

Early American printing was in some ways a dynamic profession, as illustrated by the fact that daughters as well as wives might inherit the business. In Weyler's opinion, this arrangement, highly unusual for its time, occurred because "productive presses were deemed too necessary to the public good to allow the sex of a reliable printer-publisher to become a significant distraction." However, the openness to including women did not mean that the trade was otherwise politically progressive. As Pasley and others have observed, young printers who entered the trade during and after the Revolution soon "settled into the role of reliable auxiliaries to the victorious Whig establishment, which was growing steadily more disenchanted with the democratic, localistic political fervor the Revolution had unleashed."[21]

Most printers did not specialize in the types of material they printed—small runs and local interests dictated the scope of their productions, from which they extracted what profits they could. Newspapers were a lucrative sideline for many, their readership expanding throughout the century. In some instances, as with the *Courant*, the newspaper eventually became the main source of the printer-publisher's income and reputation, the printing business turning into the sideline. As local producers, printers focused mostly on what historian James N. Green has called "the old colonial staples of newspapers, almanacs, government printing, and pamphlets relating to current events."[22]

The cost of printers' equipment was always high. Type foundries, complex operations that relied on skilled labor and developed manufacturing, had been attempted in colonial America, but none was successful. In Connecticut in 1769, the colony's General Assembly underwrote a jeweler and silversmith named Abel Buell in his endeavor to learn the art of type-founding and establish a foundry. But his business failed, and he fled to Florida to escape his creditors, leaving his wife to cope with his debts. Back in the type foundry business after the war, Buell fared little better. Isaiah Thomas judged Buell's typefaces "much inferiour to English, and the price high." Historian John Bidwell explains, "American printers could not rely on a fully equipped, completely independent local typefoundry until the establishment of the Philadelphia firm of Binny & Ronaldson in 1796."[23]

So American printers were forced to look to Britain when they required new or replacements fonts. The uncertainties of transatlantic shipping, misconstrued orders, and dockyard theft made for risky investments. Consequently, many printers held on to their worn "sorts" (letters) well past their sell-by date. When the originals gave out, they would extend the life of the set by substituting mismatched letters, different in size or style, from another set. This made for graphically challenging reading. Ben Franklin's remark about the sorry state of the typefaces used in colonial Boston's newspapers reflects the precarious financial situation many printers found themselves in as their expensive equipment aged. Franklin complained that the city papers "perfectly blind me in endeavouring to read them." He added with characteristic wit, "If you should ever have any Secrets that you wish to be well kept, get them printed in those Papers."[24]

The printers' endless search for revenue also meant selling chocolate, spices, and tobacco in their shops, next to newspapers, broadsheets, and books, as Barzillai Hudson did. The sale of sundries alongside newspapers and magazines persists into our own day, or almost. Only with the advent of the Internet and the demise of most print periodicals has the newspaper vendor's stall, where chewing gum, breath mints, candy bars, and cigarettes nestled near the daily papers and monthly magazines, become a rarity.[25]

To assure the survival of their businesses, American printers also stocked one another's works. Isaiah Thomas wrote to Hudson & Goodwin in 1786, informing his competitors: "I wish to do all in my power to encourage book printing, and am therefore willing to exchange those I print for books printed by gentlemen in other places." This was perhaps Thomas's bid to procure copies of Noah Webster's tremendously popular Blue Back Speller, first published by Hudson & Goodwin in 1783. Certainly, that was one out-come of his gambit—large quantities of Hudson & Goodwin–printed copies of the speller were exchanged for a variety of materials printed at Thomas's Worcester and Boston presses.[26]

Exchanges of their printed works also benefited others besides the printer-publishers themselves. Historian Jack Larkin has written that "books took many paths into the American countryside," not least one facilitated by the small-town printer, publisher, and bookseller. Despite the minute scale of their individual operations, these firms taken together provided several ser-vices critical to the bottom line of major publishers from Boston, New York, Philadelphia, and Baltimore, especially in the quarter century or so after the Revolution.[27]

As we have seen with advertisements for American Cookery, small town newspapers, like their big city counterparts, promoted in their pages the almanacs, pamphlets, and books they had for sale in their shops, reaping the profits of this publicity. With the help of itinerant peddlers, the printers' goods circulated deep into rural areas, to places rarely reached directly by metropolitan publishers, creating an interest in newspaper-advertised books in the region's hinterlands and extending the market for books into some rather unlikely areas.

But with the opening of rural and small-town markets to the book trade, the issue of payment arose. Urban publishers were generally unwilling to take in trade for their merchandise the kinds of bulky, perishable commod-ities their backwoods customers had to offer in lieu of specie. Local pub-lishers were in a better position to cope with these bartering arrangements. They would purchase the major publishers' stock using their own inventory of printed books, broadsides, and pamphlets as payment. Then they would sell the purchased metropolitan stock, along with their own, throughout the countryside, trading these printed goods for various commodities that would end up for sale back on their shops' shelves. In this way, everything from locally produced Bibles and almanacs to sophisticated romantic fic-tion and fashion books reflecting the trends of places like New York and Baltimore found their way into the American countryside.[28]

This kind of exchange hardly turned villagers and country farmers into urban sophisticates, but it did give them glimpses of a glittering world that existed beyond their everyday lives. Polite conversation, another marker of elevated social status, became a hot topic in the provinces, and as a guide to manners, no book was more popular than an advice book on the proper conduct of a gentleman, *Letters . . . to His Son*, by Philip Stanhope, 4th Earl of Chesterfield. Along with Chesterfield editions published in London, Dublin, Boston, New York, and Philadelphia, two editions were produced in the Connecticut River Valley in the 1790s, one brought out by Hartford printer Nathaniel Patten in 1792, the other by Greenfield printer Thomas Dickman in 1796. A third provincial edition was printed in Walpole, New Hampshire, in 1812. Country book peddlers stocked multiple versions of Chesterfield's letters, the fancier printings and bindings appealing to those with fatter purses. Historian Richard D. Brown comments on the incongruity of this British lord's American popularity: "Ironically, republican gentility followed London models."[29]

In return for the services of country printers in hawking their wares, the big city printer-publishers acquired holdings of the works brought out by their rural associates. This led to a far wider dissemination of the country printers' stock than would otherwise have been possible. Homer Merriam, who at the turn of the twentieth century served as president of the family firm of G. & C. Merriam Company, publishers of the Merriam-Webster dictionaries, explained the exchange: "The country printer would order from the city publishers his publications as needed, he to take ours as payment. He [the city publisher] would therefore push the sales of the books published by the country printers." The advertisement and sale of the Albany edition of *American Cookery* in New York City in 1797 may well have been a case in point. Thomas Greenleaf, the proprietor of the newspaper in which the cookbook was advertised, was also a printer-publisher, and Charles R. and George Webster, the printer-publishers of the Albany edition, could have made an arrangement of this sort with Greenleaf. Merriam also painted a vivid picture of the trips into the hinterland taken by the small-time printer-publishers, who sometimes left their stock for sale with rural merchants. To collect their payments, they could be seen "often going out for a day, with a horse and wagon, visiting a circuit of perhaps three or four towns, and perhaps ten merchants in those towns, gathering up goods . . . calico for a dress . . . handkerchiefs, gloves of cotton cloth, cloth for coats or pantaloons for the apprentices . . . family stores, groceries."[30]

By this swapping process, books originally created for a select market, such as high-end English architectural pattern books and London furniture makers' catalogues, turned up around 1800 in the stock of Isaiah Thomas's and Hudson & Goodwin's shops in Walpole, New Hampshire, and Hartford. The reach of Thomas's printing business, with presses and shops extending from Boston and Springfield to the more remote towns of the Connecticut River Valley, is another example of both the printers' web of influence and the allure to country customers of a varied selection of merchandise.[31]

New England's high levels of literacy, its growing taste for luxury, and its expanding settlements, combined with a print culture that despite those laborious publishers' exchanges was still primarily local in nature, resulted in a call for more printers. Tracing printing developments in the Connecticut River Valley, Christopher P. Bickford and Jeffrey H. Kaimowitz write of a postwar explosion of demand that "lured printers up the Valley in the decades after 1783." It seemed that every new town wished to see a newspaper set up shop. Newspapers gave growing places a sense of stability and identity. Jeffrey L. Pasley maintains that a newspaper was "an essential perquisite to a town becoming a significant place." By the late eighteenth century, virtually every major settlement in the Connecticut River Valley boasted a local newspaper and a press.[32]

Yet according to historian Hugh Amory, who has studied the colonial book trade, even before the war New England was, as he phrases it, "infested" with country printers. Many migrated from metropolitan to rural areas sensing new opportunities. Others were simply trying to escape the fierce competition brought on by the concentration of printers in crowded cities. The surplus produced "Malthusian necessities that drove New England printers out of Boston and swept them up the Connecticut River from Hartford," Amory writes. The demand for books and other printed material in the countryside, especially in the Connecticut River Valley, was part and parcel of the movement at all levels of provincial society toward a more cosmopolitan outlook informed by "New York, Boston, and Philadelphia versions of London taste."[33]

But the deep ethos of religious seriousness and material restraint derived from the region's Puritan heritage was not so easily displaced. The old steady sellers—Bibles for home and school use, sermons, almanacs, and pamphlets on current events—continued to roll off local presses. Amory attests to the New England values that might be seen to have tempered the rush toward gentility: "[The] continuing importance of country printing in New England meant that a relatively high percentage of its production lay in schoolbooks and chapbooks." It was the avid consumption of such humble intellectual properties by small-town and rural readers that allowed printing in the provincial city of Hartford for a time to rival Boston's output.[34]

A look at day-to-day affairs in the Hudson & Goodwin shop, written in the late nineteenth century by Goodwin descendant James Junius Goodwin, catches the flavor of the traditional printing endeavor as it was pursued by the firm earlier in the century: "Large editions of a school Bible were printed, for which the types were imported from England, in 1809, set up and locked in iron chases, ready to be placed upon the press; the New Testament, in various sizes and styles; hundreds of thousands of Webster's Spelling-books. . . . Good presswork, type, paper, and binding with exceeding neatness and accuracy, mark all their imprints."[35]

To survive in the marketplace, printers could not restrict their trade to print products nor even to those quaint sundries and bartered goods for sale in their shops. As literary critic Michael Warner explains, well before the revolution "in the North American colonies . . . printers held a monopoly on the postal service, making them an important center of communication and public life at a time when the post roads were the main way of linking as an identifiable body colonies that occupied many times the area of England with only a fraction of the population." Such printing shop/post offices did not resemble the impersonal federal post offices of today. These were rather "centers for meetings and exchanges among those who traded in information." They were the community's water cooler, the general store at the crossroads, a status and function retained only by the smallest rural post offices today.[36]

James Junius Goodwin described how Hudson & Goodwin's newspaper office and printing shop performed this role after the war. "The leading men of the State . . . made 'The Courant' office their resort," he wrote. But his testimony also reminds us that the firm functioned not merely as host to local society; it was influential in shaping it: "'The Courant' . . . being an organ of the Federal party and the Congregational clergy, for many years it gave tone to the morals and policy of the State, and many of its leading articles gained a national reputation." The topics for those articles were undoubtedly hatched during gab-fests engaged in by the "leading men of the State" in the newspaper office.[37]

Let us peer for a moment into the Hudson & Goodwin shop to examine the stock on its shelves. In this small emporium, changes in the inventory over time tell a story. Historian J. Eugene Smith wrote of the firm's earliest days, when its shop stocked "small quantities of articles . . . taken in on barter." Most of the goods were the humblest sort—dried peas, indigo dye, linseed oil. But gradually, the shop's merchandise began to include more

FIGURE 3.1. *George Goodwin,* William Henry Brown, 1843, silhouette, cut paper on board with lithographic scene, watercolor and shadow pencil.
—Gift of William Henry Brown, 1843.34.10, Connecticut Historical Society, Hartford

expensive goods. Smith noted that even during the war, in 1779, chocolate, spices, sugar, tea, and coffee were on hand, as were "cookbooks for the housewife." By the 1790s, with a postwar economy finally revving up, advertisements for cookbooks sold at the shop appeared regularly in the *Courant.*

A customer perusing the luxury foods then on sale at Hudson & Goodwin might decide to purchase both some of the ingredients to make a fine meal and one of the cookbooks designed to teach a housewife how to cook those exotic new foods.[38]

Maintaining the printing office as a "resort" for state leaders; being willing to trade in a miscellany of small consumables, some taken in barter; printing an assortment of steady-selling Bibles, almanacs, and schoolbooks; as well as reselling the elegant imprints and imports gotten in trade from metropolitan firms were all business strategies developed by regional printers to exploit every source of profit and maximize their social prominence. Michael Warner describes one more custom of the profession that further extended the printer's influence. This was the "entrepreneurial practice . . . of capitalizing journeymen to set up affiliated shops in other towns." Writing of the prerevolutionary period but with implications for the following decades, Warner finds that a "complex system of links" derived from these satellite printing ventures. Here was another way to expand the sale of the printer's stock. After the Revolution, the generation of new printing enterprises capitalized by the owners of the old shops benefited readers at the edges of settlement in northern New England, upstate New York, and Ohio.[39]

The pace at which towns began to grow after 1783 in the Connecticut River Valley lent entrepreneurial energy to printers. Indeed, it is hard to say which came first, the printer or the town. Historian Robert A. Gross maintains that thousands of printers "joined the great migration to the West, sometimes well ahead of settlement." Whether printers arrived in advance of settlement or as part of it, they found a market for their products. Bickford and Kaimowitz describe "a remarkable pattern of decentralization in the printing trades [that] emerged as local printing competed successfully with books and pamphlets from Boston and London." It was happy days for small-shop printers as "pent up demand" erupted in the founding of newspapers and subscription libraries in many towns. The 20 or so such libraries in late colonial Connecticut, for instance, had become 250 by 1820, making them "a characteristic institution of the New England town."[40]

Former journeymen and apprentice printers from the cities, setting out to establish businesses of their own, cashed in on the expanding market for print. In the postwar period, Hartford played a leading role in supplying printers to the Massachusetts towns along the Connecticut River, as well as to outlying Connecticut towns. Bickford and Kaimowitz explain, "Diffusion of printing from Hartford was a natural result of the development of the city as a printing center. As in the case of Boston, New London, and New Haven before it, Hartford became a place where journeymen printers might find work and apprentices could learn their craft. If they were ambitious, they would then try to strike out on their own."[41]

William Butler, a former Hudson & Goodwin apprentice, set up shop in Northampton, Massachusetts, in 1786, publishing the *Hampshire Gazette* there for the next thirty years. Butler's brother Simeon was also active in the publishing and bookselling trade. He was responsible for the 1798 Hartford reissue of *American Cookery*, as this notice on its title page indicates: "Hartford: *Printed for* Simeon Butler, Northampton." Like his brother, Simeon conducted business for many years in Northampton. His shop, still in operation in 1897, was by then called "an historic store" in *The New England Stationer and Printer*, an annual directory. This volume lists the store's various incarnations over the course of a century under the Butler name: "Simeon Butler, bookseller and publisher; Simeon Butler & Son; J. H. Butler; Butler & Bridgman," after which the business left the Butler line. Simeon and his brother were the sons of Captain Daniel Butler of Hartford, so it is likely that Simeon, like William, had a connection to the original Hartford publishers of *American Cookery*, Hudson & Goodwin.[42]

In 1782, Anthony Haswell, an Englishman who was previously a journeyman with Isaiah Thomas, joined with Massachusetts native Elisha Babcock to begin a newspaper in Springfield, Massachusetts, called the *Massachusetts Gazette*. Both Haswell and Babcock had recently worked for Hudson & Goodwin and likely conceived the idea for their Springfield partnership while residing in Hartford as journeymen printers.[43]

Springfield serves as a prime example of the kind of growing Connecticut River Valley town that would attract this type of ambitious young printer. Englishman Henry Wansey portrayed Springfield in 1794 as "a very pleasant country town, the houses neat, clean, and well painted, chiefly of weather board; the streets were regular . . . it put me much in mind of Winbourn in Dorsetshire." To Wansey, a notable feature of the town was the "two newspapers printed here, three times a week." He described going into one of the printing offices to buy "a provincial almanac." While in the shop, he reported, "I collected some old newspapers there, of various parts of America; they afforded me much information as well as entertainment. . . . A weekly newspaper is published here under the title of the *Federal Spy*; an excellent paper." Springfield at this time, two years after the founding of the *Federal Spy* in 1792, was much like Hartford in 1764, the year Thomas Green introduced that community of four thousand to its first paper, the *Connecti-cut Courant,* and to the advantages of a locally operated printing press.[44]

Recall from chapter 1 that in the early national period, using American labor and materials to reprint a British title turned it into an American book. Into the 1820s, the trade held that "the maker of the book was the manufacturer, *not* the author." Also, the term "publisher" was first applied in America in the 1790s, according to James N. Green, but its definition was considerably different from ours: it was used to describe American printers who reprinted British books. Some American printers abandoned their own operations completely to concentrate on selling British reprints produced by other American "publishers."[45]

Despite the dominance of British books in the American book market, two American print products began to gain ground in the 1790s. First were those perennial local favorites—almanacs, political speeches, and sermons—which got even more traction with postwar prosperity. Second were British works lightly edited to include an American perspective. In a geography text or penmanship manual, for example, the editor might replace English place names with American ones but make no other significant changes to the work. Both types of "American" books succeeded in the marketplace.[46]

Movement toward a fully American publishing industry was slow in com-ing. Yet the textual amendments of the 1790s served, as Green writes, "as important replacement on the textual level, weaning publishers, authors, and readers alike from dependence on the authority of the mother country." For instance, American sections composed by Jedidiah Morse, America's first geographer, were added to a popular English manual, William Guth-rie's *New System of Modern Geography.*[47]

Isaiah Thomas also got into the Americanizing business. He published an English literacy manual, *The Instructor,* which focused on spelling, reading, and writing "True English." Thomas felt free to give his edition the subtitle *American Young Man's Best Companion* after he inserted into it American examples for learning to read and write English. In another example, *An Easy Introduction to the Knowledge of Nature* by Sarah Trimmer (London, 1780; Boston, 1796), the original included the fictional narrator's instruction to her son Henry to study "every country in the world" but to "love England the best." In the American edition, this exhortation became "love America the best," with the added boast, "we have the best government in the world, and no people enjoy so much liberty, both civil and religious, as we do."[48]

Works of a more original nature began to appear, but these too were often modeled on British precedents. The difference between the two types of works—British reprints that had been Americanized and American works constructed on British models—was slight. But the original works at least aspired to be American in both authorship and outlook. The quest for an American viewpoint on aesthetic, pedagogical, and even scientific matters had been inaugurated.

A final challenge remained: how to make American books, in the full sense of the term, as profitable as British imports and reprints. Most American consumers continued to prefer the quality and authority they found in British products of all sorts, from porcelain and furniture to books. While one publisher alone could not shift American attitudes, Ebenezer T. Andrews, a partner of Isaiah Thomas, was diligent in promoting homegrown works. In 1789, he published the first American novel, *The Power of Sympathy* by William Hill Brown. Each year, he published more American than foreign authors, a fact that set him apart from other American publishers.[49]

American writers "flush with hopes for a republican literary culture," as Green comments, began to challenge the economics of American publishing. Starting in the 1780s, many directly solicited support for themselves through prepublication subscriptions. Others who had the means paid to have their works printed. Connecticut writers were well represented in both groups. Within Connecticut, Hartford in particular was the center of this cultural trend. The city's inland location had spared it the devastation wrought upon coastal towns by the British during the war; it had come out of the conflict an even stronger place, both commercially and culturally. Writers therefore tended to find each other there.[50]

Among writers who underwrote their works, "in effect supplying the capital and doing much of the marketing themselves," were John Trumbull with his satirical poem *M'Fingal* (1782); Noah Webster with his hugely successful speller (1783); Timothy Dwight with his epic poem *Conquest of Canaan* (1785); Joel Barlow with his *Vision of Columbus* (1787), later recast as *The Columbiad*; and Jedidiah Morse with his *American Geography* (1789). *American Geography* would become a standard work for home and school in the nineteenth century.[51]

Noah Webster is of particular interest to our story because the publishing trajectory of his first book parallels that of *American Cookery*. His speller's first edition came off the Hudson & Goodwin press in 1783. Webster's second volume in the projected three-volume work on spelling, grammar, and reading followed in 1784, also published by Hudson & Goodwin. The third volume, with the same publisher, appeared in 1785. Beginning in 1794, these works were also published by the firm of Charles R. & George Webster of Albany.[52]

The sequence for Noah Webster's books, of first editions coming from Hudson & Goodwin's press followed by editions from the Websters of Albany, was repeated with *American Cookery*. For a small cookbook attempting to compete in a market well furnished with better-known and more smartly produced British cooking manuals, the close association between Hudson & Goodwin and the Webster firm served as an important catalyst. The intimate and overlapping worlds of printers, especially among those within the Federalist fold, helped to promote authors and their works as well as the printers' own businesses. Both the Hartford and Albany editions of *American Cookery* were brought out in 1796: "The call has been so great, and the sale so rapid," of the first edition of *American Cookery*, its author Amelia Simmons explained. But augmenting this demand was the convenient network of publishing connections, which made multiple editions and an expanded market possible for a new and mostly unknown author. Publishers' links extended in many directions—the Webster brothers of Albany were also Noah Webster's second cousins once removed.[53]

Other correspondences can be drawn between Webster's speller and Simmons's *American Cookery*. Both were notably short works: the speller's first edition was 120 pages; the first edition of *American Cookery* was 47 pages. (The second edition was longer at 64 pages but still far shorter than most British works on cookery.) Webster's Blue Back Speller acquired its nickname from the color of its cheap paper binding. *American Cookery* also made its first appearance between covers of inexpensive blue paper. The content of Webster's speller was in large measure taken verbatim from the popular English spellers by Thomas Dilworth and Daniel Fenning. *American Cookery*, as we began to consider in chapter 1 and discuss at length in a later chapter, is based on popular English precedents, especially Susannah Carter's *Frugal Housewife* and Hannah Glasse's *Art of Cookery*. While Webster transformed his speller into a more original work in later editions, *American Cookery*, with only two editions produced by Amelia Simmons, did not achieve an equivalent apotheosis. However the second edition of *American Cookery* moved in an Americanizing direction with the addition of "Independence," "Election," and "Federal" cakes.[54]

Webster rose from the position of a struggling schoolteacher to become a nationally known author, one of only two Americans of the day (Jedidiah Morse was the other) able to support himself through his writing. By the early nineteenth century, his works had sold millions of copies. Webster's financial and reputational boon to Hudson & Goodwin may have played a part in the publishers' decision to bring out another instructional manual on a practical topic—this time a cookbook. If the cookbook was mostly derivative of British sources, yet the author aimed to put an American stamp on it, the analogy to Webster's work would not have escaped Hudson & Goodwin's notice.[55]

The original title of Webster's speller, *A Grammatical Institute of the English Language, Part I*, was simplified in a 1787 edition to *American Spelling Book*. In 1829, well after its reputation was firmly fixed, it became *The Elementary Spelling Book*. But early on, the American public with its genius for simplicity had dubbed it the Blue Back Speller. In time most Americans called it simply the speller. The direction Webster's first book title had taken, from pompous to plain, may have influenced the choice of a straightforward title from the start for *American Cookery*. The story of Webster's rise from humble schoolteacher in Goshen, New York, to the acknowledged expert on American language was well known when Amelia Simmons, self-described "American Orphan," solicited the "candor of the American Ladies" regarding her first edition and imagined the possibility of future editions of her work.[56]

When Webster's speller was first printed in Connecticut, only six states (Connecticut, Massachusetts, New Jersey, Maryland, New Hampshire, and Rhode Island) had copyright laws. But intellectual property rights were on many authors' minds. They linked passage of copyright legislation in additional states to their ability to support themselves with their writing. Yet copyright law (to the modern mind an inarguable good) met with significant resistance. In the decades prior to the Revolution, many colonials began to identify with a public sphere that was larger than their local community or colony. The public, thus conceived, could observe and express opinions about political events, and these observations could often be more candid than those expressed by the nominal leaders of local communities, such as the clergy and representatives of colonial governments. This "public" was realized or encountered mostly in newspapers. Newspapers (there were thirty-eight of them in the colonies by 1775) printed the columns and stories of anonymous commentators who often wrote under what were obviously pen names. Print itself seemed to create this new source of

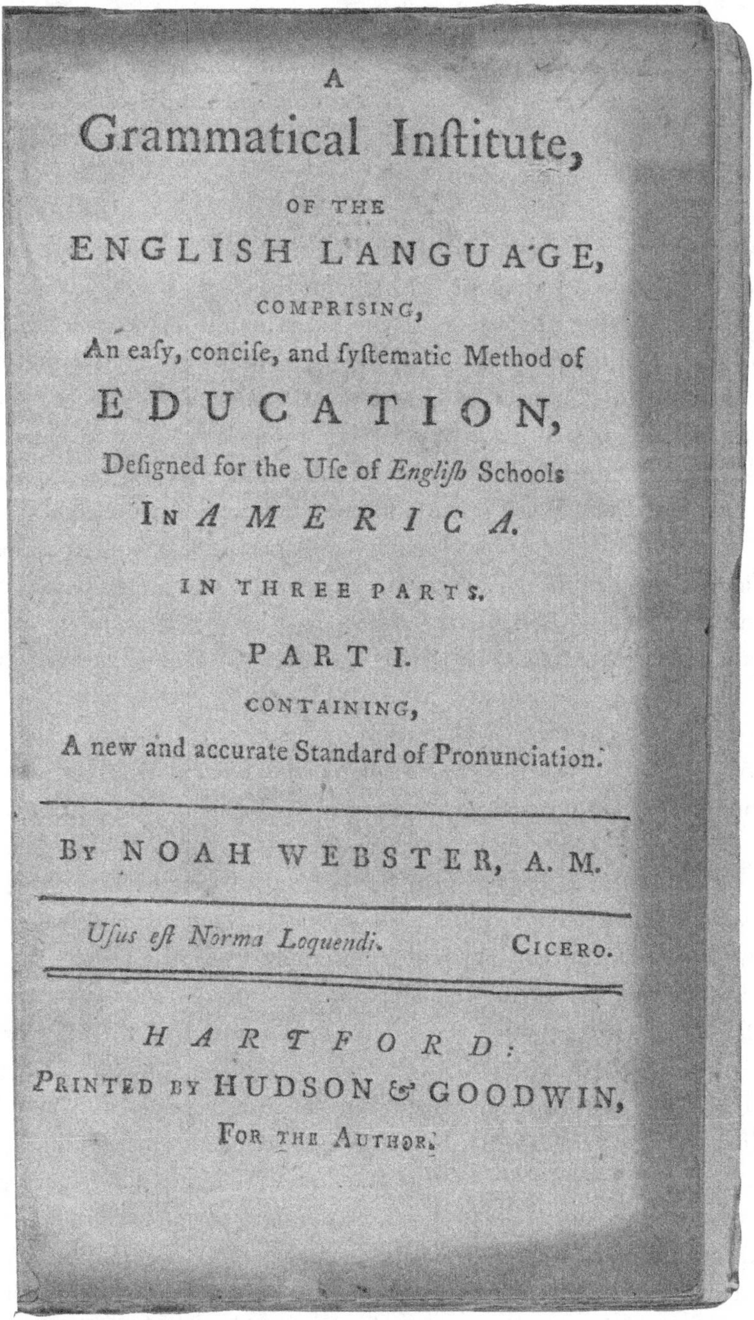

A

Grammatical Inſtitute,

OF THE

ENGLISH LANGUAGE,

COMPRISING,

An eaſy, conciſe, and ſyſtematic Method of

EDUCATION,

Deſigned for the Uſe of *Engliſh* Schools

IN *A M E R I C A.*

IN THREE PARTS.

PART I.

CONTAINING,

A new and accurate Standard of Pronunciation.

BY NOAH WEBSTER, A. M.

Uſus eſt Norma Loquendi.　　　CICERO.

H A R T F O R D :
PRINTED BY HUDSON & GOODWIN,
FOR THE AUTHOR.

FIGURE 3.2. Title page from A Grammatical Institute of the English Language, Part 1 (Hartford, 1783).
　　　　　—*AC8 W3956A 1783. Houghton Library, Harvard University

authority, one that, as Michael Warner writes, "like truth, holds validity not in persons, but despite them." The "supervision of publicity itself" seemed to many a clear benefit of this rise of a republican culture of print. Some resisted copyright protections for authors because they could threaten this newly conceived "public," even as they safeguarded an individual writer's work. Not everyone found in the emerging liberal capitalist model of the marketplace the highest good for a republican society.[57]

But by the 1780s and 1790s, with commerce ever more important and many writers casting themselves as producers in the marketplace, earlier notions of "writing as a disinterested contribution to the public from an anonymous pen," as historian Christopher Grasso puts it, began to lose ground. Sentiment had turned toward "an author's property, produced by his labor and genius, linked to his personal reputation, and up for sale in a competitive marketplace." The efforts to nationalize copyright law, the emergence of a class of professional writers, and the remaking of a loosely configured prerevolutionary press into an ever more entrepreneurial publishing industry produced the market-based conception of printing, writing, and the book trade that today is almost universally treated as self-evident regarding the nature of print.[58]

Noah Webster found the cultural atmosphere of Connecticut in general, and of Hartford in particular, highly congenial to his literary ambitions. But he chose Hartford for practical reasons as well. Only there could his burdensome financial and vocational limitations be offset. He had tried the law as a career, along with two stints at teaching, before he embarked on writing the educational treatise that would be his salvation. The few friends who were willing to aid him, financially and emotionally, were in Connecticut. He could not afford the expense of publishing his writings on his own. And he had failed to locate a publisher willing to underwrite even the first part of his planned three-part *Grammatical Institute*.

Webster's Connecticut friends lent him the money he needed to publish the first volume. His Yale classmate Joel Barlow put up five hundred dollars. Another Yale acquaintance, the poet John Trumbull, may have given a somewhat smaller amount. The funds were enough for Webster to arrange a printing contract with Hudson & Goodwin. With the standard line of the day, "For the Author," the book announces on its title page that the author paid expenses. The speller was not a sure thing, and so Hudson & Goodwin had not yet invested their own funds in it. (*American Cookery* was also published by Hudson & Goodwin "For the Author.") The first run of Webster's speller was 5,000 copies. With 500 to 1,000 sales a week, it sold out by the winter of 1783–84. Within sixteen months of publication, 12,000 copies had been sold. At the time, sales of 25,000 copies amounted to a bestseller.[59]

In 1784, when the second edition of the speller appeared, relations between Hudson & Goodwin and Webster changed considerably. The publishers no longer required the author to assume printing costs. Hudson & Goodwin had by this time acquired "sole right of printing and vending" the book. The second edition was advertised in the *Courant* on June 1, 1784. Despite the sale to the publishers of printing rights for the first part, each of the three books that made up Webster's *Grammatical Institute* continued to state that the work had been published "For the Author," a statement meaning in this instance that the author could dictate the terms for reproduction.[60]

Webster's works did remain under his control, though not solely. As sales grew, he revised his original contract with Hudson & Goodwin to allow him to work with Isaiah Thomas and Ebenezer Andrews. Thomas and Andrews would produce many subsequent editions. Furthermore, Webster retained the right to sell his work outside New England. Within New England, others who wished to print the hugely popular book would have to negotiate with Hudson & Goodwin. In 1788, a further contract revision allowed Hudson & Goodwin to retain monopoly rights in Connecticut and to sell their own imprint without restrictions throughout New England. But now their imprint would compete with those of other New England publishers. Webster was outgrowing what a regional publisher like Hudson & Goodwin could do for him. Other contracts followed, including one with the firm of Charles R. & George Webster in 1794. Two years later the Websters would try to hit the mark again with a second edition of another Hudson & Goodwin title, *American Cookery*.[61]

The early history of Webster's speller illustrates the seminal role played by Hartford printers and their extended network in making a market for American books at the close of the eighteenth century. With its six bookbinders and nine printing houses, Hartford was the publishing center of the Connecticut River Valley. Richard D. Brown describes the Hartford and regional printing phenomenon as "a polycentric rather than a centralized world of print." Boston, New York, Philadelphia, and Baltimore were publishing hubs, to be sure, but so too were smaller places such as Richmond, Charleston, Lancaster, Trenton, Pittsfield, Worcester, Litchfield, and Hartford, along with "a dozen others."[62]

Despite its influence, Hartford would never be more than a regional market center. As the industrial and transportation advances of the nineteenth century made consolidated publishing the most profitable model, Hartford lost ground to Boston, New York, and Philadelphia. But in the 1780s and 1790s, when the Connecticut Wits were writing their Federalist-inspired American epics, Noah Webster was thinking of American ways to teach reading and writing, and Hudson & Goodwin was expanding its reach by publishing new American works, Hartford could rightly consider itself uniquely important to the new national culture of print.[63]

Noted culinary historian Karen Hess was the first to propose that Amelia Simmons may not have been a native of Hartford but rather came from the Hudson River Valley. To make her case, Hess cites as evidence not only the array of New York editions but also the occurrence in the cookbook of "a number of Dutch words," such as "sla" (slaw) for salad and "cookey" instead of the English "small cake." She also argues for a connection between Simmons's use of "pearl ash" in baking and the fact that "there was a particularly active production of potash [pearl ash's base component] in the Albany area in late Colonial times." As we argue in chapter 1, the evidence for *American Cookery* as a Connecticut Federalist project by a local author includes advertisements and editions that appeared first throughout Connecticut (New Haven, New London, Middletown) and extended to areas influenced by Connecticut's diaspora, taking in the towns in New York mentioned by Hess. Such places included—besides Hess's Albany, Salem, Troy, Poughkeepsie, and New York City—Newark, New Jersey; Walpole, New Hampshire; Bennington, Brattleboro, Windsor, and Woodstock, Vermont; and as far into the western regions as Zanesville, Ohio. Even Simmons's plagiarizers, who published in New York City; Montpelier, Vermont; Boston; and Watertown, New York, offer evidence by this geographic distribution that the cultural crib of *American Cookery* was Connecticut and the Connecticut River Valley, rather than New York and the Hudson River Valley (see fig. 1.2).[64]

So, although we disagree with Hess on the question of Simmons's origins (in chapter 8 we pursue leads about the author's identity), we agree that New York and Albany hold a place second only to Connecticut and Hartford in the making of *American Cookery*. The connection between the two places is printing, and in particular the Hartford printing firm of Hudson & Goodwin and the Albany printing firm of Charles R. & George Webster.

The relationship between the two printing concerns follows the pattern we presented earlier of established printers underwriting satellite ventures begun by their former apprentices and journeymen. In early youth, Charles Webster experienced the sudden impoverishment of his family. His father had pledged surety for a stranger, an Englishman, who failed to repay the loan. The elder Webster found himself responsible for a debt he could not pay, and as Joel Munsell, Charles R. Webster's biographer, wrote, "All that he had was sold, even to the cow." As a result, Charles, age seven, was indentured until the age of twenty-one to the firm that would become Hudson & Goodwin. In the same shop was George Goodwin, likewise indentured and twelve years old at the time Webster entered into employment.[65]

Hartford was the home of Charles Webster's maternal grandfather, William Pratt, so it is possible that someone in his family secured for the child (and his family) this position with a prosperous Hartford company. Opportunities for Webster to attend school amounted to "scarcely more than one or two quarters." But as Munsell reported, the boy's exposure to books at the printing office seems to have "furnished him with a competent acquaintance with the ordinary branches of knowledge."[66]

Webster was nineteen in 1781 when the Connecticut militia was called up. How he managed release from his indenture is not clear, but he marched with the Connecticut contingent to New Haven under Captain Hezekia Wyllys. His unit remained under arms for fifteen days before being disbanded. After the war, Webster saw an opportunity to resume his career as a printer in Albany. There were no print shops in the Hudson River Valley north of Fishkill (about seventy-five miles north of New York City). The printers in Albany before the war had been Tories who fled when their allegiances made them unpopular.[67]

Albany's inhabitants presented a challenge to a printer from New England. The city was dominated by the Dutch "in language and customs as well as in descent." There was a smattering of other ethnic and religious groups—Reformed Germans, German Lutherans, English Episcopalians, and Scottish Presbyterians—but these were in a distinct minority. In any case, as Munsell testified, "To all of these, a Yankee was unacceptable, in manners, speech and modes of thought." But Webster persevered, and through sheer strength of character, according to his biographer, "all joined in admitting that although he was a Yankee, they liked him."[68]

So in his early twenties, Charles Webster established a printing business. His partner in this enterprise was Solomon Balentine, an Englishman. Webster's association with Balentine appears to have been motivated by the fact that the Englishman owned as many types "as a squaw could carry in her bag." The young and ambitious but undercapitalized Connecticut printer produced with his co-owner at least one work, a pamphlet entitled *Plain Reasons*, written by Reverend Thomas Clarke. It was printed at Albany in 1783. A year earlier, they had also begun a newspaper. But the partnership terminated, owing to what Munsell described as Balentine's "uncongenial habits."[69]

Webster then moved south to New York City, where he entered into partnership with John Lang to publish the *New York Gazette*. In the meantime, Balentine too had left Albany, and shortly after his departure, Webster's Albany friends urged him to return to their city. He took their advice and established his new Albany venture independently. In 1784, he began publication of the *Albany Gazette*. An almanac and the *New-England Primer*, both money-makers, soon followed.

Webster and his *Albany Gazette* flourished in postwar Albany. His printing firm was a success, and he became a person of note in his adopted city. He served as captain in the Independent Artillery Company and left among his papers a letter "with the autograph of John Adams" thanking him for his patriotism. On news that the United States might go to war with France, Webster had offered the services of his artillery company to President Adams. Webster also engaged in philanthropy, helping to found Albany's Mechanics' Society and Mechanics' Academy, the Lancastrian School, and the Apprentices' Library. Perhaps the last reminded him of his own early days as an unschooled printer's apprentice.[70]

Webster's political sentiments were closely aligned with his one-time fellow apprentice George Goodwin, now a partner in Hudson & Goodwin. The *Albany Gazette*, like Hudson & Goodwin's *Connecticut Courant*, was a Federalist paper. In time, Webster took as a partner in his firm his twin brother George. (The two had been born in 1762, though it was noted that Charles was the younger of the twins. His birth rank may have played a part in his parents' decision to indenture him.) He also brought his sister's three sons, Elisha, Hezekiah, and Daniel Skinner, into partnership. In many respects, he was the prototype of the ideal American man—self-made, patriotic, philanthropic, and engaged with the world through print.

One might wonder why Albany, settled since the early seventeenth century, had not developed into a magnet for printers in the way Hartford and other provincial cities had. Historian David G. Hackett posits that there was little demand for printed material because of Albany's character as a homogeneous Dutch community "where face-to-face contacts and the pervasive principles of the Heidleberg catechism predominated." But the same homogeneity (if not the same devotion to a catechism) characterized early New England, where reading flourished.[71]

The difference may be accounted for less by cultural sameness than by social insularity. The Albany Dutch, bounded by their language and unique customs, were little affected by outside influences until after the Revolution. Only then did an influx of immigrants disturb their enclave. As the population became more diverse, the city's leaders endorsed the new national principles of civic and religious liberty. The city also acknowledged a need for "knowledge and instruction" of its people. An intentional national patriotism was used to create a sense of civic harmony amid the newly diverse population. Fourth of July sermons emphasizing the shared benefits of the new American nation were among the first documents to find their way into print in Albany.[72]

Historian Michael Kammen argues that New York as a whole had begun a cultural transformation in the four decades after 1730, mostly in response to urban expansion. New York had not had New England's religiously motivated commitment to universal education. Its civic institutions were less well-formed than those of its regional neighbor. But with the growth of cities came cultural advancement. Not through formal education so much as through the informal means of newspapers, theaters, and books did early New Yorkers find the learning they sought.[73]

In the mercantile setting of Albany, where schooling had never been a legal requirement but literacy had become a necessity, the Yankee newspaperman and printer found a comfortable professional berth. Webster's ties to Hudson & Goodwin, the firm that had provided the informal school of his youth, continued as he and his company became part of its extended printers' network. This connection led to the selection of Albany as the place and Charles R. & George Webster as the printers of the second edition of *American Cookery*.

PART II
Connecticut

T hroughout the thirty-five years of its active life, *American Cookery* was printed, reprinted, pirated, advertised, and sold principally in Connecticut, the Connecticut River Valley, and the adjacent areas to which many people from Connecticut were emigrating. What was it about this region that made printers and booksellers think that such a book would appeal to its inhabitants?

One recent scholar has stated that in the early years of the nineteenth century, only "a few ladies might have owned" *American Cookery*, because conditions in Connecticut were such that "women were not expected to produce . . . complicated meals, cakes and pastry." However, the publication of a cookbook implies a belief that there were at least "a few ladies" within its projected orbit who could afford the varieties of ingredients needed to prepare the dishes it contained and who had learned to appreciate the dietary variety that would result from preparing them. These few ladies and their families were understood to be prosperous and aware of culinary and gastronomic standards.[1]

But the claim that other than a few ladies, women weren't expected and didn't wish to produce anything elaborate in the kitchen is rendered implausible by the fact of the publication of *American Cookery* in particular—that is, of a cookbook offering a prospect of culinary complexity and gastronomic pleasure in brief and affordable form. To bring out a cookbook with these properties was to suggest that those interested would not be limited to a few ladies.

In such a cookbook, by judicious simplification of individual recipes and judicious construction of a basic overall recipe profile, content was adapted downward in order to accommodate or encourage aspiration upward. Encouragement to aspiration upward was reinforced in this case, as historian Nancy Siegel has noted, by identification of the author as an orphan. In other words, not only did the publishers believe that a few ladies would buy the book because they were knowledgeable and their families prosperous;

the author and printers also believed that many more women might buy the book because they hoped, not without reason, for knowledge for themselves and prosperity for their families.[2]

In chapter 4, we show that the members of the Connecticut elite entertained a view of the social order they presided over that answered to these expectations for *American Cookery*. They believed that Connecticut was a place where their own well-being was parceled out, in due proportion, to all those who industriously pursued their callings. This was the basis of the conviction of figures such as Timothy Dwight that life in Connecticut constituted a model that Americans everywhere would be well advised to emulate. We also survey in this chapter the findings of modern social historians, which both confirm, to an extent, and challenge this upper-class self-satisfaction.

Part of the reason that *American Cookery* was initially published in Connecticut was that some of its leaders thought the state provided a fitting model for the nation as a whole. But this by itself would not have been a sufficient reason. In order for a work claiming to exemplify American-ness in the realm of food and cooking to be issued in Connecticut, households in which "complicated meals, cakes and pastry" would not seem out of place had to have existed in the state in fairly large numbers. Such households would need to be outfitted not only with the manifold ingredients needed for the recipes but also with appropriate equipment for cooking them, implements with which to eat them, furniture on which to sit and clothing to wear while consuming them, containers—houses—for all this apparatus, and types of behavior for setting the entire tableau in motion. *American Cookery* was published in Connecticut and its environs beginning in 1796 because by then a culture of domesticity composed of all of this, arising from the eighteenth-century consumer revolution in material goods and manners, was firmly in place there. In chapter 5, we immerse ourselves in this Connecticut domestic culture.

In the mind's eye of leading citizens, the economic ground on which Connecticut's prosperous and equitable society and its tasteful domestic arrangements were erected was agricultural production. Elite spokesmen boasted that the state's "houses, barns, . . . granaries, and . . . cellars . . . are stor'd / With all the sweets of life." Recent experiences justified these visions of rural plenty, they felt. Historian Richard D. Brown notes that during the Revolutionary War, the Connecticut River Valley "became New England's agricultural storehouse, and Connecticut earned the title 'the Provisions

State,'" supplying the Continental Army with large amounts of "grain, meat, butter, cheese, cider, and hides."[3]

If Connecticut farmers could produce surplus foodstuffs for export even in wartime, they certainly could produce enough to feed themselves in peacetime. Nor were they required to be the sole providers for their urban neighbors. According to Timothy Dwight, in the New Haven market at the end of the eighteenth century, ample supplies of "flesh and fish" were to be found. Vegetables and fruits were not so plentiful at market, but this was because many of the residents provided "culinary vegetables" and "very fine fruit" for themselves "from their own gardens." All in all, Dwight concluded, "an epicure may find all his wishes satisfied without much difficulty in this town."[4]

So Connecticut was perceived by influential people to be a place where one could find without undue trouble the many types of raw materials needed to prepare the recipes included even in a cookbook that was highly selective. This is the third major dimension of the area's life that made the publication of *American Cookery* seem like a propitious venture in 1796. We devote chapter 6, therefore, to an account of Connecticut foodstuff production, assessing along the way the extent to which patrician vistas of ongoing productivity and fruitfulness were valid and the extent to which they amounted to wishful thinking.

CHAPTER 4

Society and Nationality

S ometime around 1800, as he was completing a grandiose panorama of
Niagara Falls and just a year or so before his death at the age of fifty,
Ralph Earl painted two miniatures—*Portrait of a Connecticut Clock-
maker* and *Portrait of a Connecticut Clockmaker's Wife*. Earl had been a Tory
and, having fled to England, a "pupil to the celebrated [Benjamin] West."
He returned to North America after the Revolutionary War but found
himself before long in a New York debtors' prison. After Dr. Mason Fitch
Cogswell of Hartford helped secure his release in 1788, Earl spent the next
dozen years crisscrossing Connecticut, western Massachusetts, and southern
Vermont seeking out people who were eager to have their portraits painted.
As he characterized his aspirations in a 1790 advertisement in a Litchfield,
Connecticut, newspaper, "we cannot doubt, and hope, that in this age of
refinement, the well-born and well-bred of his countrymen will patronize
[Earl] in the road to fame." Many of the well-born and well-bred did indeed
patronize him. Earl executed portraits of such luminaries as the Boardmans
and Tallmadges of Litchfield, Dr. Cogswell and Colonel Samuel Talcott of
Hartford, and the Ellsworths of Windsor.[1]

But separated from his wife, struggling with alcoholism, and in constant
need of funds, Earl got to the point of being willing to portray others besides
the well-born and well-bred. In 1800, around the same time he completed
the clockmaker miniatures, he accepted a commission to paint Isaac Gere of
Northampton, Massachusetts, also a clockmaker, and Gere's wife, Jemima
Kingsley Gere.[2]

Earl's renditions of this Northampton artisan pair are in a private collection. But their Connecticut cousins, so to speak, are at home to the public
at the Smithsonian American Art Museum. We'll look first at the clockmaker's wife. There is a hint of velvety richness in the matronly decorum
of her dark gown, answering discreetly to the sheen of the conventional red
curtain behind her. She wears what looks like a muslin mobcap and has a
bright greyish, diaphanous kerchief draped around her neck and shoulders

FIGURES 4.1–4.2. *Portrait of a Connecticut Clock-maker* and *Portrait of a Connecticut Clockmaker's Wife*, attributed to Ralph Earl, ca. 1800, 10 ¼ x 7 ⅞ inches.

—Smithsonian American Art Museum, gifts of Orrin Wickersham June

and down her front. Cap and kerchief combine to make a claim to elegance that remains muted yet is a bit more distinct than the one formed by her gown and the curtained backdrop.[3]

Mrs. Clockmaker's surroundings are unostentatiously tasteful. She is seated in a chair with the slim lines and subtle curvature that had become fashionable over the past fifty years, at a simple yet also fashionably round tea table, in front of a wall on which can be seen a minimal yet distinct degree of paneling. To the left of the paneling is the corner of a framed painting. In her hand and on the tea table are books—the octavos and duo-decimos considered suitable for a woman. A plain gold wedding band is visible on the third finger of her left hand.[4]

In the accompanying pendant portrayal of her husband, the clothing and surroundings are yet more restrained. The clockmaker is outfitted in grey stockings, probably wool, and a black suit of softer appearance than the stockings. The generous collar and lapels of the coat, set off by a plain white cravat, suggest considerable prosperity, as does the plain knee buckle, just visible on the breeches. The clockmaker's chair is identical to the one in his wife's portrait, except that in his portrait the rush seat is visible. They thus have a matched set. He is at the same tea table or another one in their house in the same style. Like his wife, he holds an octavo, while on the wall behind him is a bookcase filled with tall folios. On the table are the face and works of one his clocks, along with some loose papers. Behind him to the left is the same velvety red-curtain status symbol that frames his wife. Taken together, these little portraits constitute a no-nonsense declaration of the industrious-ness, ingenuity, cultural and intellectual activity, and appropriately modest gentility of the Connecticut Yankee at the end of the eighteenth century.

Ralph Earl's 1792 portrait of U.S. senator Oliver Ellsworth and his wife, Abigail (a member of the Wolcott family long prominent in colony and state politics), is in most obvious respects a totally different proposition. To begin with, the Ellsworth portrait is more than forty times larger than the two clock-maker miniatures taken together. Abigail Ellsworth's costume is glossy and filmy from head to toe, while her husband is attired in silks, ruffles, brass but-tons, and silver buckles both at the knee and on the shoes. The pair are posed in federal shield-back chairs with upholstered and fringed, rather than rush, seats. There is an elaborately patterned carpet on the floor. In the background is seen, quasi-surrealistically, the neoclassical form of the entire stately home of which the portrayed room is a part. The Ellsworths and the clockmakers would obviously not be spending much time socializing with each other.[5]

FIGURE 4.3. *Oliver Ellsworth and Abigail Wolcott Ellsworth*, Ralph Earl, 1792, oil on canvas, 76 x 86 ¾ inches (193.1 x 220.4 cm).
—Wadsworth Atheneum Museum of Art, Hartford, Connecticut, gift of Ellsworth Heirs, 1903.7; photo: Allen Phillips, Wadsworth Atheneum

On the other hand, they do belong to the same society, for there are also intriguing similarities in the renditions of the two couples. Just as the clockmaker is shown alongside shelves of the impressive-looking ledgers by which he maintained his enterprise on a sound footing, so the lawyer and statesman Oliver Ellsworth sits in front of a bookcase filled with what look like works on the law and other weighty matters of public policy. Just as the product of the clockmaker's labor, one of his clocks, is found on the table at which he sits, so a portion of the U.S. Constitution, which Ellsworth played an important part in creating as a member of the Connecticut delegation, is partially unrolled on the table at which the senator sits. As for the wives, both of their heads are covered in bright grey mobcaps encircled by shiny ribbons.[6]

With their upholstered chairs, patterned carpets, and Palladian architecture, the Ellsworths obviously inhabited the upper reaches of Connecticut society. But they do not make a parade of it. The table at which they sit isn't a round or oval table designed for the pleasures of taking tea. It's a simple four-cornered work table. There's only a hint of carved elaboration in the frame of the sash window through which the entire house can be seen. And the fencing around the house offers everything from fancy white through unassuming red down to the thoroughly rustic unpainted rails of the outermost enclosure. If the clockmaker family was making a statement about its achievement of refinement, the Ellsworths were equally concerned not to put on airs. They wanted it known that by no means did they consider themselves worlds apart from people like the clockmaker and his wife. This matched and meshed striving and stooping amounts to a paradigm of Connecticut's image of itself in the years that saw the creation, publication, and distribution of *American Cookery*.

Was there any basis in reality for this self-image? From his analysis of abundant estate inventory evidence, social historian Jackson Turner Main concluded that in the seventeenth and eighteenth centuries Connecticut was for white men a relatively open society. Men who started out near the bottom, such as those who had been orphaned as boys, more often than not achieved success, if success is defined as "acquisition of enough property for an adequate standard of living" or attainment of "respectability of status, such as holding a responsible office. . . . Not over one in five who lived to be forty failed to overcome his humble origins." Correspondingly, a closed, hereditary elite did not develop in colonial Connecticut. "Overall, almost two out of five leaders" in the political, religious, military, and business affairs of Connecticut did not come from "families of leaders. . . . For the Connecticut boy of quality there was always room at the top."[7]

Of course, as is clear from Main's own language, a society that allowed for upward mobility could nevertheless remain, and likely did remain, hierarchical. At any point in time there are those with "humble origins" to overcome, those abiding in respectability and comfort in the middle ranks, and those occupying the "room at the top." Different people might be installed in these different positions at different times, but the positions remain.

According to historian Richard L. Bushman, Connecticut in the early years of the new American nation was clearly a social hierarchy in this sense. On the topmost level were the "River Gods . . . a handful of interwoven families who filled a high proportion of colony and county offices and who dwelt in elegant houses with the stupendous doorways that seemed to express their social and political pretensions." Membership in this small group was by this time often hereditary. As previously noted, Timothy Dwight came from a family that had played a leading part up and down the Connecticut River since the earliest years of English settlement in the seventeenth century.[8]

Bushman also writes of "a much larger group of lesser leaders who were just as entrenched in the local sphere" as were the River Gods in the larger arenas of county and state. These people, however, were for the most part not as long established as the River Gods. They "had sprung up in virtually every town by the middle of the eighteenth century," availing themselves of the upward mobility that Main discerned in the estate inventory evidence. Moreover, opportunities of the sort this group had seized upon in the previous generation remained available: "Newcomers rose economically with the older gentry, though usually not achieving political eminence. We can imagine both types emerging everywhere in Connecticut after the Revolution, elevated by the economy from their previous obscurity, ambitious for achievement, and eager to embrace the culture suitable to their position." The culture suitable to their position was the culture of gentility and refinement that we survey in chapter 5.[9]

The existence of this broader, relatively recently recruited group exercising social, economic, and political leadership in towns and villages perhaps means that John Adams was exaggerating when he alleged of Connecticut in 1808 that "half a dozen, or, at most, a dozen families, have controlled that country when a colony, as well as since it has been a state." But Adams was not necessarily overstating the case that much. There might well have been a small group that basically ran the show, doing so in such a way that its preferences and decisions were transmitted to and interpreted and implemented by Bushman's lesser and more local gentry, and also doing so in a way that facilitated, or at least did not noticeably hinder, the efforts of the majority of the population to live in a modestly prosperous manner. Is this a reasonably accurate description of Connecticut society between 1780 and 1815?[10]

We think it is. Who, for example, took the lead in establishing the new financial institutions that were perceived to be necessary in the 1790s and 1800s? Historian Richard J. Purcell long ago identified those who were instrumental in establishing Hartford's first bank in 1792, such as Oliver Ellsworth and Jeremiah Wadsworth. Purcell stressed that each of these people came to the fore in multiple ways. Besides being "a framer of the Constitution," Ellsworth was "long a judge of the state superior court, later Chief Justice of the United States Supreme Court." Wadsworth, "a commissary-general during the Revolution, at its close was estimated to be worth from sixty to eighty thousand pounds sterling. He was the largest subscriber to the Bank of North America, and in 1785 was elected president of the Bank of New York. . . . For several years he was a member of Congress and long a member of the [Governor's] Council."[11]

Among the early directors of this bank, six of them (including Wadsworth) were important figures in the establishment between 1794 and 1810 of the branch of the financial industry for which Hartford would become best known—insurance. "It is not too much to say," Purcell concluded, "that the banking, marine and fire insurance companies were controlled by the same men. Nor is it a bold generalization to add that the *status quo* eminently satisfied this group."[12]

The hereditary principle was not ignored in the selection of leaders of such institutions as the Hartford Bank. Jeremiah Wadsworth's son Daniel became a director in 1795, and Daniel was also found fifteen years later among the directors of the first fire insurance company in Hartford. Several other surnames appear repeatedly among the first four decades' worth of bank directors. For example, Oliver Ellsworth (1794-96) was followed by his sons Martin Ellsworth (1813-21), Henry L. Ellsworth (1816-19), and William W. Ellsworth (1820-28).[13]

On the other hand, the Ellsworths' presence in the Hartford Bank directorate illustrates the principle of the career open to talents. The founder of the Ellsworth dynasty, Oliver, was himself born not in the room at the top but rather into a family belonging to the lesser gentry. His father, Captain David Ellsworth, had been a prosperous farmer, a selectman of Windsor, and a militia captain. In a pattern that was fairly common in New England, Oliver was designated to be educated for the professions, while the path marked out for David's two other sons was the inheritance of land and the pursuit of their father's calling of farming. Initially intended for the ministry, Oliver became a lawyer instead, eventually achieving various political and judicial distinctions and all-around eminence.[14]

A name on the list of the first directors of the Hartford Bank of particular interest is that of one of the publishers of *American Cookery*, George Goodwin, whose tenure as a director ran from 1794 to 1817. In the same year that Goodwin stepped down as a bank director, Henry Hudson, the son of

Goodwin's partner Barzillai Hudson, began a six-year term, and in 1831, Henry Hudson's son, named for his grandfather Barzillai, in turn took up this position and held onto it for more than three decades. Meanwhile, in 1810, when the Hartford Fire Insurance Company was formed, the firm of Hudson & Goodwin subscribed to more shares of its initial stock offering than did Daniel Wadsworth, the son of the richest man in town (one hundred versus eighty shares). Henry Hudson joined Daniel Wadsworth as a director of this enterprise, the foundation on which the Hartford insurance industry would rise to national significance.[15]

The usual suspects—Jeremiah Wadsworth, Oliver Ellsworth, Barzillai Hudson, and others—are to be found in 1788 investing in an early industrial venture in Hartford, a broadcloth mill. In 1784, Hudson served on the first Hartford City Council, not only with Connecticut Wit John Trumbull but also with several of those later involved with the mill, the bank, or both. The presence on this body of such key economic players is hardly a surprise since the primary purpose of municipal incorporations of portions of Hartford and Connecticut's other leading towns was the encouragement of commerce.[16]

The interlocking directorate of early national Hartford encompassed culture as well as finance, trade, manufacturing, and politics. George Goodwin and four others of the seven trustees of the Hartford Library Company in 1797 also were, or soon would be, directors of the Hartford Bank. Shareholders in a theater established in 1795 included Jeremiah Wadsworth, Barzillai Hudson, George Goodwin, and at least four other men active in banking and/or insurance. "Among the ladies who graced" the balls organized and operated by the Hartford "Assembly" between 1791 and 1813 were the "Misses" Hudson and Wadsworth, while the subscribers to the assembly in 1807 included Daniel Wadsworth, two of George Goodwin's sons, and a generous sprinkling of surnames appearing in various other lists of Hartford luminaries.[17]

George Goodwin and Barzillai Hudson provide further illustration of the fact that the leading citizens of Hartford included men recruited relatively recently from families of modest estate. Goodwin was descended from one of the original seventeenth-century proprietors of Hartford, and some branches of the Goodwin family became notably prosperous. This does not appear to have been the case with George Goodwin's immediate line. In the 1730s and 1740s, George's father, Samuel, held various minor town offices of the sort usually reserved for young men. For instance, he was chosen as an ensign in the militia but not as a captain. The family seems to have been a few rungs down from the Ellsworths of midcentury Windsor. None of Samuel Goodwin's sons was sent to college. Instead, they all became farmers or artisans. As noted, George was apprenticed at the *Connecticut Courant* at the age of nine, showing his mettle sufficiently to be made a partner in the firm in the late 1770s when he was twenty or twenty-one.[18]

A year later, George Goodwin wed Mary Edwards, the only daughter of Richard Edwards. In 1757, Richard Edwards had been held in sufficient esteem colony-wide to be one of three men chosen to manage a lottery created to help Connecticut recover from the financial weaknesses resulting from the Seven Years' War. George Goodwin's marriage to the only daughter of a pillar of the community was, in the words of a descendant, "a fortunate and happy union, and, added to his already well-earned promotion in business, helped largely to lay the foundations of his successful life."[19]

Reviewing a few salient aspects of Barzillai Hudson's career, we recall that he was a mason who had come to Hartford from Bridgewater, Massachusetts. In 1774, Hudson moved into "a small gambrel-roof house, with a chimney at one end." The modest dimensions of the house and the marginal placement of its chimney suggest the modest circumstances of a mason plying his trade, while the gambrel roof, a distinguishing feature of genteel house design, suggests aspirations to something better. Hudson's reputation in the community was apparently solid, for in early 1777 he was chosen to lead the detachment of guards around the Hartford County Jail where British prisoners of war were being held. Young Hudson had the look of a man who didn't just aspire to something better in life but who would do what he could to put himself in a position to achieve it.[20]

One of Hudson's new neighbors in 1774 was the proprietor of the *Connecticut Courant*, Ebenezer Watson. Indeed, Hudson may have moved into the area because of the existing tie to Watson arising from the fact that Hudson's first wife, Margaret, and Watson's deceased first wife had been cousins. Watson was living with his second wife, Hannah Bunce Watson, in a house that had formerly been the residence of Reverend Thomas Buckingham of the Hartford Second Church and then of Buckingham's son, "Joseph Buckingham, Esq." It was a "two-story house of the usual pattern, with a large central chimney."[21]

As seen in chapter 3, after the death of Ebenezer Watson in September 1777 and of Margaret Hudson the following year, Barzillai Hudson married Hannah Watson in 1779. The extremely beneficial consequences of this union for Hudson were not only ascent to the more elevated occupational status of partner at the *Connecticut Courant* and in the now renamed printing concern of Hudson & Goodwin, but also a larger (and prestigious) house. Even more than was the case with Goodwin, Hudson's marriages, especially the second one, "helped largely to lay the foundations of his successful life."[22]

Early national Connecticut was a place where power was exercised and privilege was enjoyed by a group that was both small and always on the lookout for new members. This situation was not incompatible with a widely shared sense of prosperity and well-being. That is certainly what travelers thought they saw even before the Revolution. In 1760, Paul Coffin, a Harvard student, likened the Connecticut Valley landscape, with its "Hundreds of Acres of Wheat, Rye, Peas, Flax, Oats, Corn, &c.," to "a beautiful Garden, variously yet elegantly laid out."[23]

Eleven years later, John Adams waxed even more ecstatic. According to his diary for 1771, nothing was so rare as a day in June in the Hartford area. The morning of that June day was spent "Riding thro Paradise. My Eyes never beheld so fine a Country. . . . Houses all along, and a vast Prospect of level Country on each Hand, the Lands very rich and the Husbandry pretty good." He delighted in the bottom lands "loaded with rich, noble Crops of Grass, and Grain and Corn," and at the end of the day at the Middletown inn where he stayed he "regaled without Reserve" among the foods produced from this agrarian plenitude—"the finest and sweetest of Wheat Bread, and Butter, as yellow as gold, and fine Radishes, very good tea and Sugar." The "barren rocky Mountains" of his hometown of Braintree, Massachusetts, were "as great a Contrast as can be conceived to the level smoth, fertile Plains of this Country."[24]

After the Revolution, in 1788, the French traveler J. P. Brissot de Warville was just as awestruck as Adams had been. In the areas surrounding Hartford, New Haven, and Middletown, "nature and art have . . . displayed all their treasures; it is really the paradise of the United States." This was because the fertility of the valley made agriculture the source of wealth, which in turn meant that wealth was "more equally divided." There was in Connecticut "less misery, more simplicity, more virtue, more of everything which constitutes republicanism." The signs of the state's prosperity were "the number of new houses everywhere to be seen, and the number of rural manufactures arising on every side." Those such as Jeremiah Wadsworth who had reaped the greatest benefits from this republican paradise and who shouldered the heaviest responsibilities for maintaining it were carrying themselves in a truly and fully republican manner. Wadsworth "crowns all his qualities by an amiable and singular modesty. His address is frank, his countenance open, and his discourse simple."[25]

A few years after Brissot de Warville passed through, the English traveler William Strickland remarked that "wealth and want are equally rare and ignorance is unknown" in Hartford. His compatriot Henry Wansey took in Hartford around the same time, in 1794, and came to similar conclusions. He "never observed a single person in rags, or with any appearance of distress or poverty," in spite of his having "looked into all the poor habitations" he could find, "which were very few indeed." Connecticut in general was "better cultivated and more fully inhabited than any other" state, and the clergy, "chosen by the people who pay them," were as unpretentious as Brissot de Warville had found Jeremiah Wadsworth to be: "They associate much with their people," are "affable and unreserved in conversation, and very friendly to strangers." The result of the approachability of the educated elite was that knowledge was "more generally diffused among the common people than in any other state." Moreover, these common people were "thrifty and industrious." A decade later, Connecticut was still the same in the view of another English traveler, John Melish. He found in 1806 that there were "no overgrown estates on one hand, and few of those employed in agriculture are depressed by poverty on the other."[26]

Perhaps the most telling of these encomiums to early national Connecticut, both because it was eloquently understated and also because of its source, dates from 1789. In the first year of his presidency, George Washington toured New England, passing through Hartford in the latter part of October. "There is a great equality in the People of this State," he noted in his diary. "Few or no oppulent Men—and no poor." He went on to describe Connecticut domestic architecture, "the general fashion of which is a Chimney (always of Stone or Brick) and door in the middle, with a stair case fronting the latter, running up the side of the [former]." The structures inhabited by the people of Connecticut were not only solid; they were also elegant—"two flush Stories with a very good shew of Sash & glass Windows"—and spacious: "The size generally is from 30 to 50 feet in length and from 20 to 30 in width exclusive of a back shed which seems to be added as the family encreases." Connecticut clearly made an impression on this Virginian.[27]

These highly favorable accounts of Connecticut by visitors were strikingly similar—perhaps suspiciously so—to the perspectives offered by its leading citizens. Just as William Strickland thought he had found the "most exalted" version of Englishness in Connecticut, so John Adams ran into "a Gentleman" in Wethersfield who informed him that "Mr. [Jared] Ingersoll the Stamp Master told him, he had never seen in Phyladelphia nor in England any Place equal to Hartford and Weathersfield." Just as Brissot de Warville awarded the palm to Connecticut as "the paradise of the United States," so Oliver Ellsworth remarked toward the end of his life that he had "been in all the states, and Connecticut is the best state." And just as George Washington and others thought that there were in Connecticut "few or no oppulent men—and no poor," so Timothy Dwight proclaimed in his poem *Greenfield Hill* (1794) that Connecticut was a place "Where one extended class embraces all,/All mingling, as the rainbow's beauty blends,/Unknown where every hue begins or ends."[28]

Around the time of *American Cookery*'s publication, such tributes to their native place flowed in a steady stream from members of the Connecticut elite. Timothy Dwight's younger brother Theodore stated in 1801 that "Connecticut exhibits the only instance in the history of nations, of a government *purely Republican*, which has stood the test of experience for more than a century, and a half, with firmness enough to withstand the shocks of faction, and revolution." In 1787, the New Haven lawyer and frequent officeholder-to-be David Daggett professed his belief that the government of Connecticut was "the legitimate child of the people . . . more than almost any government on earth."[29]

These encomiums extended to other institutions and aspects of Connecticut life besides its government. The state's churches and schools were deemed particularly praiseworthy. "These excellent institutions are the *salt* that has hitherto preserved the body politic from putrification," said Daggett, adding that the "virtue and intelligence" that were to be discerned "in the people of Connecticut" were traceable to them. Lawyer and legislator S. W. Dana viewed this distinctly satisfactory situation from a slightly different angle, that of "manners, over which the public administration has such plastic powers, and which in turn have such influence on the public administration." Reverend Benjamin Trumbull, in an 1801 sermon, likewise applauded the "'mutual influence' of pious habits and republican institutions." In sum, as Lyman Beecher boasted in 1812, "Our fathers established, and for a great while preserved the most perfect state of society probably that has ever existed in this fallen world." Or as Trumbull put it more succinctly back in 1801, "Where is the community on earth which rivals [Connecticut]?"[30]

That last rhetorical question had been implicitly posed with rather more bite some years before, in 1789: "Where is the community in the United States which rivals Connecticut?" In his *American Geography*, which was a project of national definition similar to *American Cookery* and the writings of the Connecticut Wits and Noah Webster, Jedidiah Morse described Connecticut as the epitome of civilized order:

> The state is chequered with innumerable roads or high ways, crossing each other in every direction. A traveller, in any of these roads, even in the most unsettled parts of the state, will seldom pass more than two or three miles without finding a house or cottage, and a farm under such improvements as to afford the necessaries for the support of a family. The whole state resembles a well cultivated garden, which, with that degree of industry that is necessary to happiness, produces the necessaries and conveniencies of life in great plenty.

Moreover, Connecticut was already showing itself to be in advance of other places in the immaterial aspects of life. In politics, "that party spirit . . . which is the bane of political happiness, has not raged with such violence in this state as in Massachusetts and Rhode-Island. Public proceedings have been conducted generally, and especially of late, with much calmness and candour." The same was true of religion. The influence of the clergy "is on the increase; and it is no doubt to be attributed, in part, to their increasing influence, that an evident reformation in the manners of the people of this state, has taken place since the peace."[31]

The pointedness in Morse's account of Connecticut life and manners only becomes clear when it is compared with his accounts of other regions. He found at best a mixed bag in the middle states. In New Jersey, "agriculture has not been improved . . . to that degree which, from long experience, we might rationally expect, and which the fertility of the soil, in many places, seems to encourage." Morse attributed this deficiency to the fact that many of the inhabitants of New Jersey were Dutch, "who, although they are in general neat and industrious farmers, have very little enterprize, and seldom adopt any new improvements in husbandry." While New Jersey people were "generally industrious, frugal and hospitable," those of "the lower class," the majority, were "ignorant" and "criminally neglectful in the education of their children." Pennsylvania was somewhat better but still well below the New England and Connecticut standard.[32]

Things only got worse as one passed on to Maryland. Since most of the inhabitants resided "on their plantations, often several miles distant from each other," their lives were "very retired and unsocial." As a result, "you observe very little of that chearful sprightliness of look and action which is the invariable and genuine offspring of social intercourse." The fact that Maryland was a slave state also had baneful consequences: "As the negroes perform all the manual labour, their masters are left to saunter away life in sloth, and too often in ignorance." In the more populous parts of Maryland there was greater sociability, to be sure, but Baltimore was dominated by a crass commercialism. Very few attended church, and manners were "unsocial, unimproved, and inhospitable." In most parts of Maryland, popular education existed in name only, "so that a great proportion of the lower class of people are ignorant; and there are not a few who cannot write their names." Where indeed was the community in the United States that rivaled Connecticut?[33]

If Connecticut presented to the traveler's or geographer's eye an image of proper social and economic arrangements, and to an inquisitive mind evidence of all-but-universal good behavior, a similarly pleasing prospect was to be discerned in its political setup. The Blue Back Speller wasn't Noah Webster's only contribution to the making of American national identity, nor was it the only one published by Hartford's premier printer, Hudson & Goodwin. In 1784, the firm's *Connecticut Courant* ran Webster's "Policy of Connecticut," a four-part series of articles on current political issues, and the next year Hudson & Goodwin brought out Webster's revised pamphlet version, *Sketches of American Policy.*[34]

In this work, Webster advocated a more coherently unified government for the United States than existed under the Articles of Confederation, and he placed the current government of Connecticut at the center of his argument. Connecticut showed how power could be allocated among a central authority, subsidiary jurisdictions such as cities and towns, and individual freemen in such a way as to insure both liberty and order: "If the representation of the freemen is equal, and the elections frequent; if the magistrates are constitutionally chosen and responsible for their administration, such a government is of all others the most free and safe. The form is the most perfect on earth."[35]

In that same year, a writer in the Newburyport, Massachusetts, *Essex Journal* commented sardonically, "In the State of Connecticut they are making rapid advances towards becoming the Guide and Pattern of ALL the States, in Learning, and religious matters—they have already undertaken to dictate the manner of pronunciation, spelling and dividing of words." The writer was referring specifically to Webster's speller and to an adaptation of Isaac Watts's translation of the Psalms that Joel Barlow had just published. Had the newspaper author been aware of Webster's extending the reach of Connecticut's superiority into the realm of government, he might have allowed himself to be more broadly sarcastic: In the State of Connecticut they are making rapid advances towards becoming the Guide and Pattern of ALL the States, in ALL things.[36]

In the words of James Madison, no less, Webster's *Sketches of American Policy* called attention "at an early period" to the need for "enlarging the scope of the federal authority." This points us to the fact that the leading lights of Connecticut were, almost to a man, Federalists, from the late 1780s when that label denoted support of the new Constitution, to the late 1790s and beyond when it meant wholehearted opposition to Thomas Jefferson and all his works and ways.[37]

Those key characters in our story, Hudson and Goodwin, provide a good example. In the run-up to the 1787 Constitutional Convention, they not only published Noah Webster's preview of the revamped political order. Being proprietors of a newspaper that was viewed as the "mouthpiece for the state's socially conservative mercantile establishment," they also recruited David Humphreys, Joel Barlow, and others in the orbit of the Connecticut Wits to deploy their pens in condemnation of Shays's Rebellion in western Massachusetts, up the Connecticut River Valley from Hartford. The result was *The Anarchiad,* a labored satire modeled loosely on *The Dunciad* by Alexander Pope characterizing the Shays rebels and those sympathetic to them as enemies of all social order.

Subsequently, during the debates over the new Constitution, they refused to publish Antifederalist views in the *Courant.* Historian Christopher Grasso notes that during the later period of Federalist-Jeffersonian Republican confrontation, "Hudson and Goodwin . . . likened Republican discourse to the conspiratorial mumbling of criminals, the ranting of madmen, and the howling of rabid dogs."[38]

What was the substance of the Federalism of Connecticut's "socially conservative mercantile establishment"? The opposition between Federalists and Jeffersonian Republicans is usually portrayed in American history textbooks as one between Alexander Hamilton's emphasis on the development of manufactures and Thomas Jefferson's insistence that freehold farming must remain the basis of the American social order. This account elides the distinct agrarianism of the Connecticut Federalists. As discussed above, John Adams marveled at the fertility of the Connecticut Valley. Modern historians agree that the Connecticut Valley was North America's "first wheat belt," and that valley people had readier access to "wheaten bread" than other New Englanders.[39]

Literary scholar William C. Dowling has argued that in many of the poems of the Connecticut Wits, especially Dwight's *Greenfield Hill* and various works by Humphreys, an agrarian social vision was proposed "as a model for America in her hour of self determination." This vision comprised the sanctification of agricultural labor in Virgil's *Georgics*, the reprise of this theme undertaken by eighteenth-century English poets in combination with their critique of early capitalist "luxury and corruption," and, above all, the "organic or traditional" agrarian society of colonial Connecticut, "the solid world in which [the Wits] had grown up." As Humphreys sums up the ideal in his *Poem on the Happiness of America*, "Hail agriculture! by whose parent aid,/The deep foundations of our States are laid."[40]

In *Greenfield Hill*, Dwight repeatedly conjures up a populace of which it might be said that "Exertion strong/Marks their whole life." The "rough soil" of Connecticut "Tempts hardy labour, . . . To turn with sinewy hand, the stony glebe." What is brought forth, "every comfort from the mould,/Unpromising but kind," is all the more satisfying because of such strenuous georgic imperatives and proclivities: "Thy houses, barns,/Thy granaries, and thy cellars, hence are stor'd/With all the sweets of life."[41]

On such "deep foundations" of material plenty wrested by a rugged people from a rugged environment is built a society of middling egalitarianism:

> How bless'd the sight of such a numerous train
> In such small limits, tasting every good
> Of competence, of independence, peace,
> And liberty unmingled; every house
> On its own ground, and every happy swain
> Beholding no superior but the laws,
> And such as virtue, knowledge, useful life,
> And zeal, exerted for the public good,
> Have rais'd above the throng.

In a footnote, Dwight all but explicitly declares his agenda of offering Connecticut as "the Guide and Pattern of ALL the States" in all important matters: "The manners of New England appear to be rapidly spreading through the American republic. . . . When the enterprize, industry, œconomy, morals, and happiness, of New England, especially of Connecticut, are attentively considered, the patriotic mind will perhaps find much more reason to rejoice in this prospect, than to regret it."[42]

William Dowling's claim that the agrarian ideals of the Connecticut Federalists entailed a clear-cut opposition to early capitalism and the "luxury and corruption" supposedly accompanying it is open to question. The Federalist attitude toward commerce and even manufacturing was ambivalent. In *Greenfield Hill*, Dwight is pleased at the thought of "Rivers," that "with foamy course, / Pour o'er the ragged cliff the white cascade, / And roll unnumber'd mills; . . . or bear / The sails of commerce through the laughing groves." Dowling argues that with the image of the "sails of commerce" visible amid "the laughing groves," Dwight rescues the seagoing trade of Connecticut from the taint of luxury and corruption by suggesting a "close relationship between the georgic life of the countryside and the farthest reaches of commercial empire." As we read it, however, the imagery confers an unexplained blessing on the processes of economic development. These processes were steadily altering the rural character of Connecticut in ways that many persisted in regarding as introducing luxury and corruption.[43]

In 1795, a year after the publication of *Greenfield Hill*, Timothy Dwight was chosen president of Yale. From this position, he presided over the culture of Connecticut and Western New England until his death in 1817, earning from those who found his influence excessive the nickname "Old Pope Dwight." During his presidential tenure, Dwight developed an avocation as a traveler in his native region, for twenty years journeying through New England's Connecticut and Massachusetts heartlands, its Rhode Island black sheep zone (Dwight still regarded this state as tainted by its seventeenth-century origins in the dissent of Roger Williams and others from Puritan orthodoxy), and its emergent eastern, northern, and western colonies of Maine, Vermont, and upstate New York. First published shortly after his death, Dwight's *Travels in New England and New York* does indeed, in accordance with his opponents' view of him, savor of a potentate's record of how he progressed through and inspected his own domain.

In 1803, Dwight traveled up the Connecticut River Valley, following the river all the way to its source near the Canadian border. In his narrative of this trip, Dwight saw fit to include a survey of the valley as the locale of a coherent way of life, distinct to some degree even from the rest of New England: "The inhabitants of this valley . . . may be said to resemble each other more than their fellow citizens who live on the coast resemble them." In detailing this resemblance, Dwight paints a more detailed portrait of Connecticut and valley life in all its idealized superiority than any we have seen thus far.[44]

Right at the outset, Dwight turns what was perceived by outsiders as a defect—the region's lack of a major urban place comparable to Philadelphia, New York, or Boston—into a virtue: "They are so remote from a market as to be perfectly free from that sense of inferiority customarily felt by the body of a people who live in the neighborhood of large cities. Hence a superior spirit of personal independence is generated and cherished." Valley people aren't servile but neither is their "spirit of personal independence" of the feisty, chip-on-the-shoulder sort. Remoteness from cities combines with living "on a pleasant surface and on a soil easy of cultivation" to produce "softer dispositions and manners."

At this point, a skeptical reader might ask why the rural circumstances of the Connecticut River Valley don't engender in the inhabitants the ignorant rusticity so often reported by urban observers. Dwight has his answer ready. This problem is avoided by the fact that, more than anywhere else in New England, valley life is village life. By means of the churches that are built in these villages, families "have not only opportunity, but the most convenient opportunities, for being present at the public worship of GOD." By means of the "suites of schools" also found there, children "are sent universally at an early age to school, and begin their education almost as soon as they can speak."

The upshot is that

> the inhabitants are better educated and more orderly than in most other parts even of New England. There is no tract of the same size in which learning is more, or more uniformly encouraged, or where sobriety or decorum is more generally demanded or exhibited. Steadiness of character, softness of manners, a disposition to read, respect for the laws and magistrates, a strong sense of liberty, blended with an equally strong sense of the indispensable importance of energetic government, are all extensively predominant in this region.

We might pause briefly here to comment on some aspects of Dwight's style and rhetoric. People have "not only opportunity, but the most convenient opportunities" for going to church. Learning is not just "more . . . encouraged"; it is "more uniformly encouraged." The valley is presented as a place where everything that can possibly be thought of to make things work well has been thought of.

But we misstated things just now. Valley people don't go to church. They are "present at the public worship of GOD." The phrasing enacts the principle stated a few sentences later that in the valley, "sobriety or decorum is . . . generally demanded or exhibited." Overall, Dwight's diction and syntax are designed to convey sobriety and decorum, an onward progression of deliberate, measured thoughtfulness. The tone is such that an unqualifiedly democratic informality seems all but inconceivable.

What might be less obvious is that the tone also eschews the full-blown pomp and circumstance of the traditional hierarchies that Dwight repeatedly disparages in *Greenfield Hill.* An example of this characteristic is the final sentence of the more extended of the above quotations. It seems to be building toward an emphatic, glorious resolution and climax, but it completes itself instead in a relatively subdued, colorless manner. Dwight is claiming in the sentence that in the valley as nowhere else a reconciliation of the opposites of liberty and law has been achieved. But he opts to round things off not by stentorian proclamation but by understatement. Such a reconciliation is "extensively predominant in this region."[45]

The remainder of the passage describes the material manifestations of this spiritual equilibrium. The layout of New England villages, "and in a peculiar degree" those of the Connecticut River Valley, reflects the fact that "the intention of settling in them is not merely to acquire property, but to sustain the relations, perform the duties, and contribute to the enjoyments of life." Unlike in European villages, in which people are jammed together in dwellings "built commonly of rough stone, clay, or earth, and roofed with thatch," a house in a valley village is placed in "a convenient spot . . . at the bottom of [a] courtyard (often neatly enclosed)," on a lot of anywhere from two to ten acres. There are always "a barn and other convenient outbuildings," along with "a garden replenished with culinary vegetables, flowers, and fruits, and very often also prettily enclosed." The lot as a whole is "a meadow, richly cultivated, covered during the pleasant season with verdure, and containing generally a thrifty orchard."

The usually wood house itself is "neater, lighter, and pleasanter" than a brick or stone one and almost entirely, because of the spaciousness of the overall village layout, free from the danger of fire. Like the meetinghouse and other public buildings, it is typically "painted white," which contributes immeasurably to the "sprightly, cheerful appearance" of the landscape.

Needless to say, properties such as this are inhabited by two kinds of people: farmers "of a superior character for intelligence and good manners" and mechanics, who "have their full share of this character, and usually aim at a higher degree of respectability than in most parts of the country."

Dwight outlines a mutually reinforcing system, which forms the grounds for the claim that (as Dwight puts it in accord with William Strickland, Henry Wansey, and George Washington) "in this region poverty in the absolute sense is scarcely known." Rather,

> Every man, with hardly an exception, lives on his own ground and in his own house. Every man, therefore, possesses an absolute personal independence, derived from his earliest ancestor, and secured by the government under which he lives. It was born with him, and therefore sits upon him easily and naturally. The ancestor from whom he derived it, he respects. The government by which it is secured, he loves and venerates, and is ever ready to defend. Life here is therefore seen in all its pleasing, rural forms, and in these forms it is seen with uncommon advantage.

In associating the venerable "earliest ancestors" of the present inhabitants of the region with a government that those same inhabitants venerate, Dwight again turns what some regarded as a defect—that Connecticut was the only state whose governmental structure remained unchanged during the Revolution—into a virtue.[46]

The stability and prosperity of the Connecticut River Valley thus stretched far back into the past, and Dwight believed it would endure far into the future. In the present moment of his writing, his view takes in not only "the numerous churches lifting their spires in frequent succession," and "the neat schoolhouses everywhere occupied," but also "the mills busied on such a multitude of streams." This glimpse of the Industrial Revolution at its birth is not the serpent in the garden but merely the last in a series of phenomena by which Dwight assures his readers "that a pleasanter journey will rarely be found than that which is made in the Connecticut Valley."[47]

Dwight certainly fleshes out the assertions of Brissot de Warville and many others to the effect that Connecticut was "really the paradise of the United States." He also drops in a number of hints of "the Guide and Pattern of ALL the States" variety. Valley mechanics "aim at a higher degree of respectability than in most parts of the country." The people of Connecticut—or at least of the valley—are "better educated and more orderly than in most other parts even of New England."[48]

Predictably, the part of New England that fell the farthest short of the Connecticut standard was Rhode Island. As a traveler passing from Stonington, Connecticut, to Westerly, Rhode Island, Dwight wrote in 1800 that he "is struck with the sudden change of the whole artificial scenery. The houses, a few excepted, are small, old, and ragged. The barns vanish, and the tidy, thrifty appearance of Connecticut ceases. Everything indicates a want of energy, a destitution of all views and efforts toward improvement, a sluggish acquiescence in inconveniences and imperfections which a more vigorous disposition would easily remove"[49]

Toward the non-Connecticut Valley portions of Massachusetts Dwight was generally more respectful, though he did see room for improvement in some areas. Valley towns "taken together, are better built than an equal number in any other part of the United States, unless perhaps on the eastern coast of Massachusetts where," Dwight slyly adds, yet again turning a valley defect into a virtue, "the wealth of the inhabitants is greatly superior." Perhaps it was in consequence of this greater wealth that there was to be found among the elite circles of Boston a defective style of education that produced good breeding only in an externalized, trivialized form—"not a refinement of the taste, the understanding, or the heart" but rather "merely a refinement . . . of an imagination already soft and sickly, of a sensibility already excessive, of a relish already fastidious."[50]

Dwight made these observations about hothouse Boston gentility in the course of his first journey in 1796. Earlier in this same trip he found eastern and central Massachusetts deficient in the realm of food. As he proceeded eastward from the valley, he all but gloated about the fact that "a traveler will scarcely see a field of wheat . . . during a journey of one hundred miles." Everywhere from Worcester County in central Massachusetts on, therefore, the staple bread was made not with wheat but rather with rye. When it was necessary to stoop from wheat to rye in the valley, the bread was "made usually of what is called white rye" and was "managed with great care in every part of the process." The resulting loaf often approximated "in its color to wheat and still more in its agreeableness to the palate."[51]

But in non–Connecticut River Valley Massachusetts they used a dark, unbolted rye that was "then mixed with a large portion of the meal of maize." The baked bread was "dark, glutinous, and heavy." A visitor from the valley served such bread at an inn "looks at it in curiosity and wonder, asks what kind of food it is, and is not a little surprised when he is told that it is bread." More wondrous still was the fact that this bizarre concoction was preferred over "the best wheaten loaf" not only by "plain people" but even by the Boston upper crust.[52]

Near the outset of his account of that 1796 journey, Dwight comes close to explicitly staking Connecticut's claim to national leadership. The scene is Election Day in Hartford, marked by processions, sermons, ceremonious proclamation of the vote tallies, and formal dinners: "No public national solemnities of which I have heard or read can be compared with these for decorum. None are so productive of rational pleasure and real advantage to the community, and none are so free from that debasing licentiousness which embitters, to a virtuous man, almost all those of other countries."[53]

To make it unmistakable that the contrast between Connecticut and "other countries" includes other regions of the United States, Dwight recounts the reaction of "one of the judges of the Supreme Court of the United States" when he attended the Connecticut election day observances "a number of years since":

> As he was conversing with the governor, he said, "Pray, Sir, where are your rabble?" "You see them around you, Sir," said the governor. "Rabble, Sir," said the judge, "I see none but gentlemen and ladies." "We have no other rabble," said the governor, "but such as you see." "You astonish me," replied he. "Why, Sir, when General Washington took the oath of office in the balcony of the assembly house in Philadelphia, the chief justice, who administered it, could scarcely be heard at the distance of ten feet on account of the noise and tumult of the yard below. Among the thousands who are present, I do not discover an indecorum. These are your only rabble, Sir? Well, I will say, that the inhabitants of Connecticut are the only people within my knowledge who understand the nature of an elected government."

Dwight earlier states that during the Connecticut election day processionals, the route is lined with "several thousand spectators collected from all parts of the state, among whom there is rarely one who is not perfectly decorous. I have often been present and do not remember that I ever saw an individual intoxicated or quarreling, or that I ever heard a profane or indecent word, or even noisy conversation."[54]

So, a choice: the new national government in Philadelphia, in which solemn oaths on high are drowned out by "the noise and tumult of the yard below," or the Standing Order of Connecticut, in which "public national solemnities" are facilitated rather than hindered by farmers and mechanics "of a superior character for intelligence and good manners," standing respectfully on a level with and as a respected part of a government that they love and venerate. Which of these afforded the more auspicious model for a secure and successful republican future? To Timothy Dwight the answer was crystal clear. Connecticut's Election Day was a *tableau vivant* of Noah Webster's claim of earthly perfection for the state's political structure.[55]

Yet another nation-building initiative was undertaken in Connecticut at the beginning of the nineteenth century. In 1799, the Connecticut Academy of Arts and Sciences was created, with many of the same people, including Dwight, Webster, David Humphreys, and John Trumbull, among its founding trustees. The academy's first project was an effort "to gather information from each of [the state's] towns," in both narrative and statistical form, about such aspects of town life as farming, commerce, churches, schools, libraries, and the changes that had taken place over the past generation or so. These academicians believed that Connecticut, "in its elevation of religion, education, and good order, . . . seemed to offer an eminently suitable model to be followed." The study of Connecticut "social arrangements," made possible by the reports solicited by the academy, might yield "lessons . . . that could be applied to the country as a whole."[56]

These reports on conditions in Connecticut in the first couple of decades of the nineteenth century have been reissued in a modern edition, with an accompanying volume of analytical essays. In one of the essays, Paul E. Waggoner, drawing on the early twentieth-century work of Percy W. Bidwell, paints a rather grimmer picture of life in Connecticut villages and on its farms than one would infer from the poetic evocations of Timothy Dwight. Waggoner writes that into the nineteenth century transportation of crops to market remained highly problematic, and as a result the majority of Connecticut farmers managed to get by on no better than a hardscrabble subsistence level:

> Until 1800 they subsisted on pea and bean porridge or broth from boiled salt meat mixed with meal and sometimes hasty pudding and milk—both morning and evening. The common bread of country people away from the coast was made of Indian cornmeal and rye flour. The farmer could have carried all his tools, except the cart and harrow, upon his back. His tools included a plow, a hoe, a pitchfork, a manure-fork and a shovel. . . . A day's flailing yielded 4 to 6 bushels of wheat or 6 to 12 bushels of barley. Although Indian corn was sometimes flailed, high technology was scraping the grains from the cob across a spade. A craving for the stimulants from Connecticut's numerous distilleries arose in part from a coarse diet but "probably to a larger extent, from a desire to relieve at least temporarily the dreary monotony of village life."[57]

In another essay in the same volume, Edward S. Cooke, Jr., argues that the emphasis in the questionnaire the academy sent out to the towns reveals "the Academy's leaders to be upper-class reformers who sought to overturn what they viewed as old, inefficient farming practices." Far from standing firm in opposition to the new market economy and its possible moral ramifications, as William Dowling argues, these gentlemen believed that "new breeds, improved crops," and "enriched soil" would assist farm families in making the change from a subsistence to a "market orientation," and that such a change "would ensure prosperity, self-sufficiency, and good citizenship. Knowledge of the arts of agriculture and animal husbandry would be a pillar of the new republican government."[58]

Such aims for what became known as the Town Reports project would certainly have been in keeping with the frequently quoted passage from Dwight's *Travels* in which he observes that "a considerable number" of the settlers of Vermont whom he has been excoriating as shiftless and at best semi-civilized

> become sober, industrious citizens merely by the acquisition of property.... They sell the soil of their first farms at an enhanced price, and.... they gain for their improvements on them what, to themselves at least, is a considerable sum. The possession of this money removes, perhaps for the first time, the despair of acquiring property, and awakens the hope and the wish to acquire more. The secure possession of property demands every moment the hedge of law, and reconciles a man originally lawless to the restraints of government. Thus situated, he sees that reputation also is within his reach. Ambition forces him to aim at it, and compels him to a life of sobriety and decency. That his children may obtain this benefit, he is obliged to send them to school and to unite with those around him in supporting a schoolmaster. His neighbors are disposed to build a church and settle a minister. A regard to his own character, to the character and feelings of his family, and very often to the solicitations of his wife prompts him to contribute to both these objects; to attend, when they are compassed, upon the public worship of God; and perhaps to become in the end a religious man.

Here participation in the market in land leads inexorably to the perfected Connecticut model of schools, churches, law-abiding industry, and a secure competence.[59]

Dwight's mention of the Vermont pioneer's paying heed to "the solicitations of his wife" brings up another aspect of the Federalist social vision—that it was relatively respectful of women and their contributions. Historian Rosemarie Zagarri argues that it was the Federalists who were the primary promulgators of what historians have called Republican Motherhood, the idea that the most important part that women could play in the new nation was the nurturing of upright republican citizens. Federalist orators regularly heaped fulsome praise on women. Speaking in Hartford on the Fourth of July in 1792 (in remarks subsequently published by Hudson & Goodwin), Theodore Dwight enthused that "with minds enlarged by science, and orna-mented with every refined, dignified, and delicate sentiment, the women of America establish their sovereignty, by the united influence of beauty, modesty, and virtue. Removed from the splendour, and vices of courts, their hearts cultivate the accomplishments of peaceful, elegant, and domestic life." Even as in Timothy Dwight's account the pursuit of property was draw-ing the man toward settledness and stability, correspondingly in his brother Theodore Dwight's account the civilized pursuits of the wife were raising the man up to refinement and elegance.[60]

One of the Town Reports sent back to the Connecticut Academy of Arts and Sciences in response to its questionnaire provided a view of the benefits of market-oriented farming, property accumulation, and the role of women that was exactly in line with these various notions. In Cornwall, Connecti-cut, both the men and women of farm families, or as the author Elijah Allen respectfully entitled them, both "the Gentlemen and Ladies" of those families, were making themselves "Emminently Conspicuous" in generating "a surplus to Vend off," by which they found their "Estate Annually increas-ing." The women in particular were contributing by spinning, sewing, and dairying. By producing "greater Quantities of Butter and Cheese" to be sent "to Market for Cash," the family was enabling itself "to pay . . . Taxes for the support of Law, Order and good Government and Instruction in Church and State." That was by no means all. Industrious pursuit of market farming was creating the wherewithal for living in a refined manner: "Gold, Pearls, Silk and Embroidery . . . the Elegancies of Superb Dress" were "the Fruits of Industry."[61]

The rewards of such diligent, well-managed farming were to be found at the family dinner table as well as on the superbly dressed bodies of family members. The "Industry & good oeconomy of the Husbandman both in Grain & Grass for Mowing & Feeding Land" meant that "not only Bread, Beef, Pork, Mutton & Veal are Plenty, but also Butter & Chees are made in large quantities." These, "Joined to the great Variety of succulent Fruits, Herbs & Roots Cultivated in the Garden, the Orchard and the Field for Culinary Use," made it possible for "the Ladies . . . To Deck their Tables both for their Families and Friendly Visitants, in an Elegant manner, with Princely Fare of the most Nutricient and wholesome Viands."[62]

Elijah Allen told his interlocutors at the Connecticut Academy of Arts and Sciences exactly what they wanted to hear. One of its founding members, Isaac Beers, was the New Haven bookseller who first advertised *American Cookery*. Another member, Simeon Baldwin, the academy's recording secretary under whose name the questionnaire to the towns was sent out on January 1, 1800, had in April 1796, as clerk of the Federal District Court for Connecticut, witnessed the petition of Amelia Simmons for copyright protection of *American Cookery*. The book was published by a firm the proprietors of which, Barzillai Hudson and George Goodwin, had longstanding ties with other academy founders such as Jeremiah and Daniel Wadsworth and Noah Webster.

This little cookbook would certainly have come in handy for "the Ladies" in modest but thriving Cornwall farmhouses as they strove "to Deck their Tables both for their Families and Friendly Visitants in an Elegant manner, with Princely Fare of the must Nutricient and wholesome Viands." The leading citizens of Connecticut hoped and believed that *American Cookery* might serve this purpose not just in Cornwall, not just in Connecticut, but nationwide. In so doing, it would help to firm up support across the country for "Law, Order and good Government."[63]

But what exactly would these evocations of fine attire and cuisine have meant to a Connecticut farmer or clockmaker, as the eighteenth century drew to its close and the nineteenth century dawned?

CHAPTER 5

Domestic Culture

T he first copyright notice for *American Cookery* appeared on page three of the May 9, 1796, number of the *Connecticut Courant*. Here is what else was found on that page. Directly above the notice's position at the bottom of column two was an advertisement for "Lee and Co.," stating that this firm had "replenished their Store in West-Simsbury with a variety of GOODS suitable for the season, which are to be sold as cheap for Cash as at any Store whatever." Perusal of the wide array of ads further up and in the adjacent columns leaves one wondering just what types of goods would *not* be suitable for the season.[1]

At Buckland & Foot's in East Hartford (and in the newspaper two ads up from Lee & Co.), you could choose from "a large supply of fashionable Dry Goods," just in from New York and "selected from the latest arrivals from England." If you wanted something other than fabrics, Buckland & Foot could also provide you with "Groceries, Crockery and Hard Ware." Other merchants were more specific. In the grocery line, "Ely & Egleston" of Hartford, "at their store in Main-street, opposite Moore & Bolles's" (and in their ad just above that of Buckland & Foot), were offering "Rum, Brandy, Wines of different kinds, Molasses, Loaf, Lump and Brown Sugars; Hyson, Souchong and Bohea Teas; Pimento, Coffee, Chocolate, Pepper, Raisins, Nutmegs, Cassia, Cinnamon, &c. &c." Brown & Kimberly of Hartford (column three, four ads up from Ely & Egleston) was the place for you if you were looking for a certain set or style of crockery: "green, blue and plain edged Plates and oval Dishes of all sizes; fluted and fancy Cups and Saucers; . . . Mugs, Mustards, Salts, Peppers, Jugs, Tea Pots, Bowls, &c."

There were more notices for "fashionable Dry Goods" than for anything else. William Lawrence of Hartford (advertising immediately above Ely & Egleston) had "just received from the latest importations, a very handsome assortment of English and India Goods," such as "Ginghams, Muslinets, Dimitys, Callicoes, Chintzes" and a multitude of other types of cloth, along with "Dunstable and willow Hatts" and "a variety of ladies Shoes." In East

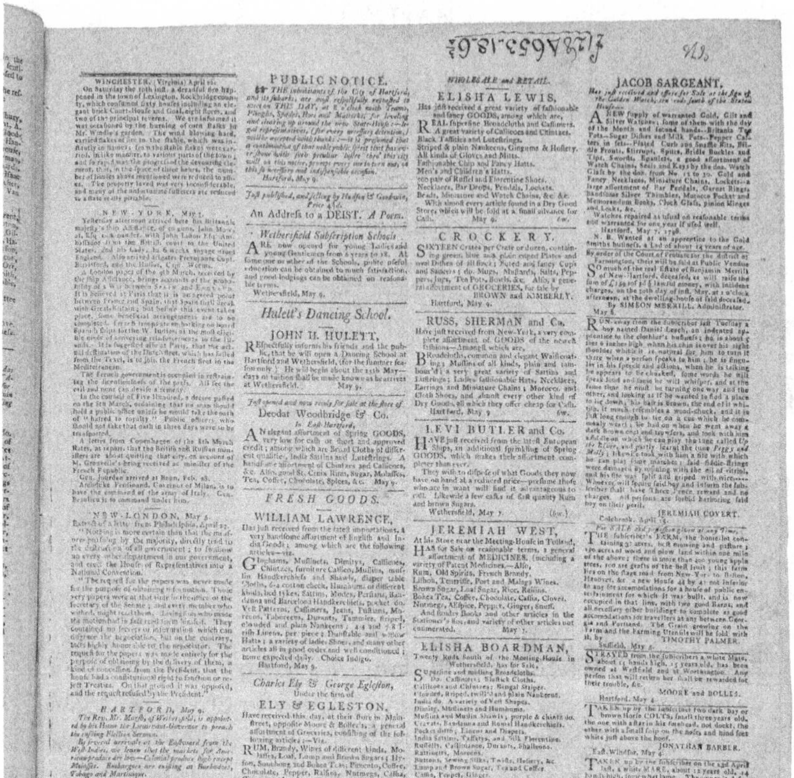

FIGURE 5.1. *Connecticut Courant*, May 9, 1796, page 3. The copyright notice for the Hartford edition of *American Cookery* is at the bottom of column two.

—Courtesy, American Antiquarian Society

Hartford (in the paper, just above William Lawrence's ad), "Deodat Woodbridge & Co." singled out for special mention their "Broad Cloths . . . India Sattins and Lut-strings." (Like their East Hartford competitors Buckland & Foot, Woodbridge sold groceries as well as dry goods—"good St. Croix Rum, Sugar, Molasses, Tea, Coffee, Chocolate, Spices, &c.") To the right in column three were five additional purveyors of textiles, four located in Hartford, one in Wethersfield. One of these, "John Dodd, Jun." of Hartford, claimed that his stock was "too extensive to enumerate."

Textiles, tableware, and groceries were far from the only consumer goods that readers of this page of this Monday's *Courant* could consider buying. In column three toward the bottom, one ad higher than those adjacent to the *American Cookery* copyright announcement, David Greenleaf of Hartford informed prospective customers that he had on hand "Gold and Silver English and French Watches from 18 to 40 Dollars each." He was also selling "Gilt and Steel Chains, Seals and Keys, elegant Ladies Necklaces of the newest fashion, Glass Gilt and enameled Pendants . . . Garnet Finger Rings, Silver Thimbles, Miniature Settings and Lockets, Pencil Cases . . . Sugar Tongs," and "Spur Buckles of all kinds." Some of the "Gold, Gilt and Silver Watches" on sale at another Hartford emporium, that of Jacob Sargeant (top of column four), had "the day of the Month and second hands." From Sargeant you could also get crockery, ladies' jewelry, equestrian gear ("Bridle Fronts, Stirrups, Spurs, Bridle Buckles and Tips"), "Swords, Epaulets," and "Morocco Pocket and Memorandum Books."

But perhaps your needs or wants were on a larger scale. The space in column three at the bottom adjacent to the *American Cookery* notice was occupied by an advertisement containing the information that there was available "To be LET and possession given immediately A Convenient two story Dwelling-House, late the property of Daniel Goodwin, deceased, situate in the north part of this city, being the same house which has lately been occupied by William Warner." In most parts of New England, a dwelling house of two stories was one that betokened prosperity and status. In Hartford, however (indeed, in the entire Connecticut River Valley), a two-story dwelling house was nothing special. Since about 1770, the great majority of the town's houses had been built two stories high. Nevertheless, a house of such a description at least signified the middling comfort and well-being that impressed contemporary travelers as the norm in Hartford and elsewhere in Connecticut.[2]

"Daniel Goodwin, deceased," the house's most recent owner, was probably the Daniel Goodwin who had passed away unmarried in 1790 at the age of forty-four. He had been second cousin to *Courant* co-owner George Good-win. His father, also Daniel, had been a selectman and deacon of the First Church. At his death in 1772, Daniel the elder had "left an estate of over £10,000." If "Daniel Goodwin, deceased" was indeed this son and cousin, then the probability was high that this "two story Dwelling-House" offered to let was a house a great deal above average, even by Hartford standards. And should you have been inclined to become the resident tenant in such an imposing structure, then you might have been interested in the adver-tisement that William Warner, your predecessor in this role, had placed at the bottom of column one, immediately to the left of the *American Cookery* copyright notice. Warner was selling a "new genteel standing top CHAISE, with Harness complete."[3]

Those interested in buying rather than renting were directed by an ad at the base of column four to consider a piece of property upriver, "about sixty rods north of the meeting-house, in the first society in Enfield," consisting of "a genteel house, with a store under the same roof, back kitchen, wood-house, barn, store-house, &c. with about twenty acres of the best of land, adjoining." The Enfield First Church meetinghouse had been the site of Jon-athan Edwards's memorable 1741 exhortation addressed to "Sinners in the Hands of an Angry God." (George Goodwin's wife Mary was a distant rela-tion of Jonathan Edwards.) By this time, more than half a century removed from Edwards's preaching, Enfield was a typical Connecticut Valley village with a goodly share of "genteel" homes. This term, when used in connection with domestic architecture, had come increasingly to denote a large two-story house having central front and back doors, a hallway extending between them, two chimneys rather than one, and four rooms on each floor.[4]

In many genteel houses, as it seems was the case with the one for sale in Enfield in May 1796, the kitchen was consigned to an ell appended to the rear of the house ("back kitchen"). This made it possible for all the rooms within the house proper to be devoted to pursuits that were exclusively genteel. A dining room could be placed where a kitchen might otherwise be needed, and the fine art of dining could thereby be separated from the rough and ready cookery operations on which it was dependent.[5]

So you have obtained your genteel house and carriage, your fashionable wardrobe, your elegant jewelry, your fancy ceramics, and your larder stocked with imported liquors, wines, teas, coffees, chocolates, and spices. If you turned over to page four for a while, you would find a few more of the essen-tials of genteel housekeeping that didn't make it onto page three, such as furniture ("AARON COLTON, . . . carries on the Cabinet Business in all its branches, in the newest, neatest and best manner") and wallpaper ("Zachariah Mills & Co. At their Paper-Hanging Manufactory, a few rods south of Major Hart's Store at the River Manufacture and keep constantly for sale, a large and handsome assortment of PAPERS").

But back to page three. What might you do with yourself once you had gotten all this set up? Your eye might wander up toward the top of column two, where you would be alerted to the local availability of refined pastimes and cultivated pleasures. Just above Deodat Woodbridge & Co.'s advertising space, "John H. Hulett, Respectfully informs his friends and the public, that he will open a Dancing School at Hartford and Wethersfield, (for the summer season only.) He will begin about the 15 May—days of tuition will be made known as he arrives at Wethersfield." Probably you knew how to dance already, but it was never too soon to get your children started. In the meantime, two spaces on up the column, Hudson & Goodwin openly advertised one of their own publications—"An Address to a DEIST. A Poem. . . . Price 4½d." Good to keep up with the controversies that Tom Paine and such were always stirring up and that you had heard your friends talking about. And even better to keep up by canvassing such issues as presented in the elevated medium of poetry.

Speaking of your children, you doubtless found the announcement that was tucked between the poetry and the dancing that "Wethersfield Subscription Schools Are now opened for young Ladies and young Gentlemen from 6 years to 18. At some one or other of the Schools, polite useful education can be obtained to much satisfaction and good lodgings can be obtained on reasonable terms."

It is clear from this survey of a couple of newspaper pages that where and when *American Cookery* was first published, the material and mental infrastructures of genteel consumerism were solidly in place. How had this come to be the case? Historians have described a "consumer revolution" that was exported to British North America from the mother country beginning in the final quarter of the seventeenth century. The first signs of these developments were detected in Boston—for example, mention in Boston probate inventories of the 1680s of "such items as pictures, timepieces, table forks, chocolate, coffee, and tea," and a 1681 Boston house plan showing a room designated for dining. In the following decade, even such a stalwart of Boston Puritanism as Samuel Sewall ornamented his new house with painted shutters, inviting his friends in to appreciate such elegancies, regaling them in a manner appropriate to the occasion with "a glass or two of wine" and "some fruit," and recording in his diary without pious disapproval the response of one of these guests: "Mr. Willard . . . was much pleas'd with our painted shutters; in pleasancy said he thought he had got into Paradise."[6]

It took a while longer for the consumer revolution to make its appearance elsewhere in New England. Historians Gloria L. Main and Jackson Turner Main argued that it spread beyond Boston "first in the towns closest to the principal waterways: on the Atlantic coast, along the Sound, and in the valley of the Connecticut River." Thus, in 1701, a Providence merchant built the first house with a dining room in that lesser seaport. And a Connecticut Valley minister, Reverend Stephen Williams of Longmeadow, Massachusetts, built in 1716 a house that was sufficiently "stately" to cause his parishioners to "speak meanly and reproachfully of me."[7]

In Worcester County, Massachusetts, an area less developed than either Boston to its east or the Connecticut Valley to its west, a similar indication of the tensions accompanying the consumer revolution came to the surface, but not until 1751. In that year, Reverend Ebenezer Parkman of Westborough built a new house outfitted with thirteen large sash windows. He noted in his diary that one of his parishioners "was very Sharp upon me about the pride of Ministers, when he saw the Window Frames." Somewhat earlier, in 1730 in another Worcester County town, it was also the clergy that took the lead in introducing the novelties of the consumer revolution to the farmers and artisans who formed the bulk of the community. Elizabeth Hall, the minister's wife, was the first person in Sutton, Massachusetts, to own and use a teapot.[8]

If the consumer revolution was making inroads into Worcester County at midcentury, it was by that time a major presence in the Connecticut Valley up and down both the river and the social ladder. As historian Kevin M. Sweeney summarizes, "The same pattern of increasing quantities of furniture, eating and cooking utensils, and modest luxuries such as looking glasses and silver spoons can be found in the river port of Wethersfield and the frontier town of Deerfield by the second quarter of the eighteenth century. . . . Merchants and professionals clearly acted as the leading consumers of the new types of goods, but the growing quantities could be found in the households of yeomen and artisans as well."[9]

Had these lesser folk not been attracted by those of the new commodities they could afford—groceries, textiles, and ceramics—there would have been insufficient demand to sustain the trading networks on which the consumer revolution was based. In the 1740s in Wethersfield, just below Hartford, onions were cultivated as a specialty crop. Gloria Main explains that the women who readied them for sale by tying them in bunches received their compensation "in the form of store merchandise, mostly luxury imports such as sugar, chocolate, pepper, rum, cotton lace, and silk romall, a silken handkerchief used as a head covering. Other goods paid for by women's onions included medicine, a pair of spectacles, and a copy of Homer's *Iliad*." Similar purchases by average people are documented in store account books from Farmington, Springfield, and Deerfield.[10]

According to Sweeney, during these same decades those on the upper levels of valley society turned to "making ambitious, public statements of status and power with artifacts. Those who could afford it, and some who could not, built large gambrel-roofed mansion houses with elaborate doorways and painted exteriors, suggesting the solidity of masonry construction." Observers from more sophisticated parts such as Boston sometimes found the valley gentry not entirely up to par in all facets of this refined style. Visiting Hampshire County, Massachusetts, in 1760, Harvard student Paul Coffin felt that "the Painting and Utensils and Furniture in the Homes do not equal outward Appearances of their Houses in this part of the Country."[11]

Even John Adams, in the course of his 1771 trip along the river, was greatly displeased with the interior of the residence of Dr. Eliot Rawson of Middletown, Connecticut. Rawson's house was "handsome without, but neither clean nor elegant within, in furniture or anything else. His dining Room is crouded with a Bed and a Cradle, &c. &c." Adams meant that Rawson's dining room was terribly old-fashioned, resembling more a seventeenth-century hall or parlor than a properly genteel contemporary dining room.[12]

Nevertheless, by the time of the American Revolution, the Connecticut River Valley, as well as other parts of Connecticut, constituted a region in which "almost every known commodity in the Western world could be obtained." In the larger towns, specialized artisanal services essential to genteel comportment and pursuits—such as wig-making, barbering, bookbinding—were also ready to hand. Dances and balls were frequently held. The villages Timothy Dwight extolled, in which as of 1774 11 percent of Connecticut's population is estimated to have lived, had become secondary hubs in the wheels of refined living. Village stores offered stocks of goods that were "surprisingly varied and complete"—textiles and wearing apparel, groceries, stationery, books.[13]

As suggested by the objections of the laity of Longmeadow and Westborough to the "pride" shown by their ministers in the designs and appointments of their houses, the consumer revolution and the refinement of New England and the Connecticut Valley were not consummated without opposition. Writers frequently denounced the phenomena as nothing but a succumbing to "luxuries," a forsaking of the "sobriety and simple manners" of the Puritan founders of New England. During the revolutionary crisis Puritan strictures on the new consumerism were reinforced by the austerities of classical republican ideology and by the boycott of British goods that was devised as a strategy of resistance to British imperial policy. To be loyal to the American cause was to be dressed in homespun "russet grey" instead of in "foreign fripperies" and to renounce "all foreign teas, china ware, spices, and black pepper, all British and foreign superfluities and manufactures."[14]

The hard times that prevailed throughout New England during most of the 1780s gave this rhetoric a postwar presence and potency. In 1785, a writer in a Boston newspaper saw, in this context of scarcity, any form of refinement as a sign of degeneration: "New amusements are invented—new dissipations are introduced, to lull and enervate those minds already too much softened, poisoned and contaminated, by idle pleasures and foolish gratifications."[15]

Over in the Connecticut River Valley, similar sentiments were expressed by "A Farmer" in August 1788 in the *Courant* (and reprinted upriver in Northampton's *Hampshire Gazette* a couple of weeks later). The writer, almost certainly a made-up mouthpiece for the *Courant's* proprietors and their elite friends and associates, explained how he and his family had for years prospered in frugal self-sufficiency: "Nothing to wear, eat, or drink, was purchased, as my farm provided all—with this saving, I put money to interest, bought cattle fatted and sold them, and made great profit." But then the farmer's wife, in the course of marrying off their three daughters, yielded to the fatal temptations of the town and consumerism. After spending sprees on "silken" gowns and cloaks, looking glasses, "china tea-gear, . . . all sorts of household furniture unknown to us before," and "a hundred other things," and after his family's adoption of fashionable styles of dress, décor, diet, and dining, the farmer found that "all my loose money is gone . . . and further what it costs me to live . . . is fifty or sixty dollars a year more than all my farm brings me in. . . . I am not alone. Thirty in our parish have gone hand in hand with me—and they all say hard times."[16]

This document, like the Connecticut Wits' *Anarchiad*, was a salvo in the campaign waged by the Connecticut establishment against Shays's

Rebellion. The hard times being experienced by the average people of the valley, which might tempt them to complain and rebel, were really their own fault, the result of their heedless, extravagant outlays on foolish things.[17]

The rhetoric of anticonsumerism took other forms as well in the Connecticut Valley of the 1780s. In November 1786, at the height of the Shays's Rebellion crisis, the "Ladies" of Hartford announced that, along with recommending renunciation to others, they would also deprive themselves of at least some of the fruits of the consumer revolution. Being "fully sensible that our calamities are in a great measure occasioned by the luxury and extravagance of individuals," they expressed the hope that "those Ladies that used to excel in dress . . . will endeavour to set the best examples, by laying aside their richest silks and superfluous decorations, and as far as possible distinguish themselves by their perfect indifference to those ornaments and superfluities which in happier times might become them."[18]

These women pledged specifically that "until the 25th of June next" they would not purchase "any Gauze, Ribbons, Lace, Feathers, Beaver-Hats, Silks, Muslins, and Chintzes, except only for weddings and for mourning." Moreover, they would "dress their persons in the plainest manner, and, encourage industry, frugality and neatness, giving all due preference to the manufactures of their own country." The consumer boycott that had helped to make the Revolution was now being enlisted in the cause of postrevolutionary law and order.[19]

But the slumping 1780s were soon succeeded by the booming 1790s, and calls for restraint began to be heard less often. Among the factors contributing to economic growth and optimism in New England was the revival of the West Indies trade. Advertisements in Worcester County, Massachusetts, newspapers in the spring and summer of 1796 displayed the same impressive stock of " 'fresh goods' from Europe, India, and the West Indies" that we saw in the *Courant* at this same time. The return of the consumer revolution in full force was accompanied by what historian Stephanie Grauman Wolf calls "frenzies of building—roads, houses, factories, public institutions, and ships." In Concord, Massachusetts, a social library, a "Harmonic Society," a "Social Club," and a volunteer fire department were all founded in the middle of the decade. Half the borrowers from the library were women.[20]

The same sorts of developments were occurring in Connecticut generally and in Hartford specifically. In New Haven, one sign of the good times that the West Indies trade brought on was increased construction. By 1798, there were 600 houses and 170 shops and stores where there had been 470 and 103 of each ten years before. Meanwhile, as noted, Hartford had emerged from the war in a relatively strong position, since unlike Connecticut's coastal cities, it had not been devastated by British raids or capture. In the 1780s and 1790s, Hartford was the home not only of the Connecticut Wits but also of an array of schools and libraries. In addition to "morning and evening schools, schools for young ladies, schools for boys, and mixed schools . . . there were teachers of French and of music, both vocal and instrumental, and those who instructed in drawing, painting, and elocution." As for libraries, a second social library was added in 1794 to the one that had been formed twenty years earlier, and commercial circulating libraries were frequently advertised in the *Courant*.[21]

Hartford's cultural vitality in the 1790s was further manifested by the opening in 1795 of a theater and in 1797 of a museum. Theatergoers could enjoy plays by Shakespeare, Sheridan, and Goldsmith. On at least one occasion, the theater doubled as a concert hall. The museum, one of the earliest in America, featured paintings by its founder, Joseph Steward, and a mix of natural and artificial "curiosities," ranging from a carnivalesque calf with two heads to items that were genuinely interesting from a scientific point of view. The location of the museum itself testified to Hartford's cultural and political stature. It was housed in two rooms in the new Connecticut State House, which had been completed just the year before. This was the first public building designed by Charles Bulfinch, and it featured a spiral staircase by Connecticut's own rising young architect, Asher Benjamin.[22]

Accompanying the renewed abundance of consumer goods, the formation of cultural institutions, and the construction of public buildings was what historian John L. Brooke has called "a broad disciplining of the countryside that began in the 1790s." Brooke describes the effect of "the erection of steeples, bells, and clocks" in Worcester County: "The sound of the bells tolling daily at twelve noon and nine in the evening and the sight of the steeple clock marking out the time at the town center would impose a new predictability and order upon the townspeople as a whole." A local clergyman articulated the ethos inspiring such initiatives when he urged farmers to build fencing that was "regular and handsome," and generally "to trim and adorn the earth . . . to pay more attention to some things for sake of ornament and sightliness."[23]

In Hartford, a similar outlook was on view in the *Courant* in 1797 in an article in favor of the construction of turnpikes. The author claimed that in areas in which turnpikes had not been built, towns had "a very deformed and unsocial appearance." He was confident, however, that the turnpike movement would continue to make headway "till the face of the country exhibits a delightful appearance."[24]

The turnpike boom facilitated the growth of Timothy Dwight's beloved villages, nodes of slightly denser habitation in the countryside that since before the American Revolution had served as farm families' points of entry into the consumer revolution. Such villages grew swiftly after 1785 in the Connecticut Valley. In village centers were found not just teapots but also the manners and decorum associated with them. The cultural dynamics observed in a bit of 1816 upstate New York satirical verse were already discernible in 1790s Connecticut, the milieu after which this early Yankee West region was patterned: "In every country village where ten chimneys' smoke perfumes the air,/Contiguous to a steeple, Great gentlefolks are found a score."[25]

Efforts in the direction of orderliness, improvement, and enhancement were made at this time in another area of Hartford's life—its food. Complaints beginning in 1791 that the city was insufficiently supplied with fowl and fruit, key items in a genteel diet, led by 1796 to the creation of "Hartford's first market house. . . . The desire for vegetables was said to be increasing daily. . . . City authorities imposed market regulations to guarantee cleanliness and the accuracy of weights and measures."[26]

Intellectual historian Christopher J. Berry stresses that an article's status as a refined or luxury good is a matter of quality, not quantity, offering examples from what are usually considered the three areas of basic human need: "It is not now a question of need—bread to assuage hunger—but of desire—for fresh bread. . . . The same applies to clothing or housing . . . not a goatskin for warmth but a cashmere coat, not a wattle-and-daub dwelling for protection but a Georgian town-house." We now survey the consumer revolution in Connecticut a bit more systematically, looking at the increasing refinement of the area's housing, furniture, clothing, and articles used to prepare and consume food.[27]

Until the middle of the eighteenth century, most upper-class houses in the Connecticut Valley were of a central chimney, two-story design, with two rooms on each floor—on the first floor the "hall" and the "parlor," on the second two "chambers." A great many of these two-on-two structures had a lean-to attached to the rear, creating the "saltbox" appearance that is considered one of the characteristic New England housing forms. During this period, the houses of yeoman and artisan families, the majority of the people, were essentially one-story versions of the same plan, with a hall and a parlor and sometimes a lean-to.[28]

Historian William N. Hosley, Jr., writes that in houses without lean-tos, whether two stories or one, the hall served as a "kitchen, dining area, and space for informal social interaction and domestic labor"—spinning, weaving, preparing food for storage. In houses with lean-tos, such as the one in Enfield mentioned above, the kitchen was placed in the lean-to, while the hall retained its other functions. The parlor was the place for more formal socializing, sometimes for taking meals with people outside the family, and also for displaying particularly valuable fabrics, metals, and other goods. Items displayed in the parlor often included the "best bed." According to historian of domestic life Elisabeth Donaghy Garrett, keeping a bed in the parlor remained a widespread practice in Hartford until the 1770s. Even as late as 1813, one wealthy resident there "yet displayed a chintz-draped bed . . . in his 'Front Room'—the most expensive bed in the house, although there were four bedchambers."[29]

Nevertheless, among the well-to-do with their two-story houses, sleeping usually took place in the upstairs chambers. These upper rooms were also used for storage and work of the same sort done in the hall. In the one-story houses of people of more modest means, both of the two available rooms had to be used for sleeping and storage as well as for any other functions. As soon as they could, the more prosperous among the yeomen and artisans added a second story or found other means of removing signs of mundane activity—tools and stored supplies—from the parlor, allowing it to serve more exclusively as the household's masthead, so to speak, its proclamation of wealth and status.[30]

At the end of the seventeenth century, the English lawyer and writer Roger North provided in his treatise "Of Building" a charming description of the communally inclusive nature of the great hall in the household of a medieval aristocrat: "In the ancient or Gothick times it was the mode for numerous families to eat in the same room at severall tables. . . . That way of a comon eating room made great halls open to the roof, with a lanthorne, to lett out smoak and stench, a laudable fashion, and consequently an indication of great dignity and plenty, and excuseth the unclenyness of it." Such openness to the life of the larger community was replicated on a smaller scale in the central-chimney houses of early colonial New England, which, as described by historian Robert Blair St. George, "retained the hall as the center of domestic functions in the public front of the house."[31]

The first steps away from such "socially open" forms of domestic architecture were taken in the south of England during the late sixteenth century. This was where and when the parlor became the norm in gentry houses; its appeal extended to the yeomanry as well. As the space in which a family's particular status was highlighted, the parlor was the room on which what North called the modern "affectation of cleanness" was first bestowed. By the time he was writing, a hundred years later, the parlor proved to have been the entering wedge for a new norm in English house design, that he described as "much variety of rooms, which the ancients had no occasion for, who cared not for exquisite neatness."[32]

The trend toward "much variety of rooms" and "exquisite neatness" showed itself in the Connecticut Valley around the end of the eighteenth century in two ways. First, the majority of the valley's population succeeded in living in two-story houses. By the 1770s in the Hartford area, the percentage of two-story ownership ranged from two-thirds in some towns to 90 percent or more in Hartford itself. Up the river in South Hadley, Massachusetts, a rate of two-thirds was achieved by 1798.[33]

The second sign of the trend toward more rooms and more distinct variation of function among rooms was the emergence around 1750 among the Hartford elite of a preference for the central-hallway, two-chimney, eight-room, kitchen-relegated-to-a-rear-ell type of house plan described earlier. From Hartford, "this new style of housing . . . was rapidly dispersed throughout the Valley region from Middletown . . . north into Vermont and New Hampshire and west to . . . towns along the Connecticut River's major tributaries."[34]

In the typical central-hallway mansion, labor and informality were consigned to the rear areas, both downstairs and upstairs, with cooking taking place in an attached ell structure. The "much variety of rooms" in such mansions facilitated entertaining small groups at teas and dinners. And, in emulation of styles first found in Boston in the early years of the eighteenth century, these rooms were laid out and decorated with "exquisite neatness"—doorways with pediments, sash windows, window caps, moldings framing the fireplaces, fielded paneling. A design and decoration feature unique to the valley was the elaborately ornamented front door, providing entrance to the central hallway.[35]

Historian John E. Crowley argues that "the new mansion style put domestic life at a . . . remove from the out-of-doors. . . . Where the central chimney of the hall-and-parlor house had symbolized the importance of being inside, the mansion house's central passage and elaborate doorways emphasized the importance of gaining admission." Nor were these structures, styles, and significances to be found only among the elite. Many of the features of the symmetrical, central hallway house are found in the two-story structures in which the majority of the valley's people lived by the time of the Revolution. For example, the two-story, six-room Deerfield, Massachusetts, home of the prosperous yeoman Sheldon family that Kevin Sweeney has analyzed, built in the 1740s and remodeled in the 1760s, is constructed on the single-central-chimney plan, rather than the central-hallway, two-chimney plan. Yet it showed "an awareness of polite architectural details," with its many large capped windows "filled with imported panes of glass," and with its pedi-mented front door. In Worcester County, Massachusetts, around this same time, there was a similar tendency among people a bit below the topmost level of society to build or remodel their houses in ways that suggested their partial acceptance of the new standards of elegance.[36]

By the end of the century, an ever increasing proportion of families socio-logically similar to the Sheldons were living in two-story, multiple chimney houses with parlors and with work spaces relegated to the rear. In 1795, fully one quarter of the houses in the Yankee West frontier village of Coopers-town, New York, had two stories.[37]

The next year, back in the area from which many in Cooperstown had emigrated, the state of Connecticut counted and ranked the fireplaces in the homes of its inhabitants. Even after allowing for the distortion caused by the presence in the group of people owning particularly grand houses outfitted with unusually large numbers of fancy fireplaces, the results of the survey suggest widespread habitation of houses with more than one fire-place of any type and a significant degree of habitation below the gentry level of houses with at least one "first-rate" fireplace. In other words, in the year that American Cookery was published, it was not that hard to find in Connecticut people whose dwellings suggested attraction to the desiderata of "much variety of rooms" and "exquisite neatness."[38]

The fault John Adams found in 1771 with the Middletown interior of Dr. Eliot Rawson's house was that it violated both these principles. With a dining room that was "crouded with a Bed and a Cradle," Rawson's interior failed on the score of much variety of rooms. It was arranged as the interior of a seventeenth-century house had been. Adams's other remark, that Rawson's house was not "elegant within, in furniture or anything else," implies that it also left much to be desired as far as exquisite neatness was concerned. What were the changes that took place in the furniture that people possessed that corresponded to the changes we have just outlined in house design?[39]

Kevin Sweeney provides the beginnings of an answer in his study of the furniture owned by people living in Wethersfield, just down the river from Hartford, between 1639 and 1800. The "heavily joined chests with drawers, chests of drawers, and oak cupboards" found in Wethersfield houses in the seventeenth century were by the middle of the eighteenth century being replaced by "lighter cases of drawers of pine, poplar, maple, and cherry, made by cabinetmakers who dovetailed and nailed their cases together." From the 1730s onward, people owned more kinds of chairs than previously, as well as hitherto unknown special-function tables such as tea and dressing tables. Most significantly, "the massive long tables and smaller square tables" of the seventeenth century were giving way to round or oval tables "as the form preferred by wealthier individuals for dining."[40]

Let's look a bit more closely at these and other items. In a seventeenth-century house, the oak cupboard and/or chest had usually been placed in the parlor and served to hold or display the family's most valued goods, such as its metalware and finer textiles. In contrast to the impression of solidity and heaviness given off by these objects, a case of drawers of the 1730s and 1740s showed what historian Edward S. Cooke, Jr., describes as a "taut, geometric symmetry." It looked light rather than heavy, here sharply angled, there delicately curved.[41]

Often acquired along with cases of drawers were dressing and tea tables and sets of matched chairs. These items were executed in the same neoclassical style as the chest of drawers. The purpose was to make a unified, harmonious aesthetic statement and thereby to show off not merely wealth and status but also cultivation. Families began owning more chairs than they needed for their own use, indicating that they intended to have repeated occasion to make such a declaration of good breeding when people outside the family came in and used the chairs.[42]

Another article that became increasingly popular in Wethersfield in the second half of the eighteenth century was the desk. Whereas only eight Wethersfield probate inventories listed desks in the 1730s, forty did in the 1790s. Slim, light, and delicate in appearance like the case of drawers and its associated pieces, the desk suggested cultivation of another sort—"literacy and economic pursuits that involve written records and accounts," in Sweeney's words. Desks were put in parlors or "best chambers" so that these meanings of desk ownership could be openly proclaimed. An item of similar significance was the candlestand, which could be construed as showing "a more than average interest in transcending localism through reading." Ownership of candlestands in Wethersfield, as seen in probate inventories, went from one in the 1730s to eight in the 1780s and then jumped to thirty-two in the 1790s.[43]

Regarding table shape, as historian Cary Carson explains, the primary function of rectangular or square tables was to accommodate the taking of meals together by members of the household. The shape constituted a map of the household hierarchy. The "most important male diner" was seated in the place defined as the head of the table, usually at one of the ends. "His dependents took their places to the right and left in descending order of precedence according to gender, estate, age, and servility."[44]

The main purpose of the new round or oval tables was different. They were for taking meals with invited guests and offered a different meaning. "Tables without corners," Carson continues, "made a closed circle of men and women whose shared commitment to the arts of civility outweighed any differences in their rank." Wethersfield probate inventories show an increase in possession of round and oval tables from four in the 1720s to eighty-nine in the 1770s. Although there was a drop-off to eighty-three in the 1780s and fifty in the 1790s, these figures still represent a quantum leap from earlier in the century.[45]

In Woodbury, Connecticut, to the west of the Connecticut River Valley in Litchfield County, tables of this sort did not begin to be owned in noticeable numbers until the 1790s. Another piece that came to be considered necessary for proper dining and that appeared in Woodbury probate inventories toward the end of the eighteenth century was the sideboard. It's likely that sideboards were owned earlier in Wethersfield. Edward Cooke describes the sideboard as "a fashionable storage area for bottles, silver, and china, and a display surface for various dining accoutrements." Much thought was devoted to the sideboard display, particularly to the utilization of candles and looking glasses for lighting theatrics. In 1803 or 1804, Anne Eliza Clark Kane of Providence, Rhode Island, recently married to the New York merchant Oliver Kane, wrote to her mother about the "elegant looking glass with candle arms" that she had arranged to have hung above her sideboard, with its "plate Vases &c."[46]

Like a round or oval table, a sideboard implied formality and ceremony in the serving of the meal. It usually meant the presence of a servant, not seated at the table in subordinate status to the head of the household but

Figure 5.2. Set of dining tables, cherry, mahogany veneer; soft maple, eastern
white pine, hickory, 28 ¾ x 40 ⅞ x 16 ⅝ inches, New England, possibly Connecticut or Rhode Island, 1800–1825. The two tables have been joined to form one oval
dining table.

        –Yale University Art Gallery, Mabel Brady Garvan Collection, 1930.2583

rather standing and moving about, transferring items from the sideboard to
the table, laboring in a status subordinated less to the household head than
to the entirety of the well-mannered company.[47]

    In keeping with the principle of "much variety of rooms," pieces of fur-
niture began to be named in accordance with their function and therefore
with their placement within the house. Some of the more carefully wrought
chairs began to be called "dining chairs," while those exhibiting less workmanship were "kitchen chairs." Tables were differentiated as dining tables,
breakfast tables, tea tables, and card tables. In price lists and newspaper
advertisements of the 1790s and the first decade of the nineteenth century,
valley furniture makers listed dining tables, breakfast tables, card tables, and
sideboards. In one from 1796, probably published in Northampton by the
printing firm of William Butler, dining tables are listed at "1 dollar 50 cents
per foot," "Plain Breakfast Tables" at "4 dollars 17 cents" for an entire table,
breakfast tables "with streatches [stretchers] and drawer" at "5 dollars" per
table, and "Kitchen Tables" at three dollars a table.[48]

FIGURE 5.3. "Cabinet Work" price list, *At a General Meeting of the House-Joiners and Cabinet-Makers in the County of Hampshire* (Northampton, Mass., 1796).

—Courtesy, American Antiquarian Society

At this time, Hartford cabinetmakers were turning out pieces of furniture exemplifying "exquisite neatness" that could withstand comparison with those produced anywhere—cherry and pine chests of drawers; mahogany sideboards; tea tables that, as historian Philip Zea notes, "offered the refinement of rotating the surface, so that the host may present the tea wares to guests without picking up the cups and saucers"; "mobile breakfast or Pembroke tables . . . with cross stretchers and a drawer"; multileaved mahogany dining tables; and tall cherry and pine clocks, including one ornamented near its base with a representation of the valley's signature fish, the shad. In 1799, Hudson & Goodwin advertised in the *Courant* an English work for sale in their shop—George Hepplewhite's *Cabinet Maker and Upholsterer's Guide*. Doubtless the title sold quite well in this particular market.[49]

So far we have not addressed the question of whether furniture of this new, refined sort was acquired by people other than those at the top, such as the great majority in Hartford that did well enough to live in two-story houses. Evidence bearing on this issue is scanty, but the available bits are quite telling. One is the 1770 estate inventory of the Roxbury, Massachusetts, barber and blacksmith Stephen Brewer. As opposed to the contemporaneous Middletown, Connecticut, Rawson dining room, in that of Brewer, writes Cary Carson, "nary a bed nor old-fashioned chest was anywhere in sight." Rather the space was filled with a properly oval dining table, a tea table, and a clock that "chimed the dinner hour and signaled teatime in Brewer's formally regulated household." In other rooms, Brewer had additional tables, enough chairs for seating guests, an easy chair, a combination desk and bookcase, and a "Case of Draws."[50]

Lest we think such subgentry gentility of taste in furniture was only to be found in sophisticated eastern Massachusetts, consider the thriving cooper and farmer James Parker of Shirley, Massachusetts, in western Middlesex County. Parker arrived in Shirley from his birthplace in nearby Groton in the 1760s. By the 1780s, he had done well enough to buy a second farm and move from his simple farmhouse of two rooms into a more spacious residence. He wallpapered at least one of the rooms in this house and placed a desk and clock in it. A few years later, having become a reader, he had a bookcase made for his ever-increasing book collection.[51]

It would be surprising indeed if Parker did not follow the same path as Stephen Brewer and make sure that his entire house was filled with the types of up-to-date pieces we have been discussing. According to Gloria Main, Parker was exceptional in rural New England only in the degree to which he enhanced his stock of furniture. In the course of the eighteenth century, "many more cushions and chairs for comfortable seating" were to be seen in farm households. The chairs were distinguished by "turned frames and woven rush seats," while the cushions were filled with feathers and adorned with needlework.[52]

Were there people in the Connecticut Valley who also went down the path taken by James Parker and Stephen Brewer? Hudson & Goodwin certainly thought there were. The "Farmer" they had speak his piece in both the *Courant* and the *Hampshire Gazette* in 1788 repented of exactly the sorts of possessions on which Brewer and Parker prided themselves, including "all sorts of household furniture unknown to us before." The very existence of newspaper advertisements and published price lists implies a pool of at least slightly down-market customers. Valley cabinetmakers didn't deal with the River Gods through the public medium of print but rather by way of traditional modes of deference and patronage. Catering to varying levels of ability to pay is exhibited in the price list instanced above, by its offering of a "Plain Breakfast Table" at a lower price than a fancier one "with streatches and drawer."[53]

These examples show some of the ways in which the achievement of genteel standards was a package deal. People like James Parker who enlarged their homes also upgraded their furniture. It's no surprise, therefore, that one of Parker's first gestures in the direction of gentility was the acquisition of "a new red jacoot" in 1774. By 1782, he owned an expensive beaver hat. In the 1790s, he was dressing himself in "a velvet jacket and breeches" and buying "silk for two Gounds" for his daughters. The downfall of the "Farmer" who spoke up in the *Courant* in 1788 began when his wife insisted that their second daughter had to have "a calico gown" and "a calimanco petticoat"; with the third daughter this escalated to "a silken gown" and "silk for a cloak." Being more within reach of people of average means than larger houses and elegant furniture, clothing made of fine fabrics, in bright colors and stylish cuts that drew attention to oneself or one's family, was therefore a more widely shared manifestation of the consumer revolution.[54]

In 1769, almost everyone wore homespun attire to Sunday meeting in Northampton, Massachusetts; fifty years later almost everyone had on clothes made with imported textiles or otherwise enhanced. In the first decade of the nineteenth century, the Farmington report in the Connecticut Academy of Arts and Sciences study of Connecticut towns noted (with regret) that for the past thirty years or so people had been "laying aside their plain apparel manufactured in their houses, & clothing themselves with European & India fabrics." These were the fabrics advertised in the *Courant* in May 1796. In the Cornwall report, on the other hand, the same trend was viewed with satisfaction. Elijah Allen stated that Cornwall's women were given to expending some of the returns from their industrious spinning and dairying on "the Elegancies of Superb Dress."[55]

John Treadwell, the academy's Farmington informant, reminisced about a local custom that had prevailed in the years before the American Revolution: "Every young lady when she had attained her stature was furnished with a silk gown and Skirt if her parents were able, or she could purchase them by dint of labour." So the consumer revolution had begun to make inroads into life in this town west of Hartford considerably earlier than in Shirley, Massachusetts, where the exceptionally prosperous James Parker didn't get silk gowns for his daughters until the 1790s.[56]

The glossiness of silk and satin might be considered the signature of the consumer revolution as far as textiles are concerned. We have seen satin advertised in the *Courant* in 1796 and seen silk on the list of things forsworn by the virtuous ladies of Hartford ten years earlier. There is hardly a single one of Ralph Earl's 1780s and 1790s portraits of members of the Connecticut elite, whether of a man or woman, that does not feature silk or satin. Daniel and Elijah Boardman of New Milford, in Litchfield County, each posed in 1789 in silk coats, vests, breeches, and stockings. The next year in the town of Litchfield, Colonel Benjamin Tallmadge did the same, while his wife, in a separate portrait done at the same time, is shown arrayed in "a formal open gown and matching . . . skirt . . . of lustrous blue satin."[57]

A silken or satiny finish is present even in portraits in which people chose to be represented in a relatively restrained manner. Earl's patron Dr. Mason Fitch Cogswell of Hartford, painted by Earl in 1791, "wears the sober dress of the professional man," but such sober dress is still "a suit of black silk cut fashionably with a high collar and tight sleeves." Senator Oliver Ellsworth of Windsor likewise showed his sobriety and dignity by wearing dark colors, and his fashion sense by wearing silk. Seated beside him, Ellsworth's wife, Abigail, wears a gown of white silk, perhaps the lustring variety found among the May 9, 1796, *Courant* textile advertisements.[58]

Glossy fabrics were only one of a multitude of ways in which the sensibility of the later eighteenth century reveled in shiny surfaces. Elisabeth Garrett explains the coordination of candles and mirrors to maximize sparkle in domestic interiors: "Glass, and particularly cut glass, was much favored for its glittering presentation of light, and pendant prisms might further refract light. Candlesticks, lamps, and chandeliers were calculatingly positioned so as to reflect in looking glasses." Historian John E. Crowley adds windows into the mix: "Contributing to the lustrous surfaces in a room was the window glass." It may be that gentry in the colonies imitated the British custom, which prescribed that the more exalted the guests the more candles lit, producing a more glamorous effect.[59]

More broadly, argues Garrett, "by the close of the eighteenth century, the reflective polish of the looking glass had become a metaphor for fastidious housekeeping." The principle that "the genteel interior was to sparkle and shine" was applied up and down the social ladder. John Singleton Copley's 1772 portrait of Rachel Skinner of Marblehead, Massachusetts, shows her sitting at a mahogany table the top of which has been polished to a "gloss like a mirror." Two years later, John Adams was pleased with an inn in Portland, Maine, in which the "desk and table shine like mirrors." And in *The Farmer's Friend*, a 1793 novel, the thriving but suitably subordinate farmer's wife is praised for the "large maple table" in the family's best room, "which for its bright polish resembled the looking glass which hung over it."[60]

Back at the apex of the social pyramid and back in the realm of attire, Garrett tells us that it wasn't only the fabrics themselves but also the accessories that were coordinated with the overall sheen of interior space. She gives examples of female costumes designed this way, but the principle was applied in men's wear as well. As costume historian Aileen Ribeiro explains, the coat worn by Colonel Benjamin Tallmadge in Ralph Earl's portrait of him "is particularly stylish with its elaborate buttons made of either diamond paste or marcasite (faceted crystalized iron pyrites) to glitter in candlelight."

Here in Litchfield, far from Philadelphia, New York, or Boston, even a bit removed from Hartford and New Haven, we find by 1789 a determination to create as harmoniously genteel an impression as possible, a goal that reached down to the smallest detail. This onetime hero of the Revolutionary War who was now rapidly getting rich as a merchant was dressed in such a way that the very buttons on his coat were integrated with the windows, mirrors, and candles in his parlor.[61]

Another item proposed to be banned in Hartford in 1786 and aggressively advertised in the city's leading newspaper in 1796 was muslin, the filminess of which was used, in both life and portraiture, to complement the high gloss of silk. Abigail Ellsworth's collar and cap were both made of "starched muslin," and muslin was worn by many others of Earl's sitters. Daniel and Elijah Boardman both have on ruffled muslin shirts in their portraits, while Mrs. Benjamin Tallmadge's costume includes "a collar of embroidered muslin with a deep frill." Mrs. Ellsworth's muslin mobcap was, according to Ribeiro, "virtually a uniform among women of her age and class." Not only of her age and class, apparently, for, as previously noted, the somewhat younger and a great deal socially inferior clockmaker's wife wore a cap that looks remarkably similar to the one worn by Ellsworth, along with a bright greyish, diaphanous kerchief.[62]

In Ralph Earl's portrait of Martha Johnston painted in England in 1785, there is shown another filmy article, a "vast gauzy scarf, the *buffon*, crossing [the subject's] bosom. The same floating and insubstantial fabric decorates Martha Johnston's hair." The transatlantic fashion for such gauzes had made its way to Hartford by 1786, for gauze, and lace as well, were on the Hartford ladies' list that year of textile goods temporarily proscribed. So were ribbons (shininess again), such as those represented by Ralph Earl as circling Abigail Ellsworth's and the clockmaker's wife's mobcaps.[63]

Additional enhancements of apparel frowned upon in 1786 were chintz, feathers, and beaver hats. Chintz was listed repeatedly in the 1796 page of the *Courant* we have examined. Atop Mary Tallmadge's hair are painted "white ostrich feathers." Daniel Boardman holds in his left hand a "hat of expensive black beaver." Since beaver hats connoted "wealth and status," such hats were acquired by those seeking wealth and status as well as by those like Boardman who already had them. We have seen that one was added to James Parker's supply of the insignia of gentility relatively early on in 1782, and John Treadwell of Farmington said that a beaver hat was part of a plain man's Sunday best garb both winter and summer in Farmington's good old days before consumerism took over. This is another indication that even back then consumerism was gaining ground in Farmington.[64]

As noted, because they were less expensive, clothing-related articles that exhibited a degree of refinement were more widely owned in eighteenth-century New England than were pieces of "exquisitely neat" furniture or houses having "much variety of rooms." However, clothing was probably not the most widely shared among the categories of new consumer goods. Gloria and Jackson Main accorded this honor to items that were "primarily associated with eating and drinking." Their research shows that by 1775, "coarse earthenware" was owned by large numbers of people in southern New England on all social levels, while "fine earthenware" and silverware were owned by significant minorities. The most dramatic increases in possession of forks and knives—from under 5 percent to about 45 percent—occurred between 1725 and 1750.[65]

Connecticut Valley estate samples from the third quarter of the seventeenth century into the first quarter of the nineteenth century show steady increases in possession of ceramics and glass. Over time, more objects were of a higher quality, and there were more and more kinds of them. The research of museum curator Elizabeth Pratt Fox shows that by the middle of the eighteenth century, the pots, basins, cups, jugs, plates, platters, porringers, bottles, and drinking glasses of the late seventeenth century were supplemented by "milk pans, punch bowls, teapots, . . . formal tableware," sugar bowls, cream pots, and more variously styled bottles and drinking glasses. Where there were some "imported Chinese porcelains and English earthenwares decorated to resemble them" in the earlier period, there was more in the later period, along with the first appearances of English stoneware. After a pause for the Revolution, these trends resumed with the appearance of such additional forms as soup plates, custard cups, coffee cups, sweetmeat dishes, and hot water platters (steam platters for keeping food warm). Also, for "the first time . . . the Valley's inhabitants purchased ceramic wares in sets."[66]

Striking as were the increases of glass and ceramic household objects in the Connecticut Valley, a review of metalwares in valley estate inventories from the 1730s reveals that these types of items, "particularly those used for food production" were most in evidence in households "in every economic category." Even those "who possessed sizable estates" were more apt in the first half of the eighteenth century to own "an array of pewter and iron" than earthenware, ceramics, or glass.[67]

To illustrate the point, museum curator Barbara McLean Ward describes the modest estate left by Andrew Robe of Simsbury, who died in 1735. He left no glassware or ceramics nor even a "hung bed" or much furniture, yet at the time of his death he was in possession of an impressive inventory of pewter: "six pewter platters, eight plates, a tankard, seven cups of various sizes, a porringer, a basin, a beaker, a grater, three old spoons, a saltcellar, two chamber pots, and other pewter." His metalware holdings didn't end there. Along with the pewter, he owned iron- and brassware that included "a chafing dish, a spit, andirons, four pairs of tongs, a fire slice, two trammels, a gridiron, a flesh fork, an iron pot, an iron kettle, two brass kettles, a skimmer, a . . . bronze . . . mortar and pestle, a warming pan, a frying pan, an iron skimmer, a chopping knife, shears, and farming tools." A much wealthier decedent from Middletown, Daniel Harris, who died the same year as Robe, owned less pewter but more earthenware, a brass skillet, and some silver plate, indicating the direction of things to come. Yet he too had little furniture beyond a hung bed.

The most intriguing items in these inventories are the costly ones owned by the poorer man. That Andrew Robe, who owned no land and whose estate didn't otherwise amount to much, had in his possession at the time of his death two brass kettles substantiates Gloria Main's statement that "ordinary households" obtained brass utensils "if cash permitted," even though they were "more than twice as expensive as cast iron." Main's explanation for this preference is of particular interest. Being "lighter and easier to handle," brass pots and pans "provided the flexibility necessary for preparing a variety of dishes." So even Robe's inventory indicates an incipient movement in the direction of refinement in diet and dining accoutrements.[68]

Lyman Beecher personally experienced the general pattern of New England tableware development during his childhood in coastal Connecticut toward the end of the eighteenth century. "We had wooden trenchers first, then pewter, then finally earthenware," he wrote. Beecher's words serve as a reminder that the progress toward what were understood as more refined containers of food and drink was full of ebbs and eddies. Some families possessed earthenware articles as early as the final decades of the seventeenth century. Others had no ceramics, only pewter, in the 1730s. And still others, such as the family in which Beecher grew up, were, after the Revolution, still using trenchers (plates) and bowls made of wood. Even in the fashionable dining room of Stephen Brewer in Roxbury, Massachusetts, in 1770, the oval table was set with old-fashioned pewter articles as well as with items made of delftware and glass.[69]

Nevertheless, things were clearly moving in the direction summarized by Beecher, indeed toward a point well beyond the ken of his remark—from wood to pewter to earthenware to creamware to the Chinese porcelain that came to New England in the direct trade with China that commenced in the 1780s. The *Courant*'s 1788 "Farmer" alluded to the final phases of tableware improvement when he complained that the "stone tea-cups" that his errant wife had brought home along with calico garments weren't ultimately good enough. Her subsequent foolish purchases, which included "silken" apparel, also involved "china tea-gear . . . with the empty purse." But if his family really couldn't have afforded "a set of chinaware which cost two hundred and fifty dollars in Canton," his wife might have settled for English "Blue printed" imitation porcelain.[70]

Domesticity and etiquette expert Helen Sprackling wrote, in agreement with the complaints of Mr. "Farmer," that in the decades spanning the eighteenth and nineteenth centuries, such "colorful ware found its way to the rural table top almost as quickly as to one in the big town. . . . Yankee merchants . . . packed their china, glass, and crockery 'in Crates, assorted principally for Country Traders.'" A more recent social historian concurs. According to Stephanie Grauman Wolf, "porcelain and its imitations were cheap enough to be purchased by those of very modest means and owned by those who were even poorer." She gives the example of the members of a "small community of nearly destitute, free black families outside of Plymouth, Massachusetts." They "possessed a considerable number of mismatched, out-of-date, fancy ceramics, no doubt obtained as gifts or 'scavange' from wealthy white neighbors or employers."[71]

That our farmer used tea-related items to represent extravagance in tableware reflects the fact that tea drinking was the type of newfangled consumption of food and drink most widely adopted throughout British North America. In a 1774 sample of estate inventories from Massachusetts, Virginia, and Maryland, 50 percent listed tea-drinking articles. "Tea led the way because the whole performance was less expensive and more easily learned than fine dining," explains culinary historian Barbara G. Carson. "The menu was simpler, the behavior less complicated, and the essential accoutrements fewer in number and thus less expensive than the equipment required for dining."[72]

Carson's contrast between tea drinking and dining may be a bit overdrawn, however. Noting that "even middling households in the wilds of Worcester county show a strong upward trend in the ownership of knives and forks along with teaware," Gloria Main believes that there was in southern New England in the eighteenth century a "gradual spread of a genteel or civilizing influence at the dining tables of ordinary farm folk." She plausibly reconstructs a situation in which the farm housewife not only superintends "the packets of tea and the pretty new dishes with which to serve it," but also "remains seated" at the dinner table "and participates in the conversation while serving her guests." Even when there were no guests, "in the most up-to-date yeoman households at midcentury, . . . everybody at the table had a knife and fork flanking his or her own [pewter or ceramic] plate." This was a big change from the days when "people had eaten from shared wooden dishes and [drunk] from a common mug."[73]

Later on and at the more exalted levels of society, dining in a room set aside for it was well established as the core component of a refined home. As Main implies and Cary Carson explicitly states, it was "genteel conversations" at the round or oval tables specifically designed to facilitate them that gave dining this focal, definitive status in the culture of gentility. In January 1800, William Williams of Dalton, Massachusetts, told his wife, Dolly, back home in the Berkshires about an "elegant dinner" in Boston at which he had been a guest. There had been "useful and entertaining conversation" at this dinner, "but not more," Williams was sure, "than is found, frequently, in a less circle in the country."[74]

But Western Massachusetts and the Connecticut River Valley could support "useful and entertaining conversation" in a large circle as well as in a "less" one. The term "circle" evokes seating at a round or oval table, and such tables were occasionally designed with multiple leaves so that they could accommodate both large and small groups of guests. Some of the tableware sets purchased by the valley elite after the Revolution contained "as many as 150 objects." A wealthy and cultivated Hartford family outfitted with a many-leaved dining table, a sideboard, and one of these ample tableware sets might also have owned the three silver skewers made by Joseph Carpenter of Norwich, Connecticut, around 1790. Philip Zea writes that these "implements of fine quality and detail . . . must have dazzled guests when placed at the side of a meat platter before serving dinner." They made even the labor of preparing the dinner "appear delicate and effortless," leaving no crude loose ends to the fabric of elegance and animated interchange of which such gatherings were expected to consist.[75]

Robert Blair St. George has called attention to the ways in which, in the second half of the eighteenth century, people at the pinnacle of the

Connecticut Valley social order strove to proclaim that such was indeed their position. They made their statements to this effect with their "large, elaborately carpentered houses," with the "doorways with which they dramatized the front (and occasionally the side) doors of these structures," with "polite furniture" inside these houses, and with objects like exquisite Staffordshire teapots that demonstrated "their interest in the world beyond the familiar faces of their towns." St. George draws a parallel between the elaborate gravestones of the elite and the elaborate front doors of their mansions. The passage into the mansion through the "ceremonial doorway" paralleled the passage from earth to heaven through the "portal of death" represented by the gravestone. Thus vast was the social distance between the refined enclaves of the upper crust and the rough-hewn world surrounding them.[76]

The cosmopolitanism and *savoir faire* implied by the acquisition of a Staffordshire teapot, giving the impression that every aspect of life was "delicate and effortless," was what distinguished a fully developed culture of refinement and gentility from the consumer revolution that supplied it with its material manifestations. And the gulf between someone who dwelt in full psychic ease among Staffordshire teapots and someone who was only beginning to learn what to do with a set of "mismatched, out-of-date, fancy ceramics" could indeed seem unbridgeable.

An 1823 diary entry made by the Kentucky-born wife of Calvin Fletcher, a Vermont-born lawyer living in Indianapolis, Indiana, in the Yankee West, helps us better understand how the situation felt to those situated toward the bottom and looking up. Fletcher, acutely conscious of the fact that his wife "had even less schooling than he," had assisted her in learning the behavior and manners required at social gatherings by having her read the work most widely used for such a purpose, Lord Chesterfield's *Letters . . . to His Son*. This did not spare Sarah Fletcher, however, from feelings of mortification at formal occasions when she "made no convercesion and [was] trembling fearing there might be some question asked that would expose my ignernce."[77]

Earlier, in 1795, and back in New England, in Walpole, Massachusetts, the Mann family experienced an excruciating disturbance one August day. Herman and Sally Mann were both orphans. Recently married and the parents of a small child, they were living on a sixty-acre farm and striving for a more cultured way of life. Apparently the effort was extremely taxing, judging from what happened when Sally placed some flowers around the house in an attempt at decoration. Herman was not pleased. He threw the

flowers on the floor, explaining, as Sally wrote in her diary, that he was
expressing "contempt" for their having been "placed there, either for ornament, use, or a sign of domestic economy." He then proceeded to feed his
pigs inside the house, deliberately covering the floor and the flowers with
their slop. As historian J. M. Opal plausibly interprets the incident, Herman
Mann was probably "ashamed that he could not provide a home where such
refinements would make sense." This struggling orphan was acting out his
frustration and rage over the degree to which he remained mired in what
felt to him like the swinish crudeness of farm labor, over how far removed
he still was from the bright realm in which everything could be made to
seem "delicate and effortless."[78]

Scenes of this sort were doubtless played out in Connecticut Valley
households. The area did not lack for people endeavoring to live in a
refined manner. Neither did it lack, as St. George argues, for people who
made it their business to flaunt their wealth and polish. The Tallmadges
of Litchfield chose to have themselves portrayed in 1790 by Ralph Earl as
what Aileen Ribeiro calls "the epitome of ancien régime grandeur," with
the colonel's glittering coat buttons and the wife's white ostrich feathers à la
Marie Antoinette. In a more mature incarnation, Colonel Tallmadge lodged
himself in the memory of Henry Ward Beecher: "We . . . should as soon
have thought of climbing the church steeple as of speaking to one living so
high and venerable above all boys." The memoirs of someone further down
the ladder than the minister's son (as Beecher was) might have recalled Tallmadge with considerably less equanimity.[79]

But most of those who have studied the culture of Connecticut and the
valley of its principal river during these early years of the American nation
have perceived its elites as bearing themselves rather differently from the
Tallmadges. Richard D. Brown tells us that part of the reason John Adams
was filled with admiration for the valley when he visited it in 1771 was that
while it was "orderly and cultivated, genteel and substantial," it was free of
"the ostentatious London patina of architectural decoration, fancy coaches,
gorgeous dress, and sophisticated snobbery that Adams detested in some of
the merchants and royal officials of eastern Massachusetts."[80]

Similarly, Kevin Sweeney concludes that "the region's gentry," in con-
structing their material culture in the eighteenth century, "rejected some
available alternatives that would have produced too 'foreign' a statement,"
such as slate headstones or brick houses marked by Palladian symmetry in
every respect and detail. Their "houses, furnishings, and gravestones . . .

were the particular expressions of a genteel, but decidedly rural life style," which combined sophistication with affirmation of regional identity.[81]

In another form of self-representation, that of portrait painting, the pillars of the Connecticut Valley community likewise saw fit to rein themselves in. Their prime portrayer, Ralph Earl, adjusted his style when he came to Connecticut from the manner in which he had painted in New York and before that in England. He "did not attempt to idealize his sitters." He showed them "in their own environments with specific regional details such as the subject's own house and surrounding lands, rooms within the house, and possessions either of local origin or associated with his or her profession." Art historian Elizabeth Mankin Kornhauser believes that this approach was taken "at the request of Earl's patrons."[82]

At least one contemporary spokesman for the Connecticut upper classes confirms these appraisals of their aesthetic and cultural preferences. John Treadwell, the author of the Connecticut Academy of Arts and Sciences Farmington report, came from modest origins as the son of a mechanic. He was sent to Yale and eventually rose to become the lieutenant governor and then governor of Connecticut. Treadwell wrote proudly, and in a vein reminiscent of Dwight's *Greenfield Hill*, that Farmington, "as its name imports, was at first, & indeed till a late period, wholly agricultural. . . . Labour has been held in reputation; none, however elevated by office or profession, have considered themselves above it. Magistrates & Ministers, when their appropriate business would permit, have laboured in the field; . . . it was honour enough to [be] esteamed the first among equals."[83]

Farmington's leading women were "no less industrious in the domestic circle," emulating their husbands in an utter lack of pretension: "On Monday they have been employed in perfect dishabille in washing their linnen & their houses & when this is done, at about the middle of the afternoon, they assume their neatest appearance, & are the perfect contrast of what they were in the morning, prepared to visit or to receive company." Clearly, Treadwell's preference, as a member of the elite, was to err on the side of under- rather than over-applying the various patinas and polishes of the culture of refinement.[84]

In Treadwell's case, as well as in that of many others on his level of the Connecticut social order, such a preference was an exercise in nostalgia, arising from anxiety about the social and economic forces that were generating the culture of refinement. Just a few paragraphs after the passages quoted, Treadwell bemoaned "the late prevalence of the commercial spirit." Where four decades earlier there had been only "a single retailer of imported goods" in Farmington, now "greater capital" was being devoted to retail trade "than in any inland town in the State."[85]

Treadwell conceded that "agriculture & commerce go hand in hand," but his heart told him otherwise: "Farmers never flourish in a populous set-tlement where the commercial character predominates." He then invoked the familiar rhetoric of anticonsumerism and antirefinement: "In homely dress & covered with sweat & dust, with weary steps returning from the field, [the farmer] sees with pain the powdered beau rowling in his carriage with horses richly caparisoned and feels himself degraded." By an inelucta-ble process, "simplicity of manners is lost, never to return." And Treadwell could compensate for his foreboding only with nostalgia: "The present time marks a revolution of taste & of manners of immense import to society, but while others glory in this as a great advance in refinement, we cannot help dropping a tear at the close of a golden age of our ancestors; while, with a pensive pleasure we reflect on the past & with suspence and apprehension anticipate the future."[86]

These complaints about the baneful effects of commercialism on farmers were voiced by a member of the same group that, as described at the close of chapter 4, was also devoting itself to promoting market-oriented agriculture. With this ambivalence in mind, we can see Treadwell's claim that Farming-ton magistrates and ministers did not like to place themselves "high and venerable" above their neighbors as a strategy for managing the changes, tensions, and contradictions that Connecticut's leaders were themselves unleashing. It amounted to the application of a different patina than the one John Adams complained about—a patina, in muted rather than bold hues, of down-home camaraderie, but an overlay and patina nevertheless.[87]

Similarly, Timothy Dwight portrayed nonelite people in Farmington, elsewhere in Connecticut, and up and down the river as being placed in situations that kept them well above the coarseness found in "many other parts of this country." Echoing the strictures of his friend Jedidiah Morse regarding Maryland, Dwight alleged that in such areas, settled in a pattern of "scattered plantations . . . a rustic sheepishness, or a more awkward and provoking impudence" prevailed. One encountered "intelligence bounded by the farm, the market, and the road which leads to it; affections so rarely moved as scarcely to be capable of being moved at all," and "conversation confined to the properties and price of a horse, or the sale of a load of wheat." Connecticut and the valley, with its villages wherein were to be found churches, "suite[s] of schools," and social libraries, presented the starkest possible contrast. There, "all the people are neighbors." They are "social beings" who "converse, feel, sympathize, mingle minds, cherish sentiments, and are subjects of at least some degree of refinement."[88]

So if the majority of ordinary people in this part of the world had been polished up at least a bit, and if the majority of privileged people had taken pains to maintain themselves in a mode as much matte as glossy, then we are looking at a part of the world in which living in a refined manner was considered a legitimate and attainable goal for those not born and bred to it. We're also looking at a part of the world in which it was understood that people not born and bred to it could achieve such an apparently "delicate and effortless" way of life only by the most strenuous effort.

John Pierce, the oldest son of a Litchfield, Connecticut, potter, rose to the rank of colonel during the Revolutionary War. He had a sister, Sarah, much younger than himself of whom he became the de facto father after their biological father died in 1783, when Sarah was fifteen or sixteen. The father-daughter complexion of the siblings' relationship is evident in a letter John sent to Sarah in New York in 1784, after he had sent her there to be educated. Besides urging her not to miss "a single dancing school," Pierce insisted that she obtain instruction "in every thing in walking standing and sitting, all the movements of which tho' they appear in a polite person natural, are the effects of art." Unless Sarah, being a "country girl," were willing to "take the utmost pains," she would "never appear natural or easy" in her gait, nor by extension in her speech and general demeanor. "I am somewhat fearful," Pierce fretted, "that your old habits at your age can not be so thoroughly removed, as to give place to a natural careless genteel air, and which totally hides all the art of it."[89]

With our knowledge of the struggles of people like Sarah Fletcher of Indianapolis and the Manns of Walpole, we can appreciate John Pierce's worries. But the modern reader of Pierce's missive to his sister is apt to ponder the origins of those feared "old habits," possessed by the sixteen- or seventeen-year-old Sarah Pierce, which threatened permanently to place her on a rung below her rightful position on the social ladder.

One possible explanation is that in their youth in a potter's household, John and Sarah were deprived of the furniture that by its very design inculcated an alternate set of habits, those leading to good deportment and the restrained self-consciousness gentility required. Elisabeth Garrett sketches the kind of eighteenth-century furnishings that provided this training

in making bodily self-incarceration second nature. "To sit in . . . uncom-
promising [parlor] chairs, with their rigid backs and firmly stuffed seats,
demanded physical and mental self-presence," she writes. In his memoir of
his childhood in late eighteenth-century Newport, Rhode Island, George G.
Channing, brother of noted Unitarian clergyman William Ellery Channing,
recalled that the family parlor was filled with glossy leather chair seats that
"sloped forward" and that therefore "required no little skill to sit upright."[90]

This continual reinforcement of genteel deportment through furniture
design was sufficiently widespread, apparently, that Harriet Beecher Stowe
knew she would hit the comedic mark in describing such instruments of
social torture in her novel *Oldtown Folks*. She writes of a typical parlor of the
time furnished with "exactly one dozen stuffed-seated cherry chairs, with
upright backs and griffin feet, each foot terminating in a bony claw, which
resolutely grasped a ball." These "high and slippery" chairs, she proclaims,
"preached decorum in the very attitudes which they necessitated, as no mor-
tal could ever occupy them except in the exercise of a constant and collected
habit of mind"—the very "collected habit of mind" that John Pierce well
knew was not a part of his or his sister's early life. Without this ammunition
lodged deep in their social arsenal, at the level of a second-nature response,
John feared that Sarah's "old habits" might not be overcome.[91]

He need not have feared. Sarah Pierce did succeed in acquiring the
requisite refinement, and she went on to establish a school in Litchfield
that became famous for imparting a similar breeding to later generations
of country girls, Catharine and Harriet Beecher among them. But for every
Sarah Pierce, how many Sally and Herman Manns were there who never
broke through to that "natural careless genteel air, . . . which totally hides all
the art of it"?

Gordon S. Wood and other historians have stressed that "printed matter
flooded the new Republic" and that not least among the motives that drove
people to become avid readers were anxieties about "acquiring gentility"
(especially if they couldn't afford in-person tutelage of the sort Sarah Pierce
received). "People wanted . . . advice and etiquette manuals for every occasion or subject—from how to write letters to friends to how to control or
clean their bodies." This was certainly true in Connecticut and the Connecticut River Valley. As we saw in chapter 3, Lord Chesterfield's *Letters . . .
to His Son*, allegedly containing "every instruction necessary to complete the
gentleman and man of fashion, to teach him a knowledge of life and make

him well received in all companies," was published three times in the valley between 1792 and 1812.[92]

It was a longing for the gentility of the table that drove printers to pub-lish and readers to purchase and use manuals of instruction in cooking. As Helen Sprackling wrote, the "words of advice" in cookbooks "were carefully calculated to help an inexperienced hostess achieve security and poise." When Thomas Greenleaf stated in his 1797 New York advertisement for *American Cookery* that "the knowledge of HOUSEWIFERY and COOKERY is absolutely necessary to EVERY FEMALE," he meant that *American Cook-ery* would endow its female, "country girl" readers with necessary knowledge for a culture that was part plain, part fancy, part republican, part genteel. But what were the raw materials available to a Connecticut reader of *Ameri-can Cookery* as she endeavored to take in the absolutely necessary knowledge that the book purported to impart?[93]

CHAPTER 6

Agriculture, Fishing, Horticulture

C onnecticut's citizens in the 1790s may have aspired to mastering
genteel deportment and surrounding themselves with the equipage of refinement, but most still passed their lives on family farms
or in small villages established to support those farms. This arrangement
was the basis of the "cooperative, Christian commonwealth" that had been
the model for Connecticut since the seventeenth century. It was a world in
which, by design, "those factors which create major class distinctions," as
historian Jackson Turner Main wrote, were kept to a minimum. Certainly
some holdings were larger and more fertile than others and could therefore
produce more surpluses. In particular, the farms of the Connecticut River
Valley were suitable for growing cereal crops, especially the most valuable,
wheat, on a large scale, making these farms unusually profitable. Still, many
more modest farm families were able to sustain themselves by working their
farms, if they combined a measure of skill with a good deal of determination. The majority of farmers outside the valley got along by concentrating
on livestock, supplementing their incomes with a variety of field crops and
orchard produce. Or at least that was the image of Connecticut its leaders
wished to project—as seen in the reports on particular towns compiled by
local luminaries and sent in the early years of the nineteenth century to the
Connecticut Academy of Arts and Sciences. Those reports are the principal
source for this chapter.[1]

Virtually from the outset, Connecticut benefited from its connection
to a sophisticated network of seaborne trade. Especially for those with
easy access to water transport, producing for markets was as important a
part of their farming activities as raising food for their families. Historian
William N. Peterson reports that southern New England's trade with the
West Indies "accounted for much of the region's overall mercantile prosperity during the Town Report period and the century before." Colonial
merchants, the middlemen between local farmers and faraway customers,
enabled the exchange between Connecticut and the West Indies. To a lesser

extent, these merchants also pursued a coasting trade with New York, the Mid-Atlantic, and the South. Connecticut's barreled beef and pork, cheese, livestock (cattle, hogs, horses, and mules), and lumber were the chief items of trade. The mixed-use nature of Connecticut farming was turned to advantage in these trading networks. Along with the major commodities, other goods were packed into the cargo holds of Connecticut ships—barrels of cornmeal, onions, potatoes, wheat flour, and even casks of bread and crackers. Rum, molasses, sugar, and tropical fruits were the main items received in exchange.[2]

Although trade was a high priority, the farmer's first concern was to produce enough food for his family. The challenges faced by settlers in early New England, including poor soil, severe weather, and periodic Indian attacks, were legendary. But it appears that most of the first European inhabitants of Connecticut were able to be self-sufficient, and this comfortable level of productivity was maintained throughout the colonial period. The diet was often simple, to be sure, but it was usually adequate. During Connecticut's first century and a half, the colony's endeavors in farming and trade resulted in what Main deemed "a respectable standard of living" for the majority of its inhabitants.[3]

In the decades after independence, although Connecticut retained many of its social and agricultural advantages, the belief that it would continue indefinitely to produce a shared prosperity was beginning to fray. The limits of productivity for its farms and fisheries were coming into view. Amid the various conditions that created difficulties for Connecticut agriculture, three stand out: too little land for the number looking to farm, soil that had become infertile from overuse, and increasing market pressures.

Overpopulation was perhaps the single most significant problem Connecticut grappled with at the turn of the nineteenth century. Certainly contemporaries wrote with dismay of the number of young inhabitants of the state forced to emigrate, mostly north and northwest into New Hampshire, Vermont, and upstate New York, to secure their economic survival. But many who began life on Connecticut farms also moved into the growing cities in search of work and would never again return to farming.

Even for those whose freeholds were secure and relatively productive, farm life could be harsh and margins of profit slim. Decreasing soil fertility led more and more farmers to fish seasonally for shad and other local catch, only to find that the fish stocks in Connecticut's rivers and streams were also in decline. The search for greater crop yields led many to experiment with new methods. Manufactured plows and other farm implements began to replace the hand-hewn goods of the local blacksmith. But new machinery often put farmers in debt and required a higher level of skill to maintain than most of them possessed.

Some attempted to augment their revenue by recruiting the women of the household to do piecework in their homes. By their kitchen hearths, even in their front parlors, after the daily round of household duties was done, mothers and daughters were kept busy making such items as yarn, cloth, and soap. Much of this labor was outwork commissioned by merchants and overseen by rural agents. Women with home dairies increased their output as the demand for their products, especially cheese, grew to feed swelling urban populations. Historian J. M. Opal and other scholars agree that at the beginning of the nineteenth century, there were "intensifying demands on women and dependents within an increasingly commercial landscape."[4]

These pressures were eroding the relative equality and homogeneity of colonial times and creating a widening gap in wealth and holdings between the well-to-do and everyone else. Even as some families fell behind financially or left the state entirely, others surged ahead in the race to greater fortune. These lucky few were situated on better land with larger holdings or were able to make a success of new crops or new methods. The wealthiest farmers benefited from the same intensifying market competition that weighed heavily on so many others. They were the victors in what has been called the market revolution. This new gentry class of highly successful farmers and merchants threatened to upset the state's social balance not from the low but from the high end of the scale. Historian Catherine E. Kelly notes that a few families "amassed a level of wealth that would have been unthinkable in their parents' or grandparents' generation."[5]

Our story takes place as Connecticut found itself at this tipping point. And if these social fissures were not enough, an even greater change was on the horizon. The Industrial Revolution was in its infancy, with small "manufactories" beginning to spring up along rivers and byways. We have already heard Timothy Dwight quietly but approvingly incorporate the "unnumbered mills" into his vision of Connecticut's future in *Greenfield Hill*. Dwight may have imagined the mills as just another benign manifestation of the state's varied productivity, but of course these embryonic industrial enterprises were destined to transform, and in many cases deform, the waterways and agricultural regions they supported, turning river falls into industrial engines.[6]

Dwight, at least, took note of the new industries. The Town Reports, by and large, ignored them. Although eager to tally substantial crop yields and report favorable commodity prices, the authors of the reports mainly conveyed the impression that small town and farm life continued to predominate in the Connecticut of 1800. Here still, the reports seem to say, despite the many political changes of the last quarter century and the environmental and commercial challenges the state faces, is to be found a land of golden fields of grain, lush orchards, bountiful kitchen gardens, and sparkling dairies. So, was it the best of times or the worst of times for Connecticut's farmers? Timothy Dwight wrote of the fortunate ones who inhabited the Connecticut River Valley: "Every man, with hardly an exception, lives on his own ground and in his own house." But Dwight's description of this modest yet secure "every man" left out one important detail: these valley farmers acquired independence not through self-sufficiency but rather by marketing much of their agricultural production. Dwight himself, in his town report on New Haven, catalogued the agricultural surplus exported from that port city. He examined shipping books and custom-house data with a sharp eye, itemizing major goods, "together with sundry small articles . . . all [of which] amount[ed] to 466,367 dollars."[7]

Despite his penchant for poetry, as a town reporter Dwight's outlook was far from romantic. As with the other reports, his is full of hard-nosed data about agricultural production and exports. Nevertheless, the overall impression the reports give is a romantic one of town and farm life in Connecticut. These contradictions and complexities must be kept in mind as we examine the detailed accounts of the state's agriculture in the Town Reports.

The cereal and field crops most likely to have been grown in Connecticut were the standard European varieties—wheat, rye, oats, peas, barley, buckwheat, flax, and hay. The one addition, which was also the best-growing crop, was Indian corn or maize. The region's food crops likewise played an important role as animal fodder. Farmers were in a constant struggle to keep down the costs of producing them. Azel Backus of Bethlehem remarked that farmers in his town weren't able to fatten their hogs "as easily as they do where Corn is raised with less expence of ploughing and manual labor." Yields on the food and fodder crops also varied from town to town, although Indian corn usually came out at or near the top. As one author wrote, corn was "the crop best suited to the Nature of the soil." Vying for second place were wheat and rye. The most highly valued grain of all was wheat, but it was apt to fall victim to disease and predation. Next came oats, peas, barley, and buckwheat, in no particular order, and finally a grain newer to American farmers, flaxseed or linseed. Flax was used both for food and as a fiber to make clothing and other textiles. Lastly came hay, which farmers grew in their fields and meadows to feed their livestock.[8]

David McClure of East Windsor listed the grains raised in his town as Indian corn, rye, wheat, oats, and barley: "The average quantity from an acre, are 25 to 30 bushels of corn, 12 of rye and 18 of wheat." He didn't give yields on oats and barley. All told, East Windsor harvested about 100,000 bushels of grain annually. William Miller testified that in Wintonbury yields were higher: "Wheat, on new land, will yield twenty five bushels per acre, by the piece; and Indian-corn, on old land, highly manured, from thirty to forty bushels per acre."[9]

Azel Backus reported for Bethlehem that rye yields were from ten to thirty bushels an acre, and corn from fifteen to forty. The uncertainty of wheat yields because of pest and fungus depredations had "nearly discouraged the farmers of late years from attempting it on a large scale." Farmington's John Treadwell left wheat out of his list altogether, reporting that "the crops which labour produces are Indian Corn, Rye, Oats, & Flax."[10]

The reports tell a story of Connecticut agriculture in which many farmers grew some cereal crops but found the most valuable of them, wheat, the least productive and reliable. Wheat's failure was, according to some, a relatively new development. To others in certain parts of Connecticut, growing wheat had long presented problems. David D. Field wrote that it had once been the leading crop of Middlesex County. Then in 1777, the "Hussein-fly," as he called it—better known as the Hessian fly—began to ravage the county's fields. At the time of his writing, about 1830, Field was optimistic that wheat might be revived, despite the Hessian fly "& other evils to which the crop is exposed." Sadly, it was not to be, largely because of that little fly.[11]

Hezekiah Frost dated the arrival of the Hessian fly in his town of Westminster to 1788. Elkanah Tisdale also complained of the fly's destruction of crops in Lebanon, but he did not give a date for the pest's arrival. And Aaron Putnam wrote that Pomfret had raised little wheat since the "the Hessian fly, or Bug" for many years had "much annoy'd" the crop.[12]

That indefatigable traveler of the region, Timothy Dwight, gave the fullest account of the damage caused by the "small, white maggot." His researches led him to believe that an encampment of Hessian soldiers was to blame. In relating the story of the fly's destructive capabilities, Dwight highlighted the disparity between the size and appearance of the enemy and the extent of the damage it caused:

> So far as I have been able to learn, this insect, so insignificant in its appearance, and yet so important by its ravages on the labors and happiness of mankind, was first found in a field of wheat on or near the Hessian encampment in the neighborhood of Brooklyn, and opposite to the city of New York. This was in the year 1784. . . . The Hessian fly, as I observed, is less than a gnat; and, when settled in its usual manner on the ground, is commonly invisible, being seen only as it rises in small clouds immediately before your steps. It is feeble and helpless also in the extreme, defenseless against the least enemy, and crushed by the most delicate touch. Yet for many years it has taxed this country annually more perhaps than a million of dollars.

Because of the Hessian fly, Dwight concluded, "in Connecticut, the cultivation of wheat has for more than twenty years been in a great measure discontinued."[13]

But the Hessian fly was not the only impediment to growing the one grain that most people wished to eat. Historian Christopher Clark writes that "wheat rust," also known as "stem rust," "black rust," or simply "the blast," infected the wheat fields of southern New England after the Revolution. In fact, farmers everywhere in New England, although to a lesser extent in the Connecticut River Valley, had had to fight this fungal disease since the first years of settlement. Facing the difficulties of low yields caused by these factors, many farmers had simply given up on wheat.[14]

Yet the desire to grow wheat—and the desire to consume it—never waned among the English-descended, bread-loving inhabitants of the region. For them, wheat was the indispensable ingredient in the best of breads. In their quest for wheat, some, like Dwight, thought that dressing fields with either fresh or "lixiviated" (leached) wood ashes would provide a prophylactic against the blast. "Wheat is very rarely blasted on grounds dressed with ashes," he rhymingly advised, though there is little evidence to support his claim.[15]

Jackson Turner Main contended that colonial farmers sensed a connection between the barberry bushes that grew adjacent to many wheat fields and the appearance of this disease. Their impression was correct. Like wheat, the barberry bush is host to the deadly fungus. But, despite the farmers' efforts to destroy the offending bushes, "wheat returned only gradually, primarily near the coast."[16]

The inability to grow wheat in New England continued to perplex the ever-optimistic Dwight, whose appreciation of the crop's economic (and gustatory) advantages led him to seek a solution to the problem. However, despite attempting to delimit the area in which wheat crops tended to fail, namely in "the country lying eastward of a line which may be fixed about thirty miles east of Connecticut River"; despite mulling over numerous possible causes of this failure, such as the nature of the soil, the proximity of fields to the ocean, the climate in general, the farmers' method of tillage, the barberry bush, and the use of cow manure as fertilizer; and despite touting at one time or another various improbable remedies such as leached wood ashes, in the end Dwight could only conclude that "wheat cannot be cultivated with success" in most parts of Connecticut and New England.[17]

The fly and the fungus may have contributed to a reduction in the overall percentage of acreage devoted to raising grains, but for most towns in Connecticut, as for other regions of New England, the percentage of farmland devoted to tillage had always been considerably less than that devoted to grazing. The one place where the ratio was reversed was on the rich ground of the Connecticut River Valley, which was universally acknowledged as the region's one "wheat belt." There, half the land was tilled, as compared to 13 percent used for pasture.[18]

Many have noted the exceptional quality of the valley's alluvial soil. Main remarked that the wealthiest farmers of "productive northern Valley soils . . . clearly engaged in large-scale sale of specialties such as wheat, flax, or cider, a concentration uncommon in most of New England." He calculated valley wheat yields at seven bushels per acre from 1750 to 1774. "In general," he reported, "a farmer could make the most money bringing in a wheat crop, with corn, meslin [wheat and rye mixed], and flax next, while peas, oats, and barley brought up the rear." But he noted that even in parts of Connecticut outside the valley area, such as in the southern district of New Haven, wheat did moderately well before the invasion of the Hessian fly; there it comprised one-third of the grains grown at the end of the colonial period.[19]

A generally high level of fertility and minimum amounts of crop disease or predation made colonial Connecticut an advantageous place for settlers. Main's data suggests that yields per acre "of the familiar cereal crops" actually increased through the third quarter of the eighteenth century, before the appearance of the Hessian fly. After this time, things changed. Thirty-five or so years later, Daniel N. Brinsmade of Washington, Connecticut, gave the relative value of his town's grain crops. By then, scarce wheat was worth twice as much as more plentiful rye and three times as much as the most easily grown crop, Indian corn.[20]

To fertilize their fields, the majority of farmers continued to rely on the old-fashioned, laborious method of applying stable manure. William Miller considered such manure the best for Wintonbury's "clayey loamy soil." Some turned to wood ashes as fertilizer, hoping to provide a defense against the blast while also encouraging plant growth. John Treadwell, for one, recommended using "ashes in their natural state" on Indian corn and garden vegetables, but only after the plants had sprouted. He wrote, "The alkaline salts which abound in them, attract and neutralize the nitrous salts which float in the air, & increase the food of plants as an agent." Ashes, he contended along with Dwight, defended against those unwanted insects. He concluded that the use is "now so much practised, that the manufacture of pot & pearl ashes is, with us, wholly discontinued" because the ashes were of greater value as manure.[21]

Potash and pearl ash, chemicals made from leaching ashes, were used in making bleach, glass, and early forms of baking soda. (The first use of pearl ash as a raising agent in baking is found in *American Cookery*.) Treadwell didn't mention the downside of using ashes as fertilizer and crop protection—the labor required to procure them. Ashes as fertilizer never caught on because farmers, knowing how hard they were to come by, tended to apply them too sparingly to be effective. The ultimate utility of ashes aside, Treadwell's reasoning about them is an example of the belief shared by the authors of the Town Reports that scientifically based methods of farming were the key to the success of agriculture in the state.[22]

Daniel Brinsmade further reported on the variety of approaches to fertilization adopted by farmers in his town of Washington: "The manures are, barn litter or stable manure; gypsum or plaster, ashes; the black soil dug from swamps and marshes, & clover suffered to rot on the land without feeding." After the town's grassland was plowed and planted with corn but before the first hoeing, "the plants are manured with ashes or gypsum." David Field struck out in a different direction, stating that rye crops in Middlesex County were manured principally with fish. Timothy Dwight, ever attentive to the best agricultural practices, attested that fish were also used successfully on nearby Long Island.[23]

Notwithstanding the efforts at pest control and fertilization by farmers and their advocates, Connecticut after the colonial period, and except for the fertile valley, would never be home to amber waves of grain. English traveler William Strickland, surveying agriculture in New England and New York in the 1790s, found New England to be a "grazing country" that grew little grain except Indian corn, which he considered unpleasant food. He found cornbread and corn whiskey too coarse for an English gentleman's refined tastes. He discounted New England altogether as a producer of cereal crops, prophesying that New York State would become "the granary of America." The acres of new fields being cleared in upstate New York had the potential to supply Europe's insatiable hunger for wheat, which was Strickland's main concern.[24]

With their desire for wheat often thwarted by fungus, fly, and unsuitable soil, most late eighteenth-century Connecticut farmers and their dairying wives would undoubtedly have nodded in agreement with the sentiment expressed by Elkanah Tisdale of Lebanon: "This town is better calculated for making beef, butter & cheese than any thing else, & this begins to be more practised than formerly." Azel Backus of Bethlehem saw the commercial advantages of producing the state's second most important meat product, pork, despite the high cost of fodder. His town annually sent 250 barrels of pork to market. James Morris of Litchfield wrote that from his town, too, pork "in considerable quantities" was exported, as it was from Washington, a bit farther south.[25]

Although pork was exported in quantity, and served the farm family well as everyday food, beef brought the greatest profits. So an even larger quantity of beef than pork—four hundred barrels—left Bethlehem in trade each year, and a similar amount was probably barreled for sale in Norfolk. In 1800, a little over eight thousand barrels of beef were exported from the port of New London; for pork the figure was a little over four thousand barrels.[26]

Daniel Brinsmade found that in Washington, "cattle are generally driven off on the leg," probably because of bad roads. Chauncey Prindle of Watertown boasted of the two hundred beef cattle that grazed in his town and were eventually sent to market. Prindle also wrote of Watertown's eighty head of "Shipping Oxen." Oxen were used as draft animals and for food, sometimes one animal serving both purposes. John Treadwell noted that "oxen when so old as not to be profitable to keep for cultivation may be fatted so as to produce a profit to the owner."[27]

The emphasis on husbandry was not new. A concentration on livestock farming had distinguished the first English colonists to America from those arriving from elsewhere in Europe. In her account of the role of livestock in the settlement of New England and the Chesapeake, historian Virginia DeJohn Anderson explains that England in the early seventeenth century had a higher rate of domestic animals per cultivated acre than anywhere else in Europe except the Netherlands. In the new American environment, other factors came into play. But tradition cannot be overlooked as part of what tilted the agricultural balance in favor of livestock. Colonists who came from the north and west of England, for instance, were accustomed to a mixed agriculture of "immense open pastures where large numbers of sheep and cattle were driven for communal grazing. Interspersed among the meadows were arable fields where farmers grew wheat and other grains." Many set out to replicate this model when they emigrated to New England.[28]

Most English colonists were also familiar with what has been called wood-pasture land management practices. In this system, woodlands provide shelter and forage for livestock as well as forest products for building and fuel. Elkanah Tisdale's conclusion that his town of Lebanon was "better calculated for making beef, butter & cheese than any thing else" can also be read as a statement placing Tisdale and his fellow townspeople safely within their cultural comfort zone.[29]

In colonial Connecticut, hogs and sheep were kept in roughly equal numbers, but pork was more prominent than mutton in the colonial diet and in the marketplace stalls. There were several reasons for this discrepancy. First, pork was uniquely suited to preservation, taking well both to dry salting and brining, which made it easy for a small farmer to store and transport it. The relative distribution of the two species also played a part in putting more pork than mutton on colonial plates. Sheep tended to be concentrated among a few owners who kept large herds, whereas a hog or two could be found in just about every farmyard. After slaughtering and dressing some of his hogs each fall for his family's needs, a farmer might still have meat left over to sell. Eventually, these differences between the two species led to far larger numbers of hogs than sheep on farms in Connecticut and throughout New England.[30]

The main factor determining if a given farmer would produce a marketable surplus, whether of cereal crops or livestock, was the extent of his acreage. With beef and pork as Connecticut's chief exports, livestock numbers, which were closely related to the size of the farmer's landholdings, serve as the best indicators of his wealth. Jackson Turner Main analyzed colonial livestock holdings in this light; his findings can be extrapolated to the first decades after independence.[31]

Throughout the colonial era, farmers with holdings of fewer than forty acres tended to own about six cattle, often including two oxen, a cow, a calf, and two heifers. Such farmers were unlikely to raise livestock for sale. Their excess barreled pork might occasionally have been sold or bartered, but these easy-to-raise farmyard animals were generally not counted in livestock inventories. Overall, the stock on these small farms went to support the farm's residents.[32]

Farmers at the next level of wealth, those with forty to eighty acres of land, tended to hold double the number of cattle, but they usually had the same number of hogs as their poorer neighbors. On these farms, a saleable surplus of pork was likely, perhaps because the farm family had other meat resources for themselves besides pork. Farmers with 80 to 120 acres of pasture generally had three more head of cattle and two more hogs than the previous group. They produced even more surplus.[33]

Finally, those with more than 120 acres at their disposal had far more of every form of livestock—on average seventeen cattle, twenty-four sheep, and eight hogs. They tended to grow more grain for home consumption, fodder, and local sale. These farmers, in other words, had plenty to eat and plenty to sell. The correlation between the size of a farmer's freehold and the likelihood of his having surplus inventory is clear.[34]

According to historian Paul E. Waggoner, at the end of the eighteenth century Connecticut farmers devised ways to get around transportation impediments and improve their meat sales: "A Connecticut specialty was drying or curing meat to make it lighter per dollar and lessen the deterioration per mile." But on-the-hoof trade was also profitable, and Connecticut had a reputation for selling high-quality horses, mules, cattle, and live hogs. Most of this stock went to West Indian planters. After 1790, New York City merchants acted as the chief middlemen for Connecticut's maritime trade, marking a further shift toward major commercial centers as the destination for the state's agricultural commodities. Connecticut farmers found themselves doing a brisk business in supplying food to the growing towns and cities within their orbit, from regional centers like Hartford and New Haven to the rapidly expanding metropolis of New York City.[35]

In some Connecticut towns, dairy farming, the woman's domain often viewed as a sideline, was in fact the most profitable branch of the generally lucrative field of husbandry. In Litchfield, for example, James Morris explained that most families "turned principally to dairies." William Miller approved of dairy farming for his town of Wintonbury but regretted the shortsightedness of the town's farmers in turning their milk into butter rather than cheese: "Ready money, once a week, is a temptation, which induces a market man to overlook his greater interest in the well-managed, but long delayed cheese market."[36]

But Wintonbury appears to have been the exception to the rule in its preference for making butter over cheese. In his consideration of Connecticut farmers' difficulties in transporting goods to market, Waggoner notes that "the quintessential Connecticut way to higher value per pound was transforming short-lived gallons of milk into long-lived pounds of cheese." Of southern New England's roughly 486 tons of annually exported cheese, Waggoner estimates that "Goshen provided nearly 200 tons and neighboring Norfolk, 100 tons." Timothy Dwight believed wholeheartedly that Goshen was correct to focus on dairy farming: "The wealth of Goshen is one proof of the superiority of grazing ground to that which is devoted to tillage . . . and the inhabitants are probably more wealthy than any other collection of farmers in new England."[37]

Although they remained in the background in the Town Reports, as they do in most accounts of colonial and early national farming in Connecticut, the women who managed the dairies were as responsible for the wealth produced on the farm as the men who tended the herds. Some authors did mention their contributions. The women of Goshen, for instance, were notably expert in the production of butter and cheese. Lewis Norton credited their "judgement, neatness, industry and experience" for making cheese a staple commodity and source of wealth for the town. As we heard at the end of chapter 4, Elijah Allen of Cornwall found a strong chain of causation between female production of "greater Quantities of Butter and Cheese" and the essential components of the Connecticut way of life. Market sales of these dairy products enabled Cornwall farm families "to pay . . . Taxes for the support of Law, Order and good Government and Instruction in Church and State."[38]

With over 150 miles of coastline, Connecticut might have been expected to maintain a saltwater fishing industry comparable to the vaunted cod fisheries of colonial Massachusetts. But Connecticut's coastal and off-shore fishing differed considerably from their Massachusetts equivalents. Most importantly, Connecticut did not share its northern neighbor's easy access to productive fishing banks. It was not until the end of the eighteenth century that the state saw the development of "a nascent deep-sea fishery," as William N. Peterson explains. Most of Connecticut's coastline looks onto Long Island Sound, which is, in the words of historian Daniel

Vickers, "from the fisherman's standpoint more like a massive bay. The waters are shallow, protected, and variable in temperature, and there are no banks directly offshore." Such conditions meant that "nowhere within it did there exist massive stocks equivalent to those of the great fishing grounds that sit on the continental shelf to the north and east." In the days before overfishing had decimated their stocks, Georges Bank, the Grand Banks of Newfoundland, and the Nova Scotia and Labrador banks all yielded historic numbers of cod, mackerel, halibut, hake, and pollock. But the natural range of the most valuable of all the cold water species, cod, did not extend as far south as Long Island Sound.[39]

Nevertheless, colonial Connecticut did engage in commercial fishing, taking particular advantage of the spring runs of shad in the Connecticut and other rivers. Unfortunately given the great numbers of these fish migrating upriver in the spring, shad, unlike cod, are highly perishable, even when salted. As a result, shad remained a commodity best suited for regional sales rather than distant markets. Still, Connecticut shad made its mark. Boston merchants were known to have had it for sale as early as the 1730s, and it remained popular almost a century later, being listed in 1815 on New York's current price lists. Other Connecticut fish also had the potential to be profitable, a fact that lay behind the 1819 complaint of Middletown's David Field that the state's waters, once full of salmon, bass, alewives, pike, carp, and perch, had been largely emptied of these species. Fish populations had been reduced by overfishing and habitat degradation.[40]

In the late eighteenth and early nineteenth centuries, the commercial value of many kinds of fish, including those previously neglected, likewise increased. In places like New York City, "sizeable populations [were] hungry for any kind of fresh, palatable food," Vickers writes. With all fish, even bony fish like shad, commanding unprecedented prices, farmers more frequently turned to fishing to supplement their incomes. David Field maintained that as of 1819, there were "nearly eighty places in Middlesex [County] where shad are now caught in the season of fishing," by which he meant the time from mid-April to mid-June when shad spawn in northern rivers and estuaries. Shad fishing was just as successful in Saybrook in 1817, when 2,194 barrels of shad were salted. Haddam and East Haddam could account for far fewer fish, but even they proudly reported putting up 146 and 169 barrels of shad, respectively. Field estimated the total quantity of fish caught in his county that year at over 5,000 barrels.[41]

Given the rising value of fresh fish, Field, like many others, regretted that past practices, especially river dredging and land clearance undertaken to improve farming, seemed to have inadvertently reduced stocks. Once, he wrote, there were "salmon, shad, bass, alewives, pike, carp, perch, &c, which cast their spawn on logs, and objects along the shores." These spawning grounds produced massive schools of fish, but earlier generations of New Englanders had been largely indifferent to the freshwater bounty. He acknowledged his ancestors' "general prejudice" against the most common of these fish, "either because they were so generally used by the Indians, or from some other cause which I am unable to assign."[42]

Witnesses from those days who were still living in Field's time attested that "there was little demand for salmon, and as for shad it was disreputable to eat them." The danger of eating shad in particular, with its many small bones, may have contributed to its reputation as poor people's food. Field wrote that the causes of the shad stock's precipitate decline could be attributed to

> the use of very long seines, particularly about the mouth of the river, by which the shoals are broken and prevented entering and ascending the river; the almost perpetual attempts to take them in the season of fishing . . . the removal of logs, roots, and other objects from the shores on which spawn are cast, and the disturbance of these objects where they remain, by boating and navigation; the erection of locks on the river, and dams on its tributary streams, by which their ascent to the regions beyond them is partially or wholly prevented.[43]

David McClure of East Windsor agreed that shad and alewives were "caught in plenty in the spring, although not so abundantly as in years past." His attitude toward freshwater fish was markedly different from that of earlier generations: "Thus providence brings to our doors, the delicious treasures of the sea." Despite his acknowledgment of declining fish stocks, he called the sea an "inexhausted store house" from which "multitudes of the human race are fed and supported." Yet he admitted that "twenty years ago Salmon were taken in great plenty; but they have of late nearly forsaken the river." Like Field, he believed that construction, such as "the great dam, across Connecticut river, at Hadley falls," was the cause.[44]

Changes to habitat did disturb the lifecycles of various fish species and consequently reduce their numbers. But Daniel Vickers argues that "the truly devastating blow to all of the fish populations of the northwest Atlantic and eastern North America over the past two hundred years has been, not the degradation of their marine and riverine environments, but rather

the creation of gigantic domestic markets for fish and fish products." So
it was the farmers-turned-seasonal-fishermen themselves and their hungry
customers in places like New York City, rather than the seines, locks, log
removals, and dams, that caused the fish to disappear.[45]

Several other Town Reports also list fish and seafood among their towns'
expanding commercial resources. Philo Shelton, writing about Stratfield,
Newfield, and the East River, catalogued the species found as "alwives or
herring . . . some Sea perch, Crabs & Oysters . . . long clams, some round
ones, flatfish, yellow fin, Bass, Scollops." Levi H. Clark of Haddam recorded
that "30,000 shad have been taken in a season." Vickers points out that
Connecticut shad required capital investment in boats, seines, barrels, and
salt, and provided the kind of return associated with commercial rather
than subsistence enterprises. "Shad may have been considered a poor man's
food—indicative of one's inability to afford salt pork—but it clearly found
customers."[46]

Vickers also finds implausible the notion of some historians that "fish
were caught mainly for home consumption" and that fisheries were treated
as "a common resource to be husbanded for the public good." He argues
that such "perishable foods that present[ed] themselves in great abundance
for short periods of the year" had always been exploited for the profits they
brought.[47]

This was also the case with the oyster fishery, which Vickers characterizes
as a "market-driven innovation of the early national period." Before the mid-
eighteenth century, colonists had enjoyed oysters only occasionally. Commercial demand rose later in the century, until harvests of 400,000–500,000
bushels were not unusual. Some Connecticut oysters "made it no farther
than the New Haven market." But much of the catch, raked, shucked, and
barreled by families living near the oyster beds, was transported in winter
throughout Connecticut and Massachusetts to as far away as Vermont and
New Hampshire and, of course, the insatiable maw of New York City.[48]

These fishing endeavors, much as they had grown, were still conducted
on a smaller scale than the vast industry of the Massachusetts cod fisheries.
The difference between the scope of fishing in the two states adds to the
evidence that the Massachusetts economy was consolidated, highly developed, and hierarchical, while Connecticut was a place where the individual
producer, whether fisherman or farmer, could function as an independent
agent. This relative independence (though always tenuous and becoming
more so), along with a general sense that profits from farming and fishing

were widely shared, formed the basis of the Town Reports authors' often self-congratulatory tone.

Fruits and vegetables grown in Connecticut served mainly to improve the quality of life of the state's residents, not to advance the economy. Only apples, turned into potable, portable, and relatively long-lasting cider, had any significant value in trade. Yet the authors of the Town Reports were both detailed and lyrical as they catalogued the various fruits and vegetables grown in the state. Historian Tamara Plakins Thornton, who writes about Boston's elite gentlemen farmers in the period 1785 to 1860 (a group similar in many respects to the authors of the reports), helps explain the impetus behind these meticulous lists of fruits, vegetables, flowers, shrubs, and ornamental trees.

Thornton argues that these gentlemen farmers were motivated by the relationship between "agricultural improvement and the rhetoric of patriotism and benevolence that informed these innovations." Imitating English aristocrats, who likewise took a keen interest in agriculture, but also conscious of the challenges facing their young nation, these Americans set out to translate the English preoccupation with landscape and agriculture into a concern to support and encourage the independent farmer. They were particularly interested in improving the food supply.[49]

The Boston-area Federalists sincerely desired to be comprehensively "improving" farmers. They experimented with crop rotation, the application of fertilizers, livestock breeding, and dairying. But from the beginning, horticulture figured prominently in their rural pursuits. Boston merchant Joseph Barrell typified the group in lavishing attention on his orchards and hothouses. Thornton relates that in 1806, "the Federalist network [was] enlisted in the task of procuring grafts of Swaar apples for Fisher Ames," and that Ebenezer Preble "imported no fewer than 150 varieties of fruit trees to his Watertown estate in 1805."[50]

She chronicles the evolving attitudes of the group toward horticultural pursuits: "When it was first introduced to the Boston elite, the cultivation of flowers, fruits, vegetables, and ornamental trees was represented as if not quite as virtuous as experimental farming, then at least a 'blameless luxury' with potential for practical application." In time, however, the Boston gentlemen scaled back their involvement in the grittiness of field agriculture, with its pests, diseases, sterile soil, and often uncooperative, backward farmers. They found it more pleasant to concentrate on gardens and orchards.

Yet their zeal for scientifically based agrarian improvement, combined with their patriotism, meant that they were reluctant to abandon the American farmer altogether. Orchard fruit, it turned out, was the answer to their dilemma. It "represented just the right combination of utility, still valued in a republican nation and a mercantile society, and beauty." The apple, in particular, which is neither so commonplace as a vegetable nor so frivolous as a flower, yet beautiful in all its stages of growth, nourishing, and suitable for conversion to a beverage, became the focus of their attention.[51]

There is no direct evidence that the agricultural enthusiasts among the Connecticut elite of the same period, many of whom wrote the Town Reports, elevated horticulture over agriculture and husbandry so distinctly. But there is plenty of indirect rhetorical evidence, embedded in the topics that captured the Town Reports authors' interest. It was vegetables and fruits, especially fruits, and among fruits especially the apple, about which these early agronomists waxed most enthusiastic.

John Treadwell recorded his town's garden produce with great care. Farmington's beets, he wrote, were of several colors and types—red, blood, white, yellow, and "scarcity." Its carrots came in orange, purple, and yellow. Its radishes were also of various hues—salmon, scarlet, and purple. There were as well the "turnip" and "horse" radish. The turnip (as opposed to the type of radish called turnip) came in common, cabbage, and "french" varieties. Parsnips were of both the common and smooth types, the latter a new variety.[52]

This was an abundance of detail about a few varieties of vegetable, to be sure. But Treadwell had barely begun. The riot of color and variety continued with white and red artichokes; red, white, and top onions (the latter "produces the onion upon the top of the stalk" with bulbs that replace the flowers); "vegetable Oyster, or sal suffee" (salsify, a root similar to a parsnip); "Pulse & other Hortulan Vines"; beans of the early bush, cranberry, frost, and English varieties; and peas of the "early June, Strawberry, Marrowfat, Rouncival," and "Ramshon" varieties. There were also crookneck, "chubb," winter, summer, and lemon squash, "a good kind & peculiar for not degenerating." Cucumbers yielded early June and long green varieties, while Farmington's melons consisted of common watermelon ("the Yellow cored do [grow] very long, & the flesh of which is very rich & melting"), "Smoodi Muskmelon," "Rusticoat muskmelon," cantaloupe, and citron.

Treadwell next itemized Farmington's "Herbs & Plants—esculent & medicinal." Here were found red cabbage for pickling, plus drumhead, early or June, yellow, and Savoy cabbage. Then there were asparagus, several kinds of lettuces, peppergrass, parsley, burnet, chives, coriander, white or "English" mustard, black mustard, common sage, and another type of sage, "the red a very large excellent kind & propagated only by the root." Treadwell pressed on with additional herbs: sweet marjoram, thyme, rue, hyssop, balm (both bee balm and balm of gilead), saffron, tansy, wormwood, and the ever-popular, ever-useful variety known as "&c."

With equal glee, Treadwell described the fruits grown in Farmington. We needn't enumerate them at any length but they include all those fruit trees and shrubs—quince, plum, pear, peach, nectarine, apricot, apple—that can be "cultivated in the borders of the Kitchen & flower Garden, or in yards devoted wholly to them." The berry shrubs and plants he catalogued included red and white currants; white gooseberries; black, red, and white raspberries; and strawberries. Some of the specimens, he noted, had only recently been introduced and had not yet "come to maturity." In other words, as of February 1804 when he submitted his report, there were yet more in store for the next growing season in this gardeners' utopia.

In the same vein, Timothy Dwight wrote of "the city of New-Haven [which] contains, probably, as many good kitchen gardens as any town in the state." In itemizing his town's plant richness, he devoted lengthy columns to the fruits and vegetables to be found in its private gardens, including most of those on Treadwell's list, as well as a few others, such as "coleworts," endive, "nasturtions," and "tomatoes, or love apples." He also offered horticultural tips, recommending, for instance, that the English brown raspberry be planted because it was the variety that produced the most berries, something he had learned from experience. He pointed out the difference between the field and meadow strawberry: the field variety ripened ten days earlier and was sweeter than the meadow type, although the field strawberry's size was unlikely to increase with cultivation. He deduced the latter from having grown the variety himself for the past eight years. The advantage of the Madeira grape, he declared, was that it could withstand Connecticut winters. Dwight reported that potatoes were so commonly grown that the acreage of land planted with them was rarely recorded.[53]

Regarding the apple, that ideal "combination of utility . . . and beauty," William Miller of Wintonbury noted the market value of "cyder, cyder brandy, and apples." He estimated that four thousand barrels of Wintonbury cider were produced annually and all of it was "esteemed of the best kind, in market." He described the best soil for growing apples, pears, peaches, and plums as "high, strong, dry, deep red loam intermixed with a little gravel." From this soil, the farmer would get "quick and vigorous growth, with little expense," along with "the richest flavored fruits, in a great perfection."[54]

Because the way to make apple cider was common knowledge, as was the way to brew beer, Azel Backus described how to make the less-familiar potato liquor in terms of those two procedures: "The process is to wash and grind them like apples, ferment as beer, and then distil." Samuel Goodrich of Ridgefield reported that "there is plenty of Apples for the inhabitants & this season there is a still set up in the town for distilling cider." Philo Shelton of Stratfield described the best method for preserving apples: "Pick them from the boughs before they are ripe with the frost in a dry Season, & Secure them from the air in as cool a place as you can find without having the frost injure them." He also advised against pruning the apple tree "after it has got its growth except it be dying, or some young Sprouts Starting, which should ever be kept from increasing, & let your pruning be in the month of February, before the sap begins to run." For the year 1799, Stratfield exported 815 barrels of cider and 237 barrels of "Cider Spirits."[55]

Lewis M. Norton of Goshen admitted that in his town, "the quantity of apple cider made does not much exceed the home consumption." He doubted that there was ever a cider distillery in the town. James Morris of Litchfield, on the other hand, placed apples at the center of his town's agrarian productivity. He was proud that in Litchfield, "lands are much better cultivated than formerly; more attention being paid to manure, particularly to the use of plaster," with the result that "land in this town, within thirty years past, has increased in value nearly one hundred per cent." This doubling of land values was due not only to improved fertilization but also to putting every inch of land in Litchfield without housing on it into cultivation. This was where the apples came in. As Morris explained, "lands, which are not arable, answer well for orchards." Apple trees "prosper on stony and ledgy lands, and generally do best in a western or south-western exposure." They should be manured to loosen the soil around them, and "sheaves of flax are found to be beneficial, when spread under apple-trees." Morris also instructed his readers on how to make cider, writing that the apples should be "well ground" and that the resulting pomace should be allowed to stand for twenty-four to forty-eight hours (depending on the weather) before pressing. He also recommended "unslacked stone lime," calling it "an excellent thing to cleanse cider casks which are musty."[56]

Other Town Report authors joined in singing the praises of their towns' apple orchards. From Washington, Milford, Lisbon, New Haven, and Pomfret, we hear much the same. In fact, there is nary a report through which the apple, of untold varieties, does not wend its fruitful way.[57]

Amid the heady fragrance of apples, it might be prudent to remind ourselves of the point with which we began this chapter—that the Town Reports' generally rosy picture of Connecticut agriculture should be viewed with some skepticism. Paul E. Waggoner emphasizes "the isolation of a farm and the loneliness of life on it as late as 1850." He also writes of the toil required to extract the abundance the reports accentuate. The lack of good roads, for example, made it nearly impossible to transport firewood any distance. Even moving a cord or two as little as three miles required a herculean effort. Such unremitting labor took a continuous and terrible toll on the farmer, his sons, and his hired hands, all of whom were pressed into service—and away from their myriad other tasks—to keep the farm household supplied with wood for heating and cooking.[58]

A farmer's woodlot certainly could provide extra income, but only if the wood could be efficiently harvested and transported. Waggoner notes that "until a canal opened in 1807 in neighboring Massachusetts, an immense quantity of lumber was still useless because it lacked an easy passage to market." He points out that as late as 1797, roads were so uneven and stony that travel by horse could prove deadly. In 1800, Ridgefield farmers found it impossible to get their potatoes to market in Manhattan, forty miles away. In the same year in the town of Washington, cattle were transported "on the leg" because barrels full of meat were apt to be damaged or split open as carts bumped along bad roads. Driving live cattle, of course, entailed its own set of dangers and reduced the cattle's weight, which reduced profits.[59]

As these examples indicate, all the improvements in farming and all the surpluses in livestock would bring "a more abundant and cheerful life only if farmers endured a long haul to market." Between 1791 and 1805, the median distance farmers in rural Massachusetts transported produce was still only twenty miles. Rural Connecticut would have been no different. Waggoner's emphasis on isolation and missed opportunities is not completely absent from the boosterist Town Reports, but it is far from prominent.[60]

Several analysts have maintained that most farmers did not even attempt the improvements that would promote surpluses. Historian Richard J. Purcell wrote regarding early national Connecticut that "knowledge of improvements in English farming had no effect. . . . The small freeholder, with his farm of 50 to 150 acres, could not afford to be progressive." Rather than invest his labor and paltry savings in better "implements, stock, seed, and fertilization," this farmer, according to Purcell, "continued to scratch the top of an exhausted soil with an antiquated plow, sow home-grown seed on unharrowed fields and await the harvest." Certainly not the picture of a go-getter.[61]

While Purcell acknowledged that "in the aggregate the production of butter and cheese was large," he drew a bleak scene of rusticity: Indian corn "cultivated as the aborigines had taught the first settlers," small apple orchards for local production of "cider-brandy," cattle of the "mixed 'native' variety, neither beefers nor milkers," sheep that were "a mongrel type, producing little wool," and a breed of horse, the Narragansett, that was "too small" for farm work.[62]

Yet the key problem with farming in Connecticut wasn't so much the character of the farmer as the number of people trying to extract a living from a finite amount of cultivable land. Historian Albert Laverne Olson wrote of the late eighteenth century, "Contemporaries were well aware of the decline of Connecticut agriculture and the exhaustion of its soil." Historian Kenneth Lockridge, investigating land use throughout New England from 1630 to 1790, concluded that the main causes of the decline in fertility were population pressures—for instance, there was a fourfold population increase in Connecticut between 1715 and 1756—and partible inheritance, the system of land division among heirs that left virtually no farms intact.[63]

Even earlier in the eighteenth century, a few observers sensed that things were starting to go wrong. In 1721, a writer calling himself "Amicus Patriae" was already noting that "living upon small shares of land" was the norm for many New Englanders. With a population disinclined to emigrate despite these mounting pressures, the result was, as historian Charles S. Grant wrote of Kent, Connecticut, "economic opportunity, bright in 1751, included a growing class of propertyless men by 1796." Lockridge saw the same pattern at work in New England as a whole: "Ultimately, the collision of land and population may have been polarizing the structure of society, creating an agricultural 'proletariat' and perhaps even a corresponding rural 'gentry.'" He noted that those caught in this dilemma were "not perceptibly better off as a result of the long-ago emigration of their great-great-grandfathers."[64]

Yet to illustrate the complexity of the situation, we turn to Timothy Dwight's description of the efforts of migrant farmers relocating *to* rather than *from* Connecticut. Or, perhaps it is more accurate to say, to Connecticut temporarily, then on to lands farther west. Dwight looked in particular at the conditions in Stonington, Connecticut, in 1800. He found there a soil that "was rich and almost everywhere well cultivated."[65]

Those who farmed their sixty- to three hundred-acre lots in the large Stonington township were mostly tenant farmers, poor country people originally from Rhode Island, who were "accustomed from their childhood to labor hard on a sterile soil, and to live on very scanty means of subsistence." These classic hard workers, finally meeting up with favorable growing conditions and by dint of their "assiduous industry, and a minute frugality," were gradually able to save enough to move on and "purchase farms in the wilderness." As they migrated, other poor farmers "from the same state" took their place. (By "from the same state," Dwight undoubtedly means the relatively poor state of Rhode Island, but the phrase can also be taken to mean that the new farmers arrived from the same "state" of penury as their predecessors.) This is hardly Purcell's picture of a Connecticut of backward farmers and infertile land, although it is one of grueling labor, diligent thrift, and only gradual improvement.[66]

There is another aspect of Connecticut life at the turn of the nineteenth century that is minimized in these Academy of Arts and Sciences reports. The number of skilled craftsmen towns could support varied according to the situation and wealth of each region, subregion, and town. Craftwork was at first mostly taken up as a way to supplement farm income, although in time some of these workers abandoned farm life completely in favor of the artisan's workshop. Jackson Turner Main argued that "the towns almost from the first supported" some who "depended for their income primarily upon their specialized skill." These skilled artisans often kept their hand in at farming, however. Owning and working small farms on the side was a way to provide relatively inexpensive food for their families.[67]

Yet the Town Reports generally neglect such enterprising artisans. Historian Edward S. Cooke, Jr., writes that "there is little mention of the blacksmiths, joiners, or shoemakers who worked in each town, or the coopers, saddlers, tailors, hatters, potters, pewterers or silversmiths who worked in many of the towns." This omission occurred because "a certain hierarchy existed in the minds of the Academy's founders and the respondents who compiled the reports" in which "agriculture was given top billing." The omission of any acknowledgment of the part skilled craftsmen played in the economy and life of the state is even more egregious when we consider that among the artisans "noticeably absent from the Town Reports" are the masters of the Connecticut federal style. As the number of hogs, barrels of beef, and casks of cider were being duly—and minutely—accounted for by the authors of the Town Reports, these experts were busy producing the furniture, silver, clocks, and other artifacts that are now universally acknowledged as among the earliest and perhaps greatest examples of American decorative arts. The academy overlooked them.[68]

With only two questions about mills and factories, even less detail about these emerging economic powerhouses is found in the reports. Yet in the decades that followed the reports' publication, mechanized industry would bring changes to all aspects of life. Farm work became more machine dependent. Daily life altered in ways that were visible to all, as such personal articles as clothing and furniture ceased to be homespun and homemade and emerged instead, mass-produced, from factories.[69]

For the first time as well, the appearance of people, houses, and town centers was becoming standardized. This sameness of appearance struck many as odd and unnatural. While improvements to the quality of life were obvious, many found the uniformity of goods made by machine unsettling. Whatever one's attitude toward such changes, all agreed they were profound.[70]

As Cooke emphasizes, the Town Reports were written in such a way as to give agriculture "top billing." Their authors certainly took the greatest interest in farming as a commercial venture. But agriculture also had a more direct and immediate impact on people—it dictated what they ate.[71]

Contemporaneous testimony about the quality of the food available to average people varies. For the upper ranks of society, occupied by the likes of Timothy Dwight, overabundance rather than scarcity seems often to have been the problem. Dwight quoted English traveler John Lambert on the subject of the tavern food he experienced as he toured lower Canada and the northeastern United States. Lambert complained, "But their meals I think are composed of too great a variety, and of too many things to be conducive to health." He speculated that Americans' diseases are "engendered by gross diet." The American habit of using "animal food at every meal" he considered especially ill advised. He found that many prosperous families "live nearly in the same style as at these [taverns], and have as great a variety upon their tables." But he was happy to report that "the best old fashioned New England inns were superior to any of the modern ones," in no small part because the food, though ample and of the best quality, was not excessive.[72]

Dwight was "entirely of Mr. Lambert's opinion that our meals are very often composed of too great a variety to be conducive to health." He believed that "a simpler mode of living would naturally prevent excess in eating and drinking." He regretted that the markets he visited were "almost glutted with everything which can be eaten or drunk." Yet national pride compelled him to point out to Lambert that "in fine fruits, it is unnecessary to say, our country incomparably exceeds yours, both as to their richness and variety." He singled out the fruits available in New England that were "brought hither in profusion" from the West Indies.[73]

Although concerned about Americans' health due to their excessively rich diet, Lambert favorably compared their "luxurious manner" of eating with his own country's "meager repasts." Speaking of the American experience, he claimed that "food in the richest variety has always abounded in this country, and has been within the reach of every man possessed even of moderate property." Contemporary observers generally agreed with Lambert's assessment, noting that American farmers, mechanics, and artisans, if they were "in easy circumstances," ate on a par with English gentlemen, a state of affairs to be found nowhere else in the world. Lambert met one such comfortable farmer, who, being worth "perhaps from twenty to twenty-five thousand dollars," a considerable amount for the time but nothing compared with the wealth of the English squirearchy, nevertheless "kept as good a table as any man whom I ever knew."[74]

The profusion of American food that Lambert and Dwight described for the first decade of the nineteenth century is attested to as well in the Connecticut of the late eighteenth century by Mason Fitch Cogswell, the physician and patron of painter Ralph Earl. A native of Windham County in eastern Connecticut and a graduate of Yale living in New York, Cogswell was in the autumn of 1788 thinking of moving to Hartford. In pursuit of this plan, he visited both Hartford and his native region at that time, socializing with a number of prominent citizens, many of whom were old friends. A journal he kept during his visit mostly concerned Thanksgiving as it was celebrated that year.[75]

In the entry for November 26, 1788, he wrote from Scotland, Connecticut, in Windham County: "In the evening as a prelude to Thanksgiving I went up and drank a mug of flip with Esq. Devotion, and ate pompion pie with his wife. . . . How cold it grows! I am too dull to write in my journal. . . . Perhaps the flip has run round my intellects, or, what is worse, the pompion pie." Cogswell returned to the household of Ebenezer Devotion to partake of Thanksgiving dinner, where he again drank flip, but this time as an accompaniment to a feast of turkeys, pigs, apple pies, tarts, and "pompion pies." On Friday, November 28, he dined at the home of a Major Backus, probably Revolutionary War veteran and merchant Ebenezer (or Elisha) Backus. At Backus's well-stocked board Cogswell found "pompion pies again in abundance."[76]

Early the next week, the popular and peripatetic Cogswell declined invitations to dine with friends so "that I might eat turkey with the Governor. Thanksgiving not gone yet, for we had flip and pompion pies both." The governor in question was Samuel Huntington, who was also Cogswell's former guardian. Cogswell was back to dining with slightly less august acquaintances a few days later, this time with wealthy businessman William Leffingwell. They consumed "a full grown turkey, and more pompion pie." There was more of the same the next day at a Mr. Breed's, probably the Honorable John McLaren Breed, descendant of a prominent Connecticut family. Cogswell's testimony gives us a glimpse of the profusion of regional specialties—especially pumpkin pies and turkeys—that were on offer at his level of society during the harvest celebration.[77]

Cogswell's appreciation of such local specialties was echoed several decades later in the sentiments expressed by John Treadwell, as he recalled the Connecticut settlers from whom he was descended. He described them as having worn homespun because of "their moderate circumstances & agricultural state." Despite—or perhaps because of—their rusticity, his ancestors' manner of living was one Treadwell particularly admired and wished to revive. For him, the rural ideal was expressed in the image of the farmer who went daily into his fields to labor with his sons and hired servants. They dined together at noon each day "on their plain fare, under the covert of some thick shade, where, on the green grass, they might enjoy the luxury of the free air, with more sincere delight, than the greatest modern epicure at a civic feast." Treadwell feared that "the late prevalence of a commercial spirit" would cause this rural scene centered on the farmer to be replaced with one focused on "the powdered beau rowling in his carriage." The farmer's "plain fare" was obviously based on local bounty, just as were the turkeys and pumpkin pies celebrated by Cogswell.[78]

But we have just heard Timothy Dwight acknowledging that the abundance on the American table was in part based on trade—those West Indian fruits "brought hither" to New England. Were those trade goods mere augmentations to the local and traditional diet celebrated by Treadwell and Cogswell, or were they an integral part of it? While Treadwell doesn't tell us exactly what his mythical farmer and company dined on, we do know that most New Englanders, who drank flip and at least occasionally ate pumpkin pie, in fact had long since integrated into their diet a fairly lengthy list of imported goods, just as Dwight implied.

For instance, those "pompion pies" were made with spices and sugar. A November 29, 1784, advertisement for a Hartford grocery store in the *Courant*'s competing newspaper, the *American Mercury*, illustrates the point. The ad lists "excellent Alspice, Ginger, Pepper, and every foreign article requisite to furnish a complete PUMPKIN PIE, RAISINS for the CAKE; SUGAR and choice SPIRITS for the PHLIP," emphasizing not merely the suitability but the indispensability of those extras for celebrating Connecticut's harvest holiday. The pumpkin pie, the cake, and the flip must be made just so.[79]

And "just so" required not only pumpkins from local fields but also luxuries obtained from global trade—spices, sugar, raisins, and of course those "choice" spirits. Such an eye-catching statement as this advertisement would have been hard to miss. It functioned as a community memo of sorts, enforcing the standards for making a "complete" pumpkin pie, as well as "the" cake and "the" "flip," all of which were required for a proper Connecticut Thanksgiving celebration. The grocery store, in its announcement that it sold "every foreign article" to "furnish" the pumpkin pie, became the delivery system that joined world trade to local agriculture.

While the critic William C. Dowling interprets Timothy Dwight's approach to commerce in *Greenfield Hill* as conciliatory and accepting, so that "an agricultural society need not, to remain virtuous, remain either rustic or wholly agrarian," we sense in these examples of the types of foods consumed in Connecticut and the rest of the region a shifting emphasis. By the early nineteenth century, as historian John E. Crowley points out, luxuries were being referred to as "conveniences" and "decencies." And with that slight but telling turn, the agrarian way of life, such as that expressed symbolically by the harvest pumpkin, the homespun cloth, and the hand-made chair, had begun to be eclipsed. But perhaps the eclipse of the pastoral was already further along than it seemed. A survey of the topic of drink suggests that it may well have been.[80]

While some towns prided themselves on their wheat and corn, others on their pork, beef, and cheese, and yet others on their fruits and vegetables—all of which found its way onto local dining tables and much of which found its way into ship's holds—just about everyone agreed that producing apples for making hard cider and cider brandy, as well as getting hold of spirits in almost any other form, made for a better life. The temperance movement that would alter drinking behavior by the end of the century was a long way off. Alcohol was consumed liberally on social occasions, of which there were many, by people at all levels of society, and by men and women alike.

An example from the Boston upper classes in the first decade of the nineteenth century can be found in the practices of minister William Emerson, who, as well as being the father of Ralph Waldo Emerson, was also the pastor of the renowned First Church of Boston. Historian Phyllis Cole informs us that "copious dining and sociability" accompanied the many "intellectual and cultural organizations" in which Emerson participated. Such social occasions included drink, as, for example, when "every Sunday evening the deacons and other friends enjoyed wine and spirits, arrayed in gleaming decanters on the sideboard" in the Emerson dining room.[81]

Nor was the Emerson practice in any way unique. In Connecticut around the same time, Lewis Norton complained that his countrymen "seem unable to perform the most trifling business of life without the help of artificial stimulus." For Goshen, Connecticut, in 1811, Norton estimated the "per family" annual consumption of "distilled spirits" (including rum, gin, French brandy, and cider brandy) at twenty-four gallons, costing each family twenty-five dollars for the year. The disapproval Norton conveyed in citing these numbers may have been one of the first volleys in the war against alcohol that would rage as the century progressed.[82]

Still, most social authorities found nothing wrong in the enjoyment of a drop. Timothy Dwight remarked favorably on the "vast abundance" of wines sold "on very moderate terms" in the remote New England towns he had recently visited. He wrote that cider was "the principal drink of the inhabitants" of the region, but catalogued other favorites as well: "Wine . . . is extensively used; so in the mild season is punch. Porter also is drunk by fashionable people; and in small quantities, ale." In the same period drinking glasses, tumblers, and wine glasses began to appear more often in estate inventories.[83]

Historian William J. Gilmore reports that New Englanders drank both West Indian and New England rum and spirits, as well as sherry, brandy, and Malaga wine. As these freely imbibing descendants of the Puritans perhaps knew, brimstone was not only a preacher's metaphor for hell but also a preservative used in wine-making. The global reach of trade and the inroads made by luxury were probably experienced by most people most often through the imported wines and spirits they bought. Even in New England's smallest towns and villages, an array of strong drink from distant climes was for sale. Gilmore, describing the "commodities from around the world" that by 1810 filled general stores in Vermont and New Hampshire, includes wine from Teneriff, gin from Holland, brandy from France, and rum from Jamaica. From the "gill" of wine in the stuffing for roast turkey, to the half pint of wine in the batter for "plumb" cake, to the wine and brandy combined in a custard, *American Cookery*'s recipes reflect the general high esteem in which alcohol in that period was held.[84]

The changing circumstances of farm life at the turn of the nineteenth century presented challenges, both practical and intellectual, not only for farm families themselves but also for Connecticut's learned elites and civic leaders, who sponsored and wrote the Town Reports. In the idealized version of the story, the Connecticut independent family farm, small but managed efficiently and actively engaged in trade through merchant middlemen, would produce a surplus of nature's best offerings and a measure of comfort and gentility for its inhabitants while avoiding the snares of luxury that plagued more sophisticated but also more socially stratified societies. Those who were behind the reports believed it was possible to achieve this balance for Connecticut. Indeed, they thought their agriculture-and-trade vision for society—what William C. Dowling calls the "notion of trade or commerce rendered innocent by its vital relation to agriculture and the life of the soil"—presented the best hope for the future of the new republic. From their perspective, the greatest reservoir of American cultural and economic capital was still to be found on—and could still be exported from—the farm.[85]

These Connecticut Federalists were convinced of a position more often identified with Thomas Jefferson's party—that the nation's future well-being depended on securing a central place for agriculture in the national economy and the national psyche. But their agricultural vision came with a commercial twist absent from the Jeffersonians' support of the yeoman farmer. So while the reports convey a greater interest in what Edward Cooke describes as "the processing of natural resources and agricultural products" than in "the application of technology or workmanship to transform the materials into household goods," they also place a high value on trade and "mechanical invention." They even acknowledge, grudgingly, the "growing

FIGURE 6.1. Engraving of Massachusetts Society for Promoting Agriculture medal, 1804, appearing as an illustration in *The Miscellaneous Works of David Humphreys* (New York, 1804), between 356 and 357. In both Connecticut and Massachusetts, Federalist gentlemen believed that the United States should continue as a primarily agrarian society.

—Courtesy, American Antiquarian Society

importance of manufacturing." But the Federalists' curiosity about these new endeavors was limited by their overriding belief in the enduring central-ity of the small producer.[86]

In essence, the reports express trust in agriculture's continuing prestige and primacy even as their writers witnessed the punishing level of commer-cial competition many farmers experienced, the outsized wealth accruing to large landowners and merchants, the loss of a younger generation to cheaper land on the frontier or to city jobs, and the emergence of mills and facto-ries. We can read in their resistance to change a hope that the new republic would be a place where "agriculture & commerce go hand in hand," as John Treadwell put it, though agriculture's hand would be on top.[87]

Why did sophisticated Federalist professionals, writers, and merchants insist on narrating the story of Connecticut as a story of the independent farm? The answer lies in a persistent irony. Notions about improving agricul-ture have tended to arise, as we have seen, from within the higher levels of society, the mercantile, political, and intellectual classes, not from the rustic life of the farm itself. In more recent times, an analogy can be found in the American environmental movement that began in the 1960s and 1970s, which was the brainchild of highly educated social activists rather than of rural populations living closest to the sites and species to be rescued. So it was from among the learned class—those who derived their inspiration from their libraries of classical literature as much as from their appreciation of and desire to retain the way of life of an agrarian society—that the "taming hand of husbandmen" found its greatest ally at the dawn of the Industrial Revolution.[88]

The search for direction led the Federalists back to Virgil and antiquity rather than forward to an uncertain, industrialized future. The centralizing narrative of the farm and its spiritual and material bounty was the most powerful imaginative force available to those Connecticut leaders who wished to influence the direction their new nation would take. It informed other Federalist literary productions as well, including a small, practical work on the subject of cooking.

PART III
American Cookery, by an
American Orphan

T he first edition of *American Cookery* reads like two books, and the second edition even more so. The whole of the first edition is only forty-seven pages, but the preface and an errata page (appended to later printings of this edition) are so distinctive in voice and different in subject matter from the rest of the book that they seem to constitute almost a separate work. As noted in an 1876 article in *Scribner's Monthly*, the preface (mostly about the disadvantages of orphanhood) is made "the means of conveying to . . . readers sentiments whose connection with cookery does not now seem very plain." With the second edition, the disjointedness between the frontmatter and the body of the text, far from being rectified, is extended and deepened. Yet again the author's personal saga, in this instance the grievance she expresses against the anonymous person allegedly responsible for errors in and unauthorized alterations to the first edition, is as memorable as it is distant from the substance of the book—its recipes.[1]

What comes across most distinctly in this front- and backmatter are feelings, rather incoherently expressed, of anxiety, resentment, anger, and perhaps a touch of paranoia. The author—Amelia Simmons—is convinced that the errors introduced by the unnamed amanuensis of the first edition were no mere accidents. They were made with the intention of hurting the sale of the book. Authors everywhere can feel her pain. But then, since she's making her complaint in the preface to a second edition, sales presumably had been at least respectable, if not good enough to mollify the author.

So here we have it: two opportunities to introduce her opus to the world, and to tell of her particular style of cooking in the new *American* mode, and Amelia Simmons opts instead to hold forth, first on the trials of female orphanhood and second on the harm done to her by an unfaithful assistant. Thus *American Cookery* walks onto the stage of history.

The tensions and contentions such as those that leak out of *American Cookery* via its front- and backmatter simmered just below the surface in many aspects of late eighteenth-century Connecticut life. For example, luxury purchases like the English cookbook imports, bought with the intention of ennobling dinner tables with genteel repasts, were beginning to weigh families down with the social obligations and financial burdens that accompanied rising status. Such a state of affairs is suggested in the 1797 *Greenleaf's New York Journal* advertisement for *American Cookery*. The ad pressures readers into believing that "the knowledge of HOUSEWIFERY and COOKERY is absolutely necessary to EVERY FEMALE," while acknowledging that "the foreign essays on Cookery come high charged." The dilemma is solved by *American Cookery*, where such necessary knowledge is "compressed into a small compass" and offered at a "cheap" price. But the deeper, and unresolved, dilemma is conveyed by the tone and manner of this and other injunctions to consumers to be ever on the lookout for ways to obtain such knowledge and skills.[2]

From the testimony of travelers to probate evidence of the steady increase in ownership of forks, fashionable furniture, and two-story housing, it appears that the highly positive view of Connecticut taken by its leaders was not without foundation. On the other hand, as we have seen, there were many ways in which Connecticut's suitability as a model for the nation was open to question. Open to question as well were the benefits of political independence to disenfranchised groups.

The forces contending within Connecticut society—agrarian versus commercial and nascent industrial interests, the established social hierarchy versus the lower orders—can be discerned throughout postrevolutionary America. With the national repository of knowledge still in the making, even a project as seemingly simple as the composition of a cookbook could involve complex and sometimes emotionally charged choices, which a closer look at the contents of *American Cookery* reveals.

In chapter 7, we consider in detail the ways in which *American Cookery*, through the nature of the cuisine it offers, was part of the Connecticut Federalist project of "laying the foundations of American greatness." By comparing the book with contemporary manuscript cookbooks from Connecticut and elsewhere, we assess the degree to which this cuisine was typical of its time and place. However, the sense of balance and unity of purpose conveyed through these dimensions of the work is greatly complicated by various features of the presentation arising from the author's social deficits as an ill-educated female cook.[3]

In chapter 8, we explore more fully the disjunction between *American Cookery*'s pleasing, even luxurious recipes and the uncomfortable personal and publishing circumstances of the individual presenting them. We weigh the evidence regarding the issue of whether Amelia Simmons was a real person or an invented persona, and we tease out the various rhetorical effects of an authorial self-portrait that consists of two compressed yet potent narratives, one about orphanhood, the other about betrayal and victimization at the hands of collaborators in the publication enterprise.

Chapter 9 is devoted to *American Cookery*'s post-1796 existence. First we profile two readers of *American Cookery* in the 1810s and 1820s. Then we examine the book's reprintings and piratings between 1798 and 1831, most of which were issued from the districts to the north and west in which Connecticut people were resettling during those years. We correlate *American Cookery*'s later incarnations with the measures taken by the Connecticut establishment to insure that the migration of Connecticut people into New Hampshire, Vermont, and New York State would also constitute an expansion of the Connecticut way of life into those areas. Thus did the imbibing of "every species of useful knowledge" that Timothy Dwight advocated in 1776 continue to be encouraged by the Connecticut Federalists for a considerable period after they had suffered decisive political defeat in 1800.[4]

CHAPTER 7

The Cookbook

Social historians Debra Friedman and Jack Larkin remark that the title of *American Cookery* "doubles as [a] table of contents": "American Cookery, or the Art of Dressing Viands, Fish, Poultry and Vegetables, and the Best Modes of Making Pastes, Puffs, Pies, Tarts, Puddings, Custards and Preserves and All Kinds of CAKES, from the Imperial Plumb to Plain Cake. Adapted to This Country, and All Grades of Life." Their statement is broadly true in terms of the major categories of dishes included in the book, though even in this respect several qualifications are required. In the first edition, for example, there is only one recipe for fish; in the second, there are no recipes for vegetables, unless we count the three for preserving them that have no section of their own. The misused term "Viands" makes sense as a table of contents item only if it means flesh meat. (In the second edition, another mistaken usage in the title, "Pastes, Puffs," is corrected to "Puff-Pastes," but the blunder with "Viands" is allowed to stand.)[1]

For neither edition is the title particularly accurate as a guide to the actual sequence in which the various types of foods are presented. Both begin with meat, followed by poultry rather than fish. In the first edition, the next major grouping is pies, first savory, then mince, then fruit. Inserted before the pies in the second edition are several fish recipes. After pies in the first edition come puddings, many of them to be baked in pie crusts, the recipes for which are given in the subsequent "Pastes" section. Next come custards and tarts. In the second edition, the order is reversed—first custards and tarts, then puddings and pastes. The remaining major categories are cakes and preserves, appearing in both editions in that order. The meaning of the changes in recipe order in the second edition is elusive, though it appears overall that systematization was the goal.

However, *American Cookery* is even less neatly structured than this summary might make it seem. In the first edition, additional meat recipes are found after those for poultry, and between these and the savory pies are placed two long, elaborate sets of instructions, "To dress a turtle" and "To

183

dress a Calve's Head. Turtle fashion." In the second edition, the arrangement is made somewhat more rational in that almost all the meat recipes
are moved in front of the poultry recipes. On the other hand, the early part
of this later edition suffers from its own disorders: one meat recipe is left to
be inserted after the turtle and the mock turtle, and recipes for meat-based
soups and boiled ham and poultry also intervene between the turtle duo
and the fish section. Arbitrarily placed between the fish and the pies are the
procedures "To keep green Peas till Christmas."

In the remainder of both editions, culinary categories are more often,
though not invariably, respected. Both give recipes for syllabubs (wine and
milk drinks) and creams just before launching into cakes. But in both editions, the final section on fruit preserves and fruit preservation also includes
recipes for pickles. In a further surprise, at the end of this fruit section,
the first edition fulfills the title's promise of information about the art of
dressing vegetables, with six recipes for boiling them. (In this edition the
Christmas peas are dropped, somewhat less haphazardly, into this group.) In
the second edition the boiled vegetables are eliminated.

The preserves section of the first edition is rendered distinctly startling
by the presence within it of recipes for "Alamode Beef" and "Dressing Codfish." In the second edition, these are removed into their respective categories toward the front of the book. On the other hand, the second edition's
idea of preserves is broad enough to encompass not only the first edition's
pickle recipes but also instructions for making bush beans and parsley last
a long time. Both editions conclude with two anomalous items, explaining
how to brew spruce beer and how to make "emptins," a type of yeast grown
from the lees of beer, ale, or wine casks.

In the second edition, ten first-edition recipes are omitted and thirty-six
new recipes are added. Forty-three of the recipes common to both editions
are altered. Some of the revisions are designed to clarify confusing aspects of
the recipes or to amplify aspects insufficiently explained. Among the recipes
that are revised, either in the ingredients used or in their amounts, most
are altered toward greater affordability and consequently toward diminished
culinary richness. In many cases, for example, the second edition calls for
milk where the first edition calls for cream. Or the second-edition version of
a pudding or cake will use less sugar or butter or fewer eggs.[2]

Another look at the subtitle reveals that the book is divided into two
parts: part 1 is "the Art of Dressing Viands, Fish, Poultry and Vegetables,"
while part 2 consists of "the Best Modes of Making Pastes, Puffs, Pies, Tarts,

Puddings, Custards and Preserves and All Kinds of CAKES, from the Imperial Plumb to Plain Cake." Except for the inclusion of various savory pies in part 2, this division corresponds to one that had emerged in French and English cuisine over the course of the seventeenth and eighteenth centuries between savory and sweet foods.

Three times as many of the words in the subtitle are devoted to sweet as to savory dishes, corresponding to the approximately 70 percent of the recipes within the book itself that are reasonably classified as sweet, leaving 30 percent or so as savory. The largest single type of food, justifying the highlighting of it in the subtitle with enlarged typeface, is cakes, with forty-eight recipes. The second largest is dressed meat, poultry, and fish, for which, taken together, there are thirty-eight recipes. The third largest, with twenty-nine recipes, is puddings.

How would one of the first readers of *American Cookery* have used the book? Our guess is that she would have made a mental division of the recipes into groups, but the groupings would not necessarily have been by food type. Instead, we think she would have categorized the recipes according to their levels of enrichment and degrees of refinement. Plain, everyday recipes would stand apart from those to be used to assert the family's prosperity, and both groups would be distinct from those used to display a higher level of elegance or to celebrate festive occasions.

The modestly prosperous housewife or the cook in a slightly more affluent household would have used the plain recipes when few ingredients were to hand, or when the family budget required them. Nothing in these dishes demands the exertions—or extra cash—needed to obtain exotic ingredients, and all can be accomplished in a relatively few simple steps. Among these recipes is stew pie: pieces of boiled veal shoulder are buttered, seasoned with salt and pepper, mixed with slices of salt pork, and layered with biscuit or biscuit dough in a pot; the pot is then covered and simmered inside a kettle full of water. If, as often happened in autumn, a young calf was culled from a family's herd, or its meat was sold in the market at a reasonable price, then this veal shoulder dish, made of an inexpensive cut of inexpensive meat (though meat nonetheless), could be produced with the addition of common ingredients like butter and salt pork and covered with a good but unexceptional dough.[3]

In this plain category the user of *American Cookery* would also place "A boiled Flour Pudding," a recipe included in both editions. This is as plain as Simmons's recipes get, calling for a quart of milk, nine eggs, nine "spoons" of flour, and a little salt, which is "put into a strong cloth" and boiled "one and a half hour." The batter is not sweetened, nor is sweet sauce suggested as an accompaniment. Neither butter nor flavoring livens up the dish. To modern tastes, there is little to recommend a plain batter of boiled flour, eggs, salt, and milk, solidified by boiling. But Simmons gives it her imprimatur. She is saying to the American housewife that here is a simple but substantial dish. It can be put together with little expense and requires only a pot of boiling water to cook it over the fire, perhaps while other components of the family meal are also simmering.[4]

When she wanted to participate more fully in the newfound sense of optimism and the new prosperity abroad in the land, the same housewife or cook would turn to the "prosperous" recipes in the book that call for more ingredients, some of them a bit costly, and more elaborate steps to prepare. If the ingredients were few and the preparation simple, those particular recipes would nevertheless be understood by all to connote domestic comfort and well-being.

The first recipe in the book in both editions, "To Roast Beef," is an obvious example of this second type of prosperous yet fairly simple recipe. Roast beef was by this time long-established in the eighteenth-century English Atlantic world as the core nourishment of Anglo-American people and the central culinary symbol of English and to a lesser extent colonial British American society. Examples of the more involved type of prosperous dish could be any of the three apple pies, in which the apples are enhanced by spices, sugar, citrus (usually lemon peel and juice), and (in two of the three) rosewater. All three of the pies are to be baked in the third of *American Cookery*'s nine rich "Puff Pastes for Tarts."[5]

When she reached even higher than she did with such displays of middling prosperity, whether for a special occasion or to impress diners at her table with her household's elegant manners and ways, the housewife or cook would choose one of the "festive" or "elegant" dishes. Such dishes require multiple ingredients, a fair share of them relatively expensive, and elaborate preparation techniques. For instance, on festive occasions, the cook might go to the trouble and expense of mixing a stuffing and inserting it into a cut of meat or a fowl before proceeding to give it a good, prosperous roasting. *American Cookery* has two recipes for stuffed turkey, one for stuffed goose, one for stuffed chicken, one for stuffed pig, and one each for stuffed legs of veal and pork. Its three recipes for beef alamode all require that a stuffing be placed in holes or incisions in the meat.[6]

On both sides of the Atlantic, a turtle feast always signaled luxury and a celebration of British maritime prowess. The notoriously elaborate recipe "To Dress a Turtle," which Simmons cribbed from Susannah Carter, covers two-and-a-half closely printed pages in the Albany edition and requires a large number of spices and herbs, "forcemeat balls made of veal," eggs, and generous doses of Madeira.[7]

On the sweet side of the savory-sweet divide, one of the elegant dishes is the lemon pudding. Some of the requisite steps in its preparation are complex and delicate: "Take two whole lemons, roll under your hand on the table till soft, taking care not to burst them." The recipe calls for grated lemon peel and lemon juice, "soft wheat bread," white wine, egg whites and egg yolks, and plenty of butter and sugar. This rich filling is to be placed in either the fanciest of the book's pie crusts, the "Royal Paste," or in one almost as fancy. The reader is advised to be as imaginative as she wishes, after the pudding is baked, in decorating it with "pieces of paste."[8]

By our reckoning, a little over 10 percent of the recipes in *American Cookery* belong in the plain category and a little under 30 percent in the festive or elegant category. This leaves the clear majority, about 60 percent, representing prosperity. The contents of this cookbook are thus consistent with the broader middling tendencies we have been discussing, both those seen in the eighteenth-century English cookbook tradition outlined in chapter 2 and those defining the rosy but not entirely well-founded perceptions of Connecticut society and culture entertained by its leaders as described in chapters 4, 5, and 6.[9]

Extremes of luxury and subsistence are implicitly addressed in the title page proclamation that the contents of the book are "Adapted to This Country, and All Grades of Life." However, the sociology suggested by Simmons's phrasing is less radical than Timothy Dwight's celebration of steady-habit Connecticut as a place where "one extended class embraces all, / All mingling, as the rainbow's beauty blends, / Unknown where every hue begins or ends." *American Cookery* promises something for all, within a hierarchy expressed as distinct "Grades of Life." But within each type of food the book gives the impression of an embrace of all, or almost all, classes.[10]

Thus, cakes do indeed run "from the Imperial Plumb," the "Rich," the "Queen's," the monumental and glitteringly dressed "Independence," the exquisite "soft . . . in little pans" and "light . . . in small cups"—all clearly genteel productions—down to tea cakes, "wiggs," cookies, gingerbreads, "plain cake," and "cheap seed cake," and further down to "Johny Cake," "Indian

Slapjack," and "Buck-wheat Cakes." Puddings include both simple flour and "cheap" rice puddings; midrange bread, cream almond, and carrot puddings; and rich concoctions such as quince pudding, Marlborough pudding (made with custard and apples), and the lemon pudding already described.[11]

The principle of appealing to all grades of life in the book operates on a more specific level as well. If a housewife had the wherewithal and so chose, she could make a fancy mince pie (using foot or tongue meat and wine). If she didn't have the wherewithal or simply chose otherwise, she could make a simpler one (with boiled beef and cider). The most notable examples of *American Cookery*'s inclusive approach are the recipes for Indian and "pumpkin" puddings. A housewife could make a boiled Indian pudding, with a salted and sweetened mixture of cornmeal and milk, or instead bake one that's enhanced with eggs, butter, molasses, and "spice sufficient." Alternately, she could go all out and bake one that's filled with even more eggs, costly sugar instead of cheap molasses, and raisins. As for "pumpkin"— both involving crust and therefore in our terms pies—this is offered either in simpler form with molasses, no top crust, and any old bottom crust (this version is the original of our now-standard Thanksgiving pumpkin pie) or in a more elaborate version with sugar, a puff-paste bottom crust, and an equally sumptuous, ornamented puff-paste top crust.[12]

To recur to Timothy Dwight's language in *Greenfield Hill,* not only does *American Cookery* "embrace" what the book calls "all grades of life" in its recipe selections. It also, by its placement of recipes, encourages these "grades" to be "All mingling." The "cheap" rice pudding is not put at the very end of the sequence of six rice puddings. It is surrounded by richer, wine-, raisin-, and complex spicing-enhanced versions.[13]

Similarly with cakes. In the Albany edition, the first three cakes neither descend nor ascend. Rather, "Plain Cake" is put between the plum cake, which the title page had trumpeted as "Imperial," and "A Rich Cake." "Another Plain cake" pops up a few pages later between quite rich loaf cakes (the one immediately preceding it involves wine, rosewater, and brandy) and the festive "Election Cake." A couple of pages of culinary wealth and elegance intervene between the humble johnnycake and Indian slapjack and the recurrence of such rusticity in the form of the buckwheat and "Federal" pancakes.[14]

Both the practices and arrangements we have been describing—the embrace of "all" (or at least several) "grades of life" in recipe options and the "mingling" of diverse "grades of life" in recipe placement—are on view in the three recipes for "alamode" beef. These three items are *American Cookery*'s principal venture into the domain of English adaptations of French cuisine. As discussed in chapter 2, subtly seasoned and long-simmered meat, poultry, or vegetable stews became in the seventeenth and eighteenth centuries the hallmark of French cooking. Such dishes were widely copied, imitated, or simplified in virtually all eighteenth-century English cookbooks.[15]

Of *American Cookery*'s three alamodes, the most complex one uses a stuffing of pork, bread, butter, hard-boiled eggs, an array of herbs and spices, and wine. This mixture is placed inside holes cut in the beef, and the beef is then simmered in a watered wine. There is attention to presentation (and an extravagant use of twine) in the instruction that "if you wish to have the beef [in a condition to be served] round when done, put it into a cloth and bind it tight with 20 or 30 yards of twine." Another of the alamodes is somewhat plainer, simmered only in water, with salt pork substituting for butter and without hard-boiled eggs. But in this version, a stuffing made with beef rather than the less costly salt pork and a precise cooking technique that relies on steam ("3 pints hot water" to begin, and more added as needed) establish that this, too, is a dainty dish. In the third version, while wine is brought back as a component of the simmering liquid, the stuffing is pared down to seasoned salt pork.[16]

In the Hartford edition, the two simpler alamodes appear as the conclusion of a sequence of stuffed and either roasted or stewed poultry and meat dishes. They are followed by the dressed turtle. The more complex alamode is placed haphazardly near the very end of the book, in the section on preserves, pickles, and vegetables. In the Albany edition, the two simpler alamodes are moved closer to the beginning, immediately after the opening sequence of roasts, as if to say at the outset, "This book will supply you with the basics of well-bred, well-balanced English cooking—roasts and a limited, judicious sampling of the French influence." The more complex alamode is moved to a position just after the recipes for turtle and mock turtle made with "Calve's Head." Thus it rubs shoulders there with even more high-class fare. But it also "mingles" in this spot with its plebeian successor, a "beef's hock" soup in which the beef is boiled with rice, potatoes, carrots, and onions in water seasoned only with salt.[17]

In the English cookbooks that served as the principal sources for *American Cookery*, such as Hannah Glasse's *Art of Cookery Made Plain and Easy* and Susannah Carter's *Frugal Housewife*, the projection of class structure through discursive structure works somewhat differently. In these texts, there is no explicit acknowledgment of class and hierarchy on the title page, just as there are proportionately far fewer references in recipe titles to the relative expense and complexity, and therefore to the social position, of dishes. In Glasse's book, which contains many more recipes than either edition of *American Cookery*, only five recipes, the same number in absolute terms as in *American Cookery*, are labeled "plain" or "cheap," and with one of these the gesture toward the low end is negated: "*To make a fine* Plain Pudding." In Carter's *Frugal Housewife*, likewise filled with many more recipes than *American Cookery*, there are only three recipes so designated: "A Plain boiled Pudding," "A plain baked Pudding," and "A Poor Man's Pudding."[18]

Both Glasse and Carter do suggest an awareness of class issues in their overall titles. To claim to make "the art of cookery . . . plain and easy" is to offer a path of upward mobility within a hierarchy that need not be explicitly referred to because it was taken for granted. In a similar spirit, a "frugal housewife" would help her family to maximize resources and position within that same hierarchy. *American Cookery*, on the other hand, with its overt insistence on social positioning in book title, recipe titles, and recipe arrangement, reflects both the early national situation of an American social order under construction and the Federalist model of what that social order should look like: hierarchical, but moderately elastic, with the "grades of life" communicating and sharing freely with each other. That, at least, was the implicit promise of an "American" cuisine consisting of a potpourri of "all" types of dishes.

Along with categorizing the recipes according to their expense and complexity, the user of *American Cookery*'s first two editions would have become intimately aware of the ingredients and techniques within the recipes, as she planned and prepared meals for her household.

Nothing marks Simmons's cookbook more as a product of the eighteenth century, before industrialism brought cast iron cookstoves into middle-class American kitchens, than its first recipes. At the outset, the housewife finds succinct instructions for roasting meats—beef, mutton, veal, and lamb. In the book's opening declaration of Anglophone prosperity, "To Roast Beef," Simmons gives "general rules" for achieving the best results: have a "brisk hot fire"; place the beef on a spit or, in the first edition, hang with twine over the fire; baste with salt and water; and allow the age of the meat to determine the length of time it roasts. "Tender beef" requires less than the standard quarter of an hour per pound, while "old tough beef" requires more. Pricking the meat with a fork "will determine you whether done or not." And should the housewife be in doubt, Simmons assures her that "rare done" is healthiest and "the taste of the age."[19]

But perhaps the family had lamb on hand for dinner. Then the cook was to "lay down a clear good fire that will not want stirring or altering." Simmons's recipe for roast lamb is based on one of Susannah Carter's, but where Carter accompanies her roast with a "nice" salad, Simmons ups her game (in the Albany edition) with one that is "elegant." She also recommends dusting the meat with flour while it roasts, a touch not found in the Carter recipe. In both of these recipes, as in those for roast mutton and veal, the prosperous housewife or her cook found reliable methods for preparing main dishes that reflected the family's comfortable social position.[20]

Should the housewife (or cook) be preparing a more elaborate dinner, she might prefer to present as the centerpiece of the meal one of those beef "alamode" dishes, perhaps "To alamode a round." If she had a copy of the Hartford edition, she would be adding an onion to season the cooking liquid—a quart of "Claret wine" and a quart of water—then covering the cooking pot with dough to "stop tight," meaning to trap in the steam, and finishing the meat, once it has steamed for hours, with a topping of grated bread crust and a final browning before the fire. If the housewife had a copy of the Albany edition, preparations would be somewhat simpler: no onion in the cooking liquid (still a quart of claret but now three pints of water); no dough to seal in the cooking juices, just a recommendation to "cover close"; no top crust of grated bread; no final browning of the topping and beef before the fire.[21]

Despite a less complex method of preparation and simpler seasoning, perhaps the final product would be just as delicious, for fat pork (an unspecified amount in the Hartford edition; a half pound in the Albany) is present in both recipes, as are the herbs, sweet marjoram and thyme, and the spices, cloves and mace (only the nutmeg in the Hartford version is absent from the Albany one). Along with pepper, these herbs and spices season the fat pork that is stuffed into incisions in the beef the night before cooking. The claret, water, and bones on which the meat rests while cooking are all there in both recipes. And the cooking time in the Albany one, though reduced from the four hours in the original to three, is still long enough to produce a meltingly tender piece of beef.[22]

Simmons doesn't offer guidance about what size the piece of meat undergoing these preparations should be. But the preceding recipe in both editions, "To alamode a round of Beef," may offer a clue. Here the beef round, which should weigh fourteen to sixteen pounds, takes four to five hours to cook. So three to four hours cooking time might imply that the cut for the housewife's round of beef would be slightly smaller, twelve to fourteen pounds.[23]

On some occasions, a buttery chicken pie, full of six jointed chickens, bones and all, and covered top and bottom with a thick crust before baking ("A Paste for Sweet Meats," no. 8), might take the place of roast beef, and a stuffed turkey might replace the alamode beef. There are many options, from plain to fancy, for dressed meat, poultry, and fish in *American Cookery*. Which one to choose would simply depend on the family's circumstances and the occasion.[24]

Between May and November, when striped bass was found in the coastal waters of New England, a well-to-do housewife of the late eighteenth century might have served Simmons's "To dress a Bass," a lovely baked dish of highly seasoned and stuffed fish. But she would only be aware of the dish if she possessed the Albany edition of *American Cookery*; it doesn't appear in the Hartford edition. With either the Hartford or the Albany volume in hand, she might decide to dress her everyday salt cod according to Simmons's methods, by washing it in cold water, putting it to soak in scalding water in a pot hung by the fire for six hours, removing it to clean warm water again, and scalding a final time for an hour. With neither seasoning, sauce, nor stuffing, this very plain codfish would be unlikely to appear on the table when the housewife was entertaining.[25]

For the family wishing to express its aspirations to refinement at the dinner table, most of *American Cookery*'s many puddings—rice, apple, bread, carrot, "potatoe"—with their generous quantities of eggs, butter, milk, or cream, would fill the bill. When baked in one of Simmons's lavish puff pastes they would become an even more fitting symbol of the household's prosperity. The well-designed recipe for Marlborough pudding, with its twelve spoons of stewed apples, wine, sugar, melted butter, and beaten egg, plus a little cream and spice, would perhaps have been too stylish for anything but a truly sophisticated display. Yet when the time was right it was there in the housewife's repertoire, courtesy of Amelia Simmons.[26]

A complex, carefully constructed, and precisely managed world of preparation lay behind every splendidly arrayed table of the eighteenth century. *American Cookery*'s many recipes for extending the life of fruits and vegetables—for preserving quinces, strawberries, cherries, "plumbs," currants, and mulberries; drying peaches and apples; pickling melons, barberries, and cucumbers; and keeping green peas until Christmas—reflect these realities. The cook or housewife who had filled her snuff bottles with boiled damsons (they would keep twelve months if the bottles had been stoppered tight), had put up her raspberry preserves in glasses, or had doled out her fine, clear currant jelly in china cups covered with brandy-soaked papers, essentially had an arsenal of gentility in her cold room. She need only repair to her pantry to put on polite airs when circumstances demanded.[27]

There is no one food, however, that more perfectly embodies *American Cookery's* culinary culture than cake. In variety and number, Simmons's cakes express the range of intentions that make up her collection of recipes. A republican spirit is conveyed with johnnycake, federal pancake, buckwheat cakes, and Indian slapjack. For "Johny Cake, or Hoe Cake," a pint of milk is scalded and put to three pints of Indian meal and half a pint of "flower." It is baked "before the fire," both a homely image and a precise direction for where to place the dough for baking. Simmons then gives an alternate method: the cornmeal is scalded with hot milk or wet with boiling water, then salt is added, as is molasses and shortening. This dough is worked "pretty stiff" with cold water and then baked before the fire.[28]

The Indian slapjacks consist of cornmeal, milk, eggs, a small amount of flour, and salt. The batter is baked on "gridles," fried in a dry pan, or baked in pans that have been greased with suet, lard, or butter. At the other extreme of complexity and luxury, "Queen's Cake" begins with half a pound of butter whipped to a cream, to which is added a pound of sugar, ten eggs, a glass of wine, half a gill of rosewater, and spices to taste. This is worked into a mere one and a quarter pounds of flour, then put into pans, covered with paper, and baked in a "quick" (hot) oven for "12 or 16 minutes." "Soft Gingerbread baked in pans" is another flour batter made rich with butter, sugar, and eggs, to which milk, rosewater, and ginger are added.[29]

Based in part on a recipe by E. Smith but modified to make it her own, Simmons's "Plumb Cake" (Hartford version) exemplifies the kind of recipe the book offered the striving housewife when she wanted to produce a showstopper. It calls for a pound each of expensive ingredients—currants, citron, candied orange peel, bleached almonds—adds these and spices (nutmeg, mace, cinnamon, salt) to six pounds of flour, twenty-one eggs, a quart of lively ale yeast, half a pint of wine, three pints of cream, and as many raisins as the cook would like to throw in. These directions produce a dense, fruit-packed, yeasted batter whose wine-and-cream flavoring, subtle spicing, and minimal sugar bake up into a fragrant, plummy, and wholly eighteenth-century cake.[30]

American Cookery's generous and varied offerings extend beyond cake to all sweet dishes. Puff paste appears in multiple forms, as do other pie crusts. There are pies, puddings, syllabubs, and creams galore. Currants, apples, lemons, pumpkins, oranges, raspberries, almonds, and gooseberries are all enlisted to sweet ends. The resolute and pennywise housewife who purchased Simmons's paperbound book from a bookseller in New York, Massachusetts, or Connecticut, or from a peddler in Vermont, upstate New York, New Hampshire, Maine, or Ohio, was not misled by the cheap binding, low price, and obscure author of the cookbook she brought home. When she cracked open *American Cookery*, she knew she had in her possession a guide to the better life that was the promise of a new country.

Considering what is left out of *American Cookery*, along with what is put into it, gives us a sharpened sense of the social positioning and cultural impact at which the work aims. For a small example, let's turn one final time to those alamodes and compare the book's most elaborate alamode, "Alamode Beef," with the alamode in Elizabeth Raffald's *Experienced English Housekeeper* of 1769. Raffald's "To à-la-mode Beef," simple in an English context, even simpler in a French one, is complex compared to the version in *American Cookery*. In the American recipe, the marrow Raffald calls for is omitted from the stuffing. Gravy is also absent, whereas Raffald adds pickled morels (quite fancy mushrooms) to her gravy. Raffald also, as her alamode is being served, encircles it with forcemeat balls. Forcemeat is found only twice in *American Cookery*, most prominently when the book strives for its highest level of elaboration and sophistication, in the dressed turtle and imitation turtle recipes.[31]

More broadly, *American Cookery* takes much, both outright plagiarized and adapted, from its primary English source, Carter's *Frugal Housewife*. What it does *not* take is the most Frenchified aspects of this work. There is nothing from Carter's sections on the French-derived hashes, fricassees, and ragouts, all of which gained acceptance in England even among relatively no-nonsense, mildly Francophobe upper-class types. Nor does *American Cookery* select at all from among those of Carter's pies that incorporate truffles, artichoke bottoms, morels, and other extras suggestive of the French style.[32]

In England, French cooking in unadulterated form was associated with the stratospheric reaches of the aristocracy. It was thought to be patrician through and through. By keeping to an absolute minimum even the most simplified versions of French cooking, *American Cookery* is silently repeating what Timothy Dwight stridently proclaims in *Greenfield Hill,* that such thoroughgoing social stratification was not to be permitted on these shores.[33]

What else doesn't find a place in *American Cookery?* The most revealing of the other omissions are found at the other end of the scale. There are no simple dishes of boiled meats and root vegetables such as novelists Lydia Sigourney and Harriet Beecher Stowe represented as the staple fare of the lower orders at this time. Boiled ham and boiled poultry served with root vegetables do make appearances in *American Cookery*'s Albany edition, as do boiled vegetables in the Hartford edition. But in all these instances care is taken to avoid crudeness. The ham is "a sweet repast," boiled turkey can be made with "forced meat in his craw," the turnips served with the boiled fowl are mashed and joined by stewed oysters, and the boiled vegetables are all, except for cabbage, such higher-order edible flora as French and broad beans, peas, and asparagus.[34]

Another interesting exclusion is "bean porridge" or pottage. This was the staple sustenance of New England commoners from the seventeenth century until it began to be superseded by boiled dinner. Even though it was by this time evolving into a more refined incarnation, as baked beans, it had not altogether escaped its associations with hardscrabble living, devoid of both culinary enhancements and table manners. From the vantage point of the middle of the nineteenth century, Seth Sprague of Duxbury, Massachusetts, remembered childhood breakfasts that consisted solely of bean porridge with bread crumbled into it: "My father and mother would eat out of one bason, myself and two sisters out of the other."[35]

The most intriguing of the omissions of this sort from *American Cookery* is that of cornmeal-based pottages and porridges. Like bean porridge, these evoked rural subsistence and the absence of amenities. The recollections of John Weeks of Salisbury, Vermont, regarding one type of cornmeal pottage, samp, are quite similar to those regarding bean porridge. Weeks had been "both a witness and a participator in the custom of setting the large six-quart dish in the centre of the table, while half a dozen or more children stood around it, each with a spoon, partaking of this homely but healthful repast of samp and milk."[36]

In 1834, the author of a history of three towns in Essex County, Massachusetts, listed cornmeal pottage along with bean porridge and boiled salt meat as constituting until quite recently the Spartan diet of the area:

"The suppers and breakfasts of our former inhabitants have been very much altered. For more than a century and a half, the most of them had pea and bean porridge, or broth, made of the liquor of boiled salt meat and pork, and mixed with meal, and sometimes hasty pudding and milk,—both morning and evening."[37]

It's the absence from *American Cookery* of hasty pudding, that most intrigues us. No doubt hasty pudding didn't make the cut for the same reason that boiled dinner and bean porridge didn't—too plebeian. But there may be something else involved as well.

Some relatively plebeian dishes are included in *American Cookery*, as we've seen. But almost invariably they make their appearances after having been somewhat elevated. The simpler of the pumpkin pudding/pies, itself not barebones, is ennobled by its association with a more genteel version of the same dish. The same procedure is used with the one kettle-cooked cornmeal dish found in *American Cookery*, boiled Indian pudding. It enters in company with two baked versions, one greatly enriched, and shares with them in the dignity conferred by the variant headings in the two editions—"nice" and "tasty."[38]

Other cornmeal foods more or less on a par with hasty pudding earn a place in *American Cookery* after they have been made more presentable. Because of the difficulty of growing wheat in the region, the everyday bread of colonial New England was made with cornmeal and rye and was called "Rye and Indian" (i.e., Indian corn). Rye and Indian turns up in the Albany edition as "Federal Pan Cake." Although not particularly enhanced (rye flour and cornmeal mixed with salt and milk and fried in lard; no eggs), the name- and shape-shifting practiced on rye and Indian in making it over into federal pancake disguises its denseness and heaviness and links it not to farm life and labor but rather to the new constitutional order wholeheartedly supported by both of *American Cookery*'s publishers. These maneuvers anticipate the colonial revival's more thoroughgoing and ingenious transformation, a century later, of this everyday loaf into highly sweetened, soda-leavened Boston brown bread.[39]

The one cornmeal item included in *American Cookery* without being cleaned up and/or placed in good company is johnnycake. Perhaps it was felt that nothing needed to be done to make it presentable. Benjamin Franklin might have been giving voice to emerging elite attitudes when in 1765, using phrasing and orthography quite close to that found in *American Cookery*, he stated that "johny or hoecake, hot from the fire, is better than a Yorkshire muffin."[40]

According to culinary historian C. Anne Wilson, hasty pudding was a dietary staple among the common people in the northern and western regions of Great Britain in the eighteenth century. It was as simple as simple could be—oatmeal salted and boiled in plain water until thick, eaten with milk, beer, butter, or molasses. As with *American Cookery*'s approach to a variety of cornmeal and other homespun dishes, British hasty pudding was found in British cookbooks mostly in enhanced form. There are such recipes in both of *American Cookery*'s two principal sources other than Susannah Carter, E. Smith's *Compleat Housewife* and Glasse's *Art of Cookery*. In two of the recipes found in Smith, one with a breadcrumb base, the other with wheat flour, the grain component is boiled in cream or milk rather than water. Other enrichments include eggs, sherry, orange-flower water, cinnamon, and sugar. As for Glasse's recipe, it first flavors the milk in which the wheat flour is to be boiled with laurel leaves and then, after the flavored milk and flour have boiled and thickened, stirs in butter, sugar, nutmeg, egg whites, and egg yolks.[41]

American Cookery makes a point of taking humble dishes, many made with cornmeal, and dignifying them. Two of *American Cookery*'s principal sources do exactly the same thing with hasty pudding. Yet hasty pudding is left out of *American Cookery*. The mystery appears to deepen when we recall that around this time a work was published in a New York magazine celebrating hasty pudding as the best of all the wonderful dishes made with cornmeal and as the quintessentially American food:

> My father lov'd thee thro' his length of days;
> For thee his fields were shaded o'er with maize;
> From thee what health, what vigor he possest,
> Ten sturdy freemen from his loins attest;
> Thy constellation rul'd my natal morn,
> And all my bones were made of Indian corn.
> Delicious grain! whatever form it take,
> To roast or boil, to smother or to bake,
> In every dish 'tis welcome still to me,
> But most, my Hasty-Pudding, most in thee.

These lines are from "The Hasty Pudding" by the onetime Connecticut Wit Joel Barlow. Although Barlow wrote the poem in France in 1793, it was first published in the January 1796 issue of the *New York Magazine*, four or five months before *American Cookery* was brought out by Barlow's own former publisher, Hudson & Goodwin of Hartford.[42]

In his study of the New England literary tradition, critic Lawrence Buell characterizes the poem as a "mini-mock-epic." However, no irony is to be detected in the passage just quoted. Nor is there much to be found in these lines:

> To mix the food by vicious rules of art,
> To kill the stomach and to sink the heart,
> To make mankind to social virtue sour,
> Cram o'er each dish, and be what they devour;
> For this the kitchen Muse first fram'd her book,
> Commanding sweat to stream from every cook;
> Children no more their antic gambols tri'd,
> And friends to physic wonder'd why they died.

Barlow upends the boastful titles and subtitles of such cookbooks as Glasse's *Art of Cookery*, Carter's *Frugal Housewife . . . Wherein the Art of Dressing All Sorts of Viands . . . Is Explained*, and (in advance) Simmons's *American Cookery; or, The Art of Dressing Viands*. The art purveyed in these productions of "the kitchen Muse" consisted, according to Barlow, of "vicious rules" that "kill the stomach" and "sink the heart."[43]

This passage versifies the sentiments expressed in the prose preface to the poem. "A simplicity in diet, whether it be considered with reference to the happiness of individuals or the prosperity of a nation, is of more consequence than we are apt to imagine," Barlow begins. His purpose in his "little piece" of verse is to "combat" certain "vicious habits" that had arisen in America due, perhaps, to "the interest which certain families may feel in vying with each other in sumptuous entertainments." Barlow is confident that "there are very few persons but what would always prefer a plain dish for themselves, and would prefer it likewise for their guests, if there were no risk of reputation in the case." Those in a position "to take the lead in forming the manners" of the fledgling United States should, as they model the "domestic virtues," be particularly concerned to set an example of cooking and eating simply and plainly.[44]

"The Hasty Pudding," composed in revolutionary France, published as the opposition in the United States between Hamiltonian Federalists and Jeffersonian Republicans was distinctly emerging, espouses hostility to all artistry in cooking, all sophistication in diet. *American Cookery*, and the Connecticut Federalist perspective that informed it, is grounded in a tempered and moderated artistry in cooking and a tempered and moderated sophistication in diet. We think it's likely that hasty pudding is by design absent

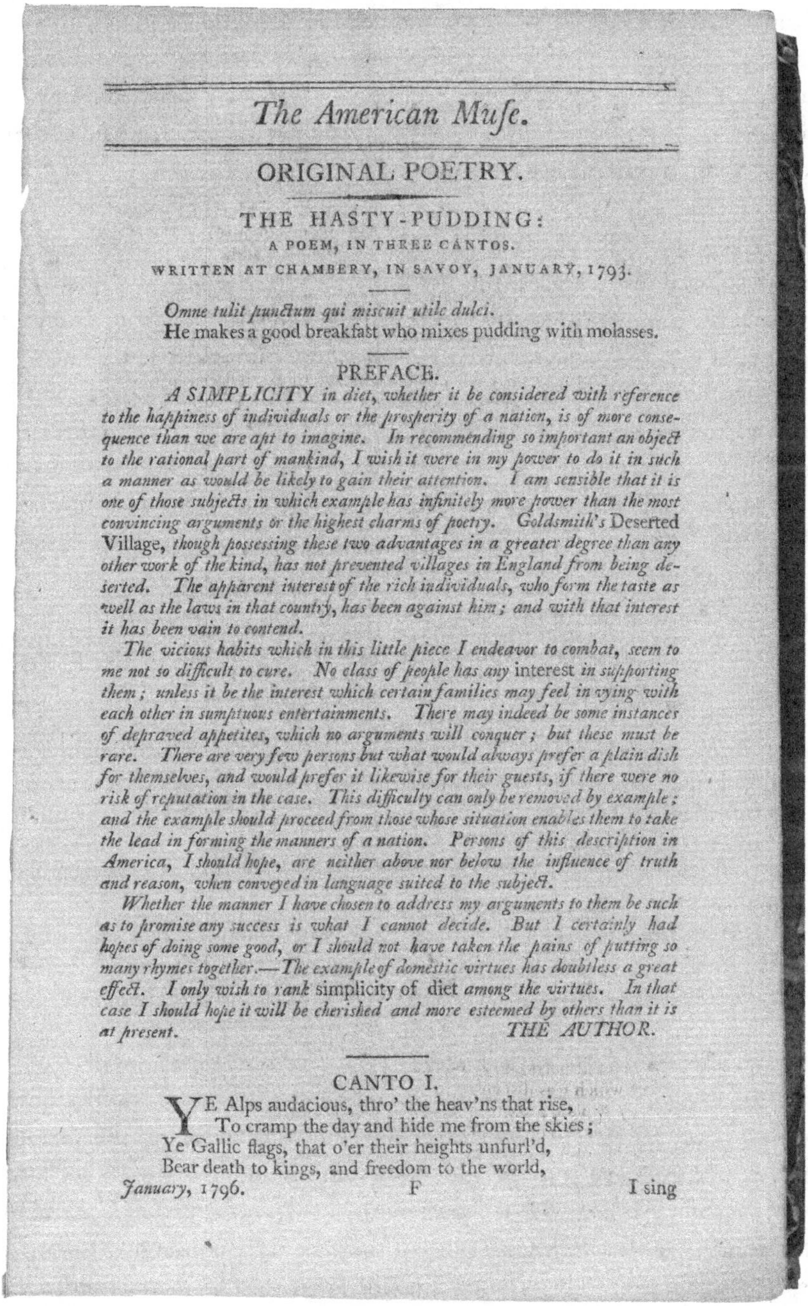

The American Muse.

ORIGINAL POETRY.

THE HASTY-PUDDING:
A POEM, IN THREE CANTOS.
WRITTEN AT CHAMBERY, IN SAVOY, JANUARY, 1793.

Omne tulit punctum qui miscuit utile dulci.
He makes a good breakfast who mixes pudding with molasses.

PREFACE.

A SIMPLICITY in diet, whether it be considered with reference to the happiness of individuals or the prosperity of a nation, is of more consequence than we are apt to imagine. In recommending so important an object to the rational part of mankind, I wish it were in my power to do it in such a manner as would be likely to gain their attention. I am sensible that it is one of those subjects in which example has infinitely more power than the most convincing arguments or the highest charms of poetry. Goldsmith's Deserted Village, though possessing these two advantages in a greater degree than any other work of the kind, has not prevented villages in England from being deserted. The apparent interest of the rich individuals, who form the taste as well as the laws in that country, has been against him; and with that interest it has been vain to contend.

The vicious habits which in this little piece I endeavor to combat, seem to me not so difficult to cure. No class of people has any interest in supporting them; unless it be the interest which certain families may feel in vying with each other in sumptuous entertainments. There may indeed be some instances of depraved appetites, which no arguments will conquer; but these must be rare. There are very few persons but what would always prefer a plain dish for themselves, and would prefer it likewise for their guests, if there were no risk of reputation in the case. This difficulty can only be removed by example: and the example should proceed from those whose situation enables them to take the lead in forming the manners of a nation. Persons of this description in America, I should hope, are neither above nor below the influence of truth and reason, when conveyed in language suited to the subject.

Whether the manner I have chosen to address my arguments to them be such as to promise any success is what I cannot decide. But I certainly had hopes of doing some good, or I should not have taken the pains of putting so many rhymes together.—The example of domestic virtues has doubtless a great effect. I only wish to rank simplicity of diet among the virtues. In that case I should hope it will be cherished and more esteemed by others than it is at present. THE AUTHOR.

CANTO I.

YE Alps audacious, thro' the heav'ns that rise,
To cramp the day and hide me from the skies;
Ye Gallic flags, that o'er their heights unfurl'd,
Bear death to kings, and freedom to the world,

January, 1796.   F   I sing

FIGURE 7.1. First page of Joel Barlow, "The Hasty Pudding," *New York Magazine*, January 1796, 41.

from *American Cookery*. With the publication of Barlow's poem, this dish came to represent an explicitly antirefined, aggressively plebeian outlook on cuisine. As such, it could have no place in a work that defined "American cookery" as part of an endeavor to integrate all grades of life, from plebeian to patrician, in middling well-being and harmony.[45]

There is ample evidence that *American Cookery*'s emphasis on a cuisine of middling well-being placed the book squarely in the New England main-stream. In 1774, John Adams wrote to his wife, Abigail, from Falmouth, Maine, about a "very genteel Dinner" to which he had been treated by a local gentleman, Richard Codman. The scene was socially tip-top, as Cod-man was possessed of "a large spacious, elegant House, Yard and Garden &c." Indeed, enthused Adams, he thought he had "got into the Palace of a Nobleman." The menu for this "very genteel Dinner" served in this facsim-ile of "the Palace of a Nobleman" included "Salt Fish and all its apparatus, roast Chickens, Bacon, Pees, as fine a Salad as ever was made, and a rich meat Pie—Tarts and Custards &c., good Wine and . . . good Punch."[46]

Several decades later, Timothy Dwight offered this description of "the food of the inhabitants" of New England "at large":

> At dinner, the vegetables . . . continually succeed each other in their vari-eties. Fruits also, which . . . are here very numerous and various, as well as very rich and luscious, are brought upon the dinner table. . . . Supper in most parts of the country . . . is made up partially of preserved fruits, different kinds of cake, pies, tarts, etc. The meats used at breakfast and supper are generally considered to be dainties.
>
> Puddings formed of rice, flour, maize, and sometimes of buckwheat very frequently constitute a part of the dinner. . . . Wine, which is here very cheap, is extensively used; so in the mild season is punch.[47]

Even after allowing for the passage of thirty or forty years as well as for the fact that Dwight is striving to make New England appear to prospective English readers in the most favorable light, what is most striking about this juxtaposi-tion of John Adams's "very genteel Dinner" and Timothy Dwight's account of New England everyday fare is the similarity between the two. It was not only in the pages of *American Cookery* that foodways were converging toward the middle, that fancy food was being simplified and plain food enhanced.

As noted earlier, the postrevolutionary Connecticut elite strove to comport themselves in a manner that would display both a cultivated ele-gance and an accessible simplicity. In having their portraits painted, for example, they insisted on integrating recognizably local details into their self-representations, such details sometimes injecting an element of rusticity into a milieu otherwise depicted as sumptuous and refined. Correspondingly, these leading citizens believed that they had constructed an independent freehold, village-centered social order in which those well below the highest levels were put in positions that allowed them to achieve "at least some degree of refinement."[48]

Furthermore, a parallel set of developments occurred in the English culinary tradition. From the middle decades of the eighteenth century onward, the gastronomical consensus among the English upper classes gravitated toward a less Francophile and courtly, a more native and "country" set of preferences. The cookbooks attracting the most readers supplemented dishes based on French sources with others believed to be of native origin. In many cases, such works also toned down the Gallic aura of the French-descended dishes they did include.[49]

Diaries of country clergymen toward the end of the eighteenth century reveal a food world in accord with these cookbook trends, one in which "hashes and fricassees [i.e., some French dishes] were acceptable" but in which the greatest pleasure was taken in "simple things, such as the first peas or strawberries of the season, and fine fruit to finish a meal." Such middle-class and sub-gentry English people were, culinary historian Gilly Lehmann states, made "uncomfortable" by "too great a display of sophistication."[50]

Connecticut's leaders likewise wished to avoid "too great a display of sophistication" in diet and cookery as well as in other areas. Their food-ways were similar in style to those of their English counterparts. In his diary account of his visit to his home turf in Windham County during the 1788 Thanksgiving season, Dr. Mason Fitch Cogswell reported being regaled in at least five wealthy households, including that of the governor of the state, with both turkey and pumpkin pie. The upper crust, so to speak, partook without reserve of foods that were understood to belong to the entire community.[51]

A story and obituary that appeared recently in the *New York Times* demonstrates the durability of this preference of the Connecticut well-fixed and well-bred for combining refinement with simplicity. Robert Hatfield Ellsworth was a dealer in Asian antiquities, legendary for his erudition as well as for his personal collections of such objects. His net worth at the time of his death in 2014 was more than $200 million. Ellsworth was a descendant of the Constitution framer and Hartford grandee Oliver Ellsworth.[52]

As we have seen, Oliver Ellsworth and his wife, Abigail, allowed, if not requested, the inclusion of a roughhewn rail fence among the details in the rendering of their mansion grounds in Ralph Earl's 1792 portrait of them. Just so, neither the wealth nor the exquisite taste in art of their descendant Robert Hatfield Ellsworth prevented this latter-day Ellsworth from dining for many decades, twice a day, four days a week, at an unassuming steak-house furnished with old-fashioned "channel-quilted vinyl" booths. The family-owned restaurant, Donohue's, is located on Lexington Avenue in New York City, not far from Ellsworth's twenty-two-room Fifth Avenue apartment, which was filled with priceless Asian art, European paintings, and antique English silver.

At Donohue's, Ellsworth dined on his "standing lunch order" of "grilled cheese and bacon with a side of coleslaw." For dinner, he had the house steak. Decades after other New York eateries, and indeed most American dining establishments, even quite modest ones, had discarded such plain fare in favor of trendier cuisine, this haunt of Ellsworth featured among its offerings "home-style $19.95 Yankee pot roast" and "$17.95 Maryland turkey with cranberry sauce." Restraint in food continued to appeal to New England descendants like Ellsworth, the determination to bring together luxury and modesty a not insubstantial part of their inheritance.

We see a corresponding picture of the inclinations, tastes, and (from this point of view) aspirations of people in eighteenth-century New England if we look from the bottom up rather than from the top down. Just as those in the upper reaches eschewed "too great a display of sophistication," so too did those farther down do what they could to live with "at least some degree of refinement." For example there is evidence that in the second quarter of the eighteenth century the proportion of average households possessing forks increased dramatically. This was, according to Gloria L. Main, part of a "gradual spread of a genteel or civilizing influence at the dining tables of ordinary farm folk."[53]

There is telling anecdotal evidence regarding the degree to which these endeavors toward refinement influenced the actual cooking and eating of ordinary New England farm folk. In rural Maine in the 1790s and early 1800s, the midwife Martha Ballard expressed pleasure concerning note-worthy meals of which she partook with both family and friends. In 1790, she enjoyed at a neighbor's house "what cherries and currants we wisht for and other handsome entertainment." In 1808, she dined with her son on

"Beautiful rice puding and Calvs head and harslett [organ meats]." As historian Laurel Thatcher Ulrich comments, "This was a rural feast."[54]

Lydia Sigourney portrayed some ordinary farm folk in the course of her 1824 novel *Sketch of Connecticut, Forty Years Since*, set in the 1780s. The people involved, "Farmer Larkin" and his family, are not even freeholders. They are tenants of the novel's main character, the benevolent "Madam L——." In the Larkins' "south-west room" are to be found a "buffet, or corner-cupboard" (displaying pewter plates, earthenware cups and saucers, and a tin teapot), a "chist o' draws," and a tea table, the surface of the latter displaying "a commendable lustre."

We meet the Larkins while they are at dinner, the first indication of which to the visiting Madam L— is "the clattering of knives and forks." The dinner, partaken at a table "covered with a coarse white cloth," consists of "boiled beef and pork, served up in a huge dish of glazed ware, of a form between platter and bowl. . . . A mass of very fine cabbage appeared in the same reservoir . . . flanked with parsnips and turnips." At the other end of the table sits "an enormous pudding of Indian meal, supported by its legitimate concomitants, a plate of butter, and jug of molasses." Dense enough to be served in slices, the pudding has doubtless been boiled rather than baked. There is also a "large loaf of brown bread," meaning the staple bread rye and Indian. For drink there are "brown mugs of cider."[55]

Boiled dinner, minimally enhanced Indian pudding, and bread without wheat—all represented as large and clumsy. Thus far the family board exhibits only the most minimal degree of refinement. However, when the Larkins discover at the conclusion of their repast the eminent personage who has favored them with a visit (Madam L— has been too polite to announce herself before her tenants have finished eating), they show, in a manner consistent with their possession and polishing of a tea table and their dining with knives and forks, that they are prepared to offer what the arbiters of culinary refinement would consider appropriate. The oldest daughter "produced with great rapidity a plate of *nut-cakes* and cheese, a basket of fine apples, and a glass of metheglin [mead]." Two of the younger children "ran to add a 'saacer of presarved barberries,' from the jar, which was filled with fruit gathered and prepared by their own hands, for a dessert on extraordinary occasions."[56]

The diet of typical Connecticut commoners is represented in the novel as consisting of plain preparations, the kinds of foods that would be found in the everyday category of dishes included in *American Cookery* or beneath it. Nevertheless, such people are also represented as participating in the range of culinary norms that *American Cookery* codifies. When necessary—for instance, when entertaining a visiting dignitary—they are able to set out on the spot a spread consisting of the dignified fare with which *American Cookery* concludes. Just as Mason Fitch Cogswell and his associates stooped to conquer with *American Cookery*'s "pompkin," so the Farmer Larkin family ascends for the moment into the realm of cultured "entertainment" with *American Cookery*'s "CAKE" and "Preserves."

We haven't yet directly addressed the issue that has been central to every discussion of *American Cookery* since Mary Tolford Wilson revived interest in the work in 1957: the extent to which *American Cookery* is a book offering instruction in distinctively American cookery. We're now in a position to reframe this question. It is most fruitfully approached, we believe, not by looking at the *extent* to which, but rather at the *way* in which, *American Cookery* is a book of American cookery.

Wilson was certainly correct to emphasize the work's insistence on American terms and phrases such as molasses, emptins, slapjack, shortening, cookie, and slaw. Is the fine hand of Noah Webster to be detected here? Webster was established by this time as the leading advocate for the development of a distinctively American language. He was also the prize author of *American Cookery*'s first publisher, Hudson & Goodwin, and the cousin of the proprietors of its second publisher, Charles R. & George Webster. Maybe Webster was consulted on matters of diction, maybe not.[57]

Another aspect of *American Cookery*'s vocabulary is the use of it to suggest the overcoming of regional, ethnic, and sectarian divisions. This is surely part of the point of the most famous term on Wilson's list of Americanisms, cookie, derived from the Dutch term *koekje*. With the inclusion as well of a "Christmas" cookie, the ecclesiastical establishment of Puritan New England, traditionally hostile to this "popish" (if not pagan) holiday, extends a hand to Anglicans, a not insignificant minority in Connecticut and more important and influential the farther south one traveled. The cornmeal cake that was called johnnycake in New England was called hoe cake in Virginia. Merging these variant regional names into a single recipe title, "Johny Cake, or Hoe Cake," brings the two most powerful and prestigious parts of the new nation together in offering readers this most assertively American item in the entire book.[58]

What must be primarily addressed, however, is not the language in which

American Cookery is couched but rather the culinary content of the menu it puts forward. This menu is overwhelmingly English. Almost half the recipes are plagiarized or closely adapted from English cookbooks. About the same number are versions of dishes well-established as part of the tradition of English cooking. Even many of the remaining 20 percent or so of the recipes for which we could find no obvious English antecedent, such as stuffed and roasted goose or loaf cake, should also be viewed as essentially English in origin.

By the most generous reckoning, there are only about 20 recipes out of the 192 in the two editions of *American Cookery* that can reasonably be construed as "American," that is, as utilizing ingredients and/or procedures that were familiar on the American side of the Atlantic and unfamiliar on the English side. So, if the recipes that comprise *American Cookery* were presented in the form of a restaurant menu, the "English" and "In the English manner" columns would take up both of the menu's inside pages and over half of the back page, leaving the remainder of the space on the back for the "American" fare of this purportedly American establishment.[59]

The issue can be cast in a different light, however, if we focus on the particular sources on which *American Cookery* does and does not draw. The three bestselling cookbooks in eighteenth-century England were E. Smith's *Compleat Housewife,* Hannah Glasse's *Art of Cookery Made Plain and Easy,* and Elizabeth Raffald's *Experienced English Housekeeper. American Cookery* makes considerable use of the first two of these. It makes even more extensive use of a work that was itself heavily dependent on Smith and Glasse, Susannah Carter's *Frugal Housewife.* In contrast, there is but one instance where *American Cookery* definitely borrows from Raffald's *Experienced English Housekeeper.*[60]

Why Smith, Glasse, and (especially) Carter, and not Raffald? To begin with, the Carter book was frequently reprinted in America—in Boston in 1772, in New York in 1792, and in Philadelphia in 1796. In view of the belief among American printers at this time that by reprinting an English book, they were turning it into an American book, filling *American Cookery* with recipes taken from Carter (and from Smith and Glasse by way of Carter) might have been understood as filling it with American cookery.[61]

However, even if this line of thought were given credence, the result would only be to increase somewhat the numerical proportion of American dishes. The way in which *American Cookery* accomplishes the task of presenting American cooking remains unaddressed. A description of how the

English cookbooks that were important to *American Cookery* resemble and differ from each other brings us closer to the heart of the matter.

Smith and Glasse both show a profound ambivalence about one of the forms the consumer and refinement revolutions took in England. On the one hand, they denounce French food as extravagant and luxurious. On the other, they fill their books with French food. In the terms and categories that we have been using throughout this book, they shuttle back and forth between refinement and simplicity. By Elizabeth Raffald's time, however, the English had been struggling with this ambivalence long enough to have begun to work it out. *The Experienced English Housekeeper* projects not fretful indecision regarding simplicity and refinement but rather a calm, confident synthesis of them. As Raffald puts it, her purpose is "to join Oeconomy with Neatness and Elegance."[62]

In our view, *American Cookery* avoids Raffald and turns instead to Smith and Glasse as transmitted through Carter because it is endeavoring to strike a balance between refinement and simplicity not in Raffald's English terms but rather in American terms, "adapted to this country." The Indian and pumpkin puddings, the broiled shad, the johnnycake, and the other American dishes that are strewn strategically throughout the book serve the same purpose as the clearly rendered Connecticut landscapes and interiors in Ralph Earl's portraits of Connecticut's leaders. They keep the work, with its strong element of English culinary refinement, from seeming to be putting on airs and thereby giving offense to emergent American egalitarianism. Keeping some distance from a well worked out English synthesis, such as Raffald's book offers, helps stabilize this early attempt at building a truly American cuisine, however slapdash that new construction might seem.[63]

The reading we have just completed finds a coherent social rationale in the book's culinary content. We have argued that the context in which the book was created warrants such a reading, and so we have presented many aspects of that context—the expansion of Anglo-American cookbook publishing, the culture of print in New England, the social structure of early national Connecticut, the evolving American codes of refinement and egalitarianism, and the practices and attitudes relating to agriculture and trade in the region.

But an approach that stresses the cultural framework of the Connecticut Federalists may slight the nonconforming aspects of the text, the tones and elements that resist this interpretation, that are discordant, that provide evidence of pressures which may be about to erupt from below the Federalist mean. A stratified society, even if it particularly prizes those in the middle, may seem, to someone below the first rung of the ladder, such as a woman, a servant, and an orphan, not an invitation to equilibrium but rather a sentence of exclusion. Is there evidence that these sentiments as well color the text?

There is of course the issue of the parts of the book that frame the recipes—the errata page, with its declarations of the author's educational deficiencies and the transcriber's misdeeds, and the two prefaces with their contradictory, emotionally volatile, and sometimes inscrutable passages. This front- and backmatter, far from advancing the purposes of the text, shrink the culinary main section, making it seem less a book than a book-within-a-book.

But even apart from this extra-culinary material, considered more fully in the next chapter, there is the additional problem of the awkward organization of the recipes themselves, the casual breaching of food categories, with alamode beef and dressed codfish showing up amid pickled barberries, pickled cucumbers, boiled beans, and asparagus. Also, in places the prose style is virtually telegraphic, so that some recipes seem oddly truncated or rushed, more like the notes of a working cook than instructions to the novices the book proclaims its primary audience to be.

An example of this elliptical style is the recipe for "Pompkin. No. 2." It consists in its entirety of the following: "One quart of milk, 1 pint pompkin, 4 eggs, molasses, allspice and ginger in a crust, bake 1 hour." The sequence in which ingredients should be mixed and the quantities of molasses and spices are left to the cook's judgement.[64]

Another recipe, for "Biscuit," is similarly condensed: "One pound flour, one ounce butter, one egg, wet with milk and break while oven is heating, and in the same proportion." In the Albany edition, one ounce of butter is silently increased to two, which might well be an improvement in the final product. But the cryptic direction to "break . . . in the same proportion" while the oven is heating remains unexplained. We presume the author means that the biscuit dough should be "broken" into pieces of equal size, but a kitchen rookie might well be baffled.[65]

What accounts for this shorthand style? Consider the experience of the English cloth manufacturer Henry Wansey during a trip to the new nation in 1794. Wansey stayed at a Boston inn called the Bunch of Grapes, which catered to commercial travelers. Dinner was served to paying guests promptly at 2:00 p.m. "Five shillings currency" per day paid for this meal, along with "breakfast, tea, supper, and bed." The notable part of Wansey's dining experience was the speed with which his fellow boarders consumed their food and then departed: "In half an hour after the cloth was removed every person had quitted table, to go to their several occupations and employments, . . . for the Americans know the value of time too well to waste it at the table."[66]

These ambitious Americans would no more linger for postprandial chats than the author of the recipes in *American Cookery* would bother to take the time to spell out her instructions for how to make pumpkin pie and biscuits. Speed—or, put judgmentally, haste—was so pronounced a feature of life in the new nation that in the course of the nineteenth century it would come to be a defining quality of the American character. We wrote a few paragraphs back that the sense of haste conveyed by many of the recipes was "virtually telegraphic." Although the telegraph itself would be one of the many inventions of nineteenth-century America, its hurried mode was anticipated at the end of the eighteenth century at both a Boston inn and in the pages of the first American cookbook.

This angle on *American Cookery* highlights those elements that do not exactly contradict but do not particularly further what we might call the book's first-level, Federalist agenda. In this view, the book's random organization, stylistic anomalies, contradictions, and discordances are foregrounded. What results is a perhaps less coherent statement of national culinary style alongside an unconscious but distinctive enactment of an emerging American individuality. There is yet another way to interpret the staccato and disjointed notes of the text. It involves seeing the work in mostly personal rather than ideological and cultural terms. Emphasizing *American Cookery* as the creation of an ill-educated yet highly ambitious orphaned female makes it predictably rather than intentionally disorganized, an intended cooking treatise whose tale/tail of woe has begun to wag the dog. In this approach, the cookbook is an amateur work by a semiliterate author, brought haphazardly before the public in the hope that its appealingly modest price and repackaging of mainly British favorites—together with its new "American" branding with a few dishes—would cause consumers to overlook its shortcomings. After a limited run, it fell into disuse—until resurrected by a much later generation in search of America's imaginative origins. Supporting this inexperienced-author reading is the book's heavy reliance on plagiarized material. In Britain, such inexpensive compilations of favorite recipes taken from more costly works often sold well.

While such commercial factors were doubtless involved, there are deeper sources for the discontinuities exhibited by *American Cookery*. Historian Karen A. Weyler describes the ways in which ordinary working people participated in print culture in the decades after the Revolution: "Even the minimally literate and the illiterate understood the potential for print to be life changing, and outsiders shrewdly employed strategies to assert themselves within collaborative dynamics." Weyler points out that while opportunities for writers increased after the Revolution, these chances for authorship were mostly open to "free, independent white men. Women, the poor, the illiterate, the unenfranchised, and the unfree still struggled to gain access to print."[67]

But sometimes "outsiders" did get into print, and when they did, the marks of their outsider status, of their inordinate struggle for achievement, and of the necessity they were under to resort to "collaborative dynamics" were likely to be discerned in textual and tonal anomalies such as those on display in *American Cookery*. Among these irregularities are the most forceful rhetorical aspects of the book, the ones that make it compelling to readers who no longer need instruction in late eighteenth-century genteel cooking, nor aspire to participate in the Federalist middle way.

The rhetorical fissures in the text that reveal a stew of anger, resentment, pride, and discomfiting servility also reveal an author's depth of culinary knowledge in her selection and recasting of classic British dishes, which she calculated to have commercial appeal, interspersed with American originals, which she knew to be both simple and delicious. The unintelligibility of a persona who seems incapable of staying in the background, even in a purportedly instructional cooking manual—a persona perhaps more accurately described as changeable than inscrutable, trundling between roles as a bereft orphan one moment and a confident professional the next—is now to be read not for any of these ever-changing identities but for her single public accomplishment, her *American Cookery*. Through it she speaks not only *to* Americans, whether impoverished young women, great ladies, Federalist social leaders, or later generations, but also in herself *as* an American.

This image of the successful female outsider author writing for an upwardly mobile American audience is an appealing one. But before concluding that such an emphasis, in conjunction with the Federalist cultural framework, points the way toward the fullest understanding of *American Cookery*, we offer one additional perspective, opened up by placing the book in the company of two manuscript cookbooks produced in the same region and around the same time.

As *American Cookery* has assumed greater prominence within the canon of founding era documents, its status as a "first" in national printing history has sometimes been conflated with the idea of its singularity as a collection of recipes exemplifying early national cuisine. On the contrary, the practice of collecting recipes into household manuscripts continued after the Revolution to be an important means of preserving favorite local dishes and disseminating the most popular local and printed recipes. Two manuscripts in particular, one dated 1789 and the other from the period 1813–21, confirm that the culinary content of our printed text, *American Cookery*, was not unique.

The 1789 manuscript is described in the Connecticut Historical Society catalogue as "a small, handwritten, hand sewn notebook containing 'useful receipts in modern cooking.' Includes puddings, biscuits, methods of preserving fruit, stewing oysters, and making bacon." The precise wording on the manuscript's cover is "Useful Receipts in Modern Cookery, 1789." The artful hand in which the title is written—even the fact that the collection is given a title—and the bold triple line underscoring the title at the bottom of the page seem designed to imitate the conventions of a printed title page. The same pseudo-print style is continued throughout the manuscript, with the collection's title, slightly truncated, repeated at the top of the first page of text, and with double lines used throughout to highlight recipe titles and separate one recipe from the next.[68]

Along with the foods mentioned in the catalogue entry, there are fifteen cake recipes, a large number considering the brevity of the manuscript. Some of the types and names of cakes and smaller baked goods are the same as those in *American Cookery*: loaf cake, pound cake, election cake, biscuits, and gingerbread, including the soft kind found in *American Cookery*. There is also a recipe for "Diet Bread," as in *American Cookery* a cakelike confection made of flour, sugar, and eggs but lacking butter or lard. (The "diet" designation meant that the dish was good for invalids or others following a "dietetic regimen" for health reasons, not that it was appropriate for weight loss.) The 1789 version is flavored with mace and rosewater, while in *American Cookery* the mace is replaced with cinnamon and coriander. In other words, there is little difference between the two. In addition to election cake, the manuscript includes another cake with a name that evokes national or regional pride, "Connecticut Cake."[69]

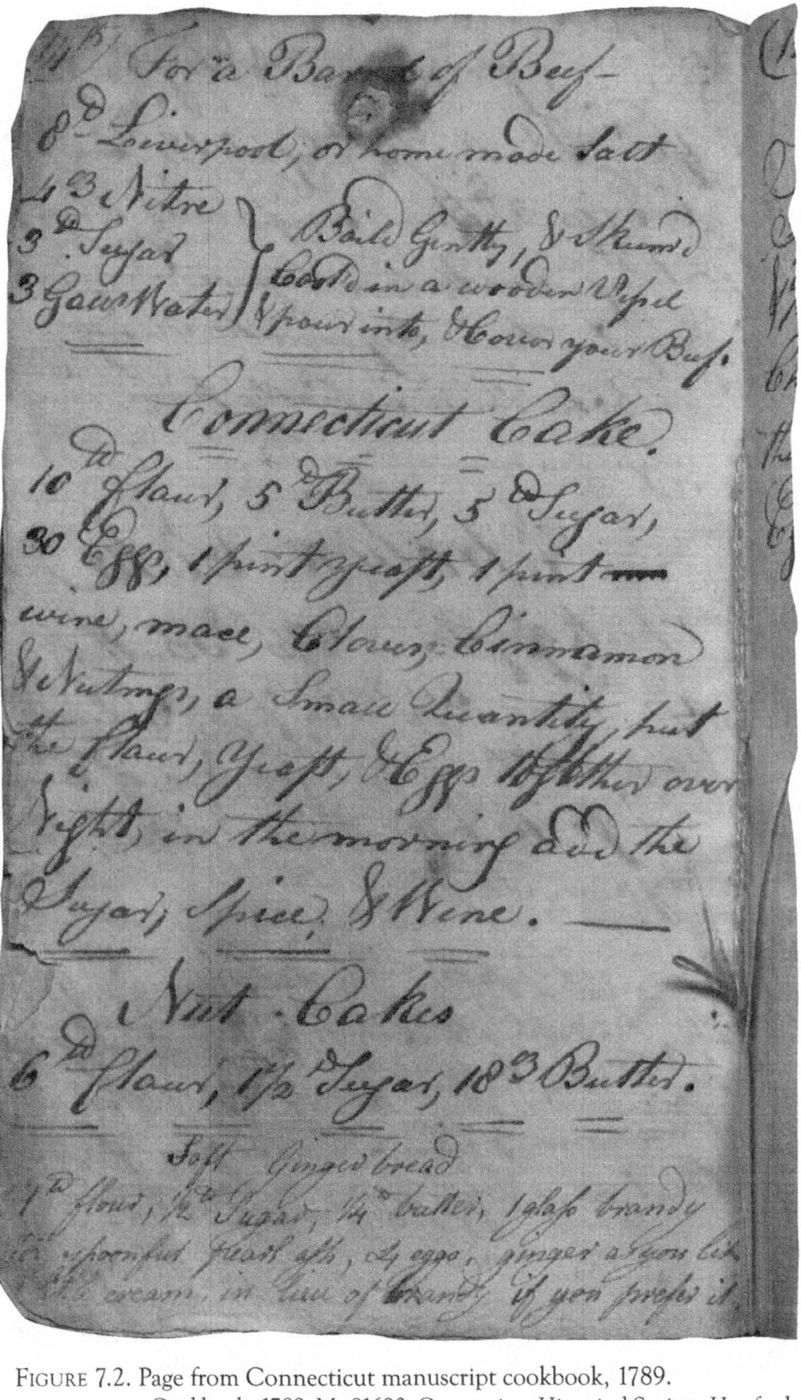
For a Barrel of Beef-
8 lb Liverpool, or home made salt
4 oz Nitre
3 lb Sugar
3 Gall Water } Boil Gently, & Skim'd Cool'd in a wooden Vessel & pour into, & Cover your Beef.

Connecticut Cake.
10 lb flour, 5 lb Butter, 5 lb Sugar, 30 Eggs, 1 pint yeast, 1 pint wine, mace, Cloves, Cinnamon & Nutmegs, a Small Quantity, put the flour, Yeast, & Eggs together over Night, in the morning add the Sugar, Spice, & Wine.

Nut Cakes
6 lb flour, 1½ lb Sugar, 18 oz Butter.

Soft Gingerbread
1 lb flour, ½ lb Sugar, ¼ lb butter, 1 glass brandy, 1 spoonful pearl ash, 4 eggs, ginger as you like, the cream, in lieu of brandy if you prefer it.

FIGURE 7.2. Page from Connecticut manuscript cookbook, 1789.
–Cookbook, 1789, Ms 81690, Connecticut Historical Society, Hartford

With twelve recipes in all, preserves, jellies, and pickles constitute another major food category in the 1789 manuscript. There are also several recipes for preserving or smoking meat. The manuscript includes two recipes for savory pie. Finishing the collection is one recipe for meat, one for fish, one for custard, one for pie crust, and one for that festive favorite, syllabub, which appears in *American Cookery* too, as it does in most eighteenth-century recipe books.

Although the second largest category in *American Cookery*—dressed meat, poultry, and fish—is underrepresented in the 1789 work, the similarity between the two works resumes with puddings, the third largest category in *American Cookery* and the second largest in the manuscript, with fourteen recipes. Indeed, the manuscript begins with this kind of food. In a beautiful hand, the first recipe in the collection is for "Rice Pudding." This is followed, on the same page, with recipes for "Biscuit Pudding" and "flour Pudding." The theme continues on the next two pages with recipes for boiled, lemon, Marlborough, and carrot pudding, followed by another rice pudding. Almost every one of these puddings is also included in *American Cookery*.

The pudding streak is broken by directions on how to preserve quinces (another standard of British cookbooks) and then by one of the savory pies, a "Chicken Pye," yet another dish similar in substance and identical in name to one in *American Cookery*. The interest in preserves does not end with quinces. Again, as in *American Cookery*, much space in this compact manuscript is devoted to preserving fruit, including peaches, cherries, barberries, and currants. In all, although much briefer than *American Cookery*, the 1789 collection resembles it in the preponderance of sweet over savory dishes, and in an emphasis on puddings, cakes, biscuits, and fruit preserves. It also resembles *American Cookery*'s approach to sprinkling vernacular recipes such as Indian pudding here and there throughout the collection.

Thirty-seven of the fifty-one recipes in the 1789 manuscript use titles that are similar to or the same as ones used in *American Cookery*. While the dishes themselves are not identical, so many are of the same type that we might suspect that the two works share common sources. In fact, the manuscript relies on many of the same British writers that Simmons would later use in 1796, primarily E. Smith, Hannah Glasse, and Susannah Carter, but also Sarah Harrison and others. For instance, the manuscript's "Boiled Pudding" is taken from E. Smith's *Compleat Housewife*, where it appears as "A good boiled Pudding." The manuscript's "Potatoe Pudding" appears to be an amalgamation of Hannah Glasse's three potato pudding recipes. The manuscript's "Jelly of Hartshorn" resembles two recipes in Sarah Harrison's *House-Keeper's Pocket-Book*. There is a similar, though longer, recipe for making hartshorn jelly in Glasse's *Art of Cookery*. The 1789 manuscript's "Whip Syllabub" shares similarities in ingredients and instructions with the Carter recipe of the same name, which Simmons copied. The "Genuine Whigs" recipe in the 1789 work makes half as many little cakes as the "Wiggs" in the second edition of *American Cookery* but is otherwise quite similar. Both recipes might well derive originally from Penelope Bradshaw's *The Family Jewel*.[70]

Looking at the two books side by side, one manuscript, the other print, reveals physical as well culinary likenesses. The famous printed work is a slight, cheaply bound recipe collection with an elegant title page. The obscure manuscript work is an equally slight recipe collection, this one hand-sewn and handwritten but with an equally elegant title page done up as best the "author" could in an accomplished hand.

Now to the second volume that amounts to an unpublished companion piece to *American Cookery*. This work, dating from 1813 to 1821, is most curiously bound within a cover made from a musical score for an 1800 Federalist campaign song, "Adams and Liberty." The manuscript's place of origin is specified in the Connecticut Historical Society catalogue record as Colchester, a small farming community southeast of Hartford. Although lacking the elegant script of the 1789 manuscript, this work's contents are also presented in a graceful hand. The Colchester manuscript has more recipes all told than the 1789 manuscript, and more per page as well, giving it a more workaday feel and also, in this respect, a greater similarity to *American Cookery*.[71]

Some of the recipes in the Colchester manuscript are identical to or closely modeled on recipes in *American Cookery*, as we show in detail in chapter 9. Beyond this, the number of dishes of the same type in the two works is striking. Like *American Cookery*, the manuscript contains recipes for "Quince Pudding," "Shrewsbury Cake," Minc'd Pie," "Plumb Cake," "Queens cake," "Loaf cake," "Whigs," "Beef Alamode," "Carrot Pudding," "Lemon Pudding," "A Trifle," "Ginger Bread," "Rice pudding," "Apple Pudding," "Indian pudding," "Potatoe pudding," "Rich cake," "Cookies," "Cup Cake," and "Soft Gingerbread." Both also have recipes for preserved strawberries, whipped syllabub, "Jumbles" ("Tumbles" in *American Cookery*), and the classic dressed meat dish "Calves Head," garnished with forcemeat

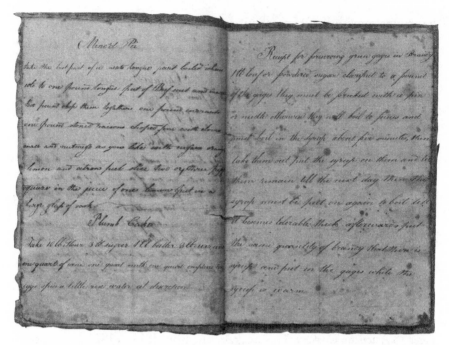

FIGURES 7.3–7.4. Facing pages from Connecticut manuscript cookbook, 1813–21.
—Cookbook, 1813–21, Ms 92208, Connecticut Historical Society, Hartford

balls, designated as "Turtle fashion" in *American Cookery* and "stewed" in the manuscript.

Simmons's "Marlborough Pudding" appears in her second edition. The dish in the Colchester manuscript is given as "Malbury pudding." Both the Simmons and Colchester versions, like the 1789 one, are variations on the traditional apple custard pudding used to fill a puff-paste shell. Traditional spice cakes also appear in both Simmons's work and the Colchester manuscript. Simmons's "Election Cake" from her second edition is absent from the Colchester manuscript, but the latter does include a similar if unfruited "Connecticut cake" (essentially a scaled-down version of the one in the 1789 manuscript), as well as a "Republican cake," also an unfruited spice cake. The massive eighteenth-century cakes made for colonial election days and known therefore as "Election" cakes were being replaced in the nineteenth century by smaller cakes, as in the Colchester example, but this standard item on Connecticut tables for election day and other celebrations went by either its old-fashioned appellation (Election) or equally evocative political names (Connecticut, Republican).

While Simmons's "Currant Jelly" is missing in the Colchester manuscript, there is a comparable "Grape Jelly." Simmons's recipe "For brewing Spruce Beer" is replaced by a Colchester recipe for "Ginger Beer." Where Simmons's two editions include recipes for "Plain Cake," the Colchester work reduces the name for the same kind of cake to the even plainer "Cake." Both works include directions for extracting "Emptins" from beer or wine casks.

In other words, the cuisine of the Colchester manuscript follows the contours of *American Cookery*, just as *American Cookery* follows the contours of the 1789 manuscript. Whether influencing each other or merely derived from the same sources, all three recipe collections present essentially the same foods, which are Anglo-American in origin, are rich though not overly elaborate, and emphasize sweets, especially cakes, puddings, and pies. They also offer many practical techniques for preserving and pickling delicate fruits, berries, and other harvest bounty, as well as tropical fruits like limes and mangoes that were gotten from maritime trade with the Caribbean and elsewhere. In all three as well, the particular combination of British specialties interspersed with local favorites like Indian pudding identify the time of their production as the late eighteenth and early nineteenth centuries and the place of their production as the region of New England.

So, from the whipped syllabub and election cake found in the 1789 manuscript cookbook and in similar recipes in *American Cookery* to the soft gingerbread in *American Cookery*, similar to one found in the Colchester manuscript of 1813–21, we see that the publication of *American Cookery* may have been a distinct achievement for a female American author, and part of a promotional plan by her Connecticut Federalist backers, but it was not, for all that, a singular production within Connecticut's contemporaneous culinary culture. Manuscript collections had been the principal source of printed English cookbooks since the seventeenth century, and they had been kept as well by colonial housewives. Indeed, in the colonies, the practice of keeping cooking manuscripts did not fall from fashion among wealthy colonial dames, as it had among the upper classes in Britain, by the late eighteenth century.

It should not surprise us to find such handmade works in dialogue with *American Cookery*. Of course, the particular manuscript cookbooks that *American Cookery* resembles were not put together by sixteenth-, seventeenth-, or eighteenth-century English aristocratic women, nor even by wealthy colonial merchants' wives like Anne Gibbons Gardiner. These Connecticut manuscripts signal in their form and content the genteel aspirations of middling and below middling Connecticut women. By the early national era, these women were collecting recipes that answered to their desire for a "modern" form of dining, one that included some local dishes based on native foods such as corn and cranberries, but that was mostly made up of standard British dishes for the prosperous set. The women who collected and cooked such recipes represented the "rising generation" to whom *American Cookery* was directed.

These Connecticut productions contrast with a more thoroughly refined style of manuscript created in more thoroughly sophisticated surround-ings, such as Boston, as is evident from surveying a manuscript cookbook compiled in 1801 by Ruth Haskins Emerson. She was the wife of William Emerson, the minister of Boston's prestigious First Church. In time, Ruth Emerson would bear eight children, among them a fourth son named Ralph Waldo. Her collection of "Receipts" is dated November 11, 1801. At the time, she had been married for five years and had born three children (one, William, that same year). The year before, she and her husband had buried their two-and-a-half-year-old daughter Phebe. Sadness and distress would dominate Mrs. Emerson's life in years to come—another child, John Clark, would die in 1807; a son, Bulkeley, would be born with a mental disability, also in 1807; and her husband would die prematurely in 1811, an event that would leave the family in a permanent state of anxiety about finances.[72]

But in 1801, the concerns of a decorous, well-to-do, metropolitan young wife were to the fore as she put together a domestic manual reflecting her tastes and interests. In its culinary aspects, the collection is composed mostly of old-fashioned British dishes (a minor irony considering that much later Ralph Waldo would disavow the imaginative creations of the Old World in favor of indigenous American productions). Ruth's choices reflect a pen-chant for prosperous, housewifely preparations in the British style, such as Hannah Glasse's "Calves Feet Jelly," and even for more high-class fare, such as "Beef Bouilli." Recipes for "Calves Head Turtle fashion" and "Plumb Cake" (in multiple versions) bespeak the demands placed on a prominent minister's wife to entertain in a suitably stylish fashion. Also included in the collection are a number of medicinal and household preparations, such as those for cementing broken glass and chinaware, removing "Spots of grease on printed books," and making "Varnish for Mahogany Furniture."[73]

Ruth Haskins Emerson's manuscript conveys her interest in presenting a highly polished exhibition of domestic decorum, in part because she herself had grown up in such circumstances as the daughter of a wealthy Boston merchant but also because her husband's social success would require such a display. Although a few economical dishes, such as "Cyder Cake," are part of her repertoire, and although several of the cakes and puddings are similar to those found in the Connecticut manuscripts and *American Cookery*, the overall impression made by her manuscript is of a life lived in more fashionable and comfortable circumstances than those of the Connecticut housewives. To anyone reading the Emerson Boston manuscript in conjunction with the manuscript and print cookery of Connecticut origins, the most striking contrast between the two places is the absence from the Emerson compilation of the "American" dimension found in all the Connecticut material. Emerson, for instance, did not record a favorite recipe for Indian pudding or for cakes associated with republican values or customs.[74]

So it is the Connecticut manuscripts, whose compilers were no less ardent in their desire for social advancement if considerably less well-connected, that are in direct dialogue with *American Cookery*. What these Connecticut texts reveal is that the intended audience of Simmons's little book may also have been its source. Manuscript works such as these seeded the cuisine that became associated with Connecticut. Getting one of these manuscripts—or a work based on one of these manuscripts—into print, and proclaiming it *American*, would perhaps be a logical next step. Is that manuscript-to-print story the genesis of *American Cookery*?

First, the evidence *for* a manuscript source for *American Cookery*. As we have just seen, one point of great similarity is the array of foods in both the manuscripts and *American Cookery*—the dishes are remarkably alike, with sweet puddings, cakes, biscuits, fruit preserves, and prepared meats predominating. But there are other striking similarities too. The book's organization (or lack thereof), with various unrelated recipes seemingly interjected willy-nilly throughout the work, also resembles the manuscripts. Perhaps Simmons's best intentions to group similar foods together were defeated when she came across a new but unrelated recipe in a book on loan to her. Whatever the reason, as in the manuscripts, recipes are sometimes added haphazardly. Both *American Cookery* and the manuscripts also add random dishes at the end of the work. In the Albany edition, these appear in a font distinctly smaller than that used in the rest of the text, giving the same impression as in one of the manuscripts, where the last recipes are squeezed in using smaller writing.

Many of the manuscripts' recipes are presented in a shorthand style similar to that of many of the recipes in *American Cookery*. The printed work thus comes across like the manuscripts as the working document of a skilled and busy cook—in essence a cook's kitchen notebook. All three are in the same mode as dinner at an inn of the day. The accommodation of dining customs to the hurried schedule of the commercial travelers whom Englishman Henry Wansey encountered in Boston in 1794, and the accommodation of writing style to the needs of a busy kitchen, are examples of the partiality to productive work over custom and convention that would distinguish American from English manners.

There is another point suggesting that *American Cookery* is a manuscript cookbook brought to print, or is meant to appear so. Simmons writes that her transcriber was "entrusted with the receipts, to prepare them for publication." She also describes her book as "being an original work in this country," which can be seen as a way of saying that here is her own collection of recipes. Of course a great many of the recipes are not original but rather copied or adapted from Carter and others. But perhaps, as the recipes were copied or adapted from one cook to the next, Simmons no longer knew their original—and mostly British—sources.[75]

On the other hand, if, as we discuss in the next chapter, the author could read but not write, she could not have compiled the manuscript herself. *American Cookery* would then, in a strict sense, not be based on a manuscript cookbook, or at least not on one compiled by the author. Perhaps an important clue to what may have taken place is to be seen in Simmons's entrusting her transcriber "with the receipts." Plural. She gave this person a sheaf of recipes. She had not written down the recipes with her own hand, but nevertheless these were dishes for which she had collected recipes, had repeatedly cooked, and had thereby, in her own eyes, made her own.

How did the sheaf of recipes come into existence in the first place? Perhaps Simmons's mistress or other servants in the household functioned as transcribers at an earlier stage in the process, copying some of the recipes out for her from the English cookbooks she was using. For dishes that were adapted from these sources or were Simmons's own more or less original creations, these copyists may have taken down the recipes from the semiliterate cook's oral dictation. It thus seems probable that if *American Cookery* was created from a manuscript cookbook, it was created from one requiring collaborative compilation. Such a set of circumstances—loose sheets of paper, many hands involved in their production—was likely to result in errors and misunderstandings. It's time to scrutinize more closely the authorship and publication of *American Cookery*.

CHAPTER 8

The Author and the Printers

W ho was Amelia Simmons—this "American Orphan" who memo-
rably obtrudes her vulnerabilities and, in the second edition of
American Cookery, her grievances into the reader's consciousness
before she has offered even a single word of culinary instruction? Before we
can consider this question with any profit, we must first consider a prior
question: was *American Cookery* written by Amelia Simmons? Scholars Mary
Tolford Wilson and Karen Hess both acknowledged that "little is known of
Amelia Simmons" beyond the title page proclamation of her status as "an
American Orphan." Both nevertheless assumed that the book was written
by a real person so named, and both went on to draw such inferences about
that person's character and history as seemed reasonable from whatever
might be gleaned from the prefaces and main texts of the two editions.
Wilson emphasized the prefatory mention of the author's limited education
and stated, on the basis that the book was published "For the Author" at a
low price, that Amelia Simmons must have been "a down-to-earth person,
shrewd and practical."[1]

From a comment in the first-edition preface about female orphans "going
into families in the line of domestics," Hess proposed that Simmons may
have been "unmarried and had to earn her living, most likely as a servant
cook in a fairly ordinary household." More speculatively, she suggested that
the publication of the second edition in Albany, the publication of several
later editions in that same area, and "the presence in her work of a number
of Dutch words" all point to the probability that Simmons was a native not
of Connecticut but rather of the Hudson River Valley.[2]

But is it valid to assume that Amelia Simmons ever existed at all? Writing
in 1985, before Hess propounded her hypothesis regarding Simmons's
New York State origins, historians Christopher P. Bickford and Jeffrey H.
Kaimowitz stated that "if Amelia Simmons lived in Connecticut in 1796, she
has managed to elude all genealogical research." This raises the possibility
"that the name was a pseudonym."[3]

Such an idea is certainly as plausible as the faint traces of a life sketched by Wilson and Hess. *The Compleat Housewife,* the first English cookbook to receive an American imprint, was purportedly authored by an individual, "E. Smith," with a suspiciously generic surname and a first name that has never been definitively established, due to the same dearth of genealogical evidence as in the case of Simmons. The source of what is "known" of "Smith" is the same as for "Simmons," unsubstantiated statements made in the preface of the work allegedly written by her.[4]

Among cookbooks subsequent to *American Cookery,* the authorship of the *Complete Culinary Encyclopedia* (1832) is highly dubious. "Mrs. N. K. M. Lee" is as absent from the genealogical record as "Amelia Simmons." Her title page authorial representation resembles that of Simmons in that her name is augmented by a social or occupational status indicator. Where "Simmons" is identified as "an American Orphan," "Lee" is said to be "a Boston Housekeeper." No independent evidence of the presence in the world of a Mrs. N. K. M. Lee, whether a Boston housekeeper or a zookeeper, has ever turned up. Amelia Simmons could be similarly phantasmagorical.[5]

Here is one indisputable fact: Simeon Baldwin, clerk of the "District of Connecticut" of the federal judiciary, attested publicly that on April 28, 1796, someone going by the name of "Amelia Simmons" and presenting herself as a resident "of the said district" filed a copyright claim as the author of *American Cookery.* This evidence casts doubt on Hess's case for Simmons as a New Yorker. At the time of *American Cookery*'s first publication in Hartford, Simmons lived in Connecticut if she lived anywhere.[6]

This would be in keeping with the pattern noted by historians James N. Green and Robert A. Gross, that "most printers produced strictly for a local market." In smaller communities—anywhere besides Boston, New York, Philadelphia, or Baltimore—most of what printers published above and beyond such standard fare as almanacs was "written locally." Gross's description of much of the typical output of a small printer, "pamphlets written and financed by aspiring authors in the vicinity," suggests that the aspiring author of the pamphlet-like cookbook *American Cookery* lived in the vicinity of Hartford in the spring of 1796.[7]

Karen Hess might rejoin that Simmons could have moved to Connecticut from New York, then went back to her home region for the second edition of her work. After all, she had every reason to be dissatisfied with Hudson & Goodwin, her Hartford printers. They had allowed her transcriber to plant numerous errors in several recipes in the first edition and to insert there as well an entire unauthorized section on purchasing foodstuffs. However, such an argument would be rendered dubious by two factors. First, the Albany printer, Charles Webster, whom Simmons chose for her corrected and revised edition, had gotten his start in the printing trade alongside George Goodwin. If she were all that put out with Hudson & Goodwin, one would suppose that she would have chosen someone with no ties with that firm.

Second, many people were moving from Connecticut to New York at this time in search of increased opportunity and a better life. Simmons is just as likely to have been a Connecticut native participating in this wave of westward migration as she is to have been a New York native going back home. As for Hess's emphasis on the Dutch-derived terminology in *American Cookery*, this is better accounted for rhetorically than biographically: "slaw" and "cookies" are part of the work's somewhat token attempt to project an inclusively American cookery, embracing geographic, cultural, and religious diversity. Moreover, as noted in the previous chapter, the Dutch derivation of "cookie" had become attenuated by the time *American Cookery* was published, since this Anglicized form of the Dutch term *koekje* had been in use in British works since at least midcentury.[8]

Amelia Simmons was very likely a native of Connecticut, if she existed at all. Some may wish to use as an argument against her existence the idea that in 1790s America, a female orphan would have had great difficulty in becoming a published author, even of a cookbook. However, historian Karen A. Weyler's *Empowering Words* describes many instances of "outsider authorship in early America," including several that involved collaborative arrangements similar to the one Simmons implied she entered into with her transcriber.[9]

These facts and factors—that "Amelia Simmons" filed a copyright claim in the U.S. District Court in Hartford on April 28, 1796, and that a female orphan could have become a published author in early America—leave unaddressed the problem posed by Bickford and Kaimowitz in 1985: the absence of genealogical evidence. In the second decade of the twenty-first century, when the digital revolution has significantly enhanced the efficacy of genealogical research, such an absence is even more striking. Our search of genealogical databases and other online and print sources has produced no one by the name of Amelia Simmons who could have been the author of *American Cookery*.

We did find one intriguing item, however, in the *Connecticut Courant* itself—that is, in the newspaper owned and operated by the same firm that published *American Cookery*. In the issue of November 28, 1796, there appears the following: "DIED . . . at New-York, Miss Amelia Simons, late of Windham." This date is seven months after the copyright filing of the first edition of *American Cookery* and four weeks after the second edition was advertised in the *Albany Gazette*.[10]

For Amelia Simons of Windham, Connecticut, there is confirming genealogical evidence. She was born in Windham in 1769 to Gideon Simons and Ann (or Anna) Ginnings (or Jennings) Simons. Amelia was not an orphan, as the term is now understood, but her parents had divorced in 1789, due to Gideon Simons's desertion of his wife. Literary scholar Cheryl L. Nixon stresses the somewhat unstable meaning of "orphan" in the eighteenth century. It could mean a child who has lost both parents, but it could also mean "a child who has lost one parent." It might "even be applied to a child whose parents are living but have given the care of the child to another." Legally, it was the loss of the father that made a child an orphan.[11]

It's not out of the question that Amelia Simons, imperfectly educated, made her way in the world in the 1790s, while in her twenties, as a cook. Having turned her experience and skills toward compiling a cookbook, she might have stretched the meaning of "orphan" by having it refer to a young woman of nineteen or twenty deserted by her father, and she might well have felt free, given this circumstance, to take liberties with her surname by adding a second "m," without venturing into outright pseudonymity. She might have become persuaded, or might have been persuaded by someone who was encouraging her or with whom she was collaborating on the text, that turning Amelia Simons the child of desertion and divorce into "Amelia Simmons, An American Orphan" would be a good marketing strategy for the book she—or they—had determined to produce. When she "DIED . . . at New-York," was she in that region still to promote her work or to settle her publishing affairs, having overseen the release of the second edition in Albany?

That a real person named Amelia Simons wrote as Amelia Simmons remains conjectural. As a tantalizing possibility, it relates to a wider phenomenon of the time in British North America—that of anonymous and pseudonymous publication. The majority of articles and letters in the newspapers of the day were either unsigned or signed with transparently fictional names. It was a bogus "Farmer" who inveighed in the *Connecticut Courant* in 1788 against the ruinous effects on ordinary people of their lusting after refined ways of living. In another skirmish in the luxury wars in Boston in 1785, participants in the letters columns gave themselves such names as "Candidus."[12]

These examples both involve letters. Longer articles and essays were just as apt to draw a veil around authorship. Literary critic Michael Warner notes that Samuel Adams disguised his revolutionary writings behind "more than twenty-five pseudonyms," and other leaders remained similarly hidden. By making the case for rebellion either "anonymously or under false names," the Whigs sought to give the impression that, in Benjamin Franklin's words, "the discontents were really general . . . and not the fiction of a few demagogues."[13]

In 1784, Noah Webster published a series of articles in the *Courant* under the title "Policy of Connecticut." They appeared without his name attached to them. A bit later in the 1790s, Theodore Dwight and Richard Alsop, of the second generation of the Connecticut Wits, produced anonymous versified political satire, such as *The Political Green-House for the Year 1798*, published by Hudson & Goodwin and featuring a vitriolic attack on Joel Barlow.[14]

The women who wrote and published around this time were as apt to deploy pseudonyms as were male authors. In the early republic, upper-class female writers such as Judith Sergeant Murray and Sally Sayward Barrell Keating Wood published under such names as "Constantia," "The Gleaner," and "A Lady of Maine." In at least one instance, a woman played a key role in determining the norms of anonymous or pseudonymous publication. Clementina Rind, the editor of the Williamsburg *Virginia Gazette* in the 1770s, printed letters and articles in which the authors' identities were disguised but required that the authors reveal themselves to her, "so that she could verify the veracity of their submissions." She did not allow "anonymous attacks on named individuals."[15]

Ladylike pseudonyms such as those utilized by Murray and Wood were not the only types used. In many cases the social position of the purported author was left as vague as possible. During the Revolution, there were any number of publications similar to the 1780 broadsheet *The Sentiments of an American Woman*, in which the author was unnamed. The practice continued after the war, as in the 1787 pamphlet *Women Invited to War*, which was signed by "a Daughter of America." The war in question was to be waged against sin. Occasionally, women likely to be of more humble origins were projected as authors. In 1794, "an Aged School-Mistress, in the state of

Massachusetts" contributed her bit to the cause of true religion with *An Explanation of the Ten Commandments*.[16]

Easily the most noteworthy female pseudonym was one appearing much earlier than any of the above examples, in 1722 in Boston's *New-England Courant*. The paper ran a series of commentaries on such issues as the failure of Harvard to exemplify an ideal of "broad learning," the subjugation of women, and the liberty of the press. In fact written by sixteen-year-old Benjamin Franklin, younger brother and apprentice of the *Courant*'s printer and editor James Franklin, the pieces were presented as the work of a widow by the name of Silence Dogood.[17]

The prevalence in eighteenth-century discourse of writings that went unsigned or were attributed fictitiously had multiple sources. Due to prevailing gender prejudices, British cookbooks written by women were sometimes published anonymously. Alternatively, they were attributed to "A Lady." This particular pseudonym was a manifestation of the upper-class tradition in which publication to the world in general, in propria persona, was viewed as less desirable than the circulation of one's work semiprivately to a select audience of the knowing and sophisticated. Another form this tradition took was claiming that the primary source for a printed cookbook by a male author was a manuscript cookbook by an anonymous noblewoman. It was this tradition that Judith Sergeant Murray and other elite American women invoked and adapted when they "employed filters such as pseudonyms . . . between themselves and the reading public."[18]

But the preponderance of eighteenth-century American anonymous and pseudonymous writing was grounded in what Michael Warner has called "the republican ideology of print." According to this outlook, the concealment of the writer's personal identity was a sign that his or her discourse was not distorted by self-interest. Rather, it was put forward as a rational contribution to the public good. In refusing to print anonymous personal attacks, as opposed to anonymous discussions of issues and policies, Clementina Rind was adhering to this republican print ideology.[19]

Warner analyzes Franklin's Silence Dogood papers in detail, stressing the lack of status and connections of the supposed female persona. She has, in her words, "no Relation on Earth." Rather, demonstrating that hers is the voice of pure reason, Dogood states that she passed her younger days "with the best of company, *Books*." It is precisely the absence of position, power, and prestige that guarantees the validity and worth of Mistress Dogood's utterances.[20]

Examining the career of *M'Fingal* author John Trumbull, historian Christopher Grasso argues that it exemplified the way in which several models of discourse and authorship coincided in postrevolutionary Connecticut. In a pseudonymous column in the *Connecticut Courant*, Trumbull "worked to establish a civic forum in the local press," thereby promoting "the ideals of republican print." Also active in Connecticut at this time was "a conception of literary practice drawn from the sociable community of polite letters"—the genteel mode of semipublic, semiprivate sophistication mentioned above.[21]

Grasso describes two additional types of discourse and authorship in which John Trumbull was involved. One looked back to the past, the other ahead to the future. In *M'Fingal*, Trumbull portrayed the older world of "face-to-face communication" represented by the New England town meeting. But if the content of *M'Fingal* was retrospective, its existence as a published entity was exactly the opposite. It was printed by Hudson & Goodwin in 1782, at a time when there was no copyright protection for authors. The poem was therefore promptly reissued in pirated editions from which Trumbull never benefited. In response, Trumbull argued in the *Courant* for a copyright law. In so doing, he anticipated "the liberal public sphere" that has since become the dominant model, in which writing provides pleasure and/or instruction to individual readers and financial gain and cultural prestige to individual authors.[22]

So for anyone interested in writing and in having his or her writing appear in print, Hartford in the 1780s and 1790s was a world of what Grasso calls "overlapping and even concurrent possibilities." A writer might operate, as John Trumbull apparently did, in accordance with first one model, then another. But the options were such that a writer might instead choose to craft his or her own synthesis of self-presentation, combining elements of gentility, republicanism, and wave-of-the-future self-promotion.[23]

We do not know whether the author of *American Cookery* was some as yet undiscovered person named Amelia Simmons or perhaps was Amelia Simons of Windham, Connecticut. Or she could have been someone else altogether, such as Hannah Bunce Watson Hudson. In 1777 and 1778, after the death of her first husband, Ebenezer Watson, she edited the *Connecticut Courant*. In this role, she almost certainly did some writing, and she may well have continued to make contributions. Or maybe the author of *American Cookery* was George Goodwin, apprentice and then printer, impersonating a female of low social standing, as had his illustrious predecessor Ben Franklin. Whoever the author was, she was presented to the public in a certain way, one that did indeed weave together strands of republicanism, gentility, and individualized career construction.

In the preface to the Hartford edition, "Amelia Simmons" actually says nothing directly about herself. Rather, she talks of female orphans generically, and even that discussion is at first less than emphatic. It is all but buried in the convoluted opening sentence, which starts out by saying that the book is intended "for the improvement of the rising generation of *Females* in America," in other words, for the improvement of all American young women. Orphanhood is mentioned almost as if in passing, as one of any number of misfortunes that might befall such young women: "Many hints are suggested for the more general and universal knowledge of those females . . . who by the loss of their parents, or other unfortunate circumstances, are reduced to the necessity of going into families in the line of domestics, or taking refuge with their friends or relations." That the writer is herself an orphan the reader knows from her title-page identification as such, but a more explicit connection is not made in the first preface between the author's social status and her purpose in writing this book.[24]

In colonial America orphans who had lost both parents, and many of those who had lost only one, were usually placed with relatives or other families. Whether or not a formal apprenticeship agreement had been drawn up, orphans from the lower ranks would be expected to be part of the household labor force. In the case of boys, this usually meant work as a farmhand. For girls, it meant the manifold "inside" domestic tasks of the typical farm household. Of approximately 1,100 poor boys and girls apprenticed by the Boston Overseers of the Poor between 1734 and 1805, around 40 percent of the boys were "put out to learn husbandry," while girls "were apprenticed chiefly to serve as household maids." There is reason to believe that at least one-third of the children in this sample were orphans.[25]

So the statement in the Hartford edition preface about young females who had lost their parents, or had otherwise suffered deprivation, being required to go "into families in the line of domestics" is in accord with the social realities of the day. And evidence is available that the "more general and universal knowledge" such young females were expected to possess included knowledge of cooking. In midcentury England, the novelist Henry Fielding's brother John put forward a scheme for a "House of Refuge for Orphans and Other Deserted Girls." The girls were to be trained in such a way that "a supply of diligent and sober domestics" would be "provided for the public." Specifically, "a Number of Girls" were "daily to attend in the Kitchen," to be instructed "in the Knowledge of plain Cookery," such cookery being further specified as "dressing *Victuals, Brewing, Baking.*"[26]

At the time *American Cookery* was published, advertisements for "Maids" or "House-Maids" in Connecticut newspapers emphasized that applicants should "understand" or be "well acquainted" with "Cookery." Clearly, orphaned or not, the young women of the eighteenth-century Atlantic world who were apprenticed as maids were taught something about cooking.[27]

The second sentence of the Hartford edition preface addresses the condition of being an orphan more coherently: "The orphan, tho' left to the care of virtuous guardians, will find it essentially necessary to have an opinion and determination of her own." This seems to align *American Cookery*'s outlook on orphanhood with Cheryl Nixon's analysis of the major role played by the orphan figure in the eighteenth century's "emerging discourse of individualism." Nixon argues that in eighteenth-century English novels featuring orphans, as well as in many eighteenth-century English lawsuits involving orphans, the orphan is "a hyper-individual of sorts, defined by qualities that might characterize any individual but are made more dramatic by orphaning, such as the experience of loss or displacement, the need to overcome social barriers, and the re-creation of self and family. . . . The orphan, with no one else to turn to, emphasizes that . . . narrative and social construction must originate within the self."[28]

However, the writer of the *American Cookery* preface immediately retreats from any innovative implications the phrase "an opinion and determination of her own" might convey. For the remainder of the paragraph, what Nixon calls "self-invention" is ruled out of bounds. The only options presented are to "conform to the ruling taste of the age in cookery, dress, language, manners, &c.," and to adhere "to those rules and maxims which have stood the test of ages, and will forever establish the *female character*, a virtuous character." The author hastens to explain that she means by "having an opinion and determination" no more than adherence to those rules and maxims. Thus, individualized self-determination figures in neither aspect of the female orphan's life possibilities. She submits both to time-tested, quasi-eternal moral truths and also, in the less significant sphere of everyday self-presentation, to whatever "fashion" dictates.[29]

The constraints on the female orphan become a virtual straitjacket in the ensuing paragraph. Lacking "parents, or brothers, or riches, to defend . . . indiscretions," the "poor solitary orphan . . . must depend solely upon *character.*" Essentially, an orphaned young woman cannot make a single false move without risking utter ruin: "How immensely important, therefore, that every action, every word, every thought be regulated by the strictest purity, and that every movement meet the approbation of the good and wise."[30]

Having proclaimed as emphatically as possible her subordination to prevailing codes and customs, it is only fitting that our "American Orphan" should conclude her prefatory statement by registering her subordination to her social superiors as well, "the American Ladies" whose "candor" is now "solicitously entreated by the Authoress." As she does so, we're reminded that such overt social deference frames the entire preface. The syntactically governing phrase of the opening sentence had been that "the Lady of fashion and fortune will not be displeased" by a little book that will help orphans and others down on their luck learn "those things which are really essential to the perfecting them as good wives, and useful members of society."[31]

The talk of "the *female character,* a virtuous character"; of "indiscretions" on the part of young women; and of "the strictest purity" that an orphaned young woman must maintain might seem gratuitous in the preface to a cookbook, as *Scribner's Monthly* recognized in 1876. But it was not necessarily gratuitous in the preface to a cookbook by a self-proclaimed "American Orphan." It all clearly refers to the framework within which more high-ranking female orphans were viewed in the novels and court cases studied by Cheryl Nixon.[32]

As Nixon writes, "Because she lacks a protective family structure, the orphan heroine is open to sexual advances. The contradictory aspects of individualism . . . the need to engage in the sexual contract, the need to rebel, the need to preserve virtue—are heightened in the female orphan." The storylines of novels grounded in these conventions are replete with devious assaults on the chastity of the protagonist. In Elizabeth Inchbald's *A Simple Story* (1791), for example, the heroine "is kidnapped by . . . a suitor whom [she] has rejected and who, as a result 'laid the plan of an open violation of all right, all power, to bear away that prize by force, which no art was likely to procure.'"[33]

A Simple Story was widely advertised in New England and New York throughout the 1790s, in newspapers and in booksellers' and library catalogues, including Hudson & Goodwin's *Connecticut Courant,* the Webster brothers' *Albany Gazette* (at least twice), and catalogues of libraries in both Hartford and Albany. Of the thirty-six English novels or memoirs with orphan plots or narrative threads discussed by Nixon, at least nineteen were offered for sale or circulation in New England and New York in the latter part of the eighteenth century.[34]

An American version of a novel devoted to female orphanhood is *The Hapless Orphan*, by "an AMERICAN LADY," published in Boston in 1793. Advertised in New England and New York alongside *A Simple Story* and other English titles on Nixon's list, it concerns a high-born young woman named Caroline Francis who is orphaned as an infant, inherits a fortune, and then has her kindly guardian uncle and aunt die on her at just the wrong time: "By the death of my uncle and aunt, I was left . . . at an age most necessary to be protected, exposed to the attack of every seducer."[35]

As that sentence promises, *The Hapless Orphan* is constructed in strict accordance with the formulas governing the female orphanhood novel in the eighteenth century. Caroline becomes smitten with "a young gentleman," Clarimont, who makes it clear that he returns her affections. Unfortunately, however, he is already engaged to another young woman by the name of Eliza: "Friends and parental wishes have long since deprived me of the choice." A few days later, Clarimont, despondent over his realization that he and Caroline, his true love, can never be united, shoots himself to death, whereupon Caroline receives a letter from Eliza. She states in the correspondence that the night before Clarimont's suicide, she had found him wearing Caroline's "hated picture hanging around his neck. This memento of his baseness I tore from him: It is now in my possession, where it shall ever remain an indubitable evidence of your treachery and deceit; and you may be assured the vengeance of Eliza shall ever follow Caroline."[36]

The balance of the story, intermixed with various subplots, portrays poor Caroline's entrapment in the measures Eliza takes to implement this vow. Eliza concocts a series of elaborate schemes involving kidnapping and accusations of sexual impropriety. These maneuvers on the part of the orphaned heroine's implacable enemy lead eventually to Caroline's demise. She dies "with a broken heart," and Eliza has been the cause of it all: "Her artful and revengeful mind, has been continually creating some malignant design against [Caroline], in which she has finally been too successful."[37]

The setting of *The Hapless Orphan* is the middle states of the new American republic. The scene shifts among Philadelphia, New York City, and various places in New Jersey, Delaware, and Maryland. Clarimont, a student at Princeton, is from Virginia; another suitor of Caroline's is from Boston; and "the Western Country" is occasionally reported on offstage as the locale of wars with the Indians. But the main action takes place in the middle states.

American Cookery "by . . . an American Orphan" of 1796 exists in intriguing dialogue with *The Hapless Orphan* "by an AMERICAN LADY" of 1793. With orphan author "Amelia Simmons" articulating the highest standards of rectitude, with Simmons's aim of helping readers along the road to becoming "good wives, and useful members of society," and with her enlisting of "the American Ladies" in this good cause, *American Cookery* corrects the malignancy and melodrama of an America following the "Guide and Pattern" of Philadelphia, New Jersey, and Maryland—where things are never as they seem and disaster and ruin are ever poised to strike—with the sobriety and good order of an America following instead the guide and pattern of New England and in particular Connecticut.

But of course if the rhetorical frame of *American Cookery* is a Connecticut Federalist retort to Mid-Atlantic cultural norms, then the book as a whole begins to look like a calculated work and the persona of the emotionally volatile, inexperienced author starts to turn into a character mask constructed to obscure a practiced authorial hand that is not only literate (a transcriber) but also literary (a concealed creator).

So we must ask if the fractures in the text highlighted in the last chapter are the naive responses they purport to be or carefully devised melodrama? Then again, might they not be both? Perhaps what we are seeing is the result of an uneven collaboration between powerful and established Federalist printers and transcribers, who were accustomed to controlling the texts they produced, and an almost, but not quite, powerless social interloper—a female orphan cook, who was in possession of the culinary skill her collaborators lacked. Vectors for social advancement, such as publishing, that the revolutionary upheaval had opened up were not yet smooth flight paths for outsiders, but neither were they so easily controlled as they once had been by a privileged minority.[38]

As Mary Tolford Wilson noted, there came to be two different printings of the first, or Hartford, edition of *American Cookery*. At the back of the second printing was appended an "Advertisement" on "a sheet of obviously dissimilar paper." The advertisement consists of a list of errata correcting cooking times and amounts of ingredients, preceded by the following: "The author of the American Cookery, not having an education sufficient to prepare the work for the press, the person that was employed by her, and entrusted with the receipts, to prepare them for publication, (with a design to impose on her, and injure the sale of the book) did omit several articles very essential in some of the receipts, and placed others in their stead, which were very injurious to them, without her consent—which was unknown to her, till after publication."[39]

A few months later, in the preface to the second, or Albany, edition, inserted between the reprinted preface to the Hartford edition and the main text, the complaints against Simmons's collaborator are both toned down and intensified. The first edition is described as full of "egregious blunders, and inaccuracies." These "were occasioned either by the ignorance, or evil intention of the transcriber for the press." So this person did not necessarily act by "design" or "evil intention." It might have only been due to "ignorance."[40]

Thus far the transcriber is treated more gently. On the other hand, there is now a new complaint added to that of botching or tampering with the recipes. "Nearly the whole of 17 pages in the first edition" was devoted to advice on shopping for foodstuffs. This is "a matter, with which the Authoress does not pretend to be acquainted, much less to give directions to others." Indeed, "the Authoress" does not think that shopping is in "any way connected . . . with that branch" of household operations "which she has undertaken," namely cooking. The marketing section of the first edition was inserted "by the transcriber, without her [the author's] knowledge or consent; and may with propriety be considered as an affront upon the good sense of all classes of citizens." Such citizens know from "long experience . . . how to distinguish between good and bad, as to every article brought into market."[41]

How does her reproof of the transcriber modify Simmons's self-representation in the first version of the Hartford edition as a deferential, determinedly virtuous, orphaned young woman? Before this question is pursued, it is worth noting that there were other instances from this period of public disagreement between an author and his or her collaborator in the writing and printing process. We learn from Weyler that in 1785, a free African American named John Marrant "orally delivered" to a London evangelical audience a narrative of his conversion to Christianity and his captivity among the South Carolina Cherokee. Two members of his audience each "rushed into print a version of this narrative," one in prose and one in verse.[42]

There is no direct evidence that Marrant was dissatisfied with how these unsought collaborators presented the discursive material that he had made available to them. But there is the powerful indirect evidence that he saw fit to publish his own version, "Enlarged by Mr. MARRANT, and Printed (with Permission) for his Sole Benefit." The key way in which Marrant enlarged his own version of his own story was by including an episode that "exposes the racism of some white Christians, while also establishing his authorial independence" from his prose collaborator. His rebuke of that collaborator was no less firm for being left implicit.[43]

More famously, in 1776 in Philadelphia, Thomas Paine became embroiled in a heated controversy with Robert Bell, the first printer of *Common Sense*. Bell angered Paine by bringing out a second edition without first consulting him. Paine engaged another printer, and for months there were dueling editions as well as a "loud commercial dispute" carried on in the pages of the *Pennsylvania Evening Post*. Paine attacked Bell for bringing out "a new edition unknown to the author," despite the author's having "expressly directed him not to proceed therein without orders." Bell shot back with a combination of vitriol ("rascally PUPPY," "wretched reptile," "villainous thief") and minimizing Paine's role in the publication process. He was not "the author," as Paine would have it, but rather "the ostensible," "the would-be," "the Foster-Father Author," no more than an "Amanuensis to a group of authors." Historian Trish Loughran writes that "this squabble was in many ways as crucial" to the "celebrity" of *Common Sense* "as were its arguments for independence." Indeed, it is likely that the quarrel increased sales, at least in Philadelphia.[44]

The only information we have about the sales of *American Cookery* is Simmons's claim in the Albany preface that, despite the flaws of the Hartford edition, "the call" for it had been "so great, and the sale so rapid," that she found herself "under a necessity of publishing a second edition." Did "the sale" get more rapid after the outraged "Advertisement" was appended to the second printing of the first edition? And was the still righteously aggrieved preface to the second edition inserted to help sustain this commercial momentum?[45]

We don't know for sure, of course, but we can assess the probable effect of Simmons's contretemps with the transcriber on the reading public's perceptions of her. The first additional fact about herself that she reveals is that she lacked "an education sufficient to prepare [*American Cookery*] for the press." Since her remedy for this deficiency was to hire a transcriber, it seems reasonable to infer that, while Simmons may have been able to read, she did not know how to write.[46]

Historian E. Jennifer Monaghan has shown that in the Atlantic world of the seventeenth and eighteenth centuries, while boys were frequently taught not only to read but also to write, usually girls were taught only to read. As Monaghan explains, writing was "a male job-related skill, a tool for ministers and shipping clerks alike." Since girls were educated "not to hold jobs, but to be successful homemakers, penmanship was an irrelevant acquisition for them." For girls, the advanced skill equivalent to what writing was designed to be for boys was sewing. Girls were more likely to produce letters by using a needle to create a sampler than by using a pen to create words on a sheet of paper.[47]

In spite of this tradition, the rates for "rudimentary" writing literacy, as well as reading literacy, among women in New England increased throughout the eighteenth century, from 30-40 percent early in the century to 60 percent in the 1760s to 80 percent or more in the 1790s. In Vermont, to which large numbers of people from Connecticut migrated, the rate stabilized in the 70-80 percent range from the 1790s onward. Monaghan herself notes that while for most of the century the Massachusetts Poor Law stated that girls placed in apprenticeships be taught only to read, in 1771 writing was added to the requisite educational attainments for female apprentices. In historian Lawrence W. Towner's research sample of apprenticeships filed by the Boston Overseers of the Poor between 1734 and 1805, it was stipulated of girls as well as boys that they be taught writing as well as reading. Indeed, between 1786 and 1792, girl apprentices were even promised instruction in arithmetic, hitherto reserved for boys only. In the provincial town of Providence as far back as 1757, at least one apprenticed girl demonstrated an ability to write.[48]

In these statistics, literacy is measured by the ability to sign one's name. The proportion of New England women who could write a letter, let alone compose a book manuscript, was doubtless considerably lower than 80 percent in the 1790s. In Litchfield, Connecticut, in the 1780s, James Morris, the local schoolmaster and later one of the authors of the Connecticut Academy of Arts and Sciences' Town Reports, recounted the prevailing opinion in the area that "girls need not learn to write, if they knew enough about it to write their names it was sufficient." Nevertheless, Morris set about to teach all subjects, including writing, to both girls and boys.[49]

Simmons concludes the Albany preface by asking readers to make allowances for "all those disadvantages, which usually attend, an Orphan." Among the disadvantages of which her readers would by this point be aware were not only that of being someone who was "poor" and "solitary" but also that of being someone who could not write and therefore had to call upon the assistance of a transcriber to get her book into print. But when *American Cookery* was published, it was becoming distinctly less unusual for women, even nonelite orphaned women, to be able to write. According to one study of female literacy in New England, "women born shortly after 1765 and who reached age 25 after 1790 may have been *nearing* something like universal literacy—with perhaps 80–90 percent literate," as measured by the same sort of signature evidence used in the studies cited above.[50]

Amelia Simons of Windham, Connecticut, whom we speculate may have been Amelia Simmons, was born in 1767. By divulging her semiliteracy through the painful tale of the errors and possible misdeeds of her tran-scriber, Simmons (or Simons) would have elicited the sympathy of contem-porary readers. Most of them would have taken pride in what a 1794 booklet called "those advantages for acquiring knowledge, which many of the fair Sex, at this day enjoy." Simmons may have managed to make herself seem not only more exotic and deserving of sympathy but also more deserving of congratulations, for overcoming her outdated circumstance of illiteracy and becoming, though an orphan, an "Authoress."[51]

Further aspects of the controversy between the author of *American Cookery* and her transcriber reveal that at this time literacy was viewed not only favorably, as a desirable "advantage," but also by some with suspicion. The allegation in the "Advertisement" that the transcriber acted from "a design" to harm the author is inserted parenthetically. By placing this accusation apart from and thus interrupting the main current of the syntax, Simmons calls particular attention to it. She is emphatic that the errors in the recipes were the result of the transcriber's deliberate "design." Although in the Albany preface she allows for the possibility of the transcriber's "ignorance," she doesn't retract the charge of malice aforethought altogether. The errors still might have arisen from "evil intention." Indeed, this remains the most likely description of the transcriber's motives, since what we next hear is how the transcriber added the marketing section to the Hartford edition without the "knowledge or consent" of "the Authoress." Such a major initiative, constituting "an affront upon the good sense of all classes of citizens," could only have been deliberate.[52]

What is the effect of these fighting words? Most immediately, in relation to the author's identity as "an American Orphan," the insistence on evil "design" puts us in mind of the conventions of the eighteenth-century orphan novels discussed above. Caroline Francis of *The Hapless Orphan* was the victim of her nemesis Eliza's "malignant design."

Equally present is an element analogous to the hostility to lawyers that persisted from colonial times into the early republic. Jackson Turner Main recounted that, especially during the hard times of the 1780s, New Englanders and other Americans viewed lawyers as "designing, cheating vultures." Just as the special knowledge of lawyers engendered suspicion on the part of those who lacked such knowledge, so too the special skill of writing could engender suspicion on the part of those who lacked this skill, or were only imperfectly equipped with it.[53]

In the 1760s, in a prolonged dispute between Reverend Ebenezer Parkman of Westborough, Massachusetts, and his parishioners, a subsidiary source of controversy was Parkman's transcriptions of testimony and his overall documentation of what was occurring. At one point, one of the laymen opposing Parkman stated that a resolution of the major issues that had been agreed upon would hold good only "if there be no writing." A bit later there was a ceremonial burning of some of the contested documents. With her seemingly gratuitous imputing of malicious scheming to the transcriber, the semiliterate author of *American Cookery* appears to have been articulating a similar sense that those able to write were bound to use this ability to put one over on those like her who were unable to do so.[54]

The animus toward lawyers and that of nonwriters toward writers were manifestations on the part of the unlearned of a perspective that, according to historian Gordon S. Wood, was deeply rooted in eighteenth-century thought. It had become a commonplace of the age, Wood writes, that "when things happen in society, individuals with particular intentions, often called 'designs,' must be at the bottom of them." Far too often, "designs" were malicious, since far too many of "the learned few, the gentlemanly elite, those who directed political affairs," were "men, not of principle but of 'policy,' or concealed intentions." They "exploited their reason and learning shrewdly and artfully to bring about selfish and wicked ends."[55]

During the American Revolution, this outlook was particularly in evidence. One example among multitudes is found in *The Crisis* of 1775, a series of oppositional British essays widely reprinted in British North America. In the fourth installment, there appears the following statement: "The steady and uniform appearance in a regular plan of despotism, since the commencement of this reign, makes it evident to the meanest capacity, that a design was formed . . . for subverting the religion, laws, and constitution of this kingdom, and to establish upon the ruins of public liberty, an arbitrary system of government." Similar rhetoric was forthcoming from the revolutionary committees that were formed at the time in nearly every community in resistance to British policy: "The British Administration have long been plotting against the liberties of America . . . the cursed plans of a tyrannical ruler and an abandoned ministry."[56]

When the voice heard in the front- and backmatter of the two editions of *American Cookery* says that she has been the victim of "a design to impose on her," she is associating herself with the patriots who made the American Revolution and with the core beliefs and principles of the new American nation. The linkage is amplified with her words about the marketing section's having been included in the Hartford edition "without her knowledge and consent." As Michael Warner states, "Republican political rhetoric insists on the foundation of politics in popular sovereignty and popular consent." Thus the marketing section is "an affront upon the good sense of all classes of citizens." Amelia Simmons is not only an American orphan authoress. She is also an American orphan republican authoress.[57]

About the marketing section. The stated reasons for its removal from the Albany edition—that shopping is irrelevant to cooking, and that everybody already knows how to shop—can hardly be the real reasons. The first one makes no sense, and the second is highly debatable. Like a great many of the recipes in both editions, parts of the advice on purchasing meat, poultry, and eggs were copied from English cookbooks. These cookbooks frequently included such advice, confuting Simmons's claim that the marketing section is an inappropriate excrescence.[58]

The real reason, we believe, for consigning everything about shopping to the cutting-room floor was the voice heard in the discussion of vegetables and fruits: "We proceed to ROOTS and VEGETABLES. . . . *Potatoes*, take rank for universal use, profit and easy acquirement." This is not the stiff tone heard in the prefaces and "Advertisement," not the tone of a young woman venturing for the first time into the arena of published expository discourse. It is certainly not the tone of someone who, when the time came to put together the revised Albany edition, was revealed as lacking "an education sufficient to prepare the work for the press." Instead, it's the tone of experience and confidence.[59]

As we read on about potatoes, we soon find that what we are hearing is experience and confidence of a particular sort. The writer begs to be pardoned for observing "that the Irish have preserved a genuine mealy rich Potatoe, for a century, which takes rank of any known in any other kingdom; and I have heard that they renew their seed by planting and cultivating the *Seed Ball*, which grows on the tine."[60]

Although the author desists from further exploration of this particular point, "better suited to a treatise on agriculture and gardening," the discussion thereafter is filled with gardening wisdom: "Onions grow in the richest, highest cultivated ground. . . . *Beets*, grow on any ground, but best on loom, or light gravel grounds. . . . The Water Melons is cultivated on sandy soils only, above latitude 41 1-2." And so on. There is even a detailed account of the author's ingenious method of making parsley available year round, so successful that "during the winter, I clip with my scissars the fresh parsley, which my neighbors or myself have occasion for."[61]

In the horticultural portions of the Town Reports, some of which are described in chapter 6, similar gardening details are given. Farmington's gardens produce three varieties of onion, for instance, and its lemon squash is "a good kind & peculiar for not degenerating." Its "Yellow cored" watermelons grow "very long, & the flesh . . . is very rich & melting." New Haven's horticulturalists find that "cauliflowers are less prosperous here, than in a moister soil. The best mode of cultivating them, is to sow the seed as early, as the season will permit and to set out the plants in trenches, dug to the depth and width of a spade, with a covering at the bottom of three inches of manure, and three inches of earth spread over the manure."[62]

Who were the authors of the Town Reports? Clergymen and other elite professional men. John Treadwell was the lieutenant governor of Connecticut at the time that he wrote about Farmington's squashes and watermelons. Timothy Dwight was the president of Yale when he saw fit to explain how best to grow cauliflowers in New Haven. When *American Cookery* was published, it was almost exclusively one type of writer who offered knowledgeable, lovingly detailed discourses about vegetables and fruits, and this type was the educated gentleman. Indeed, having the wherewithal to discuss the cultivation of vegetables and fruits was one of the surest signs that the writer was himself fully cultivated. The type of writer who could produce appropriate discourses on this subject was certainly not a young orphaned woman who did not have an education sufficient to write a book without help. The marketing section was deleted from the Albany edition of *American Cookery* because of this jarring inconsistency of authorial identity.[63]

Yet rhetorical inconsistencies continued to be tolerated elsewhere in both editions. So we might entertain one additional motive for the removal of the marketing section when *American Cookery* was published in Albany. A book that begins with a lengthy section showcasing the refined diction and polished sensibility of the educated gentleman discoursing on the goods on display at the town's emporia was far more likely to sell in Hartford, New Haven, Boston, New York City, and the older eastern districts than in what amounted to a frontier settlement at Albany. The English-dominated Albany that would replace the old Dutch trading center was in 1796 a work in progress. The determined pioneer or frontier family, not the settled household, still dominated a city in transition.

To point the contrast further, recall that Hartford at that time had recently rebuilt its central market in conformance with new, higher standards for cleanliness and order. Albany's market exchanges, on the other hand, were characterized by at least one Yankee observer, Jedidiah Morse, as "a heterogeneous collection of people, invested with all their national prejudices, eager in the pursuit of gain, and jealous of rivalship." To leave out a discussion of marketing altogether might well have seemed the safest course.[64]

Another adjustment was made in the Albany edition—on the title page. On the Hartford title page, the font used for the words "Amelia Simmons" mimics handwriting. The implication is that "Amelia Simmons" knows how to write, a claim that the subsequent revelation of her need to employ a transcriber shows to be untenable. Hence, "AMELIA SIMMONS" steps forward on the Albany title page in plain print, dressed up only by lettering that is all upper case.[65]

This change is not as insignificant as it may at first seem. Historian Tamara Plakins Thornton explains that different types of cursive script, different "hands," were considered appropriate for different types of people. A gentleman "signaled his social superiority to his private secretary when he signed a letter in an au courant italic, leaving the body of the letter unmistakably the product of a hired hand who had been relegated to the old-fashioned, workmanlike secretary hand." An entire letter written out by this gentleman was easily distinguished from one written by a merchant or his clerk, which was "executed in a round hand."[66]

The gentleman's letter would also "not be confused for one by his wife, which would have been executed in a ladies' roman." The roman or Italian hand had begun to be associated with women at the beginning of the seventeenth century, and by the beginning of the eighteenth century, "it was considered appropriate only for the ladies." This was because it was "diminutive and ornamental, like the ladies themselves, lacking both power and utility." Writing masters looking to attract female clients stressed that a "fair hand" was an "accomplishment" comparable to "dancing, music, or, most appropriate, needlework." All in all, "fine penmanship" in the roman or Italian hand was a sure sign of a woman's high social status and therefore of her "fine breeding."[67]

FIGURE 8.1. "Italian Hand," from George Bickham, *The Universal Penman* (London, 1741), 211.

−TypW 705.41.210. Houghton Library, Harvard University

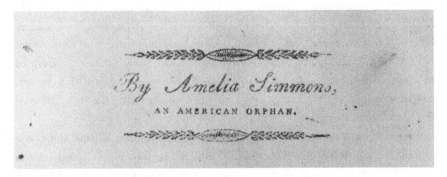

FIGURE 8.2. Close-up of *American Cookery*, Hartford edition, title page author identification, 1796.

−Courtesy, American Antiquarian Society

Printers' fonts were developed that reproduced these various standardized styles of penmanship, and Thornton provides an illustration from the mid-eighteenth century that we reproduce here, along with a reproduction of the mimic-cursive form taken by the font for "Amelia Simmons" on the Hartford title page. Clearly the "Amelia Simmons" font is identical to the "Italian Hand" in Thornton's illustration. The Hartford authorial signature was thus a faux pas on a par with the Hartford marketing section. Where the marketing section represents Simmons as one type of upper-class person, a gentleman, the title page signature represents her as another type, a lady. This is an implicit representation of an "accomplished" woman fully capable of writing not just her own name but also a manuscript cookbook full of recipes such as those to be found within, recipes moreover preponderantly for the types of "confectionery" preparations deemed suitable for such a well-bred female. The Amelia Simmons of this authorial signature is thus one of those "American Ladies" to whom, on the contrary in the preface, Simmons as "an American Orphan" acknowledges her subordination. Would not the potential purchasers of the work in Albany and its environs also be more comfortable buying an inexpensive compendium of proper cookery that was free of the more ostentatious marks of refinement which they either could not or did not wish to emulate?[68]

So, once again, who was Amelia Simmons? A plausible case can be made for the idea that the creation of *American Cookery* involved collaboration among printer, transcriber, and author. Karen Weyler has shown that collaborative authorship was widely practiced in early America. Her most telling example is the partnership between the cross-dressing Revolutionary War soldier Deborah Sampson and the Dedham, Massachusetts, printer and editor Herman Mann. In the realm of cookbook authorship, there is the precedent of the mutual assistance exchanged between Elizabeth Raffald of Manchester, England, and Joseph Harrop, her publisher and the printer and editor of the *Manchester Mercury*.[69]

Let's suppose, then, that Amelia Simons of Windham, Connecticut, was a skilled cook in an elite Hartford, Connecticut, household. Also on the scene in Hartford was Dr. Mason Fitch Cogswell, the son of Reverend James Cogswell of one of the parishes of Windham. A Yale graduate, Cogswell was friendly with the Connecticut Wits and moved in the orbit of Hartford's leading printer, Hudson & Goodwin. He had already established his credentials as a patron of the arts, having rescued the portrait painter Ralph Earl from a New York debtors' prison.

Through Cogswell, Amelia Simons may have come to the attention of Hudson & Goodwin and its stable of writers. In this milieu there was awareness of the recent publication of *The Hapless Orphan* "by an AMERICAN LADY" and also of the near-simultaneous publication of *The Farmer's Friend; or, The History of Mr. Charles Worthy . . . a Poor Orphan*. Hudson & Goodwin decided that the time was ripe to assert the New England and Connecticut version of American-ness in yet another area. Both complementing *The Farmer's Friend* and sharply contrasting with *The Hapless Orphan* would be *American Cookery* "by an American Orphan." New England female orphanhood and its nurturing of true domesticity would be paired with New England male orphanhood and its nurturing of true yeomanry. This type of female orphanhood would be shown to be as disciplined, upright, and flourishing as the type apparently prevailing in regions farther south was frivolous and wretched.

George Goodwin and/or his author associates, clustered around a newspaper named the *Connecticut Courant,* were also well acquainted with Benjamin Franklin's Silence Dogood papers, published decades before with great commercial success in the *New-England Courant.* They knew that the character Franklin invented as the author of these articles was an orphan. Silence's father died at the very moment she was born. Her poverty-stricken mother had her "bound out Apprentice," and after two more years the mother died, leaving Silence Dogood "as it were by my self, having no Relation on Earth within my knowledge."[70]

Goodwin and the others in on this project were further aware that the name Silence Dogood was a play on the Puritan practice of naming girls for abstract qualities and virtues, such as Faith, Hope, Patience, and Desire. The young woman who had come within their ken already had a name, Amelia, that was in accord with the current fashion for "pretty names," often from the heroines of novels such as Henry Fielding's *Amelia.* They decided to play with her surname by turning "Simons" into "Simmons," and they chose to exploit the broadest definition of orphanhood, which included parental desertion, so that the abandonment of her family by her father made of her "An American Orphan."[71]

"Amelia Simmons" proceeded to work with George Goodwin and any others who were part of the authorial team on the compilation of *American Cookery.* Amelia appeared in court to file her copyright claim before Simeon Baldwin, another Yale man well known to the Connecticut Wits and Hudson & Goodwin. The book was published. But unfortunately there were a couple of slipups that could not be ignored. Some of the recipes were incorrect. Moreover, this young orphan woman wielded her pen with much too elegant a feminine hand on the title page and sounded too much like a gentleman farmer in the book's opening section. Enter the scheming "transcriber," who provided the pretext for a redone edition in which these errors could be corrected and from which these inconsistencies were removed.

Those involved in the project were well aware, having followed Thomas Paine's and other writers' careers, of the boost to sales that controversy, whether real or fabricated, could provide. They were also aware that not only writers but also printers could generate publicity through controversy, in the Franklin-Dogood manner. So they did not tone down much Amelia Simons's genuine anger over the unsatisfactory aspects of the first edition.

The new edition was brought out at a safe distance from all this behind-the-scenes maneuvering by the Websters of Albany, known and trusted by Hudson & Goodwin of Hartford.[72]

These last few paragraphs are conjectural of course, but they express the kinds of social relations, literary tropes, and printer's gambits that would have been familiar to any late eighteenth-century Anglo-American reader; they condition any conclusions modern readers may wish to draw about the "real" Amelia Simmons. What indisputably remains is the persona "Amelia Simmons" as self-represented in the first two editions of *American Cookery*: a female orphan who follows the path marked out for her kind, devoting herself with sufficient energy and application to domestic work to have become expert at one branch of it, cooking. She believes that her expertise in this field is of an order such that others, whether themselves orphans working as "domestics" or any member whatsoever of "the rising generation of *Females* in America," would benefit from being instructed by her, becoming not only good cooks but also "good wives, and useful members of society."

This young orphan is deferential. She entreats the good opinion and patronage of "the American Ladies" above her. But this doesn't prevent her from being ambitious. The "domestic" is now also an authority who makes it clear that she is keeping her eye on how well her book is selling. In the respects and to the degree that she has improved herself, while persisting in her calling and remaining sensible and upright, she has made herself a credit to her "American" nation. Conversely, the American nation is implicitly advised to follow the example of this young woman and the region that she, by virtue of her venues of publication, represents. Upward mobility was to be countenanced insofar as it was not overdone, insofar as it was not disruptive of the good order long established in Connecticut and emerging in the Yankee West.

Finally, when imposed upon, "Amelia Simmons" would stand up and fight for her rights, however much she might seem to be, like her American nation a quarter century before, the underling and underdog. In the article upon which we drew earlier regarding the contemporary social and political meanings of "design," Gordon Wood notes that "throughout the 1790s the Republicans . . . accused [the Federalists] . . . of fomenting beneath their high-sounding professions of devotion to the new republic secret designs for monarchizing American society and government." Thus, there is at least a partially Jeffersonian sound to Simmons's blunt claim that the transcriber had acted "with a design to impose on her, and injure the sale of the book."[73]

Yet *American Cookery* was published in both Hartford and Albany under Federalist auspices. Barzillai Hudson and George Goodwin may have considered Jeffersonian rhetoric to be the equivalent of "the conspiratorial mumbling of criminals, the ranting of madmen, and the howling of rabid dogs," as Christopher Grasso characterizes their attitude. But they let this bit of Republican-ish scrappiness out into the world under their imprimatur, or perhaps actively contrived to bring it forward into the world, just as their brethren in Albany, the Websters, allowed or arranged for Simmons to speak with equal Republican spunk of a social superior's "evil intentions" of trampling on her rights to knowledge and consent, which constituted an affront to "all classes of citizens."[74]

A brief comparison with the Federalists of eastern Massachusetts is instructive. In 1792, in their capacity as gentlemen farmers, the Massachusetts Federalists founded and thereafter sustained the Massachusetts Society for Promoting Agriculture. The society encouraged agricultural innovation and improvement. Experiments undertaken by its elite members and their friends were reported in the pages of its publications. Tamara Thornton summarizes the society's goals: "Gentlemen farmers would act as a kind of leaven in the agricultural populace, stimulating practical farmers to abandon their backward techniques for more successful ones pioneered by their well-to-do neighbors."[75]

But the society, though elitist, did not wish to treat ordinary Massachusetts farmers as totally passive recipients of wisdom from on high. Its trustees encouraged ordinary farmers to engage in agricultural experimentation and submit the results to the society for publication. In 1796, concerned that such people of lower rank might be reluctant to offer their work for publication, as they were "lacking education" and therefore might be afraid of being ridiculed, the trustees "volunteered their editing skills." Those who made submissions could "rely with confidence," wrote the trustees, that the trustees would "never suffer an [ingenious] mind to be wounded by committing to the publick any communications, without such corrections as shall not expose them to the sneers of the weak and uncandid." The response to these overtures was muted at best.[76]

At least in this instance, the Massachusetts Federalists, for all their benevolent intentions, could not get beyond a fairly blatant condescension. Participation from below was to be accompanied by ritual enactment of subordination. In contrast, the Federalists of Connecticut and its hinterlands put forward a minimally educated representative of the lower orders speaking in her own voice. Although this voice was for the most part defer-ential, some of what it had to say might have grated harshly on the ears of those who provided it with a public platform. But provide such a voice with a public platform the Connecticut Federalists nevertheless did. Over the long haul, in a society where the cat of popular assertiveness had once and for all been let out of the bag, the Connecticut group, opting for deflecting potentially rebellious impulses into safe channels, had devised the shrewder strategy for holding onto position, privilege, and power.

CHAPTER 9

The Readers and the Editions

W ho were the actual readers of *American Cookery*? Two Connecticut manuscript cookbooks point us toward people who had
access to the printed work, either directly or indirectly. One from
Colchester, Connecticut, discussed in chapter 7, compiled between 1813
and 1821, contains a verbatim copy of the recipe for Shrewsbury cake in
the Hartford edition of *American Cookery*. Of the several recipes for "Plumb
Cake" in the manuscript, one of them is closely modeled on the Hartford
edition's version. Nine other recipes are loosely based on recipes for the
same items in *American Cookery*: those for "Whigs," "Whip Syllabub," "Beef
Alamode," gingerbread, Marlborough pudding, "Mrs. Coits Loaf Cake,"
cookies, and two for "Potatoe Pudding."[1]

Another contemporaneous manuscript cookbook, by Zeloda Barrett of
New Hartford, a village twenty miles northwest of Hartford, includes three
recipes copied from *American Cookery*: "Cookeys," bread pudding, and rice
pudding. Seven others are adaptations of *American Cookery* recipes: "Diet
Bread," pound cake, "Pudding," "Cake," gingerbread, "Puff paste," and
"Loaf cake."[2]

So, fifteen to thirty years after publication, material from *American Cookery* was still circulating in the Hartford area. We cannot say for certain that
Zeloda Barrett or the anonymous compiler in Colchester owned copies of
the work themselves. The fact that the Colchester compiler got her *American Cookery*-derived loaf cake from "Mrs. Coit" may suggest that there
was one shared copy in the neighborhood. Similarly, Barrett identifies as
"Mrs. Yale's receipt" the gingerbread recipe derived from *American Cookery*'s
"Molasses Gingerbread." Mrs. Yale was doubtless the wife of Cyrus Yale, the
minister of the New Hartford Congregational church that Zeloda and her
sister Samantha regularly attended. It could well be that the minister's wife
owned a copy of *American Cookery* and either lent it out to her husband's
parishioners or shared material from it with them. But it is also quite possible that Zeloda Barrett had her own copy of the book.[3]

245

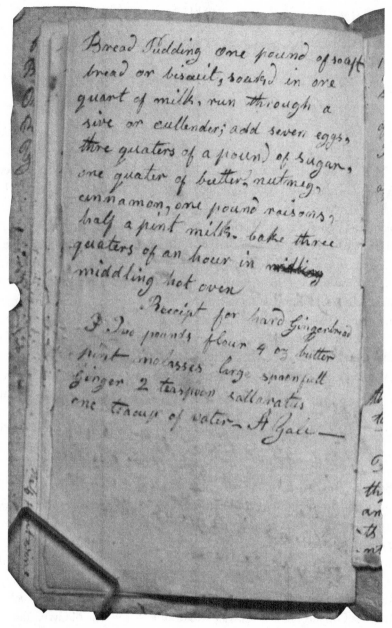

Bread Pudding. one pound of soft
bread or biscuit, soaked in one
quart of milk, run through a
sive or cullender; add seven eggs,
three quaters of a pound of sugar,
one quater of butter, nutmeg,
cinnamon, one pound raisons,
half a pint milk. bake three
quaters of an hour in ~~middling~~
middling hot oven
            Receipt for hard Gingerbread
3. Two pounds flour 4 oz butter
pint molasses large spoonfull
ginger 2 teaspoon sallaratus
one teacup of water ~ A Gale —

FIGURE 9.1. Page that includes the "Bread Pudding" recipe from Zeloda Barrett's manuscript cookbook, 1820s (?). The recipe is all but identical to the bread pudding recipe in *American Cookery*.

—"Bread Pudding" and "Receipt for hard Gingerbread" recipes kept by Zeloda Barrett, Zeloda and Samantha Barrett Diaries, 1804–31, Ms 45572, Connecticut Historical Society, Hartford

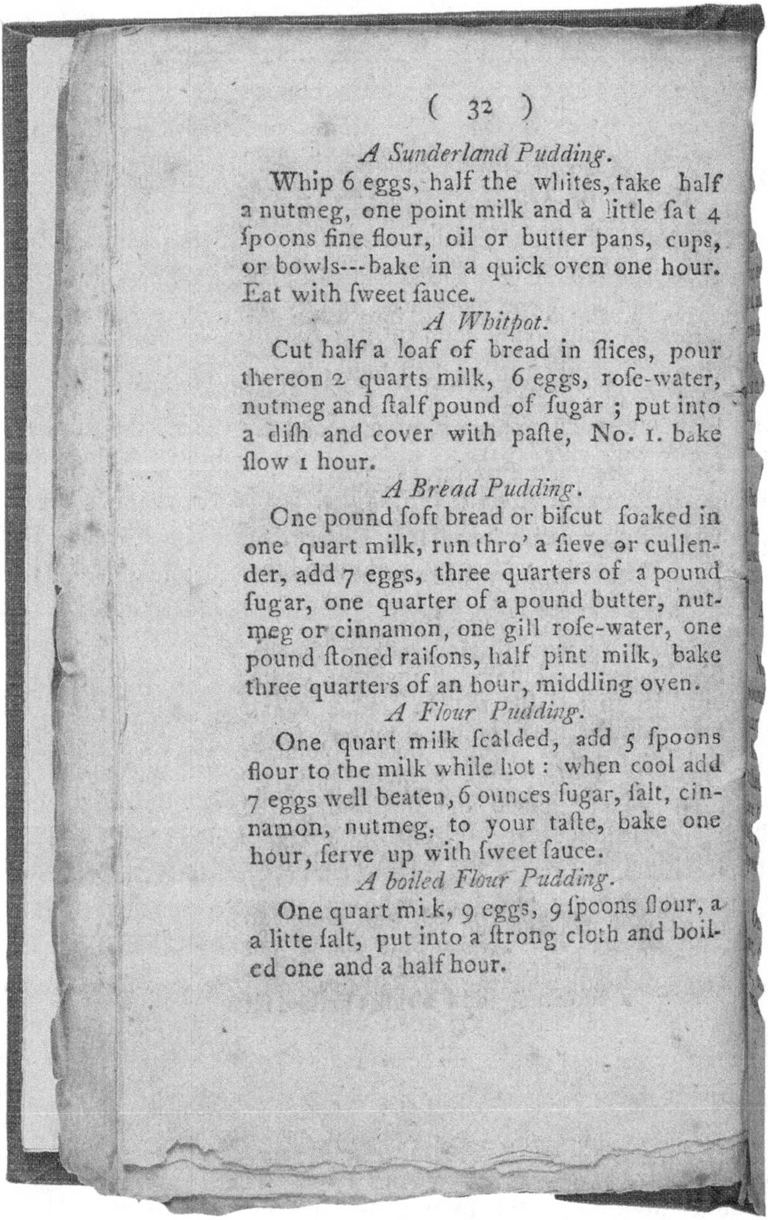

A Sunderland Pudding.

Whip 6 eggs, half the whites, take half a nutmeg, one point milk and a little fat 4 fpoons fine flour, oil or butter pans, cups, or bowls---bake in a quick oven one hour. Eat with fweet fauce.

A Whitpot.

Cut half a loaf of bread in flices, pour thereon 2 quarts milk, 6 eggs, rofe-water, nutmeg and ftalf pound of fugar ; put into a difh and cover with pafte, No. 1. bake flow 1 hour.

A Bread Pudding.

One pound foft bread or bifcut foaked in one quart milk, run thro' a fieve or cullender, add 7 eggs, three quarters of a pound fugar, one quarter of a pound butter, nutmeg or cinnamon, one gill rofe-water, one pound ftoned raifons, half pint milk, bake three quarters of an hour, middling oven.

A Flour Pudding.

One quart milk fcalded, add 5 fpoons flour to the milk while hot : when cool add 7 eggs well beaten, 6 ounces fugar, falt, cinnamon, nutmeg, to your tafte, bake one hour, ferve up with fweet fauce.

A boiled Flour Pudding.

One quart milk, 9 eggs, 9 fpoons flour, a a litte falt, put into a ftrong cloth and boiled one and a half hour.

FIGURE 9.2. "Bread Pudding" recipe, in *American Cookery*, Albany edition, 1796.
—Courtesy, American Antiquarian Society

Two pieces of extra-culinary information are available regarding the Colchester compiler. One is that she (as we assume) read the January 21, 1820, issue of the *New York Evening Post,* for the manuscript includes that issue's instructions on how "to cleanse the Mouth & improve the Breath." On August 15, 1820, the compiler went on a stagecoach "excursion . . . to the Neck" with "Mrs Taylor," who favored her along the way with a recipe for "Cup Cake." The Neck was perhaps what is now Selden Neck State Park, on the Connecticut River, eighteen miles from Colchester. These stray facts are enough to suggest a certain level of education and the possession of means sufficient to engage in leisure activities.[4]

We know much more about the New Hartford compiler, beginning of course with her name. Zeloda Barrett was born in 1786, the third of five children of William and Susanna Barrett of New Hartford. William Barrett had traveled across the Atlantic during the Revolution as a member of the British Army. Taken prisoner and temporarily held at New Hartford, Barrett escaped but did not return to the British forces. Rather, he lingered for the duration of the war in the neighborhood where he had made his escape, eventually marrying a local girl and becoming a farmer.[5]

Neither Zeloda nor her younger sister Samantha ever married. After the death of their father in 1821, they managed the eighty-five-acre family farm, having doubtless taken over most of its operations before his death. Zeloda's diary for 1820 records such activities as picking potatoes and apples, picking and husking corn, slaughtering livestock (with the help of men in the neighborhood), and boiling cider "for molasses." After finishing the corn husking in late October, Zeloda expressed satisfaction at having "a very fine crop considering the work which was done."[6]

Samantha Barrett's diary for 1828 likewise refers repeatedly to the multifarious tasks of a mixed-use, midsize Connecticut family farm: plowing the garden, planting peas and beans, exchanging pork and apples with neighbors, driving livestock to and from the village common, erecting sheds, and turning slaughtered livestock into salt meat and sausage.[7]

From these diaries, we also learn of the village culture in which farm and family were immersed. During the first few months of 1804, when she was seventeen or eighteen, Zeloda recorded, besides domestic chores, regular attendance at Sabbath services and school (Sabbath entries include quotations of the scriptural texts on which the minister preached), evening reading of improving books (some specifically meant for young people), evening letter-writing, and regular exchanges of visits with neighbors. One

Friday evening in late January, Zeloda saw fit to "take down the heads of the discourse" during a visit from "Mr. Eliphlet Ensign . . . 1st was about Swine. 2 Demicrat pigs. About Mr. Spencer & Mr. Smith's arbitration. Mrs Ensign sore finger—Colonel Kellogg's commission for a General. About the meeting house being seated. Seat mates &c &c &c."[8]

Samantha Barrett's account of her life as a member of the village community a quarter of a century later, in 1828 and 1829, was essentially a list of the same activities: participation in church life ("a meeting for prayer and to choose a new Deacon" in January 1829 included "some conversation respecting the low state of the church"), frequent visiting ("evening visited Mrs. H . . . Mrs Rogers calld"), evening reading ("evening read about the Greeks"), sharing of books ("lent Laura my 3 to reed"), and evening letter-writing ("sent a letter to Grove" [her nephew]). The Barrett sisters' culinary endeavors involved them in such central community rituals as Thanksgiving and Election Day.[9]

In just about every key respect, the self-portraits left behind by Zeloda and Samantha Barrett of New Hartford conformed to the Connecticut Federalist ideal—agrarian industry and independence combined with village piety, rectitude, bookishness, earnestness, and sociability. The Barretts also participated in the consumer culture of the day, purchasing at general stores in the neighborhood such items as a silk shawl, a pocket handkerchief, fish, wine, rum, a "vinegar cruise" (a small cup), fine wire and ribbon for a bonnet, and a set of knives and forks. As of 1820, the Barretts had installed a cast-iron cookstove in their kitchen: "Mr. Ladd fetchd our stove & set it up we are a little disappointed as it does not bake as it used to & troubled a little with smoke."[10]

These Barrett self-portraits also reflected the realities of the early national rural economy. An essential element in maintaining the Barrett farm as a subsistence-plus enterprise was engagement in domestic manufacture. The sisters functioned as a textile production team, with Zeloda specializing in spinning and carding and Samantha in weaving. Their output consisted primarily of blankets, bedcovers, handkerchiefs, towels, aprons, and table linen. In 1815, their income from textiles was over six hundred dollars. The Barrett sisters also devoted themselves to one of the other major forms of female domestic manufacture at this time, dairying. They sold or bartered butter and cheese at the local store and to neighbors, sometimes spending the proceeds on such items as tea and "pepper and spice."[11]

It is clear that the culinary content of *American Cookery* found a comfortable niche within a Connecticut milieu of middling, hard-working, modestly thriving households. Another user of *American Cookery* is found through an inscription in the American Antiquarian Society's copy of the 1816 Windsor, Vermont, printing of the book. The inscription reads: "This was the book Grandma [illegible] had after her marriage." The volume was thus deemed suitable for a young woman embarking on household pursuits. It was apparently hoped that *American Cookery* would indeed, as the book's preface puts it, assist this bride in "doing those things which are really essential" to becoming a "good wife" and a "useful member of society."[12]

The copy of *American Cookery* that became a part of one family's culinary legacy was printed neither in Hartford nor Albany but rather in Vermont. The location of the printing suggests that the young woman began her married life somewhere in the Connecticut diaspora. From a geographical point of view, *American Cookery* essentially spent three decades traveling up the Connecticut River (Northampton, Massachusetts; Brattleboro, Vermont; Walpole, New Hampshire; Windsor and Woodstock, Vermont) and two decades traveling up and down the Hudson River (Albany, Troy, Poughkeepsie, New York City), with a journey into the West (Zanesville, Ohio) thrown in for good measure.[13]

If we take account of other manifestations of *American Cookery*'s presence in a given locale, such as plagiarisms of its contents or advertisements of its availability for sale, our geographic perspective extends eastward as far as Portland, Maine; southwestward to New York City; westward through Pittsfield, Massachusetts, and Albany, Herkimer, and Cooperstown, New York, on out to Geneva, New York; and northwestward through Montpelier, Vermont, up to Plattsburgh, Ogdensburg, and Watertown, New York. A breakdown by direction from the original place of publication of all the post-1796 editions and plagiarisms, and of the post-1797 advertisements that we have been able to find, shows eight *American Cookery* appearances to the east, five to the southwest, one to the west, fifteen to the north, and twenty to the northwest. The latter two directions, into western Massachusetts, New Hampshire, Vermont, and upstate New York, thus account for almost three-fourths (thirty-five of forty-nine) of *American Cookery*'s appearances between 1798 and 1831 (see fig. 1.2).[14]

In this pattern of publication and distribution, *American Cookery* was following the well-established routes of emigration from New England generally and from Connecticut specifically. Timothy Dwight, having reached the terminus of his 1803 "Journey to the Canada Line," enthused over "the efforts of the New England people in colonizing" Maine to the northeast and the Massachusetts Berkshire country, New Hampshire, Vermont, and New York to the north and west. These efforts had begun around 1760, Dwight thought, at which time these outlying regions were still "an absolute wilderness." Dwight's dating of the process is consistent with the fact that the first road connecting Hartford and Albany was built in the 1760s.[15]

The road almost immediately fell into disrepair, but this was only a small hindrance to the major movements of peoples along its route and many others roughly adjacent to it. By 1774, Connecticut had contributed so significantly to population growth in New Hampshire, Vermont, New York, and northern Pennsylvania that, according to Jared Ingersoll, a Connecticut native residing in Philadelphia, people there viewed "the Northern New England men as a Set of Goths and Vandals who may one day overrun these Southern Climes unless thoroughly opposed." What non–New Englanders contemplated with foreboding the Connecticut-born father of American geography celebrated with gusto. Jedidiah Morse boasted in 1789 that "New England may, with propriety, be called a nursery of men, whence are annually transplanted, into various parts of the United States, thousands of its natives," especially into Vermont and "the northern parts" of New York.[16]

The degree and direction of emigration from specific places was one of the questions posed in the Connecticut Academy of Arts and Sciences' Town Reports project. Respondents to the survey confirmed the broad patterns just outlined. John Treadwell believed that the 775 people who had emigrated from Farmington between 1783 and 1802 "are principally gone into the States of New York and Vermont, tho some few" had gone farther west.[17]

Lewis M. Norton, reporting from Goshen, thought that the "very numerous" emigrations from that town had been "first" to Berkshire County, Massachusetts, "then to Vermont, afterward to Bloomfield N. York [near Rochester], and to the town of Hudson in the Connecticut western reserve [northern Ohio]. There has lately been a large emigration to the flats on the Gennessee river." David D. Field, reporting on Middlesex County in 1819, stated that people had been "perpetually removing" from there since about 1740, first "to the county of Litchfield in this State, and Berkshire in Massachusetts; then to New-Hampshire and Vermont. In later years they have removed to New York, and to the western States and Territories."[18]

Descriptions of New England outmigration by modern historians run parallel to these contemporary accounts. Historian Christopher Clark says that in the second half of the eighteenth century, many Connecticut and

Massachusetts families moved into New Hampshire, Maine, and Vermont. Beginning in the 1780s, "as the new political framework opened access to regions to the west, migration began into upstate New York and to the Ohio Valley." In 1790, the population of New York State was 340,000. By 1810, largely as a result of this influx from New England, it had almost tripled, reaching 959,000.[19]

Clark illustrates the process with the example of the Connecticut native Jedidiah Baldwin, born in 1769. First apprenticed to a clockmaker in Norwich, Connecticut, Baldwin later moved to Northampton, Massachusetts, and then, in 1793, on up the Connecticut River to Hanover, New Hampshire, where he set up his own clock-making workshop. Sometime after 1807, Baldwin moved westward to New York State "in an effort to reestablish his business there." Baldwin's relocations around 1780 to 1810, from a long-settled part of Connecticut, up the Connecticut River Valley, and then into New York State, match quite closely the zone in which American Cookery repeatedly surfaced between 1796 and 1831.[20]

In characterizing as "an absolute wilderness" the areas settled by Yankee New Englanders in the second half of the eighteenth century, Timothy Dwight was hiding from view in this coveted territory the presence of Native American peoples and their long-established ways of life. He was not the first New Englander to do so. The original governor of Massachusetts, John Winthrop, had come up with the necessary "cant of conquest" on the eve of the 1630 Great Migration. Winthrop defined as a wilderness any area in which the natives "inclose noe Land, neither have they any setled habytation, nor any tame Cattle to improve the Land by." Relying on these Eurocentric standards, Winthrop believed that the English were justified in expropriating as much of the Native zone of habitation as was needed to establish what they considered a superior civilization.[21]

Winthrop promised that the New English would leave the Natives "sufficient" land "for their use, . . . there being more then enough for them & us," but by this time, such restraints had long since been brushed aside. Contemplating in 1811 the progress of New England settlement along the westward route from Albany to the Genesee River, Dwight exulted in how "a numerous train of churches, and those often handsome buildings, are planted on the very ground devoted a little while since to the ravages of the scalping knife and the celebration of the powwow."[22]

This replacement of Native superstition and idolatry with Christianity in

its highest Yankee Protestant form was, Dwight felt, the crowning achievement of the immigration into the area since 1784 of almost 300,000 New
Englanders. "The efforts by which" these settlers had transformed New
York's "vast forests into fruitful fields and gardens" were "unparalleled perhaps in the world. . . . A great number of beautiful villages have risen up as
by the power of enchantment; and the road for one hundred and twenty
miles is . . . lined by a succession of houses, almost universally neat, and
frequently handsome." The culture of the Connecticut River Valley that
Dwight repeatedly extolled, with its neat and handsome homes, its schools
"established with a celerity delightful to the eye of benevolence," and its
well-proportioned churches had been transplanted intact in this westerly
district. Truly this was "the utmost degree of improvement hitherto attained
by civilized men."[23]

In New York State, it wasn't only Native Americans who were to be displaced or subdued. The Dutch people occupied the Hudson River Valley,
squarely across the path that Yankee New Englanders needed to tread to
reach the fertile fields farther west. In the 1780s and 1790s, Albany, long
the capital of Hudson Valley Dutch culture, also became the place through
which Yankee migrants passed, at a rate of several hundred a day, on their
way westward.[24]

And just as Native Americans were not in fact being left unmolested on
land "sufficient for their use," so Albany and the Hudson Valley were not
going to be permitted to remain a peninsula of Dutch hegemony jutting
into a sea of New England-ness. In *American Geography*, Jedidiah Morse took
on the task of ideological demolition. He found that the Dutch along the
Hudson were even more sadly lacking than the New Jersey Dutch, quoting
Swedish naturalist and traveler Pehr Kalm's assessment that these people
were "every where well known for their avarice and selfishness. They are
unhospitable, and never disposed to oblige beyond a prospect of interest."
Another of the sources on which Morse relied found that the avarice of the
New York Dutch was hindered by their "want of enterprize," and that their
relations among themselves soon degenerated into continual "slandering
and injuring each other's characters."[25]

Albany, in particular, presented Morse with a sorry spectacle. The houses
there, though they were "kept very neat," had "but little convenience, and
less elegance." Moreover, the people persisted in the ridiculous practice of
building all houses with projecting "watergutters or spouts." These rendered
it "almost dangerous to walk the streets in a rainy day." The perils of Albany

perambulation were compounded by the fact that the neatness with which
the houses were kept was "not observed in the streets, which are very muddy
most of the year, except those which are paved; and these are seldom swept,
and very rough."[26]

As for manners, the judgment of a "gentleman of observation and dis-
cernment, who resided some time in Albany," was that the people of Albany
were basically lacking in gentility. They knew "nothing of the little plays
and amusements common to small social circles." They "seldom drink to
intoxication," except when they most especially should not, "in company,
or on public occasions, when it is thought to be no disgrace." Their wedding festivities typically concluded with "a shocking specimen of human
depravity." Funeral observances likewise ended in conversations devoted to
"promiscuous subjects, however improper, and unsuitable to the solemnity
of the occasion, and the house of mourning is soon converted into a house
of feasting."[27]

Finally, the social structure of Dutch Albany was the antithesis of that of
Connecticut. In Connecticut there were, as George Washington remarked
in the same year that *American Geography* was published, "few or no oppulent men—and no poor." Albany society, on the other hand, was identical
to that of the European *ancien régime* that Timothy Dwight would castigate
a few years later in *Greenfield Hill*: "The best families live extremely well,
enjoying all the conveniences and luxuries of life; but the poor have scarcely
the necessaries for subsistence."[28]

A boorish and unjust society such as this could not withstand the incur-
sion of representatives of a well-ordered, energetic, and fairly allocated society. In 1794, a Yankee immigrant castigated the Albany Common Council
for its hostility to economic initiative and enterprise. By 1798, however,
according to Dwight, the leaders of the Albany Dutch community had
begun to acknowledge New England superiority. They were building "handsome houses in the modern English style" and adopting "in their furniture,
manners, and mode of living . . . the English customs." By 1805, the English
ethos of "rapid improvement" had fully taken hold. The English takeover of
Albany was essentially complete by 1820, when the Dutch proportion of the
population had dwindled to 5 percent, and "Yankee shops and stores lined
the main streets."[29]

The conquest of what we will henceforth call Greater Connecticut was
brought about by deliberate initiatives and policies. In 1807, Timothy

Dwight referred to what was doubtless the most significant of these in the course of his musings about Vermont. "Frequent and considerable revivals of religion have contributed not a little to increase the number of clergymen and change the moral aspect of the country," he observed. Among those converted by these revivals, "neither enthusiasm nor superstition has soiled their profession." Rather, these born-again Vermont Christians had shown themselves to be "sober, rational, essentially amended in their character, and visibly reformed in their conduct." Dwight anticipated a broadly beneficial effect on Vermont society: "Should this happy influence, so desirably begun, become generally prevalent, its effects on the good order, peace, and prosperity of the state will be such as to preclude the necessity of all other means of melioration."[30]

In this description of the desired effects of carefully focused religious indoctrination and exhortation, Dwight was echoing the mission statements of the Connecticut Missionary Society, founded in 1798 by the General Association of the Congregational churches of Connecticut. The society's express purpose was secular as well as religious: "The civil and political as well as the religious welfare of our brethren in the New Settlements require that the gospel should be preached to them."[31]

Lay members of the Connecticut Federalist elite endorsed these goals. In the year the Connecticut Missionary Society was founded, Daniel Noble wrote to his friend and Williams College classmate Thomas Robbins, scion of an old Connecticut clerical family, congratulating him on his decision to become one of the society's missionaries: "In this demoralizing age of the world the profession [of missionary] which you have chosen is the great stay and support of order, government and social happiness." The Federalist establishment's backing of the project to civilize Greater Connecticut extended well beyond mere verbal encouragement. The first chairman of the Missionary Society's board of trustees was John Treadwell, lieutenant governor and then governor of Connecticut, and author of the Farmington Town Report. Another trustee was Oliver Ellsworth, a national political leader in numerous capacities, a fixture in Hartford's emerging array of economic and cultural institutions, and, thanks to Ralph Earl's memorable portrait, an embodiment alongside his wife of subdued yet impeccably tasteful gentility.[32]

The Connecticut ecclesiastical authorities sponsored revivals in at least twenty Connecticut towns in the final years of the eighteenth century, and, with its new Missionary Society getting underway, revivals also took place in northern Vermont, New Hampshire, and the New York State Gene-see country. In keeping with the conservative auspices under which they occurred and the overall missionary goal of bolstering "order, government and social happiness," these religious awakenings were not what one histo-rian characterized as "the noisy, tumultuous exhibitions which flourished elsewhere on the frontier." Rather, they were, in the words of contemporary revival chronicler Bennet Tyler, "like showers of rain, which refresh the dry and thirsty earth. . . . Their fruits were permanent. By them the churches were not only enlarged, but beautified and strengthened." Exactly as Dwight boasted, "a benign influence was exerted on the community around."[33]

A modern historian of Vermont has described more analytically why par-ticipation in religious and church life encouraged moral probity and social respectability. For anyone of significant economic standing in a community, being a church member meant that any questionable actions would be sub-jected to the scrutiny of other members: "The presence of such sanctions was important in a business environment in which good will and reputa-tion counted for so much." Ordinary farmers and farmhands who joined churches had likewise accepted the apparatus and procedures of moral review and were therefore also more likely to remain reliable and upright.[34]

We have heard Timothy Dwight stating that successful religious revivals could bring about such a degree of "good order, peace, and prosperity . . . as to preclude the necessity of all other means of melioration." But we have also almost always heard him lauding churches and religious worship not in isolation but rather in conjunction with "other means of melioration"—in particular, schools and "handsome" or at least "neat" houses. Religion, education, and a certain plateau of domestic refinement constituted the three key components of the Connecticut Way that needed to be recreated to the north and west in Greater Connecticut. Just a few pages before his passage on revivals, Dwight pondered the benefits of "the exchange of . . . log huts for decent houses. . . . The comfort, the spirit, the manners, nay even the morals of [a forester's] family, if not of himself, are almost of course improved. The transition from a good house is, by the association of ideas natural to the human mind, a very easy one to good furniture, a handsome dress, a handsome mode of living, better manners, and everything else con-nected with a higher reputation."[35]

Just as Dwight was at one with the rest of the Connecticut ecclesiastical establishment in his emphasis on religious revivals, so he was in accord with Federalists in general in his emphasis on domestic decorum and refinement.

Historian Andrew R. L. Cayton writes that in the territory encompassed by the 1787 Northwest Ordinance, Federalists projected "an orderly, prosperous, regular world dominated by gentlemen and founded on the pillars of education, Protestantism, and government." It was to be founded as well on women. Federalist planners believed that "refined women were both evidence and bulwarks of a highly developed society. While they would attend to the business of household production and reproduction, wives and daughters also would form social circles that would contribute to the stability of the West." As early as 1788, Marietta, Ohio, was the locale of a ball graced, as one attendee reported, by "fifteen ladies as well accomplished in the manners of polite circles as any I have ever seen in our old States."[36]

The description of the ball was written by Connecticut native and Northwest Territorial judge Samuel Holden Parsons, and Connecticut was well represented among Northwest Territory settlers. We may safely infer that the vision the Federalists developed for this region was constructed from experiences and practices similar to those devised for the emigrants to the areas bordering on Connecticut whose paths we have been following. If these people were indeed, as Dwight imagined, being led from residing in a good house to an interest in good furniture, handsome clothing, "and everything else connected with a higher reputation," then they were also becoming interested in acquiring the wherewithal for good food. Were the particular features of the later printings of *American Cookery* designed to facilitate the civilizing process Dwight outlined?

Beginning with the 1798 Northampton reprint of the original Hartford edition and ending with the 1831 Woodstock, Vermont, expanded version of the Albany edition, there were in all sixteen reissues of the basic content of the first two editions. The great majority of these were reprints of the Albany edition. Twelve of them—all but Northampton in 1798, New York City in 1805, Boston in 1819, and New York City in 1822—were produced either in northern and western frontier areas or in places serving as gateways to those areas.[37]

Amelia Simmons is named on the title page in only three of the post-1798 printings—Salem/Albany, 1804; Troy, 1808; and Zanesville, 1816. In all others the name "Amelia Simmons" is omitted from the title page altogether, and, with one exception, the author is identified only as an anonymous "American Orphan." The exception is that in 1831, the printer went even further, dropping the national tag and labeling the author only as "An Orphan." Thus, the impact of the convention of the beat-the-odds female orphan who has become an "Authoress" was reduced by the failure to attribute to the author a full name or gender. But the continued portrayal into the third decade of the nineteenth century of the author as an orphan (perhaps presumed female because a cookbook author) attests to the tenacity of the trope of the orphan as the classic underdog, which had captured a broad audience in highly sexualized novels about female orphans.

But even more intriguing is the fact that the authorial attribution of *American Cookery* to someone with the given name of Amelia Simmons was, except in the 1816 Zanesville, Ohio, edition, summarily dispensed with by 1808. After that, in the book's primary region of publication, "Amelia Simmons" as the author of *American Cookery* is nowhere to be found. Can this be read as evidence that printers, who might have been in the know about the machinations of their brethren, understood that "Amelia Simmons" was either a pseudonym or a fabrication? If Amelia Simmons had in fact been a semi-pseudonym for Amelia Simons of Windham, Connecticut, then the death of Simons shortly after the publication of the second edition might well have given printers added incentive to eliminate individualized authorial identity altogether.

In no instances of the reprinting of the Hartford edition is the errata page included, and in only two instances of the reprinting of the Albany edition is the preface to that edition included. All editions and printings come with the original Hartford edition preface. Thus, in the later life of *American Cookery*, just as Amelia Simmons herself became an indistinct presence, so also did her controversy with her transcriber. What remains, between the title page identification of an orphan as the author and the orphanhood discourse of the original preface, is the initial authorial persona who is at once aspiring and subordinate.

Among the books in which the content of *American Cookery* is included without acknowledgment, *The New England Cookery*, "compiled by Lucy Emerson" and printed in Montpelier, Vermont, in 1808, exhibits many of the features of the later printings of *American Cookery* itself. Rather incongruously, it retains the orphanhood disquisition from the Hartford edition preface, even though its "compiler," Lucy Emerson had never been an orphan, had married respectably, was well educated, had worked as a schoolteacher, and, far from being from the lower orders, was the sister of a Montpelier bank president who had been one of the first settlers of the town.[38]

Between 1796 and 1812, the average price of *American Cookery*, translated into twenty-first-century terms, was about five dollars. In one advertisement, the price of *The New England Cookery* was a little over seven dollars. The price of another book in which *American Cookery* is plagiarized, *New American Cookery; or, Female Companion* (1805) was given in two advertisements as being in the nine- to ten-dollar range.[39]

In the 1807 Portsmouth, New Hampshire, advertisement discussed in chapter 1, the price of *American Cookery* was $5.20, that of Carter's *Frugal Housewife* ranged from $13.00–15.60, those of Hannah Glasse's *Art of Cookery* and Maria Rundell's *New System of Domestic Cookery* were both $20.80, and that of Richard Brigg's *English Art of Cookery* was $28.60. Clearly *American Cookery* was the most affordable cookbook on the market in the northeastern United States during the first two decades of the nineteenth century. Even its padded-out knockoffs were significantly cheaper than the competition.[40]

Another noteworthy feature of the later versions of *American Cookery* is their size. Whereas the Hartford edition is 9 inches in height, the Albany edition 7 ½ inches, and the 1798 Northampton reprint 8 ⅔ inches, all printings from 1804 onward are significantly smaller, around 6 inches in height. Even *The New England Cookery*, the Lucy Emerson plagiarism, follows the pattern, logging in at the same 6-inch height.[41]

Why dwell on such minutiae about the various reappearances of *American Cookery*? To begin with, consider the fact that *American Cookery*'s price in contemporary terms in New York City in 1797, eighteen cents, was below the "quarter of dollar" that Mason Locke Weems ("Parson Weems") defined in a letter that same year to the Philadelphia publisher Mathew Carey as the desirable price for works "on subjects calculated to strike the Popular Curiosity." Such works would, if printed on a sufficient scale and "properly *distributed*, . . . prove an immense revenue to the prudent undertakers." For the next fifteen to twenty years, the price of *American Cookery* held steady in the "quarter of dollar" range. Weems also recommended that such books be "small," and *American Cookery* met this standard.[42]

The only example Weems gave of subject matter for such books was biographies of Revolutionary War heroes, such as that of George Washington he would himself later produce. He certainly wasn't thinking of cookbooks. Nevertheless, the fact that *American Cookery* otherwise measures up to his criteria for early national mass marketing of printed material is highly intriguing. "People . . . think nothing of giving 1/6 (their quarter of a dollar) for anything that pleases their fancy," Weems concluded. The periodic reissue of *American Cookery* in Greater Connecticut at just about this price suggests that printers there thought the book would please the fancies of Connecticut and other New England émigrés to the region.[43]

What did Weems mean by "properly *distributed*"? Historian David Jaffee calls Weems "the most famous peddler in the early republic," so among other things he almost certainly meant that publishers aspiring to produce books with a good chance of being successfully marketed should design them in such a way that book peddlers could conveniently include them in their stock of goods.[44]

Among the types of books circulating in the early republic that we know were distributed by peddlers were chapbooks. A chapbook is defined by scholar Victor Neuberg as "a paper-covered book or pamphlet, usually measuring some three and a half by six inches, containing 4, 8, 12, 16 or 24 pages." Chapbooks were most often children's books or abridged versions of popular novels, but in England cookbooks and household manuals were occasionally issued in chapbook format.[45]

We know very little about how *American Cookery* was actually distributed. Newspaper advertisements invariably mention the book's availability at bookstores operated by newspaper proprietors. But it is unlikely that all copies remained on the shelves of these town and village emporia. Even the first two editions of *American Cookery* are similar to chapbooks in being paper-covered and in their even-numbered paginations, which in both editions are exact multiples of the chapbook paginations listed by Neuberg. These features are retained in most of the later printings, and in all of them the size is reduced to six inches, bringing them within the chapbook range in this respect as well.[46]

In other words, the book was made even more portable, suggesting that distribution by peddlers was not absent from printers' calculations. According to historian William J. Gilmore, writing of Vermont during the same period with which we are concerned, "the informal circulation network" that peddlers constituted "was not accessory. Rather, it was essential to bookselling during the early republic and constituted a regular part of rural northwestern New England life after 1800."[47]

The picture now brought into focus is that of a relatively small, relatively cheap book containing culinary instruction which exhibits a careful balancing of elegance and restraint. This book was written by an orphan who exhibited an equally careful balancing of aspiration and deference. It was being carried by peddlers into newly settled areas filled with households inhabited by people similar to the orphaned author, aspiring yet desirous as well of social stability. Such people were ready to make the transition from the initial rawness of the frontier to "good furniture, a handsome dress, a handsome mode of living, better manners, and everything else connected with a higher reputation." The English traveler John Lambert described such a household beginning to thrive on the shores of Lake Champlain in 1810. Lambert was surprised and pleased at the "variety of eatables" offered him at breakfast by the farmer's wife and daughters—"eggs, fried pork, beef-steaks, apple tarts, pickles, cheese, cider, tea, and toast dipped in melted but-ter and milk." He was equally pleased by the "half-barrel" device the farmer had constructed that "answered the double purpose of a churn for making butter, and a rocking horse for his children."[48]

It was for households such as this one that *American Cookery* was created and designed. David Jaffee concludes that peddlers "furthered the democra-tization of gentility that began with the eighteenth-century retail shops. . . . [They] joined storekeepers in the role of tutor with regard to the polite world of material goods." A 1787 Vermont broadside peddler's ditty boasted that the singer's bag held "Straw-hats & Bonnets for Lads & Lasses, / Good as the best, the Gentry wear." Twenty years later, peddlers' bags also held, we believe, a little book full of instructions on how to make dishes that ranged from exotic and refined "orange pudding" to familiar and comfort-ing pumpkin or Indian pudding, good as the best the gentry ate.[49]

We mentioned above that John Treadwell both served as chairman of the board of trustees of the Connecticut Missionary Society and participated in the Town Reports project. That is, he was involved in promoting both reli-gion and the material improvement of domestic and community life as stays of social order and well-being. Another Town Report author, Levi Hart, was also an officer of the Missionary Society. Yet two more such authors, Ammi Robbins and William F. Miller, presided over religious revivals in Connecti-cut, and Robbins and his son Thomas were both active in the Missionary Society. Town Report author Azel Backus was the nephew of a revival-sponsoring clergyman, Charles Backus. And report author David Hale had received his theological training from Jeremiah Day, revival clergyman and an editor of the Missionary Society's periodical, the *Connecticut Evangelical Magazine*. In a compendium of revivals that took place throughout the United States between 1815 and 1818, eleven of the places where *American*

Cookery was reprinted, plagiarized, or advertised are listed as locations where discreet, sober revivals of the sort conducted by the Connecticut ecclesiastical establishment took place.[50]

Such key spokesmen of Connecticut Federalism as Timothy Dwight and Jedidiah Morse disapproved of peddlers, who were susceptible to "the evils which are attendant upon the bartering of small wares." Nevertheless, we view the peddlers who brought *American Cookery*'s Connecticut-inflected code of restrained gentility into country households as analogous to the clergymen sent out by the Connecticut Missionary Society to enfold those same households into a Connecticut religious culture inflected in much the same way. Just as the itinerant religious missionaries were spreading the village rectitude that would become one of the two main props of Victorianism in mid-nineteenth-century America, so these itinerant book and consumer goods salesmen were missionaries for the parlor taste and decorum that would become the other mainstay of American life a few decades later. This was the cultural work that "the first American cookbook" was created to help perform.[51]

CONCLUSION

The American Dream and Its Discontents

At many points in this book we have argued that *American Cookery* was part of an effort by the prominent citizens of Connecticut to win cultural leadership of the new nation known as the United States of America. Those historians such as Joseph A. Conforti and Sam Haselby who have called attention to the part played in early national culture by Jedidiah Morse, Timothy Dwight, and others in the Connecticut circle have tended to see their work as part of a campaign to trumpet the superiority of the New England region as a whole. Conforti writes that in *American Geography*, Morse "sought to codify and stabilize the region's cultural distinctiveness while conveying his hope for the 'New Englandization' of the republic." Haselby states that the Connecticut Wits "imagined the United States of America as an idealized version of revolutionary-era New England, especially Connecticut and Massachusetts, writ large."[1]

But although New Englanders as a whole did generally agree on the superiority of their region to the other regions with which they were conjoined, they also contended for primacy among themselves. Timothy Dwight opined that the people of the Connecticut Valley were "better educated and more orderly than in most other parts even of New England." A Massachusetts newspaper editor spoke sarcastically of how the "State of Connecticut" was setting itself up as the "Guide and Pattern of ALL the States." He surely was not the only non-Connecticut New Englander who bristled at such assertions as Dwight's.[2]

The New England states competed during the first half of the nineteenth century for the role of spearheading the all–New England effort to gain cultural leadership of the United States, as literary historian Lawrence Buell has chronicled. Rhode Island's case was made at midcentury by state historian Samuel Greene Arnold. Emphasizing Roger Williams's flight from Massachusetts persecution and his founding of a settlement devoted exclusively to "the spirit of liberty, which elsewhere had no congenial home,"

263

Arnold proclaimed that Rhode Island's influence "had extended far beyond our narrow borders, . . . and already made the American Union one vast Rhode Island in principle and feeling."[3]

Unlike the Rhode Island entry, the Connecticut version of a New England model for the United States lacked a myth of seventeenth-century origin with a compelling storyline. A group of families had removed themselves and their minister Thomas Hooker from Cambridge in the Massachusetts Bay settlements to the Connecticut River Valley for reasons that have always remained unclear. Disgruntlement over land allotments? The lure of valley fertility? Theological disagreements between Hooker and other Massachusetts clergy? None of this was going to cut it in the competition for a place in national consciousness and memory.

Enter Massachusetts with far more resources at its disposal than Rhode Island and with a far better story to tell than Connecticut: its tale of the persecuted, persevering, heroic "Pilgrims" of Plymouth. Conforti recounts in convincing detail the story of the nineteenth-century crafting of the Pilgrim story. The Plymouth settlers' mostly modest social origins, relative tolerance, and purportedly friendly relations with the Native people were put to the fore to obscure the reality of the much more significant and more traditionally hierarchical and dogmatic Puritan plantations established around Massachusetts Bay a few years later. So successful was the installation of Plymouth as the default version of early Massachusetts and by extension early America that the grimmer aspects of Massachusetts Puritanism depicted in Nathaniel Hawthorne's *The Scarlet Letter* and conveyed in memories of the Salem witch trials were turned into a darkly glamorous sideshow. The dour and rigid Puritans came to serve primarily as the shadowy foil against which the valor, virtue, and amiability of the Pilgrims shone ever more brightly. The imaginative excitements of these Massachusetts narratives made everyone forget about Connecticut, "the land of steady habits." By 1865, a writer in the Massachusetts-based *Atlantic Monthly* could snidely refer to the writings of the Connecticut Wits as a "profitless employment of labor, unusual in Connecticut."[4]

Yet there is reason to believe that the social vision of the Connecticut Federalists, with its emphasis on agrarian and village freeholding, nevertheless exerted a potent influence on American culture well into the twentieth century, however much the Connecticut roots of this vision were forgotten. Historian Trish Loughran has argued that the Federalists of the 1780s and 1790s managed to carry out their plans for a national polity by virtue of sheer ideological willpower and shrewd intellectual maneuvering, success-fully imposing what was in effect a counterrevolution in spite of seemingly overwhelming material impediments and persisting regional allegiances.[5]

It was the Connecticut branch of Federalism, however, that gave this nationalizing agenda a measure of social content and appeal. The recycling of the sheet music of a Federalist campaign song for the 1800 presidential election into the cover of the 1813–21 Colchester manuscript cookbook dis-cussed earlier amounts to a symbol of the enduring influence of Connecti-cut Federalism, in spite of the national Federalist Party's decisive political defeat in that 1800 election.[6]

Timothy Dwight asserted that the Connecticut River Valley's lack of urban and mercantile locales was not a defect but rather a virtue. This meant that valley inhabitants were "free from that sense of inferiority cus-tomarily felt by the body of a people who live in the neighborhood of large cities. Hence a superior spirit of personal independence is generated and cherished." Buell finds that this distancing from urban scenes and realities remained characteristic of New England writing as a whole "through the Civil War," in spite of the fact that "New England was the nation's first region" to channel its mercantile wealth into industrialization.[7]

Connecticut agrarianism and antiurbanism faced competition, of course, from the partially similar views formulated by Thomas Jefferson and his followers. But the Jeffersonian version of what we might term ruralism was increasingly compromised by its association with slavery and then further discredited by the outcome of the Civil War.

As the nineteenth century wore on, therefore, the most influential rural-istic outlook in the United States became the one first articulated forcefully in Connecticut. Historians have generally confirmed the assertions made by contemporaries that Connecticut played a major, if not dominant, part in the settlement of upstate New York and much of Ohio. Not only did large numbers of people move from Connecticut into these areas; they also brought their institutions and ways of life with them.[8]

In the 1820s, Timothy Dwight's most prominent Yale student, his cultural son Lyman Beecher, emerged as the leading spokesman for the view that it was the mission of New England in general and Connecticut in particular to "civilize" the "West" (i.e., the Midwest). Among the measures Beecher sought to implement for civilizing the West along Connecticut lines was encouraging the founding of colleges modeled specifically on Yale. Western Reserve (now Case Western Reserve) maintained particularly close ties with Yale.[9]

A comparable commitment to the "mission to the West" is to be found among members of the succeeding generation. Lyman Beecher's biological son Edward studied at Yale under another prominent cultural son of Timothy Dwight, Nathaniel William Taylor. In 1830, Edward Beecher was appointed president of Illinois College in Jacksonville. This institution was envisioned as what historian Theodore Calvin Pease called "a new and greater Yale to be reared on the western prairies." Beecher presided over a faculty consisting primarily of the "Yale Band," a group of recent New Haven graduates who had come west to help transplant the Connecticut Way. Concurrently, efforts were made to settle the state along New England lines, with twenty-eight "colonies" started up in Illinois during the 1830s.[10]

Lyman Beecher's eldest daughter also devoted herself to western cultural missionary work. One of Catharine Beecher's many projects was the training of women to work as teachers in the West. Her efforts bore fruit with the founding in the 1850s of Milwaukee College (later Milwaukee Downer College).[11]

Just as the Plymouth settlement of the seventeenth century was not in fact the noble, harmonious community of saints of Pilgrim legend but instead a motley crew of "saints and strangers," so these Connecticut civilizing endeavors were greeted with considerable resistance by many of their intended beneficiaries, non–New England natives who did not accept the Connecticut view of themselves as in dire need of uplift. This, however, does not mean that the Connecticut missionaries were prevented from disseminating their values and ideals, any more than soberly accurate descriptions of Plymouth much hindered the propagation of the Pilgrim saga. Catharine Beecher was forced to resign from Milwaukee College, but by that time she was already influential as the author of widely read works on household management, including an 1846 cookbook that carried forward the tradition inaugurated by *American Cookery*.[12]

In 1869, Beecher revised her writings on domesticity and gave them greater currency by coauthoring *The American Woman's Home* with her even more famous and influential younger sister, Harriet Beecher Stowe. That same year, Stowe brought out *Oldtown Folks*, the one of her four post–*Uncle Tom's Cabin* nostalgic novels of preindustrial New England that most fully idealizes the same early national village that Timothy Dwight had celebrated in its heyday. So here were the Beecher sisters, true progeny of the Connecticut elite that had claimed national leadership during their childhood, offering at the very outset of accelerated industrialization and urbanization not only pleasant vistas of New England village life but also systematic practical instruction in how to carry on under modern conditions the freehold house-holding that Dwight and other Connecticut Federalists had celebrated.[13]

What all this suggests is that the Connecticut vision of independent householding, preferably in rural or semirural settings, was a principal source for what in the twentieth century came to be known as the American Dream. The creation of suburbia after World War II amounted to the mass production of the Connecticut Way—escape for a broad swathe of the populace of the United States from tenancy in the city to home ownership in the countryside. People would live "free from that sense of inferiority customarily felt by the body of a people who live in the neighborhood of large cities," in homes that they would, through the magic of mortgage financing, be able to claim independently to own. They would receive plentiful advice in mass market magazines and books about how to decorate and maintain these homes in a style of modest elegance. And advice on how to provide wholesome, nicely composed and presented meals for their families would be just as readily available from the same or similar sources.[14]

It may be that those of us living in the early years of the twenty-first century are witnessing at long last the demise of the Connecticut definition of American life. Suburbia has for quite some time been felt to be at best banal and at worst stifling. In a time of slice-and-dice mortgages and dizzyingly complex forms of real estate investment, home ownership is being steadily problematized.

And it appears to be the case at the moment that in a great many families, standards of living can be maintained only if all adults in the household are gainfully employed. The consequent minimizing of adult time and energy available for activities carried on at home has meant that home cooking is being superseded by convenience foods, fast food, and take-out from restaurants or supermarket deli counters.

Some aspects of cooking are still very much alive in the public imagination, but these have little to do any longer with the housewife's provision of three square meals a day. Instead, interest in food is taking more imaginative or theoretical forms, such as televised cooking shows and celebrity chefs, glossily produced cookbooks full of elaborate recipes, and indeed the emergence of the field of which this book is a manifestation—culinary history. Food preparation is becoming more a profession or a hobby than a necessary, integral aspect of everyday life.

As such trends toward commodifying and professionalizing the domestic arts on the one hand and trivializing them on the other continue unabated, the pleasant, quotidian civility of the carefully prepared, home-cooked meal, like the pleasant vista of the carefully manicured American lawn, is coming to seem as antique as the cuisine of alamode beef, rich custards, nice puddings, and syllabub on display in *American Cookery*.

But in a strange twist, at the moment that the principal subject of *American Cookery*—moderately refined, homemade food preparations—has come to feel removed from any convincing vision of middle-class American life, the persona inscribed perplexingly in the book's front- and backmatter has moved closer to the center of the American imagination. This semiliterate, indeed only semi-coherent, voice announced that she had been unable to master her own work as completely as she felt was necessary to both the subject and her own integrity. Nevertheless, in the act of asserting that her text was subverted, the author/cook's narrative of that subversion undermined the control of those who perhaps wished actively to injure her or who simply failed to follow her directions.

In recounting her grievances, the author also escaped from the norms of her day for cookbook writing. The writer of a cookbook was expected to be virtually indistinguishable from others doing the same kind of culinary work. A detached, practical tone and the interchangeability of many recipes within a particular cuisine encouraged the practice of recipe plagiarism in the period. Not so in *American Cookery*. Its author became a personality to be reckoned with.

The book's outsider author is what gives it staying power, as much as does its status as a "first." The unsung, the unconventional, and the unlikely are, after all, emblematically modern. To find rhetorical vestiges of these qualities in an early national work makes that work, in our post–American Dream time, not only more approachable but also more in conformity with our ideas of a valuable artistic or historic artifact.

So the legacy of *American Cookery* is not limited to the intentions of Connecticut Federalists to mold American identity. The book's afterlife is also the story of a cook's determination to buck the odds and become an author. Her fury at the errors that mar the first edition of her work, her suspicions about the intentions of the anonymous person who transcribed her recipes, her subservience to "the Ladies," her aspiration to aid a "rising generation" of American women, and her boasting about her first edition success combine to form a complex personal portrait, certainly as full and nuanced as those created for members of the Connecticut elite by Ralph

Earl. But what is most tantalizing about this combination of contradictory traits and factors is how they presage the potent brew of simmering resentments and self-determination that, many generations later, would give birth in the American suburbs of the 1960s (constructed in conformity with Connecticut's vision for the American future) to feminism's Second Wave.

Now we know the story in full. The long history of the interplay between manuscript and print recipes that produced the rise of the female cookbook author and the housewifely cookbook tradition in Britain, and the importation of those books and those modes of cooking to the American colonies, laid the foundations on which a talented female cook in the new American nation could envision a new mode of cooking, adapted from British sources and deploying American ingredients and methods. She thought—or those with elite connections around her thought—this new American cuisine worth bringing before the public. The medium of print that had enhanced the spiritual power of Puritanism and had helped bring political power to a motley collection of rebellious American colonists was to be extended to all fields of endeavor for Americans, including culinary pursuits.

The potency of print, what Karen A. Weyler has called the "potential for print to be life changing," to which must be added the particular social prestige of print in New England, seems to have inspired a semiliterate orphan to fight her way into the position of instructing the American public on the subject of its cuisine. Without the social reward of being "an Authoress" to aspire to, it is unlikely that she would have undertaken the task. Yet undertake it she did. The power of authorship to provide respect, influence, and social position, not to mention cash, may have provided her with the motivation to overcome all the obstacles in her way. But Amelia Simmons's disappearance from her own title page after the first two editions of *American Cookery* implies that something went wrong with her plan. It seems that she did not survive to enjoy the fruits of her labors. Or it may be that the speed with which her name was dropped implies that she had never been anything more than a fiction of the publishers. Does it matter? Amelia Simmons is, without doubt, a potent social metaphor for the struggling orphaned female and the socially marginal in early America, and her story is forever etched into the first American cookbook.

The other part of the story is less romantic but just as essential to the book's purpose—to assert that a life of middling prosperity, with some measure of refinement and some degree of enjoyment of "all the sweets of life," was the goal that Americans should set for themselves as they embarked on their national project. Restraint in the pursuit of happiness does not translate well into a battle cry. But it was the course the Connecticut Federalists wished the nation to steer between the dual perils of wealth and poverty. Thus did this particular American version of the social good put forward by "Amelia Simmons, an American Orphan" find its way into history.

The Sources of *American Cookery*

As discussed in chapter 1, 35 percent of the recipes in *American Cookery* are either copied word for word, or all but word for word, from recipes in English cookbooks or are closely based on recipes from the same set of cookbooks. The list below of these plagiarisms and adaptations is modeled on the two tables of "Corresponding Recipes" compiled by Jennifer Stead and Priscilla Bain for the modern reprint edition of Hannah Glasse's *The Art of Cookery Made Plain and Easy*.[1] The following abbreviations and symbols are used:

H	Simmons, *American Cookery* (introduction by Wilson)
A	Simmons, *American Cookery* (introduction by Hess)
FH	Carter, *The Frugal Housewife* (1792)
ACPE	Glasse, *The Art of Cookery Made Plain and Easy*
CH	Smith, *The Compleat Housewife*
LA	*The Lady's Assistant for Regulating and Supplying Her Table*
HP	Harrison, *The House-Keeper's Pocket-Book*
EEH	Raffald, *The Experienced English Housekeeper*
CC	*Court Cookery; or, The Compleat English Cook*
WD	*The Whole Duty of a Woman*
EH	Moxon, *English Housewifry Exemplified*
*	recipe in *American Cookery* copied verbatim from source
#	recipe in *American Cookery* altered from source only in wording
%	recipe in *American Cookery* altered from source in culinary details

The page number where the source recipe is to be found is given in the "Source(s)" column.

PAGE	RECIPE	SOURCE(S)
H 17, A 9	Roast Mutton	%FH 2
H 18, A 9	Roast Veal	%ACPE 4
H 18, A 9–10	Roast Lamb	#FH 4
H 20–22, A 15–17	To Dress a Turtle	*FH 29–32
H 25, A 30	A Rice Pudding, No. 1	%ACPE 108

PAGE	RECIPE	SOURCE(S)
H 26, A 32	A Sunderland Pudding	%LA 355–56
H 26, A 32	A Whitpot	%ACPE 79
H 26, A 32	A Bread Pudding	%ACPE 109
H 26, A 32	A Flour Pudding	%FH 143
H 26, A 32	A Boiled Flour Pudding	%FH 138
H 27, A 33	An Apple Pudding Dumplin	%ACPE 113
H 27, A 33	Potatoe Pudding, No. 2	%HP 123–24
H 27, A 33–34	Apple Pudding	%ACPE 107, CH 129
H 27, A 34	Carrot Pudding	%CH 126
H 28, A 35	Orange Pudding	#FH 145, ACPE 105–6
H 28–29, A 35–36	Lemon Pudding	#CH 144–45
H 29, A 37	Puff Pastes for Tarts, No. 1	%CH 154
H 29, A 37	Puff Pastes for Tarts, No. 2	%CH 152
H 29, A 37	Puff Pastes for Tarts, No. 3	%CH 165
H 29, A 37	Puff Pastes for Tarts, No. 5	#ACPE 75
H 29–30, A 38	Royal Paste	%FH 115, HP 88
H 30, A 28	Custards, No. 2	%FH 153, ACPE 143
H 30, A 28	Custards, No. 4 (A No. 3)	%FH 153, CH 141
H 30, A 28	Rice Custard	%FH 154, CH 141–42
H 31, A 29	Orange or Lemon Tart	%FH 125–26, ACPE 74–75, CH 153–54
H 31, A 38	Syllabub from the Cow	*FH 147–48
H 32, A 39	A Whipt Syllabub	*FH 148
H 32, A 39	To Make a fine Cream	%FH 148, ACPE 144
H 32, A 39	Lemon Cream	*FH 148, ACPE 143, CH 185
H 32, A 39	Raspberry Cream	*FH 148–49
H 32–33, A 40	Whipt Cream	%FH 149, ACPE 144
H 33, A 40	A Trifle	%FH 149
H 33	Plumb Cake	%CH 170, 171–72
H 33, A 41	Potatoe Cake	%ACPE 98
H 36, A 49	Gingerbread Cakes	%ACPE 139, HP 107
H 36, A 47	A Cheap Seed Cake	%ACPE 139
H 36–37, A 47–48	Queens Cake	%LA 377
H 37, A 48	Soft Cakes in little pans	%ACPE 140
H 37, A 48–49	Shrewsbury Cake	%EEH 137
H 37, A 49	Diet Bread	% CC 187, WD 534–35
H 40, A 54	To keep White Bullace	*FH 158–59, ACPE 157
H 40, A 54	To make Marmalade	#H%A FH 159
H 40, A 54–55	To preserve Mulberries	*FH 159
H 41, A 55	To preserve Goosberries	*FH 159–60
H 41, A 55–56	To preserve Peaches	*FH 160, ACPE 155
H 41–42, A 56	To preserve Apricots	#FH 160, 161
H 42, A 56–57	To preserve Cherries	%FH 161–62

PAGE	RECIPE	SOURCE(S)
H 42, A 57	To preserve Raspberries	*FH 162
H 42, A 57	To preserve Currants	*FH 162
H 42–43, A 57–58	To preserve Plumbs	#FH 161
H 43, A 60	To keep Damsons	%EH 161
H 43, A 60–61	Currant Jelly	#FH 152, ACPE 145
H 43–44, A 62	To dry Peaches	#FH 162–63
H 44, A 62–63	To pickle . . . Melons	#FH 164–65
H 44, A 63–64	To pickle Barberries	#FH 165–66, ACPE 134
H 44–45, A 64	To pickle Cucumbers	#FH 168
H 45–46	To boil . . . Garden Stuff	#FH 32
H 46, A 23	To keep green Peas	#FH 157–58, ACPE 156, CH 88
H 46	To boil French Beans	#FH 34
H 46	To boil broad Beans	#FH 34–35
H 46	To boil green Peas	#FH 35
H 46–47	To boil Asparagus	#FH 32–33
H 47	To boil Cabbage	*FH 35
A 20	General Rules . . . Boiling	#FH 16
A 20–21	To boil Ham	%FH 18–19
A 21	To boil a Turkey	%FH 19–20
A 40	Plumb Cake[2]	%CH 170, 171–72

TOTALS

ONE SOURCE

Frugal Housewife	29
Art of Cookery	9
Compleat Housewife	7
Lady's Assistant	2
Experienced English Housekeeper	1
House-Keeper's Pocket-Book	1
English Housewifry Exemplified	1

TWO POSSIBLE SOURCES

Frugal Housewife or *Art of Cookery*	8
Frugal Housewife or *Compleat Housewife*	2
Frugal Housewife or *House-Keeper's Pocket-Book*	1
Art of Cookery or *Compleat Housewife*	1
Art of Cookery or *House-Keeper's Pocket-Book*	1
Whole Duty of a Woman or *Court Cookery*	1

THREE POSSIBLE SOURCES

Frugal Housewife or *Art of Cookery* or *Compleat Housewife*	3

SOURCES OF THE HARTFORD EDITION
MARKETING SECTION

Some or all of the following portions of the shopping
advice in the Hartford edition are clearly derivative.

H 5	Beef	ACPE 161
H 8	Capons	ACPE 162
H 8	Goose	ACPE 162
H 8	Wild Ducks	ACPE 162
H 8	Wood Cocks	ACPE 162
H 8	Snipes	ACPE 162
H 8	Partridges	ACPE 162
H 8	Pigeons	ACPE 162
H 8	Hares	ACPE 163
H 8–9	Leveret	ACPE 163
H 9	Rabbits	ACPE 163
H 10	Eggs	CH 5

Recipes from Plain to Fancy

I n chapter 7, the culinary content of *American Cookery* is broken down into three categories: plain, prosperous, and festive or elegant. Below is the list of our assignments to these categories of all the recipes in the first two editions of the book. Each recipe in each edition is designated by the abbreviations H (for the Hartford edition) or A (for the Albany edition) followed by its page number.

PLAIN	PROSPEROUS	FESTIVE/ELEGANT
A Stew Pie H22–23 A24	To Roast Beef H17 A9	To stuff a Turkey H18 A13
A Sea Pie H23 A24	Roast Mutton H17 A9	To stuff . . . a Turkey or Fowl H18 A13
A Rice Pudding No. 5 H25 A31	Roast Veal H18 A9	To stuff . . . a Goslin H19 A13–14
A Nice Indian Pudding No. 3 H26 A31	Roast Lamb H18 A9–10	To smother a Fowl H19 A15
A Flour Pudding H26 A32	A Chicken Pie H23 A24–25	To stuff a leg of Veal H19 A11–12
A boiled Flour Pudding H26 A32	Minced Pie of Beef H24 A26	To stuff a leg of Pork H19 A12
An apple Pudding Dumplin H27 A33	Apple Pie H24 A26	To alamode . . . Beef H19–20 A10
Potatoe Pudding No. 1 H27 A33	Currant Pies H24 A27	To alamode a round H20 A10–11
A sick bed Custard H30 A28	A buttered apple Pie H25 A27	To dress a Turtle H20–22 A15–17
Johny Cake H34 A41	A Rice Pudding H25 A30	To dress a Calve's Head H22 A17–18
Indian Slapjack H34 A41–42	A Rice Pudding No. 2 H25 A30	Minced Pies H23–24 A25
A cheap seed Cake H36 A47	A Rice Pudding No. 3 H25 A30	Tongue Pie H24 A25–26
Biscuit H38 A47	A Rice Pudding No. 4 H25 A30–31	A Cream Almond Pudding H27 A33

PLAIN	PROSPEROUS	FESTIVE/ELEGANT
Butter Biscuit H38 A47	A Rice Pudding No. 6 H25 A31	Pompkin No. 1 H28 A34–35
The American Citron H40 A53	A Nice Indian Pudding No. 1 H26 A31	Orange Pudding H28 A35
For dressing Codfish H45 A22	A Nice Indian Pudding No. 2 H26 A31	A Lemon Pudding H28–29 A35–36
To boil Cabbage H47	A Sunderland Pudding H26 A32	Royal Paste H29–30 A38
Emptins H47 A64	A Whitpot H26 A32	Marmalade [Tart] H30
Chouder A22–23	A Bread Pudding H26 A32	Orange or Lemon Tart H31 A29
Potatoe Pie A27	Potatoe Pudding No. 2 H27 A33	To make . . . Syllabub from the Cow H31 A38
Buck-wheat Cakes A44	Apple Pudding H27 A33–34	A Whipt Syllabub H32 A39
Federal Pan Cake A44	Carrot Pudding H27 A34	To make a fine Cream H32 A39
Tea Biscuit A46	A Crookneck . . . Pudding H27–28 A34	Lemon Cream H32 A39
To make good Bread A50–51	Pompkin No. 2 H28 A35	Raspberry Cream H32 A39–40
A new method . . . Apples A59	Puff Pastes for Tarts No. 1 H29 A37	Whipt Cream H32–33 A40
	Puff Pastes for Tarts No. 2 H29 A37	A Trifle H33 A40
	Puff Pastes for Tarts No. 3 H29 A37	Plumb Cake H33
	Puff Pastes for Tarts No. 4 H29 A37	A rich Cake H33 A41
	Puff Pastes for Tarts No. 5 H29 A37	Loaf Cakes No. 1 H34 A42
	Puff Pastes for Tarts No. 6 H29 A38	Loaf Cakes, Another No. 2 H34 A42–43
	A Paste for Sweet Meats No.7 H29 A38	Loaf Cakes, Another No. 3 H35 A43
	A Paste for Sweet Meats No.8 H29 A38	Loaf Cakes, Another No. 4 H35 A43
	Custards No. 1 H30 A27–28	Another Christmas Cookey H35 A46
	Custards No. 2 H30 A28	Queens Cake H36–37 A47–48
	Custards No. 3 H30	Another (called) Pound Cake H37 A48
	Boiled Custard H30 A28	Soft Cakes in little pans H37 A 48
	Rice Custard H30 A28	A light Cake . . . in small cups H37 A48
	A Rich Custard H30 A28[1]	To make Marmalade H40 A54

PLAIN	PROSPEROUS	FESTIVE/ELEGANT
	Apple Tarts H30 A28	To preserve Apricots H41–42 A56
	Cramberries H30 A29	Alamode Beef H45 A19
	Appricots [Tart] H31 A29	To stuff a Pig A12
	Gooseberry Tart H31 A30	To stuff . . . four Chickens A14
	Grapes [Tart] H31 A30	Soup, of Lamb's head and pluck A20
	Plain Cake H33 A40–41	Orange Pudding A36
	Another [Plain Cake] H33	Marlborough Pudding A36
	Potatoe Cake H33 A41	Quince Pudding A37
	Another Plain cake H35 A43	Election Cake A43–44
	Cookies H35 A45–46	Independence Cake A44
	Molasses Gingerbread H36 A49	New Year's Cake A45
	Gingerbread Cakes . . . No. 1 H36 A49	Apple Preserve A58–59
	Soft Gingerbread H36 A50	Damson Preserve A59
	Butter drop do H36 A50[2]	To preserve Parsley A60
	Gingerbread No. 4 H36	Peach Preserve A61–62
	Pound Cake H37 A48	
	Shrewsbury Cake H37 A48–49	
	Diet Bread H37 A49	
	Rusk No. 1 H38 A51	
	Rusk No. 2 H38 A51	
	Rusk No. 3 H38 A51	
	Rusk No. 4 H38 A51	
	Rusk No. 5 H38 A51	
	Rusk No. 6 H38 A51–52	
	A Butter drop H38 A50	
	For preserving Quinces H39 A52	
	For preserving Quinces . . . Sugar H39 A52–53	
	For preserving Strawberries H39 A53	
	To keep White Bullace H40 A54	
	To preserve Mulberries whole H40 A54–55	
	To preserve Goosberries H41 A55	
	To preserve Peaches H41 A55–56	
	To preserve Cherries H42 A56–57	
	To preserve Raspberries H42 A57	
	To preserve Currants H42 A57	
	To preserve Plumbs H42–43 A57–58	
	To keep Damsons H43 A60	
	Currant Jelly H43 A60–61	
	To dry Peaches H43–44 A62	
	To pickle . . . Melons H44 A62–63	
	To pickle Barberries H44 A63–64	
	To pickle Cucumbers H44–45 A64	
	To boil . . . Garden Stuff H45–46	

PLAIN	PROSPEROUS	FESTIVE/ELEGANT
	To keep Green Peas H46 A23	
	To boil French Beans H46	
	To boil broad Beans H46	
	To boil green Peas H46	
	To boil Asparagus H46–47	
	For brewing Spruce Beer H47 A64	
	To broil a Beef-Stake A11	
	To dress a Beef-Stake A11	
	Veal Stake A11	
	To broil Chickens A14–15	
	Soup . . . Beef's Hock A19	
	Veal Soup A19–20	
	To boil Ham A20–21	
	To boil a Turkey A21	
	To dress a Bass A21–22	
	To dress Sturgeon A22	
	To broil Shad A22	
	Beef-stake Pie A23	
	A Lamb Pie A23–24	
	Dried Apple Pie A26–27	
	A Plumb Pudding A36	
	Plumb Pudding, boiled A36–37	
	Plumb Cake A40[3]	
	Honey Cake A45	
	Tea Cakes A45	
	Wiggs A46	
	Wafers A46	
	Tumbles A47	
	Gingerbread No. 4 A50	
	Gingerbread A50	
	Strawberry Preserve A58	
	To preserve bush Beans A59	
	To preserve Plumbs and Cherries A61	

TOTALS	NUMBER	PERCENT
Plain	25	13
Prosperous	114	59
Festive/Elegant	53	28

Works Relating to Orphanhood Available in New England and New York, 1760-1800

I n Cheryl L. Nixon's *The Orphan in Eighteenth-Century Law and Literature*, thirty-six eighteenth-century English novels or other works in which orphanhood is a significant motif are discussed or mentioned. Using the databases Early American Imprints, series 1, and America's Historical Newspapers, we searched for the presence of these works in New England and New York in the closing decades of the eighteenth century, assuming that advertisements for them in newspapers or listings of them in booksellers' and library catalogues would constitute evidence of their availability in the region. We found at least one advertisement or listing for nineteen of the thirty-six works. The absence from the northern U.S. market of the remaining seventeen English works may be due to the fact that by and large they were older, published before 1760. The themes and conventions of the nineteen English orphan works circulating in New England and New York in this period are likely to have contributed to forming regional perspectives on orphanhood.

WORK	NO. OF ADS OR LISTINGS
James Annesley, *Memoirs of an Unfortunate Young Nobleman* (1743, 1747)	1
Frances Burney, *Cecilia* (1782)	30
——, *Evelina* (1778)	43
Henry Fielding, *Tom Jones* (1749)	6
[Sarah Fielding], *History of Betty Barnes* (1753)	3
Eliza Haywood, *History of Betty Thoughtless* (1751)	6
Elizabeth Inchbald, *Simple Story* (1791)	26
Henry Mackenzie, *Man of the World* (1773)	11
The Perfidious Guardian; or, Vicissitudes of Fortune (1790)	4
Ann Radcliffe, *Mysteries of Udolpho* (1794)	7

WORK	NO. OF ADS OR LISTINGS
——, *Romance of the Forest* (1791)	14
Clara Reeve, *Two Mentors* (1783)	3
Samuel Richardson, *Clarissa* (1747–48)	5
——, *Sir Charles Grandison* (1753–54)	7
Elizabeth Singer Rowe, *Friendship in Death* (1750)	14
Charlotte Smith, *Celestina* (1791)	10
——, *Emmeline: The Orphan of the Castle* (1788)	24
Tobias Smollett, *Adventures of Peregrine Pickle* (1751	6
——, *Expedition of Humphry Clinker* (1771)	18

We also searched for advertisements and listings of the two American works of the day with orphanhood as a major theme.

Hapless Orphan (1793)	9
Enos Hitchcock, *Farmer's Friend* (1793)	9
	Total 256

The following is a tabulation of the advertisements and listings by location.

NO. OF ADS OR LISTINGS

Maine

Eastern Herald, Portland	5
	Total 5

New Hampshire

New Hampshire Spy, Portsmouth	2
New Hampshire Gazette, Portsmouth	3
Courier of New Hampshire, Concord	2
	Total 7

Vermont

Vermont Gazette, Bennington	1
	Total 1

Massachusetts

James White's Store, Boston	9
Thomas & Andrews, Boston	11
William Pelham Circulating Library, Boston	10
Selected Catalogue, Boston	4
American Apollo, Boston	8
American Herald, Boston	2
Columbian Centinel, Boston	2
Federal Orrery, Boston	1
Massachusetts Mercury, Boston	2
Total, Boston	49

NO. OF ADS OR LISTINGS

Salem Mercury	7
Salem Gazette	4
Dabney, *Salem Bookstore*	6
Total, Eastern Mass. other than Boston	17
Rural Repository, Leominster	3
Massachusetts Spy, Worcester	9
Total, Central Mass.	12
Andrews's Western Star, Stockbridge	6
Total, Western Mass.	6
Total, Massachusetts 84	

Connecticut

Hudson & Goodwin broadside, Hartford	14
Hartford Library	7
Connecticut Courant, Hartford	18
Total, Hartford	39
Middlesex Gazette, Middletown	2
New Haven Gazette	2
Connecticut Journal, New Haven	3
Litchfield Monitor	2
American Telegraph, Newfield	2
Total, Connecticut 50	

Rhode Island

Providence Gazette	11
United States Chronicle, Providence	5
Total 16	

New York

New York Society Library	1
Diary, or Loudon's Register, New York City	26
New York Packet, New York City	6
Impartial Gazetteer, New York City	2
Weekly Museum, New York City	21
New York Daily Gazette, New York City	6
Total, New York City	62
Albany Library	9
Albany Bookstore	9
Albany Gazette	11
Total, Albany	29
Hudson Gazette	2
Total, New York 93	
TOTAL 256	

Editions, Printings, and Major Plagiarisms

Editions and printings are listed first, in chronological order,
followed by the plagiarisms, also in chronological order.

Hartford: Hudson and Goodwin, 1796
Author attribution: Amelia Simmons, an American Orphan
Pages: 47; height: 9.5 inches
Notes: Author identification in cursive font; preface; section on "Directions for Catering"; total recipes: 145

Hartford: Hudson and Goodwin, 1796
Author attribution: Amelia Simmons, an American Orphan
Pages: 48; height: 9.5 inches
Notes: Identical to first printing, above, except that the forty-eighth page is an "Advertisement" listing errata

Albany: Charles R. and George Webster, 1796
Author attribution: Amelia Simmons, an American Orphan
Pages: 64; height: 7.5 inches
Notes: Author identification in small caps; "the second edition"; two prefaces; section on "Directions for Catering" omitted; total recipes: 181

Hartford: Printed for Simeon Butler, Northampton, 1798
Author attribution: Amelia Simmons, an American Orphan
Pages: 48; height: 8.66 inches
Notes: Reprint of first printing of Hartford, 1796, except that the author identification is in small caps

Salem, N.Y: Printed by Dodd and Rumsey, for Charles R. and George Webster, Albany, 1804
>   Author attribution: Amelia Simmons, an American Orphan
>   Pages: 72; height: 5.5 inches
>   Notes: Identical to the Albany printing above, though called a "third edition" on the title page

Troy, N.Y.: Wright, Goodenow, and Stockwell, 1808
>   Author attribution: Amelia Simmons, an American Orphan
>   Pages: 86; height: 5.9 inches
>   Notes: Reprint of either the first Hartford printing or the 1798 Hartford/ Northampton reprint

N.p.: "Printed for the Publishers," 1808
>   Author attribution: An American Orphan
>   Pages: 72; height: 5.5 inches
>   Notes: Reprint of Albany, 1796, or Salem/Albany, 1804, with these changes: includes only one preface, the one to the first Hartford edition
>   five recipes omitted:
>   "To broil a Beef-Stake"
>   "To dress a Beef-Stake, sufficient for two Gentlemen"
>   "Veal Stake"
>   "A Plumb Pudding"
>   "Emptins"
>   two slightly altered:
>   "To dress a Calve's Head. Turtle fashion": added at end, "put in cloves to your taste"
>   "Another *Christmas Cookey*": title altered to "Another, *Christmas Cookey*," clarifying its relationship to the preceding recipe, "Cookies"

Walpole, N.H.: Printed for Elijah Brooks, 1812
>   Author attribution: An American Orphan
>   Pages: 67; height: 5.9 inches
>   Notes: Reprint of Albany, 1796, or Salem/Albany, 1804, with the same changes as N.p., 1808, except
>   "Another *Christmas Cookey*": title altered to "Another—*Christmas Cookey*," clarifying its relationship to the preceding recipe, "Cookies"
>   "Rusk, No. 3": "wet soft with milk, and bake" altered to "wet soft with milk, bake"

Brattleboro, Vt.: William Fessenden, 1814
>   Author attribution: An American Orphan
>   Pages: 69; height: 5.9 inches

Notes: Reprint of Albany, 1796, or Salem/Albany, 1804, with the same changes
as N.p., 1808, except
"Another *Christmas Cookey*" and "Rusk, No. 3" are left as they were in Albany,
1796, and Salem/Albany, 1804
One additional change:
"Rice Pudding, No. 6": Omits "N. B. The mode . . . fine and settled"

Poughkeepsie, N.Y.: Paraclete Potter, 1815
Author attribution: An American Orphan
Pages: 72; height: 5.9 inches
Notes: Reprint of Albany, 1796, or Salem/Albany, 1804, with the same changes
as Brattleboro, 1814

Windsor, Vt., 1816
Author attribution: An American Orphan
Pages: 67; height: 5.9 inches
Notes: Reprint of Walpole, 1812; the title page of that printing is included twice
in this one, first as the cover, then as the title page; at the bottom of the cover are
the words "For sale at the Bookstore of Pomroy & Hedge, Windsor, VT"

Zanesville, Ohio: Putnam and Clark, 1816
Author attribution: Amelia Simmons, an American Orphan
Pages: 71; height: 6.3 inches
Notes: Except for one feature, identical to Albany, 1796, or Salem/Albany,
1804, though called a "fourth edition" on the title page; the added feature is a
table of contents, pp. 66–71

Brattleboro, Vt.: John Holbrook, 1819
Author attribution: An American Orphan
Pages: 48; height: 5.9 inches
Notes: Reprint of Albany, 1796, or Salem/Albany, 1804, with the same changes
as Brattleboro, 1814, and with these additional recipes omitted:
"The American Citron"
"To preserve Mulberries whole"
"To preserve Goosberries, Damsons or Plumbs"
"To preserve Apricots"
"To preserve Parsley"
After "Currant Jelly," all recipes to the end of Albany, 1796, are omitted,
including "Emptins" omitted from Brattleboro, 1814
Two recipes slightly altered:
"Damson Preserve": Omits "*Cherries* and *Grapes* may be . . . same way"
"To keep Damsons": Omits "so as no air . . . plumbs must be hard"

New York: William Beastall, 1822

    Author attribution: An American Orphan

    Pages: 72; height: 5.9 inches

    Notes: Reprint of Albany, 1796, or Salem/Albany, 1804, with the same changes
    as in Walpole, 1812, except

    "Rice Pudding, No. 6": Omits "N. B. The mode . . . fine and settled," as in
    Brattleboro, 1814

    "Loaf Cakes, No. 1": Omits "Some return the frosted . . . into the oven"

    "For Preserving Quinces": "cool dry place" instead of "dry cool place"

    Pp. 64–71 consist of additional pickling recipes from English cookbooks, the
    majority from Raffald, *Experienced English Housekeeper*

Woodstock, Vt.: A. Colton, 1831

    Author attribution: An Orphan

    Pages: 110; height: 4.7 inches

    Notes: Called "second edition improved"; original subtitle language altered to
    ". . . cakes, from plain, to the imperial, and wedding cake"; then is appended
    the following: "also the best way of curing hams, corning beef, mutton, and
    veal: together with the rules for carving at dinner parties, exemplified with
    cuts"; includes only the Hartford, 1796, preface; *American Cookery* portions of
    the main text taken from Albany, 1796

PLAGIARISMS

New American Cookery; or, Female Companion . . . by an American Lady. New York: T.
    B. Jansen, 1805

Pages: 180; height: 5.5 inches

Notes: Until p. 94, culinary content virtually identical to Albany, 1796; pp. 94–
    103 consist of additional pickling recipes; pp. 103–4 include the two remain-
    ing recipes from Albany, 1796, "For brewing Spruce Beer" and "Emptins";
    remainder of the book consists almost entirely of recipes copied from Carter,
    Frugal Housewife

The New England Cookery . . . Particularly Adapted to This Part of Our Country. Compiled by Lucy Emerson. Montpelier, Vt.: Josiah Parks, 1808

Pages: 81; height: 5.9 inches

Notes: Subtitle language altered to "the Art of Dressing All Kinds of Flesh, Fish,
    and Vegetables"; preface is thinly disguised copy of Hartford, 1796, preface;
    most of "Directions for Catering" and recipes included from Hartford, 1796;
    interspersed are additional recipes from English cookbooks, the great majori-
    ty from Carter, *Frugal Housewife*

Harriet Whiting. *Domestic Cookery.* Boston: Printed for the Author, 1819.
Pages: 48; height: 6.7 inches
Notes: Work contains "no recipe that had not appeared" in Hartford, 1796, "and
exactly as it was then printed."[1]

*The Cook Not Mad; or, Rational Cookery; Being a Collection of Original and Selected
Receipts.* Watertown, N.Y.: Knowlton and Rice, 1830.
Pages: 120; height: 5.9 inches
Notes: Portions plagiarized from *American Cookery* are based on either N.p., 1808;
Brattleboro, 1814; or Poughkeepsie, 1815, since like them, the sentence "put
in cloves to your taste" is added to "To dress a Calve's Head. Turtle fashion."
Although the later Brattleboro edition of 1819 also includes this sentence, it
omits other material from *American Cookery* that appears in *Cook Not Mad.*
Some of the material in *Cook Not Mad* that is not derived from *American Cook-
ery* is taken from such nineteenth-century English sources as Maria Rundell's
New System of Domestic Cookery and William Kitchener's *The Cook's Oracle.*

Notes

Introduction

1. Library of Congress, "Books That Shaped America."
2. Philbrick, *Mayflower*, xvii.
3. Nixon, *Orphan in Eighteenth-Century Law and Literature*, 13.
4. Franklin, *Writings*, 5-6.
5. For the material impediments to nationalizing aspirations during this period, see Loughran, *Republic in Print*, parts 1 and 2.

PART I
Cooks and Books

1. Stavely and Fitzgerald, *Northern Hospitality*, 230-31, 17, 209.
2. Lehmann, *British Housewife*, 194; Wilson, *Food and Drink in Britain*, 321.
3. Stavely and Fitzgerald, *America's Founding Food*, 234-39.
4. Warner, *Letters of the Republic*, 120.
5. Wood, *Empire of Liberty*, 476, 478.

CHAPTER 1
Adapted to This Country

1. *Connecticut Courant*, May 9, 1796; see also issues of May 16, May 23, and May 30; Peters, *Public Statutes at Large*, 125.
2. Peters, *Public Statutes at Large*, 125.
3. Green, "Rise of Book Publishing," 78.
4. *Connecticut Journal*, June 8, 1796 (also June 15, 22); *Connecticut Gazette*, July 28, 1796 (also August 4, 11); *Middlesex Gazette*, August 12, 1796 (also August 19); *Vermont Gazette*, August 26, 1796; *Albany Gazette*, August 19, 1796 (also August 22, 26).
5. Smith, *One Hundred Years of Hartford's Courant*, 12, 272n21. For the configuration of the newspaper, printing, and bookselling trades in colonial and early national America, see Amory, "New England Book Trade," 334-35, 337-38; Gross, "Introduction," 17-18; Green, "Rise of Book Publishing," 76, 78; and Larkin, " 'Printing Is Something Every Village Has in It,' " 146, 153-54. For such a configuration in place at the *Connecticut Courant* and with Hudson & Goodwin specifically, see Smith, *One Hundred Years of Hartford's Courant*, 5, 8, 16, 128-30.

6. *Albany Gazette*, October 31, 1796; see also issues of November 18, November 21, and December 5. The Websters' price for this new edition was approximately seven dollars, as compared to roughly six dollars for the first edition.
7. *Hudson Gazette*, January 2, 1797 (also January 23, 30; February 13, 27; March 6, 20; April 3); *Centinel of Freedom*, December 28, 1796 (also January 18, February 22, April 26, 1797); *Greenleaf's New York Journal and Patriotic Register*, May 3, 1797 (also May 6; April 25, 1798); *The Diary; or, Loudon's Register*, November 14, 1797 (also November 15, 18, 28, 29, 30; December 6, 11, 13-16, 21, 23, 27). Ads in the *Middlesex Gazette*, December 2, 1796; June 30, July 14, August 25, and December 22, 1797, did not specify whether it was the first Hartford or the second Albany edition that was being offered for sale. For the history of U.S. currency in the early national period, see McCusker, *How Much Is That in Real Money?* 80–83.
8. Simmons, *American Cookery* (introduction by Hess), 5; Simmons, *American Cookery* (introduction by Wilson), xviii–xix. Mary Tolford Wilson did not mention the Zanesville edition, and she believed, mistakenly, that the Albany edition first appeared in 1800. The American Antiquarian Society has a copy of the 1808 printing of the Albany edition. The title page says merely "Printed for the Publishers." The 1822 New York City and 1831 Woodstock, Vermont, editions both include supplementary material.
9. Simmons, *American Cookery* (introduction by Wilson), xix, xxii, xxiv. For a complete, annotated list of the editions, printings, and plagiarisms, see appendix 4.
10. In 1819, there were even a couple of ads outside this region. See *Alabama Courier*, April 9, 1819, and *Winyaw Intelligencer*, September 29, 1819.
11. *New Hampshire Gazette*, September 22, 1807.
12. Ibid. Contemporary prices, in New Hampshire state currency, were Briggs, eight shillings, three pence; Glasse, six shillings; Carter, bound, four shillings, six pence; Carter, half-bound, three shillings, nine pence; Simmons, one shilling, six pence.
13. Hall, *Cultures of Print*, 44. For the careers of Child, Hale, and Leslie, see Stavely and Fitzgerald, *Northern Hospitality*, 46-63, 65-80.
14. "Centennial Cookery," 892-94.
15. Taylor, "Amelia Simmons"; Thompson, *Making of the English Working Class*, 12.
16. Wilson, "Amelia Simmons Fills a Need"; Simmons, *American Cookery* (introduction by Wilson), vii-xxiv. As reprinted, Wilson's article was retitled "The First American Cookbook."
17. Simmons, *American Cookery* (introduction by Wilson), x, ix, xi-xii, xvi.
18. Simmons, *American Cookery* (introduction by Hess), xii-xv.
19. Stavely and Fitzgerald, *Northern Hospitality*, 41-45.
20. Ridley, "First American Cookbook." The idea of the orphaned author as a metaphor for the orphaned new nation is echoed in Theophano, *"Eat My Words,"* 233, 235.
21. Siegel, "Cooking up American Politics," 58.
22. Ott, *Pumpkin*, 53-55; Vester, *Taste of Power*, 29-33, 30 (quotation). Cooley, "Searching for Amelia," came to our attention too late fully to be incorporated into our presentation. Some of Cooley's research and the conclusions she draws from it are consistent with aspects of our discussion in chapters 3 and 8, below.
23. Simmons, *American Cookery* (introduction by Wilson), xi, title page; Simmons, *American Cookery* (introduction by Hess), xii-xv, title page; Carter, *Frugal Housewife* (1772, 1792, 1796), title page.
24. For a list of all the recipes that are copied or adapted, see appendix 1.
25. Simmons, *American Cookery* (introduction by Wilson), xi-xiii.
26. Yokota, *Unbecoming British*, 70, 102-4.
27. Ibid., 71, 103-4.
28. Ulrich, *Age of Homespun*, 306-9, 323, 327-28, 333-39, 308-9 (quotation).
29. Green, "Rise of Book Publishing," 79, 85-86; Gross, "Introduction," 28-29. Acquiring American-made typeface could be a problem, however. For a discussion of the difficulties involved, see chap. 3, notes 23-24, below. Wendy Wall argues that defining cuisine

in nationalistic terms first became a major purpose of English cookbooks in the eighteenth century. From this point of view, the very project of establishing an "American" cuisine amounted, paradoxically, to yet another form of following English precedent. Wall, *Recipes for Thought*, 45-48, 51, 56-57.

30. Dwight, *Travels in New England and New York*, 1:x-xi.
31. Dwight, *Valedictory Addressed*, 15-16; Kendall, *Forgotten Founding Father*, 33.
32. Unger, *Noah Webster*, 5, 7; Ellis, *After the Revolution*, 165, 172-73.
33. Ellis, *After the Revolution*, 174, 177.
34. Buel, *Joel Barlow*, 79.
35. Stavely, "World All before Them," 150. Dwight denied that his poem allegorized the Revolutionary War.
36. Humphreys, *Poem on the Happiness of America*, 51; Kornfeld, *Creating an American Culture*, 97.
37. Trumbull, *M'Fingal*, 99; Kornfeld, *Creating an American Culture*, 92.
38. For the dependence on Milton, see Stavely, "World All before Them," 148-50. In the preface to his *Lyrical Ballads* (1798), generally viewed as a founding document of the Romantic movement in English poetry, Wordsworth states that his poems are written in the "language really used by men," as opposed to the "arbitrary and capricious habits of expression" in vogue among poets, which only "furnish food for fickle tastes, and fickle appetites." Wordsworth, *Poetical Works*, 734, 735.
39. Grasso, *Speaking Aristocracy*, 318; Buel, *Joel Barlow*, 75, 80; Bickford and Kaimowitz, "Books and Prints," 446.
40. "Memoir . . . of John Trumbull," 21-22; Humphreys, *Life and Times of David Humphreys*; Fitzmier, *New England's Moral Legislator*; Unger, *Noah Webster*.
41. Trumbull, *Memorial History of Hartford County Connecticut*, 1:380.
42. Bickford, *Voices of the New Republic*, 7.
43. Haselby, *Origins of American Religious Nationalism*, 6.
44. Geertz, *Interpretation of Cultures*, 14.

CHAPTER 2
Culinary Tradition

1. Stavely and Fitzgerald, *Northern Hospitality*, 83. The sources of Gardiner's recipes are noted at several points in this work. For an English example of printed sources in manuscript recipe collections, see the discussion of Margaretta Acworth in Lehmann, *British Housewife*, 99-100. For a detailed, sophisticated treatment that is in broad agreement with the perspective presented in this chapter on the development of the English culinary tradition from the sixteenth through the eighteenth century, see Wall, *Recipes for Thought*, esp. chap. 1.
2. Lehmann, *British Housewife*, 33-35.
3. Ibid.; Stavely and Fitzgerald, *Northern Hospitality*, 10; Day, "Art of Confectionery"; Wilson, *Food and Drink in Britain*, 300; Davidson, *Oxford Companion to Food*, 57.
4. Wilson, *Food and Drink in Britain*, 300.
5. Lehmann, *British Housewife*, 70-72.
6. Ibid., 56, 99-100, 154.
7. Stavely and Fitzgerald, *Northern Hospitality*, 83-84; Hayes, *Colonial Woman's Bookshelf*, 87-88.
8. Lehmann, *British Housewife*, 33, 38-41, 56, 99-100; Spiller, "Introductory Note," xi-xiv.
9. Lehmann, *British Housewife*, 33; Davidson, *Oxford Companion to Food*, 276; Spiller, "Introductory Note," xi-xiii.
10. Lynette Hunter, "English Cookery Books—of the Period 1500-1700," in Davidson, *Oxford Companion to Food*, 276.

11. Lehmann, *British Housewife*, 30–32; Spiller, "Introductory Note," xi–xii, xiv. Jayne Archer notes that "by the mid-seventeenth century it was something of a convention for the editors and publishers of receipt books to identify the source of their publication as the manuscript receipt book of a (usually anonymous and recently deceased) noblewoman." She gives John Partridge's *The Widowes Treasure* (1586) and Gervase Markham's *The English Housewife* (1631 ed.) as examples. Archer, "Queens' Arcanum."

12. Archer, "Queens' Arcanum."

13. Lehmann, *British Housewife*, 38–39, 51–52; Willan et al., *Cookbook Library*, 136; Archer, "Queens' Arcanum"; Stavely and Fitzgerald, *Northern Hospitality*, 7, 390n2. Both Willan and Archer think it likely that W.M. was Walter Montagu. Lehmann offers no opinion. She states that *The Queens Closet Opened* "went into ten editions by 1700 and . . . was further reprinted in the eighteenth century." Lehmann, *British Housewife*, 38. But according to Archer, "Queens' Arcanum," there were "at least eighteen editions in the seventeenth century alone." Only in a later edition was the cookery section, "The Compleat Cook," added. Archer speculates that the "Queens" of the title implies plurality and that Elizabeth I and Anne, consort of James I, owned and contributed recipes to the collection before it descended to Henrietta Maria as Charles I's wife. Wendy Wall, drawing on the work of Laura Knoppers, states that a major goal of *The Queens Closet Opened* was "to 'English' the suspiciously foreign Henrietta Maria by showing her to be a woman of industry rather than a seditious plotter." Wall, *Recipes for Thought*, 34.

14. Spiller, "Introductory Note," xiii–xv; Archer, "Queens' Arcanum"; Willan et al., *Cookbook Library*, 112–14, 133.

15. Willan et al., *Cookbook Library*, 136–37.

16. Hunter, "English Cookery Books," in Davidson, *Oxford Companion to Food*, 276–77.

17. Spiller, "Introductory Note," xviii. See also Cowan, "New Worlds, New Tastes," 201–2. Lehmann, *British Housewife*, 48, 54, 56, offers examples of conduct advice given in Woolley's *Gentlewomans Companion*.

18. Lehmann, *British Housewife*, 32, 30, 56, 357; Willan et al., *Cookbook Library*, 142.

19. Markham, *English Housewife*, 209–11, 77–78; Willan et al., *Cookbook Library*, 29; Stavely and Fitzgerald, *Northern Hospitality*, 9–10, 14–15, 138.

20. Stavely and Fitzgerald, *Northern Hospitality*, 7–8.

21. Lehmann, *British Housewife*, 174; Willan et al., *Cookbook Library*, 155; Russell, "History Cook." See also, from a slightly different perspective, Stavely and Fitzgerald, *Northern Hospitality*, 14–19.

22. Willan et al., *Cookbook Library*, 195, 2, 153, 168–69, 166; Lehmann, *British Housewife*, 161–62, 173; Dods, *Cook and Housewife's Manual*, 303; Wheaton, *Savoring the Past*, 152–53; DeJean, *Essence of Style*, 118.

23. Lehmann, *British Housewife*, 101–2, 140–44, 212–13; Wheaton, *Savoring the Past*, 150; Willan et al., *Cookbook Library*, 2, 153, 166, 194–95, 216–19, 222.

24. *Oxford English Dictionary*, s.v. "made dish"; Dods, *Cook and Housewife's Manual*, 303.

25. Lehmann, *British Housewife*, 101–2, 140–44, 212–13; Willan et al., *Cookbook Library*, 166, 194, 216–19, 222.

26. Willan et al., *Cookbook Library*, 219; Lehmann, *British Housewife*, 96.

27. Glasse, *Art of Cookery*, ii; Lehmann, *British Housewife*, 92, 93, 96, 98–99, 194; Willan et al., *Cookbook Library*, 194, 195; Mennell, *All Manners of Food*, 124–27; Landau, "Eating Abroad and at Home," 168–69.

28. Ridley, "What about August 1714?"

29. Stavely and Fitzgerald, *Northern Hospitality*, 18; Lehmann, *British Housewife*, 96–99, 357–58.

30. Lehmann, *British Housewife*, 114, 104; Stavely and Fitzgerald, *Northern Hospitality*, 18–19; Raffald, *Experienced English Housekeeper*, 2–3.

31. Lehmann, *British Housewife*, 61–62, 98, 286. Willan and her colleagues cover the subject of the English women cookbook authors of the eighteenth century, with illustrations from their works. Willan et al., *Cookbook Library*, 204–7, 210–13.

32. Lehmann, *British Housewife*, 61; Willan et al., *Cookbook Library*, 204.

33. Willan et al., *Cookbook Library*, 210n, 204, 212; Lehmann, *British Housewife*, 61, 108-9; Davidson, *Oxford Companion to Food*, 339-40; Glasse, *Art of Cookery*, v-vi.

34. Lehmann, *British Housewife*, 61, 84.

35. Willan et al., *Cookbook Library*, 212; Lehmann, *British Housewife*, 129.

36. Mennell, *All Manners of Food*, 116.

37. Ibid., 118-20, 132, 127, 130, 125; Lehmann, *British Housewife*, 46-47.

38. Lehmann, *British Housewife*, 106.

39. Ibid., 64, 105, 106-7.

40. Ibid., 107-8, 287, 63.

41. Willan et al., *Cookbook Library*, 207, 210.

42. Lehmann, *British Housewife*, 131, 286-87.

43. Glasse, *Art of Cookery*, vii-xiv; Davidson, *Oxford Companion to Food*, 340; Willan et al., *Cookbook Library*, 210n; Lehmann, *British Housewife*, 109-10, 126.

44. Raffald, *Experienced English Housekeeper*, viii-xiv; Lehmann, *British Housewife*, 129-31, 287.

45. Raffald, *Experienced English Housekeeper*, viii-xi, xiii-xiv; Willan et al., *Cookbook Library*, 212-13, 210n; Stephen and Lee, *Dictionary of National Biography*, 16:602.

46. Lehmann, *British Housewife*, 131, 286-87, 278-79, 147-48; Mennell, *All Manners of Food*, 116, 127, 133; Landau, "Eating Abroad and at Home," 168-69. See also Wall, *Recipes for Thought*, 45-48, 51, 56-57.

47. Stavely and Fitzgerald, *Northern Hospitality*, 7.

48. Ibid.; Willan et al., *Cookbook Library*, 231; Hayes, *Colonial Woman's Bookshelf*, 80-82, 165n2, 166n6.

49. Willan et al., *Cookbook Library*, 231, 194, 146.

50. Hayes, *Colonial Woman's Bookshelf*, 82-85; Lehmann, *British Housewife*, 96; Willan et al., *Cookbook Library*, 231.

51. Hayes, *Colonial Woman's Bookshelf*, 82-85; Stavely and Fitzgerald, *Northern Hospitality*, 8-9; Willan et al., *Cookbook Library*, 231.

52. Hayes, *Colonial Woman's Bookshelf*, 85-87; Willan et al., *Cookbook Library*, 231.

53. Stavely and Fitzgerald, *America's Founding Food*, 83, 169; Willan et al., *Cookbook Library*, 231.

54. Hayes, *Colonial Woman's Bookshelf*, 87; Stavely and Fitzgerald, *Northern Hospitality*, 41.

55. Lehmann, *British Housewife*, 134, 116, 105; Davidson, *Oxford Companion to Food*, 340.

56. Hayes, *Colonial Woman's Bookshelf*, 82-87; Lehmann, *British Housewife*, 104-5; Stavely and Fitzgerald, *Northern Hospitality*, 293-94.

57. Main, "Standard of Living in Southern New England," 129.

58. Hayes, *Colonial Woman's Bookshelf*, 83, 166n12.

59. Lehmann, *British Housewife*, 87; Willan et al., *Cookbook Library*, 148, 155-56, 159, 202, 231, 194.

60. Willan et al., *Cookbook Library*, 204; Lehmann, *British Housewife*, 86-87, 96; Hayes, *Colonial Woman's Bookshelf*, 82.

61. Lehmann, *British Housewife*, 87, 99, 82, 83.

CHAPTER 3
Print Culture

1. Ziff, *Puritanism in America*, 3-4.

2. Eames, "Introduction," vii.

3. Ibid., v-vi.

4. Ibid., v-viii.

5. The following account of the early history of printing in Connecticut is based on

Bickford and Kaimowitz, "Books and Prints," 445–46; Thomas, *History of Printing in America* (1874), 87–89, 185; and Weyler, *Empowering Words,* 166.

6. Warner, *Letters of the Republic,* 3, 36. In England, the breakdown of traditional authority that occurred during the mid-seventeenth-century civil wars led, among other things, to early formulations of precisely the idea that variations in understanding of divine truth could be legitimate. The most noteworthy articulations of this view were produced by John Milton in *Areopagitica* (1644), and by that New England maverick Roger Williams in *The Bloudy Tenet of Persecution* (1644) and *The Bloudy Tenet Yet More Bloudy* (1652). Williams was in London for extended intervals during these decades on missions to secure Rhode Island's status as an independent plantation.

7. The vast scholarly literature on New England Puritanism now includes a number of critiques of Perry Miller's foundational description of the region as being essentially of one mind during the colonial period. We are here summarizing one of these critiques, in Stavely, *Puritan Legacies,* 101–36. For a convenient overview of the dispute over free grace and the divergent views among the ministers caught up in it, see Hall, *Antinomian Controversy,* ix–xviii, 3–23.

8. For a summary of the evidence regarding literacy and printed materials in New England in the first half of the eighteenth century, see Stavely and Fitzgerald, *Northern Hospitality,* 21–22. For the widespread circulation of devotional manuals in the region in the seventeenth century, see Hall, *Worlds of Wonder,* 51–52.

9. This further narrative of Connecticut printing and the origins of Hudson & Goodwin is based on Bickford and Kaimowitz, "Books and Prints," 446, 458–59; Smith, *One Hundred Years of Hartford's Courant,* 4–5, 13–14; Trumbull, *Memorial History of Hartford County Connecticut,* 1:160, 241, 305, 380, 606, 622; Goodwin, *Goodwins of Hartford, Connecticut,* 174, 641–42; and Grasso, *Speaking Aristocracy,* 318–19.

10. Bickford and Kaimowitz, "Books and Prints," 458–59; Munsell, "Memoir of Charles R. Webster," 5:230.

11. Bickford and Kaimowitz, "Books and Prints," 451; Smith, *One Hundred Years of Hartford's Courant,* 14; Trumbull, *Memorial History of Hartford County Connecticut,* 1:606.

12. Smith, *One Hundred Years of Hartford's Courant,* 14; Goodwin, *Goodwins of Hartford, Connecticut,* 641; Trumbull, *Memorial History of Hartford County Connecticut,* 1:606. Smith states that "at the end of the year" in which Ebenezer Watson died, that is, 1777, the widow Watson "entered into partnership with George Goodwin." However, according to Trumbull's *Memorial History,* "Watson died in 1777, and until 1778 'the widow Watson' conducted it [the *Courant*]. . . . In 1778 she took George Goodwin into partnership."

13. Smith, *One Hundred Years of Hartford's Courant,* 15–16; Trumbull, *Memorial History of Hartford County Connecticut,* 1:305.

14. Love, *Colonial History of Hartford,* 306–7n4.

15. Smith, *One Hundred Years of Hartford's Courant,* 16.

16. Ibid., 14–16, 136.

17. Bickford and Kaimowitz, "Books and Prints," 446; Smith, *One Hundred Years of Hartford's Courant,* 135.

18. Thomas, *History of Printing in America* (1874), 187–88; *Connecticut Gazette,* July 28, 1796 (also August 4, 11).

19. Weyler, *Empowering Words,* 165; Pasley, "Tyranny of Printers," 25. On the personnel needed to run pre-nineteenth-century print shops, see also Bickford and Kaimowitz, "Books and Prints," 451–52.

20. Weyler, *Empowering Words,* 165.

21. Ibid., 166; Pasley, "Tyranny of Printers," 40.

22. Pasley, "Tyranny of Printers," 24–25; Green, "Rise of Book Publishing," 78. Christopher P. Bickford and Jeffrey H. Kaimowitz describe the two almanacs published by Thomas Green during his first months in Hartford. Bickford and Kaimowitz, "Books and Prints," 457–58.

23. Bidwell, "Printers' Supplies and Capitalization," 169.
24. Ibid., 171. Although our discussion of the mechanics of American printing might seem to assume a givenness to the printer's art as it came to be practiced in Western culture, we agree with Michael Warner that printing as a technology is the result of specific "social investments" and has no "ontological status prior to culture." Warner, *Letters of the Republic*, 8-9.
25. Bickford and Kaimowitz, "Books and Prints," 457-58.
26. Ibid., 451.
27. Larkin, " 'Printing Is Something Every Village Has in It,' " 154-55.
28. Ibid.
29. Brown, "Regional Culture in a Revolutionary Era," 46.
30. Larkin, " 'Printing Is Something Every Village Has in It,' " 155. For Thomas Greenleaf, see Thomas, *History of Printing in America* (1810), 119-20. A search on Greenleaf's name in the Early American Imprints database produces a list of numerous imprints by him in the 1790s.
31. Hosley, "Architecture," 67.
32. Bickford and Kaimowitz, "Books and Prints," 445; Pasley, *"Tyranny of Printers,"* 24-25.
33. Amory, "New England Book Trade," 338; Brown, "Regional Culture in a Revolutionary Era," 46-47. Jack Larkin discusses the expansion of rural printing offices to commercial villages throughout the American countryside. Larkin, " 'Printing Is Something Every Village Has in It,' " 146.
34. Amory, "New England Book Trade," 338; Bickford and Kaimowitz, "Books and Prints," 457; Green, "Rise of Book Publishing," 76, 78; Charvat, *Literary Publishing in America,* 19.
35. Goodwin, *Goodwins of Hartford, Connecticut,* 641-42.
36. Warner, *Letters of the Republic,* 68.
37. Goodwin, *Goodwins of Hartford, Connecticut,* 642.
38. Smith, *One Hundred Years of Hartford's Courant,* 5, 8, 16, 129. However, as noted in chapter 1, *American Cookery* was not advertised in the *Courant.*
39. Warner, *Letters of the Republic,* 67-68.
40. Gross, "Introduction," 5; Bickford and Kaimowitz, "Books and Prints," 445-46.
41. Bickford and Kaimowitz, "Books and Prints," 446.
42. Ibid., 447; "Historic Store."
43. Bickford and Kaimowitz, "Books and Prints," 447.
44. Wansey, *Excursion to the United States of North America,* 37-38; "Bibliography of American Newspapers," 476; Smith, *One Hundred Years of Harford's Courant,* 4-5.
45. Green, "Rise of Book Publishing," 76, 79; Warner, *Letters of the Republic,* 121.
46. Bickford and Kaimowitz, "Books and Prints," 450, 457.
47. Green, "Rise of Book Publishing," 85-86.
48. Gross, "Introduction," 28-29.
49. Green, "Rise of Book Publishing," 76, 89-90.
50. Kornhauser and Schloss, "Paintings and Other Pictorial Arts," 136; Kornhauser, "Ralph Earl," 51; Green, "Rise of Book Publishing," 78.
51. Green, "Rise of Book Publishing," 78.
52. Monaghan, *Common Heritage,* 29-30, 81.
53. Simmons, *American Cookery* (introduction by Hess), 5.
54. Bickford and Kaimowitz, "Books and Prints," 470.
55. Ibid.; Webster, *American Spelling Book,* iii.
56. Bickford and Kaimowitz, "Books and Prints," 470; Simmons, *American Cookery,* (introduction by Wilson), title page, 4.
57. Monaghan, *Common Heritage,* 29; Warner, *Letters of the Republic,* 52-53, 61-62, 113-14, 82. On the commercialization of print, see Grasso, *Speaking Aristocracy,* 322-24, 326; Green, "Rise of Book Publishing," 100-101; and Bickford and Kaimowitz, "Books and Prints," 470-71.

58. Grasso, *Speaking Aristocracy*, 322–26. While our narrative focuses on Noah Webster, Grasso uses to great effect "the relationship between the poet [John Trumbull] and the printers [Hudson & Goodwin] . . . to reveal the changing politics of publishing in the post-Revolutionary era." Ibid., 318. We draw on his discussion of Trumbull's career in chapter 8.

59. Monaghan, *Common Heritage*, 29–31, 43.

60. Ibid., 29–31, 74; *Connecticut Courant*, June 1, 1784; Grasso, *Speaking Aristocracy*, 318.

61. Monaghan, *Common Heritage*, 73–77, 81.

62. Bickford and Kaimowitz, "Books and Prints," 447, 451; Brown, "Revolution's Legacy for the History of the Book," 68–70.

63. Bickford and Kaimowitz, "Books and Prints," 450–52; Brown, "Regional Culture in a Revolutionary Era," 46.

64. Simmons, *American Cookery* (introduction by Hess), xi.

65. In sketching Webster's life, we have relied on Munsell, "Memoir of Charles R. Webster," especially 5:230–31, 233–34. Christopher Clark describes the networks of other skilled craft workers in New York and New England as they "circulated in rural areas to seek work or practice their crafts." He notes that "migration did not just follow common patterns from countryside to frontier or town, but formed a more complex thread of connections through diversifying rural regions." Clark, *Social Change in America*, 105–6.

66. Munsell, "Memoir of Charles R. Webster," 5:230.

67. Ibid.; Amory, "New England Book Trade," 315–16.

68. Munsell, "Memoir of Charles R. Webster," 5:230–31.

69. Ibid., 5:231.

70. Ibid., 5:234.

71. Hackett, *Rude Hand of Innovation*, 191–92n63.

72. Ibid.

73. Kammen, *Colonial New York*, 242–44.

PART II
Connecticut

1. Moynihan, "With 'Unshaken Heroism and Fortitude,'" 88.

2. Siegel, "Cooking up American Politics," 61n27.

3. Dwight, *Greenfield Hill*, 14 (part 1:ll. 112–14); Brown, "Regional Culture in a Revolutionary Era," 44.

4. Dwight, *Travels in New England and New York*, 1:139, 132.

CHAPTER 4
Society and Nationality

1. Kornhauser, "Ralph Earl," 62–65, 39, 48, 45, 47, 49, 51, 52–53.

2. Ibid., 60–61, 65, 62. Kornhauser provides neither a reproduction nor a description of the Gere portraits.

3. Kornhauser does not mention the "Connecticut Clockmaker" miniatures. They were given to the Smithsonian in 1967; on the museum's website, they are listed as "Attributed to Ralph Earl" and dated "ca. 1800." See Earl, "Portrait of a Connecticut Clockmaker," and "Portrait of a Connecticut Clockmaker's Wife." For the conventionality of the red curtain, see Kornhauser and Schloss, "Paintings and Other Pictorial Arts," 137, and Kornhauser, "Ralph Earl," 41. For a discussion of mobcaps, see chap. 5, note 62, below.

4. For a brief survey of book format terminology, see chap. 9, note 41, below.

5. Kornhauser and Ribeiro, "Catalogue," 181.

6. Ibid., 181, 180: "Oliver Ellsworth was instrumental in securing the famous Connecticut

Compromise, which ended the struggle between large and small states over representation, and he was also responsible for the use of the term United States in the Constitution."

7. Main, *Society and Economy in Colonial Connecticut*, 185, 325, 333, 372. In Main's sample of orphaned boys, 58 percent of those orphaned before the age of ten were successful in terms of the above definition; for those orphaned at age ten or older, the success rate was about 10 percent higher.

8. Bushman, "Portraiture and Society," 73; Dwight, *Travels in New England and New York*, 1:x–xi.

9. Bushman, "Portraiture and Society," 73, 75.

10. Dwight, *Travels in New England and New York*, 1:xi.

11. Purcell, *Connecticut in Transition*, 100, 104–5. In current U.S. terms, Jeremiah Wadsworth was worth at the end of the war about $9 to 12 million. At his death in 1807, Oliver Ellsworth's estate was valued at $126,674.32. Kornhauser and Ribeiro, "Catalogue," 184. This amounts to about $2.5 million in current U.S. terms. The Governor's Council on which Wadsworth served was the upper house of the state legislature, renamed the Senate in 1818.

12. Purcell, *Connecticut in Transition*, 111–13; Woodward, *One Hundred Years of the Hartford Bank*, 168.

13. Woodward, *One Hundred Years of the Hartford Bank*, 168.

14. Brown, *Life of Oliver Ellsworth*, 11–12.

15. Woodward, *One Hundred Years of the Hartford Bank*, 168; Trumbull, *Memorial History of Hartford County Connecticut*, 1:500; Purcell, *Connecticut in Transition*, 112.

16. Trumbull, *Memorial History of Hartford County Connecticut*, 1:564–65, 380; Daniels, "Remarkable Complexity of the Simple New England Town," 251. The mill, called the Hartford Woolen Manufactory, supplied the cloth for the suits worn by President George Washington, Vice President John Adams, and the members of Congress from Connecticut at Washington's inauguration in 1789; see Bagnall, *Textile Industries of the United States*, 101. By 1795, however, the firm had failed. The year before, the British woolen manufacturer Henry Wansey inspected it and came away thoroughly unimpressed: "I found it much on the decay, and hardly able to maintain itself; I saw two carding engines, working by water, of a very inferior construction." See Wansey, *Excursion to the United States of North America*, 42–43.

17. *Constitution of the Hartford Library Company*, 7; Trumbull, *Memorial History of Hartford County Connecticut*, 1:581, 586–87.

18. Goodwin, *Goodwins of Hartford, Connecticut*, 626, 641; Trumbull, *Memorial History of Hartford County Connecticut*, 1:622, 606. For the branch of the Goodwin family that prospered earlier on, see chap. 5, note 3, below.

19. Trumbull, *Memorial History of Hartford County Connecticut*, 1:82; Goodwin, *Goodwins of Hartford, Connecticut*, 641.

20. Love, *Colonial History of Hartford*, 306–7; Trumbull, *Memorial History of Hartford County Connecticut*, 1:305. For gambrel roofs, see Sweeney, "From Wilderness to Arcadian Vale," 24, and Cooke, *Making Furniture in Preindustrial America*, 88.

21. Love, *Colonial History of Hartford*, 306, 306–7n4.

22. The success of George Goodwin and Barzillai Hudson in achieving full membership in the Hartford upper class makes them somewhat anomalous among printers, according to Jeffrey L. Pasley. "Though their literacy and role in publication gave them more prestige than many tradesmen, printers were nonetheless artisans, craftsmen who made their living with their hands and thus lacked one of the fundamental attributes of gentility," Pasley writes. Not only the manual nature of their craft but also their need for the social endorsement of their patrons (and sometimes their need for their patrons' financial support) left printers permanently on uncertain terrain between "the ruling, thinking, and writing classes" to which many aspired and the mass of ordinary, uneducated citizens. Goodwin's and Hudson's overcoming of these obstacles is perhaps partially explained by

the New England esteem for the printed word. See Pasley, *"Tyranny of Printers,"* 19–20, 25, and Weyler, *Empowering Words*, 165.

23. Sweeney, "From Wilderness to Arcadian Vale," 23.

24. Adams, *Diary and Autobiography*, 2:28, 30 (June 8, 1771).

25. Brissot de Warville, *New Travels in the United States of America*, 83, 85, 82.

26. Lewis, "Landscape and Environment of the Connecticut River Valley," 7; Wansey, *Excursion to the United States of North America*, 44, 41–42; Wood, *Empire of Liberty*, 712.

27. Washington, *Diaries*, 5:470–71 (October 21, 1789).

28. Brown, "Regional Culture in a Revolutionary Era," 42; Kornhauser and Ribeiro, "Catalogue," 181; Dwight, *Greenfield Hill*, 36 (part 2:ll. 172–74).

29. Dwight, *Oration, Delivered at New Haven*, 7; Fischer, *Revolution of American Conservatism*, 296.

30. Siegel, " 'Steady Habits' under Siege," 210, 215, 214.

31. Morse, *American Geography*, 218, 219. Morse did not pretend that Connecticut was without flaws. He thought that the people of the state were "remarkably fond of having all their disputes, even those of the most trivial kind, settled *according to law.*" Such a "litigious spirit" was also prevalent elsewhere in New England, and Connecticut shared with the rest of New England the fact that it was home to peddlers. These were "a class of people . . . of the baser sort, who, averse to honest industry, have recourse to knavery for subsistence." Perhaps the worst thing about peddlers was that they gave New England and Connecticut a bad name: "Other states have felt the effects of their villainy. Hence they have characterized the New Englanders, as a knavish, artful, and dishonest people." Ibid., 219, 147.

32. Ibid., 289, 292, 313.

33. Ibid., 352, 353, 356. Morse's Connecticut/New England exceptionalism was of course annoying to readers who lived elsewhere. In 1795, St. George Tucker, "a citizen of Williamsburg," Virginia, counterattacked in response to Morse's dismissal of his native place as "dull, forsaken, and melancholy," by characterizing Connecticut as a place lacking utterly in "that liberality of Sentiment which pervades and animates our Southern world." Yokota, *Unbecoming British*, 51. Two years earlier, James Freeman, a Boston clergyman, remarked that while "some readers may charge [Morse] with being partial to his native state," to Freeman it appeared "not that he has done Connecticut more, but that he has done other states less, than justice." Freeman, *Remarks on the American Universal Geography*, 52.

34. *Connecticut Courant*, February 24, March 2, 9, 16, 1784; Kendall, *Forgotten Founding Father*, 99.

35. Webster, *Sketches of American Policy*, 33–34.

36. *Essex Journal*, July 20, 1785.

37. Kendall, *Forgotten Founding Father*, 99.

38. Buel, *Joel Barlow*, 80–81; Grasso, *Speaking Aristocracy*, 320–21, 456. *The Anarchiad* was serialized in the *Courant* and other newspapers.

39. Sweeney, "From Wilderness to Arcadian Vale," 18.

40. Dowling, *Poetry and Ideology in Revolutionary Connecticut*, 7–8, 15–17; Humphreys, *Poem on the Happiness of America*, 26.

41. Dwight, *Greenfield Hill*, 14 (part 1:ll. 99–100, 108–14).

42. Ibid., 12 (part 1:ll. 42–50), 171. Similar agrarianism was espoused by other Connecticut Federalists. Noah Webster characterized New Englanders as "independent landholders, free and accustomed to manage their own local concerns." Webster, *Ten Letters to Dr. Joseph Priestly [sic]*, 9–10.

43. Dowling, *Poetry and Ideology in Revolutionary Connecticut*, 44–45, 84–87, 86 (quotation). For additional discussion of Dwight's attitudes on these issues, see Watts, "Ministers, Misanthropes, and Mandarins," 164–66.

44. The following several paragraphs are devoted to Dwight, *Travels in New England and New York*, 2:229–33.

45. For the critique of traditional European social hierarchy in *Greenfield Hill*, see Bushman, "Portraiture and Society," 81–82.

46. This political continuity was in keeping with what was, in the judgment of Jackson Turner Main, the Revolution's limited effect on Connecticut society. Since "the under-lying factors determining the social structure altered very little," change occurred "only within a fundamental continuity." Main, *Connecticut Society in the Era of the American Revolution*, 70–71.

47. Thus, as Joseph Conforti writes, while both Dwight and Jedidiah Morse described "the white village" that was becoming characteristic of Connecticut and New England, they ignored that the trim, neat village was a recent innovation, and that "dynamic com-mercial activity" was not peripheral but central to the emergence of this type of village. Conforti, *Imagining New England*, 128. Again in tandem with Morse, Dwight did not claim that Connecticut had no flaws whatsoever, particularly objecting to the peddlers the state seemed unaccountably to breed. "The consequences of this employment . . . are generally malignant," he wrote in 1796 in contemplation of the peddlers in the Suffield area. "Men who begin life with bargaining for small wares will almost invariably become sharpers." Dwight, *Travels in New England and New York*, 1:223; see also 2:33–34.

48. Dwight, *Travels in New England and New York*, 2:230.

49. Ibid., 3:20–21.

50. Ibid., 2:231; 1:370–75, 375 (quotation).

51. Ibid., 1:273–74.

52. Ibid., 1:274. For a discussion of the difficulties in growing wheat in Connecticut at this time, even in the valley, see chap. 6, notes 11–17, below. By "glutinous," Dwight prob-ably meant "sticky" or "gluey" (*Oxford English Dictionary*, s.v. "glutinous"). In the more literal sense, bread made with cornmeal and rye cannot be "glutinous," as these grains are devoid of gluten.

53. Dwight, *Travels in New England and New York*, 1:195.

54. Ibid., 1:195, 194.

55. Ibid., 1:195.

56. Bickford, *Voices of the New Republic*, 7.

57. Waggoner, "Fertile Farms among the Stones," 48–49.

58. Cooke, "Embedded Nature of Artisanal Activity," 145.

59. Dwight, *Travels in New England and New York*, 2:324.

60. Zagarri, "Gender and the First Party System," 120; Dwight, *Oration, Spoken before the Society of the Cincinnati*, 14.

61. Bickford, *Voices of the New Republic*, 99. For women's dairying activities in Connecticut at this time, see chap. 6, notes 4, 36–38, below, and Sloat, "Connecticut's Home Dairies."

62. Bickford, *Voices of the New Republic*, 97.

63. Connecticut Academy, "Original Documents"; Bickford, *Voices of the New Republic*, xiv.

CHAPTER 5
Domestic Culture

1. This and the next several paragraphs are drawn from the *Connecticut Courant*, May 9, 1796.

2. Hosley, "Architecture," 65, 69n3.

3. Goodwin, *Goodwins of Hartford, Connecticut*, 549, 553–54, 556, 625, 626, 640. In current terms, Daniel Goodwin the Elder's 1772 estate would be worth about $850,000. Accord-ing to Jackson Turner Main, this made him exceptionally wealthy compared to most of Connecticut's deacons. Main, *Connecticut Society in the Era of the American Revolution*, 46.

4. Goodwin, *Genealogical Notes*, 48–49, 52, 58; Kelly, *Early Domestic Architecture of Connecti-cut*, 14–16.

5. Kelly, *Early Domestic Architecture of Connecticut*, 17.
6. Main and Main, "Economic Growth and the Standard of Living," 41; Stavely and Fitzgerald, *Northern Hospitality*, 393n43; Sewall, *Diary*, 1:412–13 (December 17–18, 1695). If the closing years of the seventeenth century were the time when the consumer revolution first began to emerge in New England, in England itself those years saw its diffusion quite far down the social scale. For a recent survey of the evidence of improved standards of living for nonelite English people at this time, see Slack, *Invention of Improvement*, 155–59.
7. Main and Main, "Economic Growth and the Standard of Living," 41; Stavely and Fitzgerald, *Northern Hospitality*, 393n43; St. George, "Artifacts of Regional Consciousness," 346.
8. Main, *Peoples of a Spacious Land*, 219; Sklar, "Schooling of Girls," 531. For the role of ministers in facilitating the consumer revolution, and for the criticism they sometimes received as a result, see Sweeney, "From Wilderness to Arcadian Vale," 21.
9. Sweeney, "From Wilderness to Arcadian Vale," 22.
10. Ibid., 23; Main, "Gender, Work, and Wages in Colonial New England," 57.
11. Sweeney, "From Wilderness to Arcadian Vale," 24.
12. Sweeney, "Furniture and the Domestic Environment," 287.
13. Daniels, *Connecticut Town*, 147, 149–50, 157, 161.
14. Conroy, *In Public Houses*, 95–96; Stavely and Fitzgerald, *Northern Hospitality*, 29.
15. Shields, *Civil Tongues and Polite Letters*, 314.
16. *Connecticut Courant*, August 18, 1788; *Hampshire Gazette*, September 3, 1788.
17. Abigail Adams likewise alleged that Shays's Rebellion was caused by "luxury and extravagance, both in furniture and dress"; Zakim, *Ready-Made Democracy*, 31.
18. *Connecticut Courant*, November 6, 1786.
19. Ibid.
20. Appleby, *Capitalism and a New Social Order*, 99; Wolf, *As Various as Their Land*, 10, 276; Brooke, *Heart of the Commonwealth*, 273–74; Cole, *Mary Moody Emerson*, 95.
21. Clark, *Social Change in America*, 100; Kornhauser and Schloss, "Paintings and Other Pictorial Arts," 136; Smith, *One Hundred Years of Hartford's Courant*, 107–8.
22. Smith, *One Hundred Years of Hartford's Courant*, 108–10, 115; St. George, "Artifacts of Regional Consciousness," 351; Kornhauser and Schloss, "Paintings and Other Pictorial Arts," 139; Zea, *Useful Improvements*, 43.
23. Brooke, *Heart of the Commonwealth*, 239–40.
24. Opal, *Beyond the Farm*, 62.
25. Lewis, "Landscape and Environment of the Connecticut River Valley," 10–11; Opal, *Beyond the Farm*, 67.
26. Smith, *One Hundred Years of Hartford's Courant*, 103–4. According to Paul Slack, a corresponding trend toward the ordering and enhancing of communal space had emerged in England in the first quarter of the eighteenth century. Slack, *Invention of Improvement*, 219–20.
27. Berry, *Idea of Luxury*, 11. We have omitted Berry's fourth area of need, leisure, although this too was a part of the consumer revolution. Witness the dancing and theater- and concert-going already mentioned. Leisure arises in connection with cooking and eating, as in the fact that "entertainment" used to be a synonym for dining in company.
28. Hosley, "Architecture," 64; Crowley, *Invention of Comfort*, 97.
29. Hosley, "Architecture," 64; Crowley, *Invention of Comfort*, 53–54; Garrett, *At Home*, 52.
30. Hosley, "Architecture," 64–65; Crowley, *Invention of Comfort*, 98.
31. Crowley, *Invention of Comfort*, 47; St. George, "Artifacts of Regional Consciousness," 346.
32. Crowley, *Invention of Comfort*, 53, 48, 98.
33. Hosley, "Architecture," 65. One-story houses remained more common in the outlying areas of many towns; see Crowley, *Invention of Comfort*, 102.

34. Hosley, "Architecture," 66. The style also appeared in the Litchfield County towns of Woodbury and New Milford; see Cooke, *Making Furniture in Preindustrial America*, 88, and Bushman, "Portraiture and Society," 75. According to John E. Crowley, most mansions in eighteenth-century Virginia were of this design. Crowley, *Invention of Comfort*, 86.

35. Kelly, *Early Domestic Architecture of Connecticut*, 14–17; Crowley, *Invention of Comfort*, 101, 100; Hosley, "Architecture," 66. J. Frederick Kelly's typical first-floor layout for a central-hall house shows on the front a hall on the left and a parlor on the right. Kelly, *Early Domestic Architecture*, 16. However, in at least one New England instance, that of the Concord, Massachusetts, ministerial residence in the 1770s, the first-floor front consisted of parlors on each side of the central entrance hallway. Cole, *Mary Moody Emerson*, 42. Elisabeth Donaghy Garrett states that "many American homes between 1750 and 1870 could boast two parlors." Garrett, *At Home*, 39.

36. Crowley, *Invention of Comfort*, 101, 102; Sweeney, "From Wilderness to Arcadian Vale," 25; Hosley, "Architecture," 93; Main, *Peoples of a Spacious Land*, 215–20.

37. Crowley, *Invention of Comfort*, 261–62; Taylor, *William Cooper's Town*, 111.

38. Bushman, "Portraiture and Society," 72, table 2.2. The per capita figures for fireplaces of all types were as follows: for Hartford County, 1.5; for New Haven County, 2; and for New London County, 2.5. The figures for "first-rate" fireplaces for the towns of Hartford, New Haven, and New London respectively were .62, 1.75, and 1.53. Per capita rates of fireplace ownership are best interpreted in conjunction with rates of two-story-house ownership. In Hartford, the latter approached 100 percent. It is not unlikely that a typical two-story house in Hartford had a fireplace both downstairs and upstairs. It is also not unlikely that the downstairs fireplace was located in the parlor and that efforts were made to have it be "first-rate."

39. Sweeney, "Furniture and the Domestic Environment," 287.

40. Ibid., 276.

41. Ibid., 279; Cooke, *Making Furniture in Preindustrial America*, 111.

42. Sweeney, "Furniture and the Domestic Environment," 279.

43. Ibid., 284–85, 271, table 8, 278, table 11.

44. Carson, "Consumer Revolution in Colonial British America," 590.

45. Ibid., 591; Sweeney, "Furniture and the Domestic Environment," 274, table 9.

46. Cooke, *Making Furniture in Preindustrial America*, 159, 112; Garrett, *At Home*, 89–90; Bowne, *Girl's Life Eighty Years Ago*, 134n4.

47. Cooke, *Making Furniture in Preindustrial America*, 111. "The story was told in New England of a Congregational minister from Boston who, facing financial difficulties, moved in 1795 to a church in rural New Hampshire where his living costs would be low. But his family's social airs quickly put him at odds with his new parishioners. It became known, for instance, that his household servants ate separately from his family rather than at the same table, as was customary in the countryside. After a few years he gave up and returned to town, to a milieu less intolerant of his 'aristocratic' leanings." Clark, *Social Change in America*, 110.

48. Cooke, *Making Furniture in Preindustrial America*, 114–15, 121, 157, 159, 263n12; Sweeney, "Furniture and the Domestic Environment," 279; Zea, "Furniture," 189–90; Bickford and Kaimowitz, "Books and Prints," 474. As noted in chapter 3, William Butler's brother Simeon would two years later in 1798 be associated with a reissue of the first edition of *American Cookery*.

49. Zea, "Furniture," 256, 255, 251, 190; Zea, *Useful Improvements*, 55, 56, 35–36.

50. Carson, "Consumer Revolution in Colonial British America," 652–53.

51. Brown, *Knowledge Is Power*, 151.

52. Main, *Peoples of a Spacious Land*, 222.

53. St. George, "Artifacts of Regional Consciousness," 342.

54. Brown, *Knowledge Is Power*, 151; *Connecticut Courant*, August 18, 1788.
55. Brown, "Regional Culture in a Revolutionary Era," 46–47; Bickford, *Voices of the New Republic*, 50–51, 99. According to "a succinct account of the manufactures carried on in the State of Connecticut" submitted to Secretary of the Treasury Alexander Hamilton in 1791, "a great proportion of our most substantial Farmers and mechanicks appear dressed on *Sundays* and *holydays* in the manufactures of their Wives & daughters; & this is becoming every day more reputable." This suggests that homespun clothing was beginning to be made in ways that made it appear more elegant. See Cole, *Industrial and Commercial Correspondence of Alexander Hamilton*, 4.
56. Bickford, *Voices of the New Republic*, 50.
57. Kornhauser and Ribeiro, "Catalogue," 152, 156, 172, 173.
58. Ibid., 178, 181.
59. Garrett, *At Home*, 153; Crowley, *Invention of Comfort*, 129; White, "Impact of Historic Lighting," 149.
60. Garrett, *At Home*, 181, 176.
61. Ibid., 160; Kornhauser and Ribeiro, "Catalogue," 172.
62. Kornhauser and Ribeiro, "Catalogue," 181, 152, 156, 173; "Colonial Lady's Clothing"; Wass and Fandrich, *Clothing through American History*, 82–83; Earl, "Portrait of a Connecticut Clockmaker's Wife." Among our sources on women's clothing of the day, there are divergent emphases regarding the suitability of mobcaps for such formal situations as posing for a portrait. However that issue may be resolved, it is clear that the headwear worn by both Abigail Ellsworth and the clockmaker's wife matches these sources' descriptions of mobcaps in every particular.
63. Kornhauser and Ribeiro, "Catalogue," 135.
64. Ibid., 152, 173; Bickford, *Voices of the New Republic*, 50.
65. Main and Main, "Economic Growth and the Standard of Living," 43, table 5; Main, *Peoples of a Spacious Land*, 223, figure 7. See also Main, "Standard of Living in Southern New England," 133–34, table 7.
66. Fox, "Ceramics and Glass," 415–17.
67. The following discussion of metalware in the Connecticut River Valley is based on Ward, "Metalwares," 273.
68. Main, *Peoples of a Spacious Land*, 222. In an upper-class eastern Massachusetts household in the third quarter of the eighteenth century, that of the Concord minister William Emerson, "an array of brass kettles and skimmers and skewers . . . made an art of open-hearth cooking." Cole, *Mary Moody Emerson*, 42.
69. Sprackling, *Customs on the Table Top*, 6, 4–5; Carson, "Consumer Revolution in Colonial British America," 653.
70. Sprackling, *Customs on the Table Top*, 4–9; *Connecticut Courant*, August 18, 1788.
71. Sprackling, *Customs on the Table Top*, 9; Wolf, *As Various as Their Land*, 68.
72. Carson, *Ambitious Appetites*, 29, 174n11.
73. Main, "Standard of Living in Southern New England," 129; Main, *Peoples of a Spacious Land*, 223–24.
74. Zea, *Useful Improvements*, 55; Carson, "Consumer Revolution in Colonial British America," 588.
75. Zea, "Furniture," 251; Fox, "Ceramics and Glass," 417; Zea, *Useful Improvements*, 32, figure 34.
76. St. George, "Artifacts of Regional Consciousness," 340, 342.
77. Brown, "Revolution's Legacy for the History of the Book," 71.
78. Opal, *Beyond the Farm*, 48, 81.
79. Kornhauser and Ribeiro, "Catalogue," 172–73.
80. Brown, "Regional Culture in a Revolutionary Era," 43.
81. Sweeney, "From Wilderness to Arcadian Vale," 24.

82. Kornhauser and Schloss, "Paintings and Other Pictorial Arts," 137; Kornhauser, "Ralph Earl," 42.

83. Fischer, *Revolution of American Conservatism*, 292; Bickford, *Voices of the New Republic*, 433–34, 49.

84. Bickford, *Voices of the New Republic*, 49.

85. Ibid., 50.

86. Ibid., 50–51.

87. Richard L. Bushman attributes the tendency of the Connecticut upper classes to tone themselves down to wariness of an egalitarian, Jeffersonian backlash. Bushman, "Society and Portraiture," 78–80, 82–83.

88. Dwight, *Travels in New England and New York*, 1:244–46.

89. Vanderpoel, *Chronicles of a Pioneer School*, 339, 448, 347.

90. Garrett, *At Home*, 40.

91. Ibid.

92. Wood, *Empire of Liberty*, 478, 476; Brown, "Regional Culture in a Revolutionary Era," 47; Zea, *Useful Improvements*, 72.

93. Sprackling, *Customs on the Table Top*, 3; *Greenleaf's New York Journal and Patriotic Register*, May 3, 1797.

CHAPTER 6
Agriculture, Fishing, Horticulture

1. Main, *Connecticut Society in the Era of the American Revolution*, 8–9; Bickford, *Voices of the New Republic*, 1.

2. Bickford, *Voices of the New Republic*, 188; Peterson, "Ships and Shipping in Connecticut," 133–36.

3. Main, *Connecticut Society in the Era of the American Revolution*, 8; Main, *Society and Economy in Colonial Connecticut*, 78–79, 381.

4. Clark, *Social Change in America*, 105; Opal, *Beyond the Farm*, 87; Stavely and Fitzgerald, *America's Founding Food*, 129–32. On dairying in Connecticut, see Sloat, "Connecticut's Home Dairies," esp. 82.

5. Kelly, "Consummation of Rural Prosperity," 584. On the "market revolution" of the nineteenth century that was in its early stages when *American Cookery* was published, see Stokes, "Introduction." For a brief discussion of how the emergence of capitalism in England in the sixteenth and seventeenth centuries generated increasing inequality, which in turn made the prospect of resettlement in North America attractive to many English people, see Stavely and Fitzgerald, *America's Founding Food*, 119–21.

6. See chap. 4, notes 43, 47, above.

7. Dwight, *Travels in New England and New York*, 2:232; Bickford, *Voices of the New Republic*, 328.

8. Bickford, *Voices of the New Republic*, 85–86, 309. For an overview of colonial Connecticut grain yields, see Main, *Society and Economy in Colonial Connecticut*, 79.

9. Bickford, *Voices of the New Republic*, 40, 77.

10. Ibid., 85, 54.

11. Ibid., 177.

12. Ibid., 395, 402, 407.

13. Dwight, *Travels in New England and New York*, 3:210–11.

14. Clark, *Social Change in America*, 86.

15. Bickford, *Voices of the New Republic*, 310.

16. Main, *Society and Economy in Colonial Connecticut*, 79.

17. Dwight, *Travels in New England and New York*, 1:273. Dwight disputed the impression of

many farmers, confirmed by Main, that there was a link between wheat fungus and the barberry.

18. Gross, "Culture and Cultivation," 524, table 3.
19. Main, *Society and Economy in Colonial Connecticut*, 78-79, 218, 222, 223, 226, 239.
20. Ibid., 381; Bickford, *Voices of the New Republic*, 152.
21. Bickford, *Voices of the New Republic*, 77, 61.
22. Simmons, *American Cookery* (introduction by Wilson), xiii-xv.
23. Bickford, *Voices of the New Republic*, 152, 177; Dwight, *Travels in New England and New York*, 3:213. Gypsum plaster, also known as plaster of Paris because of the gypsum deposits found at Montmartre, Paris, was one of the earliest examples of a chemical used in agriculture. It was relatively easy to make by dehydrating the mineral at high temperatures then rehydrating it with water to form a paste or plaster. Its advantages as a fertilizer over labor-intensive stable manure are easy to grasp. Although in the view of William Miller of Wintonbury, as in that of many others, stable manure was a higher quality dressing than gypsum plaster, cheap and easy won the day, and many American farmers of the period took to fertilizing their hayfields with gypsum. But traditionalists like George Washington Stanley of Wallingford maintained that "no considerable improvement in Agriculture can be reasonably expected, but in proportion to the attention paid to the increase in quantity & quality of manure." *Britannica Library*, s.v. "Gypsum plaster," "Gypsum"; *Oxford English Dictionary*, s.v. "plaster of Paris"; Bickford, *Voices of the New Republic*, 77, 343.
24. Herndon, "Agriculture in America in the 1790s," 510.
25. Bickford, *Voices of the New Republic*, 402, 85-86, 142, 152.
26. Ibid., 86, 142, 365. Despite the Town Reports' general assessment that beef, not pork, was the main meat export, Jackson Turner Main contended that pork brought higher prices during the colonial era than beef. While Main's focus extended only to 1774, it is doubtful that agricultural and husbandry practices would have changed substantially after the Revolution. Main, *Society and Economy in Colonial Connecticut*, 78.
27. Bickford, *Voices of the New Republic*, 152, 156, 62.
28. Anderson, *Creatures of Empire*, 84-85.
29. Ibid., 86.
30. Main, *Society and Economy in Colonial Connecticut*, 78; Stavely and Fitzgerald, *America's Founding Food*, 178.
31. Main, *Society and Economy in Colonial Connecticut*, 78-79.
32. Ibid., 212-13.
33. Ibid., 215-16, 218.
34. Ibid., 222-23.
35. Waggoner, "Fertile Farms among the Stones," 50; Peterson, "Ships and Shipping in Connecticut," 133-34, 136.
36. Bickford, *Voices of the New Republic*, 142, 78.
37. Waggoner, "Fertile Farms among the Stones," 50; Dwight, *Travels in New England and New York*, 2:259.
38. Moynihan, "With 'Unshaken Heroism and Fortitude,'" 87; Sloat, "Connecticut's Home Dairies"; Bickford, *Voices of the New Republic*, 116, 99.
39. Peterson, "Ships and Shipping in Connecticut," 133; Vickers, "Fisheries," 127.
40. Vickers, "Fisheries," 128; Bickford, *Voices of the New Republic*, 175-76.
41. Vickers, "Fisheries," 127-30; Bickford, *Voices of the New Republic*, 175-76.
42. Bickford, *Voices of the New Republic*, 175-76.
43. Ibid.
44. Ibid., 39-40.
45. Vickers, "Fisheries," 129.
46. Bickford, *Voices of the New Republic*, 31-32, 169; Vickers, "Fisheries," 128.
47. Vickers, "Fisheries," 128.

48. Ibid., 130.

49. Thornton, *Cultivating Gentlemen*, 26–30, 32.

50. Ibid., 27, 29, 40–41, 45, 52, 44, 148.

51. Ibid., 171.

52. The next several paragraphs are devoted to Bickford, *Voices of the New Republic*, 62–63.

53. Ibid., 311–13.

54. Ibid., 77–78.

55. Ibid., 85, 25, 31, 32.

56. Ibid., 116, 131.

57. Ibid., 152, 293, 311, 358, 408.

58. Waggoner, "Fertile Farms among the Stones," 48.

59. Ibid., 48–49.

60. Ibid., 48.

61. Purcell, *Connecticut in Transition*, 159–60.

62. Ibid., 160.

63. Lockridge, "Land, Population and the Evolution of New England Society," 69, 70.

64. Ibid., 71, 74. Gloria L. Main has argued that for the prerevolutionary decades, continual population exodus from Connecticut and elsewhere in rural New England "eased pressure on the land at home." This was one of the factors contributing to an improving standard of living for those who remained. Our focus, however, is on the pressures that caused out-migration from Connecticut to intensify again at the end of the eighteenth century. Main, "Standard of Living in Southern New England," 127.

65. Dwight, *Travels in New England and New York*, 3:11.

66. Ibid.

67. Main, *Connecticut Society in the Era of the American Revolution*, 32.

68. Cooke, "Embedded Nature of Artisanal Activity," 141–48.

69. For mills and factories in early national Connecticut, see Cooper, "Technology in Transition."

70. See chap. 5, notes 23–26, above.

71. Cooke, "Embedded Nature of Artisanal Activity," 141–42.

72. Dwight, *Travels in New England and New York*, 4:182.

73. Ibid., 4:183, 247.

74. Ibid., 4:182.

75. Root, *Father and Daughter*, 31, 33–35.

76. Ibid., 29. For Ebenezer Devotion, see *Genealogical and Biographical Record of New London County Connecticut*, 698. For Major Ebenezer or Elisha Backus, see Weaver, *History of Ancient Windham*, 61–62, and *Contemporary American Biography*, 2:538.

77. Root, *Father and Daughter*, 30, 7, 31. For William Leffingwell, see Dexter, *Biographical Sketches*, 4:488–90, and Bidwell, *American Paper Mills*, 171–72. For John McLaren Breed, see Dwight, *History of the Descendants of John Dwight*, 2:1110. The "flip" that Cogswell mentioned he repeatedly drank was a popular rum-based mixed drink; see Stavely and Fitzgerald, *America's Founding Food*, 264–66.

78. Bickford, *Voices of the New Republic*, 49–51.

79. Roth and Meyer, *From Revolution to Constitution*, 69–70.

80. Dowling, *Poetry and Ideology in Revolutionary Connecticut*, 84; Crowley, *Invention of Comfort*, 143–44.

81. Cole, *Mary Moody Emerson*, 121.

82. Moynihan, "With 'Unshaken Heroism and Fortitude,'" 88.

83. Dwight, *Travels in New England and New York*, 4:247, 249; Fox, "Ceramics and Glass," 417.

84. Gilmore, *Reading Becomes a Necessity of Life*, 79, 94. For a sample discussion from this period of brimstone in wine-making, see Shannon, *Practical Treatise on Brewing*, 114, 176.

85. Dowling, *Poetry and Ideology in Revolutionary Connecticut*, 45.

86. Cooke, "Embedded Nature of Artisanal Activity," 141.

87. Bickford, *Voices of the New Republic*, 50.
88. Dowling, *Poetry and Ideology in Revolutionary Connecticut*, 7–8, 15–17, 36–39; Rhoades, *Georgics of Virgil*, 9.

PART III
American Cookery, by an American Orphan

1. "Centennial Cookery," 892.
2. *Greenleaf's New York Journal and Patriotic Register*, May 3, 1797.
3. Dwight, *Valedictory Addressed*, 15–16.
4. Kendall, *Forgotten Founding Father*, 33.

CHAPTER 7
The Cookbook

1. Friedman and Larkin, *Old Sturbridge Village Cookbook*, 5; Simmons, *American Cookery* (introduction by Wilson), title page; Simmons, *American Cookery* (introduction by Hess), title page. The first and second editions are the subject of this chapter; later printings are considered in chapter 9.
2. Our tally of the altered recipes does not include second-edition recipes that are in accord with first-edition recipes as corrected by the first edition's errata list.
3. Simmons, *American Cookery* (introduction by Wilson), 22–23; Simmons, *American Cookery* (introduction by Hess), 24.
4. Simmons, *American Cookery* (introduction by Wilson), 26, "Advertisement"; Simmons, *American Cookery* (introduction by Hess), 32. Measurements in recipes were not standardized until the end of the nineteenth century; see Stavely and Fitzgerald, *Northern Hospitality*, 107.
5. Simmons, *American Cookery* (introduction by Wilson), 17, 24, 25; Simmons, *American Cookery* (introduction by Hess), 9, 26–27. For the central place of roast beef in English cuisine and culture, see Lehmann, *British Housewife*, 355–56, 374.
6. Simmons, *American Cookery* (introduction by Wilson), 18–20, 45; Simmons, *American Cookery* (introduction by Hess), 10–14, 19–20.
7. Simmons, *American Cookery* (introduction by Wilson), 20–22; Simmons, *American Cookery* (introduction by Hess), 15–17. For turtle as party food in both England and America in the second half of the eighteenth century, see Lehmann, *British Housewife*, 258, and Daniels, *Puritans at Play*, 122.
8. Simmons, *American Cookery* (introduction by Wilson), 28–29; Simmons, *American Cookery* (introduction by Hess), 35–36.
9. See appendix 2 for placement of all the recipes in the two editions within these categories.
10. Simmons, *American Cookery* (introduction by Wilson), title page; Simmons, *American Cookery* (introduction by Hess), title page; Dwight, *Greenfield Hill*, 36 (part 2:ll. 172–74).
11. Simmons, *American Cookery* (introduction by Hess), 40–50, 30–37.
12. Ibid., 25–26, 31, 34–35.
13. Ibid., 30–31, 32–33.
14. Ibid., 40–44.
15. See chap. 2, notes 21–24, 29, above.
16. Simmons, *American Cookery* (introduction by Wilson), 19–20, 45; Simmons, *American Cookery* (introduction by Hess), 10–11, 19.
17. Simmons, *American Cookery* (introduction by Wilson), 19–22, 45; Simmons, *American Cookery* (introduction by Hess), 9–11, 15–19.
18. Glasse, *Art of Cookery*, 111, 139; Carter, *Frugal Housewife* (1792), 138, 143, 144.

19. Simmons, *American Cookery* (introduction by Wilson), 17; Simmons, *American Cookery* (introduction by Hess), 9.

20. Simmons, *American Cookery* (introduction by Wilson), 17–18; Simmons, *American Cookery* (introduction by Hess), 9–10.

21. Simmons, *American Cookery* (introduction by Wilson), 20; Simmons, *American Cookery* (introduction by Hess), 10–11.

22. Simmons, *American Cookery* (introduction by Hess), 10–11; Simmons, *American Cookery* (introduction by Wilson), 20.

23. Simmons, *American Cookery* (introduction by Wilson), 19–20; Simmons, *American Cookery* (introduction by Hess), 10. Many of the recipes in both editions, including several discussed below, are designed to produce much larger amounts of food than do typical recipes today. It was generally assumed that the cook was preparing meals for large households that included not only master, mistress, and children but also servants, help, extended family, and visitors.

24. Simmons, *American Cookery* (introduction by Wilson), 23, 29, 18; Simmons, *American Cookery* (introduction by Hess), 24–25, 38, 13.

25. Simmons, *American Cookery* (introduction by Hess), 21–22; Simmons, *American Cookery* (introduction by Wilson), 45.

26. Simmons, *American Cookery* (introduction by Wilson), 25–27; Simmons, *American Cookery* (introduction by Hess), 30–34, 36.

27. Simmons, *American Cookery* (introduction by Hess), 52–64, 23; Simmons, *American Cookery* (introduction by Wilson), 39–45, 46.

28. Simmons, *American Cookery* (introduction by Wilson), 34; Simmons, *American Cookery* (introduction by Hess), 41–42, 44. In Rhode Island, "Jonny" cake came to be fried rather than baked, so Simmons's recipe did not become standard procedure there.

29. Simmons, *American Cookery* (introduction by Hess), 41–42, 47–48, 50; Simmons, *American Cookery* (introduction by Wilson), 34, 36–37.

30. Simmons, *American Cookery* (introduction by Wilson), 33. As in many early cookbooks, the quantities called for in Simmons's recipes for baked goods, and the resultant size of the final products, were gargantuan by modern standards. The reasons are several: as mentioned earlier, households were considerably larger than today; also, bake ovens were fired up and used only once or twice a week.

31. Raffald, *Experienced English Housekeeper*, 59. For a discussion of the tradition of recipes for "alamoded" beef, see Stavely and Fitzgerald, *Northern Hospitality*, 232–36.

32. Carter, *Frugal Housewife* (1792), 79–83, 97–113, 116–20, 122–23; Lehmann, *British Housewife*, 235.

33. Bushman, "Portraiture and Society," 81–82.

34. Simmons, *American Cookery* (introduction by Hess), 20–21; Simmons, *American Cookery* (introduction by Wilson), 46–47. For Sigourney's and Stowe's depictions of boiled dinner as forming the basic diet of average New Englanders at this time, see note 55, below, and Stavely and Fitzgerald, *America's Founding Food*, 181–82.

35. Ulrich, *Age of Homespun*, 300. For the history in New England of bean porridge or pottage and its gradual transformation into baked beans, see Stavely and Fitzgerald, *America's Founding Food*, 40–41, 59–65.

36. Ulrich, *Age of Homespun*, 300.

37. Felt, *History of Ipswich*, 30.

38. Simmons, *American Cookery* (introduction by Wilson), 28, 26; Simmons, *American Cookery* (introduction by Hess), 34–35, 31.

39. Simmons, *American Cookery* (introduction by Hess), 44; Stavely and Fitzgerald, *America's Founding Food*, 23–29; Stavely and Fitzgerald, *Northern Hospitality*, 357–61.

40. Stavely and Fitzgerald, *Northern Hospitality*, 32–33.

41. Wilson, *Food and Drink in Britain*, 213; Smith, *Compleat Housewife*, 133; Glasse, *Art of Cookery*, 111.

42. Barlow, "Hasty Pudding," 44.

43. Buell, *New England Literary Culture*, 127; Barlow, "Hasty Pudding," 45.

44. Barlow, "Hasty Pudding," 41. When the work was first sent for publication to the Philadelphia printer Mathew Carey, the preface was couched as a dedication to Martha Washington. For unknown reasons, Carey did not publish the poem, and when it appeared in the *New York Magazine*, the Washington dedication was omitted; see Smith, "In Praise of Maize," 199. This dedication was not part of the poem's appearances in print until the 1820s.

45. The medium in which "The Hasty Pudding" made its first public appearance, *New York Magazine*, was largely put together by members of "the Friendly Club," a group of young literati many of whom had ties to the Connecticut Wits. Indeed, two years later, one of the most active members of the Friendly Club, Elihu Hubbard Smith, wrote a respectful biographical sketch of Joel Barlow for a British periodical. These facts may seem to cast doubt on our hypothesis that hasty pudding was left out of a cookbook published by Hudson & Goodwin because Barlow's poem was ideologically at odds with the cookbook's aims. *American Cookery* and "The Hasty Pudding" were, after all, both published under Connecticut Wit/Connecticut Federalist auspices. Moreover, Hudson & Goodwin's *Connecticut Courant* was one of the newspapers in which "The Hasty Pudding" was serialized in the summer of 1796. See Mott, *History of American Magazines*, 114–15; Cronin, "Elihu Hubbard Smith and the New York Friendly Club," 471–74; Smith, "Original Communications"; and *Connecticut Courant*, July 25, 1796, August 1, 8, 1796. However, there is no inconsistency between publishing Barlow's poem as a freestanding celebration of national pride and republican simplicity and not admitting into one's cookbook a dish that has been made to symbolize hostility to cookbooks.

46. John Adams to Abigail Adams, July 9, 1774, in Butterfield et al., *Adams Family Correspondence*, 1:134, 135.

47. Dwight, *Travels in New England and New York*, 4:249.

48. See chap. 4, notes 1–6, and chap. 5, notes 80–84, 88, above.

49. See chap. 2, notes 27–30, above.

50. Lehmann, *British Housewife*, 366–75, 375 (quotation).

51. See chap. 6, notes 75–77, above.

52. The following account of Robert H. Ellsworth is based on Trebay, "At Donohue's, a Nightly Steak, a Life Gone By," and Weber, "Robert H. Ellsworth Is Dead at 85 after a Life Devoted to Chinese Art."

53. Main, *Peoples of a Spacious Land*, 223, figure 7; Main, "Standard of Living in Southern New England," 129.

54. Ulrich, *Age of Homespun*, 303, 304.

55. Sigourney, *Sketch of Connecticut*, 143, 145; Dwight, *Travels in New England and New York*, 1:273–74. For the density of boiled Indian pudding in Harriet Beecher Stowe, see Stavely and Fitzgerald, *America's Founding Food*, 17–18; for rye and Indian bread, see ibid., 23–29.

56. Sigourney, *Sketch of Connecticut*, 148. Madam L—— is portrayed en route to the Larkin household as an exemplar of the Connecticut gentry's lack of pretension. She continues to travel in a chaise that has become comically antiquated, exhibiting "none of the light and graceful elegance of modern times." This worthy lady "declined to make her equipage the herald of her wealth" (139–40). According to the *Oxford English Dictionary*, the most common meaning of "nutcakes," especially in the United States, was doughnuts. In James Fenimore Cooper's *The Pioneers*, nutcakes appear on a Christmas Eve banquet table: "The four corners were garnished with plates of cake. On one was piled certain curiously twisted and complicated figures, called 'nut-cakes.'" Cooper's nutcakes

are clearly crullers. Two of the other three corners of the table are "garnished" with gingerbread and plum cake, items found in *American Cookery*. See Cooper, *Pioneers*, 135-35. For the recipe for "Nut Cakes" in Cookbook, 1789, Connecticut Historical Society, Hartford, see fig. 7.2.

57. *American Cookery* (introduction by Wilson), xvi–xvii.

58. Ibid., xvi; Simmons, *American Cookery* (introduction by Hess), xi. Although "cookie" became identified as an American usage, it was used by British writers earlier in the eighteenth century. See, for example, Burt, *Letters from a Gentleman in the North of Scotland*, 2:272, and Northumberland, *Short Tour*, 30. Joel Barlow also pairs the regional names of cornbread: "Some talk of Hoe-cake, fair Virginia's pride,/ Rich Johnny-cake this mouth has often tried." Barlow, "Hasty Pudding," 44.

59. See chap 1, note 24, above.

60. For a summary account of the popularity of Smith, Glasse, and Raffald, see Stavely and Fitzgerald, *Northern Hospitality*, 11–14.

61. Green, "Rise of Book Publishing," 79. The 1742 American printing of Smith's *Compleat Housewife* was probably too far back in the past to have been viewed as contributing to this form of Americanization.

62. See Stavely and Fitzgerald, *Northern Hospitality*, 16–19.

63. Richard L. Bushman likewise sees wariness of egalitarian backlash as one of the factors that led the Connecticut upper classes to tone themselves down; see Bushman, "Society and Portraiture," 78–80, 82–83.

64. Simmons, *American Cookery* (introduction by Wilson), 28; Simmons, *American Cookery* (introduction by Hess), 35.

65. Simmons, *American Cookery* (introduction by Wilson), 38; Simmons, *American Cookery* (introduction by Hess), 47.

66. Wansey, *Excursion to the United States of North America*, 21.

67. Weyler, *Empowering Words*, 2–3.

68. The next six paragraphs are devoted to Cookbook, 1789.

69. *Oxford English Dictionary*, s.v. "diet bread."

70. Smith, *Compleat Housewife*, 130; Glasse, *Art of Cookery*, 105, 145; Harrison, *House-Keeper's Pocket-Book*, 145, 147; Carter, *Frugal Housewife* (1792), 148; Bradshaw, *Family Jewel*, 61. The *Oxford English Dictionary* explains that hartshorn—powdered or shaved deer antler—jells when boiled in water and cooled, and can be flavored like any gelatin pudding.

71. The next four paragraphs are devoted to Cookbook, 1813–21, Connecticut Historical Society.

72. Emerson, Receipts, Houghton Library, Harvard University, Cambridge, Mass. For a sketch of life in the household of William and Ruth Emerson, see Allen, *Waldo Emerson*, 4–16.

73. Emerson, Receipts.

74. Ibid. In an odd twist, Ruth Emerson's recipe for "Rice Florendine Pudding," a conventional eighteenth-century dish, turns up verbatim seven years later, copied into Vermonter Lucy Emerson's *New-England Cookery*, which was in great part a knockoff of *American Cookery*. The Emersons were a large clan, and although we have found no direct link between Ruth's Bostonian husband, William, and Lucy's Vermont husband, Cyrus, Lucy Emerson's sister Eleanor also married someone named Emerson, and this Joseph Emerson was not only a distant relation of William but also an eastern Massachusetts minister. The circle in which all three Emerson wives traveled was perhaps small enough to allow for transmission of a pudding recipe among spousal Emersons. See Emerson, Receipts; Emerson, *New-England Cookery*, 45; Reed, *History of the Reed Family*, 203; and Emerson, *Life of Rev. Joseph Emerson*, 442, 445.

75. Simmons, *American Cookery* (introduction by Wilson), "Advertisement," 4.

CHAPTER 8
The Author and the Printers

1. Simmons, *American Cookery* (introduction by Wilson), x–xi.
2. Simmons, *American Cookery* (introduction by Hess), x–xi.
3. Bickford and Kaimowitz, "Books and Prints," 469.
4. On the uncertainties regarding the first name, see Lehmann, *British Housewife*, 451.
5. See Stavely and Fitzgerald, *Northern Hospitality*, 63–64.
6. *Connecticut Courant*, May 9, 1796.
7. Green, "Rise of Book Publishing," 78; Gross, "Introduction," 5.
8. See chap. 7, note 58, above.
9. Weyler, *Empowering Words*.
10. *Connecticut Courant*, November 28, 1796.
11. Magnuson, *Barbour Collection*, 322, 197; Knox and Ferris, *Connecticut Divorces*, 388; Nixon, *Orphan in Eighteenth-Century Law and Literature*, 4. According to Lisa Wilson, "desertion [was] the most common cause for divorce in eighteenth-century Connecticut." Wilson, *Ye Heart of a Man*, 102.
12. *Connecticut Courant*, August 18, 1788; Shields, *Civil Tongues and Polite Letters*, 315.
13. Warner, *Letters of the Republic*, 67–68.
14. *Connecticut Courant*, February 24, March 2, 9, 16, 1784; [Alsop and Dwight], *Political Green-House*.
15. Weyler, *Empowering Words*, 4, 179–80.
16. *Sentiments of an American Woman; Women Invited to War; Explanation of the Ten Commandments*.
17. Franklin, *Writings*, 5–42.
18. See chap. 2, notes 32–34, above; Weyler, *Empowering Words*, 10–18.
19. Warner, *Letters of the Republic*, 108 and *passim*; Weyler, *Empowering Words*, 180.
20. Warner, *Letters of the Republic*, 82–87.
21. Grasso, *Speaking Aristocracy*, 323–24.
22. Ibid., 323, 322.
23. Ibid., 324. Trish Loughran discerns similarly diverse models of authorship at play in a dispute between Thomas Paine and Robert Bell, the first printer of *Common Sense*, in Philadelphia in 1776: "Against the cult of genius that Paine was already cultivating about himself, Bell proffered a more traditional republican model of group authorship." Loughran, *Republic in Print*, 85.
24. Simmons, *American Cookery* (introduction by Wilson), 3.
25. Stavely and Fitzgerald, *Northern Hospitality*, 36–37; Towner, "Indentures of Boston's Poor Apprentices," 44–45; Nixon, *Orphan in Eighteenth-Century Law and Literature*, 52. The remaining 60 percent of the poor Boston boys were apprenticed to artisanal occupations. A sample from a less urban district would doubtless have shown a higher proportion put out to farming. The evidence regarding the proportion of apprentices that were orphans comes from early modern England. We doubt that things would have been that different in the colonies.
26. Nixon, *Orphan in Eighteenth-Century Law and Literature*, 43–44, 46, 63.
27. *Connecticut Courant*, January 30, 1797; *Norwich Packet*, May 5, 1794.
28. Simmons, *American Cookery* (introduction by Wilson), 3; Nixon, *Orphan in Eighteenth-Century Law and Literature*, 13–14, 17.
29. Simmons, *American Cookery* (introduction by Wilson), 3.
30. Ibid., 4. Karen Weyler notes that "the chartering documents" of the local mechanic societies that in this era provided artisans with opportunities for authorship "emphasize the importance of the collective conduct of artisans." As Benjamin Russell put it in his 1809 address to the Massachusetts Charitable Mechanic Association, "let your fellow citizens see in you, patterns, worthy of imitation, of all the moral and domestick virtues"; see Weyler, *Empowering Words*, 227.

31. Simmons, *American Cookery* (introduction by Wilson), 4, 3.

32. "Centennial Cookery," 892.

33. Nixon, *Orphan in Eighteenth-Century Law and Literature*, 155, 214. The corresponding set of challenges and dangers for female orphans of a lower class, particularly in urban settings such as London, involved being forced into prostitution. John Fielding's "Asylum" was specifically designed as a remedy for "the large number of young female prostitutes working in London"; see ibid., 44.

34. *Connecticut Courant*, November 23, 1795; *Albany Gazette*, February 9, 1795, July 25, 1796; *Constitution of the Hartford Library Company*, 19; *Catalogue of . . . the Albany Library*, 35. For a complete list of the Nixon orphan titles for which we found New England or New York advertisements or catalogue listings, see appendix 3.

35. *Hapless Orphan*, 1:13. The novel was advertised, among other places, in both the *Albany Gazette* (February 9, 1795; July 25, 1796) and the *Connecticut Courant* (January 5, March 2, 1803).

36. *Hapless Orphan*, 1:28, 33.

37. Ibid., 2:233.

38. Another contribution to the discussion on orphanhood in the young republic is Enos Hitchcock's *Farmer's Friend*. Just as *American Cookery* represents a female orphan fulfilling herself within the status and occupation, that of a "domestic," to which the established social order has called her, so *Farmer's Friend* portrays a male orphan rising in exemplary fashion to a similarly modest, predetermined, gender-appropriate status: "Tho' [Charles Worthy] discovered . . . a thirst for knowledge, yet he never betrayed the least disposition to quit the business he had been so far brought up in, that of farming" (40). For a comparable view of Connecticut farmers as being praiseworthy because of their commitment to living by standards of "industry and subordination, which are the germs of the strength and peace of communities," see Sigourney, *Sketch of Connecticut*, 149.

39. Simmons, *American Cookery* (introduction by Wilson), xvii–xviii, "Advertisement."

40. Simmons, *American Cookery* (introduction by Hess), 5.

41. Ibid., 5–6.

42. Weyler, *Empowering Words*, 98.

43. Ibid., 104, 110–11.

44. Loughran, *Republic in Print*, 45–50, 85–87.

45. Simmons, *American Cookery* (introduction by Hess), 5.

46. Simmons, *American Cookery* (introduction by Wilson), "Advertisement."

47. Monaghan, "Literacy Instruction and Gender in Colonial New England," 64–65.

48. Perlmann et al., "Literacy, Schooling, and Teaching among New England Women," 123; Gilmore, *Reading Becomes a Necessity of Life*, 121; Monaghan, "Literacy Instruction and Gender in Colonial New England," 63; Towner, "Indentures of Boston's Poor Apprentices," 52; Herndon, *Unwelcome Americans*, 99.

49. Opal, *Beyond the Farm*, 118; Bickford, *Voices of the New Republic*, 426–27.

50. Perlmann and Shirley, "When Did New England Women Acquire Literacy?" 64.

51. *Explanation of the Ten Commandments*, preface; Simmons, *American Cookery* (introduction by Hess), 5.

52. Simmons, *American Cookery* (introduction by Wilson), "Advertisement"; Simmons, *American Cookery* (introduction by Hess), 5–6.

53. Main, *Social Structure of Revolutionary America*, 204.

54. Stavely, *Puritan Legacies*, 180–82.

55. Wood, "Conspiracy and the Paranoid Style," 417, 422.

56. Breen, *American Insurgents, American Patriots*, 269, 238, 240.

57. Warner, *Letters of the Republic*, 110.

58. See Stavely and Fitzgerald, *Northern Hospitality*, 397n19. For a complete list of marketing section "borrowings," see appendix 1.

59. Simmons, *American Cookery* (introduction by Wilson), 10.

60. Ibid., 11.

61. Ibid., 11–13.

62. Bickford, *Voices of the New Republic*, 63, 311.

63. Katharina Vester argues that the marketing section amounts to a claim that women "were fit to engage in economic and agricultural discussions" and should be seen as "participants in public debates who could expect to be taken seriously." Vester, *Taste of Power*, 32. Our reading, however—that the voice speaking in these pages is not that of a young, half-educated woman but rather that of a mature gentleman—is more consistent with the submissively feminine disavowal of participation in "economic and agricultural discussions" in the preface to the Albany edition. Simmons states that the Hartford marketing section is devoted to matters "with which the Authoress does not pretend to be acquainted, much less to give directions to others." Simmons, *American Cookery* (introduction by Hess), 6. The marketing section's mention of how an apple tree can grow "in some otherwise useless spot" anticipates James Morris's remark in his Litchfield Town Report a few years later that "lands which are not arable, answer well for orchards"; see Simmons, *American Cookery* (introduction by Wilson), 16, and chap. 6, note 56, above.

64. Hackett, *Rude Hand of Innovation*, 64.

65. Simmons, *American Cookery* (introduction by Hess), title page.

66. Thornton, *Handwriting in America*, 23.

67. Ibid., 23, 19, 38, 8.

68. Ibid., 20–21.

69. Weyler, *Empowering Words*, 145–64. See also chap. 2, note 45, above.

70. Franklin, *Writings*, 5–6.

71. On naming patterns in New England, see Main, "Naming Children in Early New England," 23, and Main, *Peoples of a Spacious Land*, 227–28.

72. We have found no direct evidence of involvement by any of the Connecticut Wits in the writing of *American Cookery*. As it happens, one member of the circle, Richard Alsop, has been identified as the compiler of a cookbook, *The Universal Receipt Book*. This work contrasts sharply with *American Cookery* in both substance and style. Almost all the recipes require the most expensive ingredients and the most complex procedures, and the instructions are couched in polished, leisurely prose. For "Universal" in the title, read "Cosmopolitan": "Genuine Sirup of Capillaire, as made in France" (11), "Russian method of preserving Green Peas for winter" (40), "Spanish Syllabub" (128), "Excellent Turkish Dish called Yaprak" (157). On the title page of the first edition, authorship is attributed to "a Society of Gentlemen in New-York." For the second edition, this is laughingly altered to "Priscilla Homespun." For Alsop as the author/compiler, see Romaine, "Richard Alsop and His Universal Receipt Book." We thank Andrew F. Smith for calling our attention to this cookbook and the evidence that Alsop was its author.

73. Wood, "Conspiracy and the Paranoid Style," 434.

74. Grasso, *Speaking Aristocracy*, 456. A comparable willingness to traffic with the opposition is perhaps to be discerned in the fact that the most prominent advertisement for the Albany edition of *American Cookery* appeared in *Greenleaf's New York Journal and Patriotic Register*. According to Isaiah Thomas, Jeffersonians attacked "the measures of the venerable Washington with a great degree of virulence, in Greenleaf's paper." Thomas, *History of Printing in America* (1810), 119.

75. Thornton, *Cultivating Gentlemen*, 63.

76. Ibid., 64–66.

CHAPTER 9
The Readers and the Editions

1. Cookbook, 1813-21, Connecticut Historical Society, Hartford, compared with Simmons, *American Cookery* (introduction by Wilson), 37, 33, 32, 20, 35, 27, and Simmons, *American Cookery* (introduction by Hess), 46, 39, 10-11, 50, 36, 43, 45-46, 33. Regarding the plum cake, the two recipes call for the same amounts of flour, eggs, wine, candied fruit, and almonds, and for almost the same amounts of spices. Most tellingly, the manuscript recipe uses turns of phrase drawn from the *American Cookery* recipe: the flour is to be "well dry'd," the yeast is to be "1 quart new ale yeast," and spices are measured by the "drachm." While the manuscript's plum cake and Shrewsbury cake come from the Hartford edition, three of the looser adaptations, those of gingerbread, "Wiggs," and Marlborough pudding, could only have come from the Albany edition.

2. Barrett, Recipe booklet, Connecticut Historical Society, compared with Simmons, *American Cookery* (introduction by Wilson), 35, and Simmons, *American Cookery* (introduction by Hess), 32, 31, 49, 48, 40-41, 37, 42. The manuscript's rice pudding is a copy of *American Cookery*'s "No. 5, A *Cheap One.*" The manuscript's pudding, cake, gingerbread, puff-paste, and loaf cake are adaptations of, respectively, *American Cookery*'s "Flour Pudding" (baked), "Plain Cake," "Molasses Gingerbread," puff-paste "No. 1," and loaf cake "No. 1." Of these copied or adapted recipes, six appear in different versions in the Hartford and Albany editions of *American Cookery*. The Zeloda Barrett manuscript copies or adapts the Albany version in all instances but one, "Cookeys." As in Colchester, recipes from both editions were evidently known and used in New Hartford.

3. Cookbook, 1813-21; Barrett, Recipe booklet; Vinton, "Parsons Cooke," 227.

4. Cookbook, 1813-21.

5. Samantha Barrett, *Diary; Encyclopedia of Connecticut Biography*, 124.

6. Samantha Barrett, *Diary*; Zeloda Barrett, Diary, 1820, September 25-27, October 5, 6, 14, 20, November 20, Connecticut Historical Society. For turning cider into "molasses," see for example the roughly contemporaneous magazine article "Apple Molasses."

7. Samantha Barrett, *Diary*, May 6, 10, 29, June 10, July 5, October 22, November 11, 19, 1828.

8. Zeloda Barrett, Diary, 1804, January-March, Connecticut Historical Society. The "heads of the discourse" entry, including the spelling "Eliphlet" rather than "Eliphalet," is for January 27. One of the books Barrett mentioned reading on February 5 and 18, *The Life and Character of Miss Susanna Anthony*, had been issued in a reprint edition by Hudson & Goodwin in 1799.

9. Samantha Barrett, *Diary*, May 1, June 5, 6, October 15, 22, November 26, 1828, January 23, 1829; Zeloda Barrett, Diary, 1820, November 29; Zboray and Zboray, *Voices without Votes*, 47.

10. Samantha Barrett, *Diary*, June 19, July 31, September 10, October 11, 1828; Zeloda Barrett, Diary, 1820, December 25. For cookstoves being installed in homes in increasing numbers after 1815, see Brewer, *From Fireplace to Cookstove*, 81-85. Advertisements for cookstoves appeared in area newspapers as early as 1800. See *Connecticut Courant*, September 22, 1800; *Albany Gazette*, January 26, 1801; *Connecticut Gazette*, February 11, 1801; and *Franklin Herald*, January 7, 1812.

11. Mohanty, *Labor and Laborers of the Loom*, 169-71; Samantha Barrett, *Diary*, May 3, 13, July 11, November 19, December 4, 1828. In current dollars, the Barretts' 1815 income from their textile production was about nine thousand dollars.

12. *American Cookery* (1816); Simmons, *American Cookery* (introduction by Wilson), 3.

13. For a list of all the editions, printings, and plagiarisms of *American Cookery*, see appendix 4.

14. The *American Cookery* advertisements from 1798 onward that included a price are listed below; see note 39. The others are listed here. In many cases, the advertisement ran

for several weeks or even months in succession. We give only the initial appearance date in each sequence: *Otsego Herald*, September 25, 1800; February 7, 1805; July 17, 1806; *Hudson Gazette*, February 10, 1801; *Albany Gazette*, September 6, 1804; *Northern Post*, September 13, 1804; *Pittsfield Sun*, May 3, 1806; August 29, 1807; December 5, 1807; December 19, 1810; January 13, 1819; *Eastern Argus*, November 20, 1806; *Portland Gazette*, November 24, 1806; *New Hampshire Sentinel*, January 3, 1807; *Berkshire Reporter*, August 15, 1807; *Expositor*, March 9, 1808; *Herkimer Herald*, July 26, 1808; November 2, 1809; *Political Observatory*, December 5, 1808; *Middlesex Gazette*, June 29, 1809; *American Monitor*, September 15, 1809; *Old Colony Gazette*, November 10, 1809; *Weekly Wanderer*, January 12, 1810; *Spooner's Vermont Journal*, November 26, 1810; *Orange County Patriot*, August 11, 1812; *Rutland Herald*, September 20, 1815; *Berkshire Star*, February 1, 1816; *St. Lawrence Gazette*, December 16, 1817; *Salem Gazette*, July 7, 1818.

15. Dwight, *Travels in New England and New York*, 2:212; Gordon, "Travel on Connecticut's Roads," 171–72.

16. Collier, *Roger Sherman's Connecticut*, 29; Morse, *American Geography*, 144.

17. Bickford, *Voices of the New Republic*, 64.

18. Ibid., 116, 178. The reporter from Pomfret, Aaron Putnam, had a twofold complaint about the emigration from that town: first, that the departure of "Heads of Families" had left "their Places here, in ye Hands of Baptists Quakers &c," and second, that with so many young men having decamped "to settle especially on new Lands . . . its much more difficult getting Help now than formerly." Ibid., 408.

19. Clark, *Social Change in America*, 89–90. The portions of Ohio in which people from Connecticut and New England figured particularly prominently in the initial settlement did not include Zanesville, where *American Cookery* was printed in 1816. However, there was one Zanesville district that was settled at first primarily by New Englanders, under the leadership of the Revolutionary War hero Rufus Putnam, a native of Sutton, Massachusetts. Putnam's son Edwin, also born in Sutton, was in 1816 the Zanesville printer of *American Cookery*; see Putnam, *History of the Putnam Family*, 161, 287–88, and *Biographical and Historical Memoirs of Muskingum County, Ohio*, 48.

20. Clark, *Social Change in America*, 105–6. Norwich, where Baldwin served as an apprentice clockmaker, is not far from Windham, where Amelia Simons, who possibly was involved in the authorship of *American Cookery*, was born in 1767, two years before Baldwin.

21. Winthrop, *Life and Letters of John Winthrop*, 1:312. We quote in this paragraph from the title of the classic work by Francis Jennings: *The Invasion of America: Indians, Colonialism and the Cant of Conquest* (1975).

22. Ibid.; Dwight, *Travels in New England and New York*, 3:374.

23. Dwight, *Travels in New England and New York*, 3:373–74.

24. Hackett, *Rude Hand of Innovation*, 57.

25. Morse, *American Geography*, 251, 252.

26. Ibid., 258.

27. Ibid., 259.

28. Bushman, "Portraiture and Society," 81–82; Morse, *American Geography*, 259.

29. Hackett, *Rude Hand of Innovation*, 72, 57; Dwight, *Travels in New England and New York*, 2:345–46.

30. Dwight, *Travels in New England and New York*, 2:333.

31. Neen, "Creating Social Capital in the Early American Republic," 479; Rohrer, *Keepers of the Covenant*, 64.

32. Rohrer, *Keepers of the Covenant*, 64; Perry, *Williamstown and Williams College*, 234; Neen, "Creating Social Capital in the Early American Republic," 482.

33. Rohrer, *Keepers of the Covenant*, 71–72; Keller, *Second Great Awakening in Connecticut*, 90; Tyler, *New England Revivals*, vii. Thomas Robbins's grandfather Philemon had promoted revivals in his Branford parish during the midcentury Great Awakening; see Tracy, *Great*

Awakening, 312–14. Thomas's father, Ammi, oversaw them in Norfolk in 1767 and again in 1799. Keller, *Second Great Awakening*, 37; Tyler, *New England Revivals*, 179–91.

34. Roth, *Democratic Dilemma*, 84–85, 87–88.

35. Dwight, *Travels in New England and New York*, 2:328–29.

36. Cayton, "Radicals in the 'Western World,'" 82–84.

37. For documentation of this and the following paragraph, see appendix 4.

38. Emerson, *New-England Cookery*, title page, preface; Reed, *History of the Reed Family*, 203–4; Noyes, *Memorial of the Town of Hampstead, New Hampshire*, 438; Gilman, *Bibliography of Vermont*, 87. The *New-England Cookery* plagiarizes the Hartford edition of *American Cookery*. Most of the additional material in the book is taken from *American Cookery*'s own principal source, Carter's *Frugal Housewife*.

39. Contemporary prices for *American Cookery* are given in parenthesis at the end of each citation: *Connecticut Journal*, June 8, 1796 (2s/3d); *Connecticut Gazette*, July 28, 1796 (1s/6d); *Albany Gazette*, August 19, 1796 (2s/8d); *Vermont Gazette*, August 26, 1796 (2s); *Albany Gazette*, October 31, 1796 (3s); *Greenleaf's New York Journal and Patriotic Register*, May 3, 1797 (1s/6d); *The Diary; or, Loudon's Register*, November 14, 1797 (18¢); *The Hive*, February 7, 1804 (25¢); *Pittsfield Sun*, February 27, 1804 (25¢); *Farmer's Museum*, December 12, 1806 (25¢); *New Hampshire Gazette*, September 22, 1807 (1s/6d); *Brattleboro Reporter*, December 10, 1808 (25¢); *Long Island Star*, November 18, 1812 (31¢). For *The New-England Cookery*: *Vermont Centinel*, May 12, 1809 (38¢). For *New American Cookery*: *New York Gazette and General Advertiser*, January 4, 1805 (50¢); *New England Palladium* (Boston), August 2, 1811 (50¢). *New American Cookery* is cribbed from the Albany edition. As with *The New-England Cookery*, most of the supplementary material is from *The Frugal Housewife*.

40. See *New Hampshire Gazette*, 1807, note 39, above. A New Haven ad for the Rundell work from the same year likewise priced it at around twenty dollars (in twenty-first century terms); see *Connecticut Herald*, September 1, 1807 ($1).

41. Book-format terminology ("folio," "quarto," "octavo," etc.) does not, strictly speaking, denote the size of a volume but rather "the number of times the original sheet has been folded to form the leaves of a book." The size of a book in a particular format varies according to the size of the original sheet of paper. If the most common paper size in earlier times, nineteen by twenty-five inches, was used to produce the Hartford edition and the 1798 Hartford/Northampton reprint, then these were octavos. With the 1796 Albany edition, a sheet of this size would result in a duodecimo (in modern usage, a twelvemo). With the later editions and the Emerson plagiarism, the result would be a sextodecimo (in modern usage, a sixteenmo). See McKerrow, *Introduction to Bibliography*, 164–65, and Roberts and Etherington, *Bookbinding and the Conservation of Books*, 35–56.

42. Jaffee, "Peddlers of Progress," 525.

43. Ibid.

44. Ibid., 519.

45. Reilly and Hall, "Customers and the Market for Books," 391; Neuberg, "Chapbooks in America," 82, 95; Gilmore, *Reading Becomes a Necessity of Life*, 176.

46. With the addition of the "Advertisement," the second printing of the Hartford edition has forty-eight pages.

47. Gilmore, "Peddlers and the Dissemination of Printed Material," 88. Records of peddler stocks and sales indicate that "peddlers with printed matter usually carried a greater variety of imprints than general stores," though not of course than bookstores; see ibid., 80, 88. For a discussion of some of the other ways in which books were distributed in rural areas, see chap. 3, notes 27–31, above.

48. Dwight, *Travels in New England and New York*, 4:160–61.

49. Jaffee, "Peddlers of Progress," 524. In Washington in 1810, Massachusetts congressman Timothy Pickering, staunch Federalist gentleman that he was, taught his boardinghouse landlady how to make Indian pudding; see "Letters of Abijah Bigelow," 313.

50. Bickford, *Voices of the New Republic*, 420, 424, 426, 430, 433-34, correlated with Tyler, *New England Revivals*, 17-23, 179-91, 227-42, and Shiels, "Second Great Awakening in Connecticut," 408-9. The 1815-18 revival venues are listed in Bradley, *Accounts of Religious Revivals*, vi-xii.

51. Dwight, *Travels in New England and New York*, 2:34.

Conclusion

1. Conforti, *Imagining New England*, 91; Haselby, *Origins of American Religious Nationalism*, 51.

2. Dwight, *Travels in New England and New York*, 2:230; *Essex Journal*, July 20, 1785.

3. Buell, *New England Literary Culture*, 454n47.

4. Conforti, *Imagining New England*, 172-96, esp. 182, 190-96; Buell, *New England Literary Culture*, 33.

5. Loughran, *Republic in Print*, chaps. 3-5.

6. Cookbook, 1813-21, Connecticut Historical Society, Hartford.

7. Dwight, *Travels in New England and New York*, 2:230; Buell, *New England Literary Culture*, 300.

8. Mathews, *Expansion of New England*, 122-23, 136, 153-57, 159-62, 181.

9. Fraser, *Pedagogue for God's Kingdom*, 148, 151-56; Mathews, *Expansion of New England*, 189-90.

10. Pease, *Frontier State*, 437-38; Doyle, *Social Order of a Frontier Community*, 23-31.

11. Sklar, *Catharine Beecher*, 113-17, 176-78, 217-21.

12. Risjord, *Representative Americans*, 217-19; Beecher, *Treatise on Domestic Economy*; Beecher, *Miss Beecher's Domestic Receipt Book*.

13. On Catharine Beecher, Harriet Beecher Stowe, domesticity, and nostalgia for preindustrial small-town New England, see, among many other sources, Conforti, *Imagining New England*, 205-6, 225-27; Stavely and Fitzgerald, *America's Founding Food*, 140-45, 226-31; and Stavely and Fitzgerald, *Northern Hospitality*, 80-92, 98-101.

14. Suburbia was not created *ex nihilo* after World War II, of course. Scott Donaldson notes that "in the 1920s, suburbanization became a demographic process of magnitude for the first time." Donaldson, *Suburban Myth*, 35. Thus, in Sinclair Lewis's *Babbitt*, published in 1922 and set in the immediately preceding years, the realtor protagonist is involved in suburban development and lives himself in a suburb. Nevertheless, as Donaldson writes, "compared to the flight from the cities after World War II . . . the exodus of the 1920s represented only a minor trend" (35). Donaldson sees Jeffersonian agrarianism as the principal source of the suburban sensibility.

Appendix 1

1. Glasse, *Art of Cookery*, xxxi-xxxiii, xxxvi-xxxvii.

2. See appendix 2 for the reasons we consider this plum cake in the second edition to be a different recipe from the one in the first.

Appendix 2

1. Baked custard in A.

2. This recipe, placed after "Soft Gingerbread to be baked in pans," is for "Butter drop" gingerbread, with "do" short for "ditto."

3. The differences between the versions of plum cake in the Albany and Hartford editions are great enough, in our view, to warrant considering them as two separate recipes. Cream in Hartford becomes milk in Albany. Hartford's candied citron and orange peel

are omitted in Albany, as are its almonds and wine, and the number of eggs is greatly reduced. Hartford's candied fruit and its richer dairy dimension of cream and more eggs is replaced in Albany by butter and sugar. All in all, the Albany version is less elaborate and elegant, enough so to place it in the prosperous category, whereas we assign the Hartford plum cake to the festive/elegant category.

Appendix 4

1. Simmons, *American Cookery* (introduction by Wilson), xix.

Bibliography

MANUSCRIPTS

Barrett, Zeloda. Diary, 1804. In Zeloda and Samantha Barrett Diaries, 1804–31, historical manuscripts 45572. Connecticut Historical Society, Hartford.

——. Diary, 1820. In Zeloda and Samantha Barrett Diaries, 1804–31, historical manuscripts 45572. Connecticut Historical Society, Hartford.

——. Recipe booklet. In Zeloda and Samantha Barrett Diaries, 1804–31, historical manuscripts 45572. Connecticut Historical Society, Hartford.

Cookbook, 1789. Historical manuscripts 81690. Connecticut Historical Society, Hartford.

Cookbook, 1813–21. Historical manuscripts 92208. Connecticut Historical Society, Hartford.

Emerson, Ruth Haskins. Receipts. Ralph Waldo Emerson Memorial Association deposit, MS Am 1280.235 (445). Houghton Library, Harvard University, Cambridge, Mass.

NEWSPAPERS

Alabama Courier (Claiborne)

Albany Gazette (Albany, N.Y.)

American Apollo (Boston)

American Herald (Boston)

American Mercury (Hartford, Conn.)

American Monitor (Plattsburgh, N.Y.)

American Telegraph (Newfield, Conn.)

Andrews's Western Star (Stockbridge, Mass.)

Berkshire Reporter (Pittsfield, Mass.)

Berkshire Star (Stockbridge, Mass.)

Brattleboro Reporter (Brattleboro, Vt.)

Centinel of Freedom (Newark, N.J.)

Columbian Centinel (Boston)

Connecticut Courant (Hartford)

Connecticut Gazette (New London)

Connecticut Herald (New Haven)

Connecticut Journal (New Haven)

Courier of New Hampshire (Concord)

The Diary; or, Loudon's Register (New York)

Eastern Argus (Portland, Maine)

Eastern Herald (Portland, Maine)

Essex Journal and Massachusetts and New Hampshire General Advertiser (Newburyport, Mass.)

Expositor (Geneva, N.Y.)

Farmer's Museum (Walpole, N.H.)

Federal Orrery (Boston)

Franklin Herald (Greenfield, Mass.)

Greenleaf's New York Journal and Patriotic Register

Hampshire Gazette (Northampton, Mass.)

Herkimer Herald (Herkimer, N.Y.)

The Hive (Northampton, Mass.)

Hudson Gazette (Hudson, N.Y.)

Impartial Gazetteer and Saturday Evening's Post (New York)

Litchfield Monitor (Litchfield, Conn.)

Long Island Star (Brooklyn, N.Y.)

Massachusetts Mercury (Boston)

Massachusetts Spy (Worcester)

Middlesex Gazette (Middletown, Conn.)

New England Palladium (Boston)

New Hampshire Gazette (Portsmouth)

New Hampshire Sentinel (Keene)

New Hampshire Spy (Portsmouth)

New Haven Gazette and Connecticut Magazine

New York Daily Gazette

New York Gazette and General Advertiser

New York Packet and the American Advertiser

Northern Post (Salem, N.Y.)

Norwich Packet (Norwich, Conn.)

Old Colony Gazette (New Bedford, Mass.)

Orange County Patriot (Goshen, N.Y.)

Otsego Herald (Cooperstown, N.Y.)

Pittsfield Sun (Pittsfield, Mass.)

Political Observatory (Walpole, N.H.)

Portland Gazette and Maine Advertiser

Providence Gazette and Country Journal (Providence, R.I.)

Rural Repository (Leominster, Mass.)

Rutland Herald (Rutland, Vt.)

Salem Gazette (Salem, Mass.)

Salem Mercury (Salem, Mass.)

Spooner's Vermont Journal (Windsor)

St. Lawrence Gazette (Ogdensburg, N.Y.)

United States Chronicle (Providence, R.I.)

Vermont Centinel (Burlington)

Vermont Gazette (Bennington)

Weekly Museum (New York)

Weekly Wanderer (Randolph, Vt.)

Winyaw Intelligencer (Georgetown, S.C.)

BOOKS AND ARTICLES

Adams, John. *Diary and Autobiography of John Adams.* Edited by L. H. Butterfield. 4 vols. Cambridge, Mass.: Belknap Press of Harvard University Press, 1961.

Allen, Gay Wilson. *Waldo Emerson: A Biography.* New York: Viking, 1981.

[Alsop, Richard]. *The Universal Receipt Book; or, Complete Family Directory.* New York: I. Riley, 1814.

——. *The Universal Receipt Book; Being a Compendious Repository of Practical Information.* 2nd edition. Philadelphia: I. Riley, 1818.

[Alsop, Richard, and Theodore Dwight]. *The Political Green-House for the Year 1798: Addressed to the Readers of the Connecticut Courant.* Hartford: Hudson and Goodwin, 1799.

American Cookery. N.p.: "Printed for the Publishers," 1808.

——. Walpole, N.H.: Elijah Brooks, 1812.

——. Brattleboro, Vt.: William Fessenden, 1814.

——. Poughkeepsie, N.Y.: Paraclete Potter, 1815.

——. Windsor, Vt.: Pomroy and Hedge, 1816.

——. Brattleboro, Vt.: John Holbrook, 1819.

——. New York: William Beastall, 1822.

——. Woodstock, Vt.: A. Colton, 1831.

Amory, Hugh. "The New England Book Trade, 1713–1790." In *A History of the Book in America,* vol. 1, *The Colonial Book in the Atlantic World,* edited by Hugh

Amory and David D. Hall, 314–46. Cambridge: Cambridge University Press, 2000.

Anderson, Virginia DeJohn. *Creatures of Empire: How Domestic Animals Transformed Early America*. Oxford: Oxford University Press, 2004.

Appleby, Joyce. *Capitalism and a New Social Order: The Republican Vision of the 1790s*. New York: New York University Press, 1984.

——. *Inheriting the Revolution: The First Generation of Americans*. Cambridge, Mass.: Harvard University Press, 2000.

"Apple Molasses." In *The Family Magazine; or, Monthly Abstract of General Knowledge*, 394. Boston: Otis, Broaders, 1837.

Archer, Jayne. "The Queens' Arcanum: Authority and Authorship in *The Queen's Closet Opened* (1655)." *Renaissance Journal* 1, no. 6 (June 2002), http://www2.warwick.ac.uk/fac/arts/ren/projects/publications/journal/six.

Bagnall, William R. *The Textile Industries of the United States*, vol. 1, *1639–1810*. Cambridge, Mass.: Riverside Press, 1893.

Barlow, Joel. "The Hasty Pudding." *New York Magazine; or, Literary Repository*, new ser., 1 (1796): 41–49.

Barrett, Samantha. "Diary of Samantha Barrett, New Hartford, Conn., 1811 to 1829." Edited by Old Sturbridge Village. http://resources.osv.org/explore_learn/document_viewer.php?DocID=1164.

Beecher, Catharine E. *Miss Beecher's Domestic Receipt Book: Designed as a Supplement to Her Treatise on Domestic Economy*. 1846. Reprint, Mineola, N.Y.: Dover, 2001.

——. *A Treatise on Domestic Economy*. Edited by Kathryn Kish Sklar. 1841. Reprint, New York: Schocken, 1977.

Beecher, Catharine E., and Harriet Beecher Stowe. *The American Woman's Home; or, Principles of Domestic Science*. Edited by Nicole Tonkovich. 1869. Reprint, New Brunswick, N.J.: Rutgers University Press, 2004.

Berry, Christopher J. *The Idea of Luxury: A Conceptual and Historical Investigation*. Cambridge: Cambridge University Press, 1994.

"Bibliography of American Newspapers, 1690–1820." *Proceedings of the American Antiquarian Society*, new ser., 25 (1915): 396–501.

Bickford, Christopher P., ed. *Voices of the New Republic: Connecticut Towns, 1800–1832*, vol. 1, *What They Said*. New Haven: Connecticut Academy of Arts and Sciences, 2003.

Bickford, Christopher P., and Jeffrey H. Kaimowitz. "Books and Prints." In *The Great River: Art and Society of the Connecticut Valley, 1635–1820*, edited by Gerald R. W. Ward and William N. Hosley, Jr., 445–83. Hartford: Wadsworth Atheneum, 1985.

Bidwell, John. *American Paper Mills, 1690–1832.* Hanover, N.H.: Dartmouth College Press, 2013.

——. "Printers' Supplies and Capitalization." In *A History of the Book in America,* vol. 1, *The Colonial Book in the Atlantic World,* edited by Hugh Amory and David D. Hall, 163–83. Cambridge: Cambridge University Press, 2000.

Biographical and Historical Memoirs of Muskingum County, Ohio. Chicago: Goodspeed, 1892.

Bowne, Eliza Southgate. *A Girl's Life Eighty Years Ago: Selections from the Letters of Eliza Southgate Bowne.* Edited by Clarence Cook. New York: Scribner's, 1887.

Bradley, Joshua. *Accounts of Religious Revivals in Many Parts of the United States from 1815 to 1818.* 1819. Reprint, Wheaton, Ill.: Richard Owen Roberts, 1980.

Bradshaw, Penelope. *The Family Jewel, and Compleat Housewife's Companion.* 7th edition. London: R. Whitworth, 1754.

Breen, T. H. *American Insurgents, American Patriots: The Revolution of the People.* New York: Hill and Wang, 2010.

Brewer, Priscilla J. *From Fireplace to Cookstove: Technology and the Domestic Ideal in America.* Syracuse, N.Y.: Syracuse University Press, 2000.

Brissot de Warville, J. P. *New Travels in the United States of America.* Bowling Green, Ohio: Historical Publications, 1919.

Britannica Library. library.eb.com/levels/referencecenter.

Brooke, John L. *The Heart of the Commonwealth: Society and Political Culture in Worcester County, Massachusetts, 1713–1861.* Cambridge: Cambridge University Press, 1989.

Brown, Richard D. *Knowledge Is Power: The Diffusion of Information in Early America.* New York: Oxford University Press, 1989.

——. "Regional Culture in a Revolutionary Era: The Connecticut Valley, 1760–1820." In *The Great River: Art and Society of the Connecticut Valley, 1635–1820,* edited by Gerald R. W. Ward and William N. Hosley, Jr., 41–48. Hartford: Wadsworth Atheneum, 1985.

——. "The Revolution's Legacy for the History of the Book." In *A History of the Book in America,* vol. 2, *An Extensive Republic: Print, Culture and Society in the New Nation, 1790–1840,* edited by Robert A. Gross and Mary Kelley, 58–74. Chapel Hill: University of North Carolina Press, 2010.

Brown, William Garrott. *The Life of Oliver Ellsworth.* New York: Macmillan, 1905.

Buel, Richard, Jr. *Joel Barlow: American Citizen in a Revolutionary World.* Baltimore: Johns Hopkins University Press, 2011.

Buell, Lawrence. *New England Literary Culture: From Revolution through Renaissance.* Cambridge: Cambridge University Press, 1986.

Burt, Edward. *Letters from a Gentleman in the North of Scotland to His Friend in London*. 2 vols. London: S. Birt, 1754.

Bushman, Richard L. "Portraiture and Society in Late Eighteenth-Century Connecticut." In Elizabeth Mankin Kornhauser, with Richard L. Bushman, Stephen H. Kornhauser, and Aileen Ribeiro, *Ralph Earl: The Face of the Young Republic*, 68–83, 99–100. New Haven, Conn.: Yale University Press, 1991.

Butterfield, L. H., et al., eds. *Adams Family Correspondence*. 12 vols. to date. Cambridge, Mass.: Belknap Press of Harvard University Press, 1963–.

Carson, Barbara G. *Ambitious Appetites: Dining, Behavior, and Patterns of Consumption in Federal Washington*. Washington, D.C.: American Institute of Architects Press, 1990.

Carson, Cary. "The Consumer Revolution in Colonial British America: Why Demand?" In *Of Consuming Interests: The Style of Life in the Eighteenth Century*, edited by Cary Carson, Ronald Hoffman, and Peter J. Albert, 483–697. Charlottesville: University Press of Virginia, 1994.

Carter, Susannah. *The Frugal Housewife; or, Complete Woman Cook*. Boston: Edes and Gill, 1772.

——. *The Frugal Housewife; or, Complete Woman Cook*. New York: Berry and Rogers, 1792.

——. *The Frugal Housewife; or, Complete Woman Cook*. Philadelphia: James Carey, 1796.

A Catalogue of Books . . . for Sale . . . at James White's Book and Stationary Store. Boston: James White, 1798.

Catalogue of Books for Sale . . . by Thomas, Andrews and Penniman, at the Albany Bookstore, No. 45, State-Street. Albany: Loring Andrews, 1797.

A Catalogue of the Books Belonging to the Albany Library. Albany: Barber and Southwick, 1793.

Cayton, Andrew R. L. "Radicals in the 'Western World': The Federalist Conquest of Trans-Appalachian North America." In *Federalists Reconsidered*, edited by Doron Ben-Atar and Barbara B. Oberg, 77–96. Charlottesville: University Press of Virginia, 1998.

"Centennial Cookery." *Scribner's Monthly* 11 (1875–76): 892–94.

The Charter, Bye-Laws, and Names of the Members of the New-York Society Library, with a Catalogue of the Books Belonging to the Said Library. New York: Hugh Gaine, 1789.

Charvat, William. *Literary Publishing in America, 1790–1850*. Amherst: University of Massachusetts Press, 1993.

Clark, Christopher. *Social Change in America from the Revolution through the Civil War*. Chicago: Ivan R. Dee, 2006.

Cole, Arthur Harrison, ed. *Industrial and Commercial Correspondence of Alexander Hamilton*. Chicago: A. W. Shaw, 1928.

Cole, Phyllis. *Mary Moody Emerson and the Origins of Transcendentalism: A Family History*. New York: Oxford University Press, 1998.

Collier, Christopher. *Roger Sherman's Connecticut: Yankee Politics and the American Revolution*. Middletown, Conn.: Wesleyan University Press, 1971.

"A Colonial Lady's Clothing: A Glossary of Terms." http://www.history.org/history /clothing/women/wglossary.cfm.

Conforti, Joseph A. *Imagining New England: Explorations of Regional Identity from the Pilgrims to the Mid-Twentieth Century*. Chapel Hill: University of North Carolina Press, 2001.

Connecticut Academy of Arts and Sciences. "Original Documents." http://caas. yale.edu/original-documents.

Conroy, David W. *In Public Houses: Drink and the Revolution of Authority in Colonial Massachusetts*. Chapel Hill: University of North Carolina Press, 1995.

The Constitution of the Hartford Library Company; Extracts from the By-Laws, and a Catalogue of the Books. Hartford: Hudson and Goodwin, 1797.

Contemporary American Biography: Biographical Sketches of Representative Men of the Day. 2 vols. New York: Atlantic, 1895.

Cooke, Edward S., Jr. "The Embedded Nature of Artisanal Activity in Connecticut, ca. 1800." In *Voices of the New Republic: Connecticut Towns, 1800–1832*, vol. 2, *What We Think*, edited by Howard R. Lamar, 141–48, 282–83. New Haven: Connecticut Academy of Arts and Sciences, 2003.

——. *Making Furniture in Preindustrial America: The Social Economy of Newtown and Woodbury, Connecticut*. Baltimore: Johns Hopkins University Press, 1996.

The Cook Not Mad; or, Rational Cookery. Watertown, N.Y.: Knowlton and Rice, 1830.

Cooley, Pamela. "Searching for Amelia: A Quest for the Author of the First American Cookbook." 2016. https://sophiecoeprize.files.wordpress.com/2012/12/ cooley-entry-searching-for-amelia-6951-words.pdf.

Cooper, Carolyn C. "Technology in Transition: Connecticut Industries, 1800–1832." In *Voices of the New Republic: Connecticut Towns, 1800–1832*, vol. 2, *What We Think*, edited by Howard R. Lamar, 149–70, 283–88. New Haven: Connecticut Academy of Arts and Sciences, 2003.

Cooper, James Fenimore. *The Pioneers; or, The Sources of the Susquehanna*. New York: James G. Gregory, 1862.

Court Cookery; or, The Compleat English Cook. London: T. Wotton, 1725.

Cowan, Brian. "New Worlds, New Tastes: Food Fashions after the Renaissance."

In *Food: The History of Taste*, edited by Paul Freedman, 197–230. Berkeley: University of California Press, 2007.

Cronin, James E. "Elihu Hubbard Smith and the New York Friendly Club, 1795–1798." *Proceedings of the Modern Language Association* 64, no. 3 (June 1949): 471–79.

Crowley, John E. *The Invention of Comfort: Sensibilities and Design in Early Modern Britain and Early America*. Baltimore: Johns Hopkins University Press, 2001.

Dabney, John. *Additional Catalogue of Books for Sale or Circulation, in Town or Country, at the Salem Bookstore*. Newburyport, Mass.: J. Dabney, 1794.

Daniels, Bruce C. *The Connecticut Town: Growth and Development, 1635–1790*. Middletown, Conn.: Wesleyan University Press, 1979.

———. *Puritans at Play: Leisure and Recreation in Colonial New England*. New York: St. Martin's, 1995.

———. "The Remarkable Complexity of the Simple New England Town." In *Voices of the New Republic: Connecticut Towns, 1800–1832*, vol. 2, *What We Think*, edited by Howard R. Lamar, 247–54, 295–96. New Haven: Connecticut Academy of Arts and Sciences, 2003.

Davidson, Alan. *The Oxford Companion to Food*. Oxford: Oxford University Press, 1999.

Davidson, Cathy N. *Revolution and the Word: The Rise of the Novel in America*. New York: Oxford University Press, 1986.

Day, Ivan. "The Art of Confectionery." http://www.historicfood.com/The%20 Art%20of%20Confectionery.pdf.

DeJean, Joan E. *The Essence of Style: How the French Invented High Fashion, Fine Food, Chic Cafes, Style, Sophistication, and Glamour*. New York: Free Press, 2005.

Dexter, Franklin Bowditch. *Biographical Sketches of the Graduates of Yale College, with Annals of the College History*. 6 vols. New York: Henry Holt, 1885–1912.

Dods, Margaret. *The Cook and Housewife's Manual*. 8th edition. Edinburgh: Oliver and Boyd, 1847.

Donaldson, Scott. *The Suburban Myth*. New York: Columbia University Press, 1969.

Dowling, William C. *Poetry and Ideology in Revolutionary Connecticut*. Athens: University of Georgia Press, 1990.

Doyle, Don Harrison. *The Social Order of a Frontier Community: Jacksonville, Illinois, 1825–70*. Urbana: University of Illinois Press, 1978.

Dwight, Benjamin W. *The History of the Descendants of John Dwight of Dedham, Mass*. 2 vols. New York: John F. Trow, 1874.

Dwight, Theodore. *An Oration, Delivered at New Haven on the 7th of July, A. D. 1801, before the Society of the Cincinnati*. Hartford: Hudson and Goodwin, 1801.

——. *An Oration, Spoken before the Society of the Cincinnati of the State of Connecticut, Met in Hartford, on the 4th of July, 1792*. Hartford: Hudson and Goodwin, 1792.

Dwight, Timothy. *Greenfield Hill: A Poem in Seven Parts*. New York: Childs and Swaine, 1794.

——. *Travels in New England and New York*. Edited by Barbara Miller Solomon. 4 vols. Cambridge, Mass.: Harvard University Press, 1969.

——. *A Valedictory Addressed to the Young Gentlemen, Who Commenced Bachelors of Arts at Yale-College, July 25th, 1776*. New Haven, Conn.: Thomas and Samuel Green, 1776.

Eames, Wilberforce. "Introduction." In *The Bay Psalm Book: Being a Facsimile Reprint of the First Edition Printed by Stephen Daye at Cambridge in New England in 1640*, v–xvii. New York: Dodd and Livingston, 1912.

[Earl, Ralph]. "Portrait of a Connecticut Clockmaker." http://americanart.si.edu/collections/search/artwork/?id=7715.

——. "Portrait of a Connecticut Clockmaker's Wife." http://americanart.si.edu/collections/search/artwork/?id=7716.

Ellis, Joseph J. *After the Revolution: Profiles of Early American Culture*. New York: Norton, 1979.

Emerson, Lucy. *The New-England Cookery . . . Particularly Adapted to This Part of Our Country*. Montpelier, Vt.: Josiah Parks, 1808.

Emerson, Ralph. *Life of Rev. Joseph Emerson, Pastor of the Third Congregational Church in Beverly, Mass*. Boston: Crocker and Brewster, 1834.

Encyclopedia of Connecticut Biography. Boston: American Historical Association, 1917.

An Explanation of the Ten Commandments, Partly Composed, and Partly Compiled by an Aged School-Mistress, in the State of Massachusetts. Keene, N.H.: Henry Blake, 1794.

Felt, Joseph B. *History of Ipswich, Essex, and Hamilton*. Cambridge, Mass.: Charles Folson, 1834.

Fischer, David Hackett. *The Revolution of American Conservatism: The Federalist Party in the Era of Jeffersonian Democracy*. New York: Harper and Row, 1965.

Fitzmier, John R. *New England's Moral Legislator: Timothy Dwight, 1752–1817*. Bloomington: Indiana University Press, 1998.

Fox, Elizabeth Pratt. "Ceramics and Glass." In *The Great River: Art and Society of the Connecticut Valley, 1635–1820*, edited by Gerald R. W. Ward and William N. Hosley, Jr., 415–43. Hartford: Wadsworth Atheneum, 1985.

Franklin, Benjamin. *Writings*. Edited by J. A. Leo Lemay. New York: Library of America, 1987.

Fraser, James W. *Pedagogue for God's Kingdom: Lyman Beecher and the Second Great Awakening.* Lanham, Md.: University Press of America, 1985.

Freeman, James. *Remarks on the American Universal Geography.* Boston: Belknap and Hall, 1793.

Friedman, Debra, and Jack Larkin, eds. *Old Sturbridge Village Cookbook: Authentic Early American Recipes for the Modern Kitchen.* 3rd edition. Guilford, Conn.: Globe Pequot Press, 2009.

Garrett, Elisabeth Donaghy. *At Home: The American Family, 1750–1870.* New York: Harry N. Abrams, 1990.

Geertz, Clifford. *The Interpretation of Cultures: Selected Essays.* New York: Basic Books, 1973.

Genealogical and Biographical Record of New London County Connecticut. Chicago: J. H. Beers, 1905.

Gilman, Marcus D. *The Bibliography of Vermont; or, A List of Books and Pamphlets Relating in Any Way to the State.* Burlington, Vt.: Free Press Association, 1897.

Gilmore, William J. "Peddlers and the Dissemination of Printed Material in Northern New England, 1780–1840." In *Itinerancy in New England and New York,* edited by Peter Benes, 76–89. Boston: Boston University, 1986.

——. *Reading Becomes a Necessity of Life: Material and Cultural Life in Rural New England, 1780–1835.* Knoxville: University of Tennessee Press, 1989.

Glasse, Hannah. *The Art of Cookery Made Plain and Easy.* London, 1747. Reprint as *"First Catch Your Hare . . .": The Art of Cookery Made Plain and Easy.* Edited by Jennifer Stead and Priscilla Bain. Totnes, Eng.: Prospect, 1995.

Goodwin, James Junius. *The Goodwins of Hartford, Connecticut, Descendants of William and Ozias Goodwin.* Hartford: Brown and Green, 1891.

Goodwin, Nathaniel. *Genealogical Notes; or, Contributions to the Family History of Some of the First Settlers of Connecticut and Massachusetts.* Hartford: F. A. Brown, 1856.

Gordon, Robert B. "Travel on Connecticut's Roads, Bridges, and Ferries, 1790–1830." In *Voices of the New Republic: Connecticut Towns, 1800–1832,* vol. 2, *What We Think,* edited by Howard R. Lamar, 171–82, 288–89. New Haven: Connecticut Academy of Arts and Sciences, 2003.

Grasso, Christopher. *A Speaking Aristocracy: Transforming Public Discourse in Eighteenth-Century Connecticut.* Chapel Hill: University of North Carolina Press, 1999.

Green, James N. "The Rise of Book Publishing." In *A History of the Book in America,* vol. 2, *An Extensive Republic: Print, Culture and Society in the New Nation,*

1790–1840, edited by Robert A. Gross and Mary Kelley, 75–127. Chapel Hill: University of North Carolina Press, 2010.

Gross, Robert A. "Culture and Cultivation: Agriculture and Society in Thoreau's Concord." In *Material Life in America, 1600–1860*, edited by Robert Blair St. George, 519–33. Boston: Northeastern University Press, 1988.

——. "Introduction: An Extensive Republic." In *A History of the Book in America*, vol. 2, *An Extensive Republic: Print, Culture and Society in the New Nation, 1790–1840*, edited by Robert A. Gross and Mary Kelley, 1–50. Chapel Hill: University of North Carolina Press, 2010.

Hackett, David G. *The Rude Hand of Innovation: Religion and Social Order in Albany, New York, 1652–1836*. New York: Oxford University Press, 1991.

Hall, David D., ed. *The Antinomian Controversy, 1636–1638: A Documentary History*. 2nd edition. Durham, N.C.: Duke University Press, 1990.

——. *Cultures of Print: Essays in the History of the Book*. Amherst: University of Massachusetts Press, 1996.

——. *Worlds of Wonder, Days of Judgment: Popular Religious Belief in Early New England*. New York: Knopf, 1989.

The Hapless Orphan; or, Innocent Victim of Revenge. A Novel, Founded on Incidents in Real Life. In a Series of Letters from Caroline Francis to Maria B——. 2 vols. Boston: Belknap and Hall, 1793.

Harris, Thaddeus M. *Selected Catalogue of Some of the Most Esteemed Publications in the English Language. Proper to Form a Social Library: With an Introduction upon the Choice of Books*. Boston: I. Thomas and E. T. Andrews, 1793.

Harrison, Sarah. *The House-Keeper's Pocket-Book and Compleat Family Cook*. 2nd edition. London: R. Ware, 1739.

Haselby, Sam. *The Origins of American Religious Nationalism*. Oxford: Oxford University Press, 2015.

Hayes, Kevin J. *A Colonial Woman's Bookshelf*. Knoxville: University of Tennessee Press, 1996.

Herndon, Melvin G. "Agriculture in America in the 1790s: An Englishman's View." *Agricultural History* 49 (1975): 505–16.

Herndon, Ruth Wallis. *Unwelcome Americans: Living on the Margin in Early New England*. Philadelphia: University of Pennsylvania Press, 2001.

"An Historic Store." *New England Stationer and Printer* 11 (1897): 28F.

History.com Staff. "Congress Renames the Nation 'United States of America.'" A+E Networks, 2010. http://www.history.com/this-day-in-history/congress-renames-the-nation-united-states-of-america.

Hitchcock, Enos. *The Farmer's Friend; or, The History of Mr. Charles Worthy. Who, from Being a Poor Orphan, Rose, through Various Scenes of Distress and Misfortune, to Wealth and Eminence, by Industry, Economy, and Good Conduct.* Boston: I. Thomas and E. T. Andrews, 1793.

Hosley, William N., Jr. "Architecture." In *The Great River: Art and Society of the Connecticut Valley, 1635–1820,* edited by Gerald R. W. Ward and William N. Hosley, Jr., 63–133. Hartford: Wadsworth Atheneum, 1985.

Hudson and Goodwin, Have for Sale at Their Store . . . the Following Books. Broadside. Hartford: Hudson and Goodwin, [1797?].

Humphreys, David. *A Poem on the Happiness of America; Addressed to the Citizens of the United States.* Hartford: Hudson and Goodwin, 1786.

Humphreys, Frank Landon. *Life and Times of David Humphreys: Soldier–Statesman–Poet.* 2 vols. New York: Putnam's, 1917.

Jaffee, David. "Peddlers of Progress and the Transformation of the Rural North, 1760–1820." *Journal of American History* 78 (1991): 511–35.

Kammen, Michael. *Colonial New York: A History.* New York: Scribner's, 1975.

Keller, Charles Roy. *The Second Great Awakening in Connecticut.* New Haven, Conn.: Yale University Press, 1942.

Kelly, Catherine E. " 'The Consummation of Rural Prosperity and Happiness': New England Agricultural Fairs and the Construction of Class and Gender, 1810–1860." *American Quarterly* 49 (1997): 574–602.

Kelly, J. Frederick. *The Early Domestic Architecture of Connecticut.* 1924. Reprint, New York: Dover, 1963.

Kendall, Joshua. *The Forgotten Founding Father: Noah Webster's Obsession and the Creation of an American Culture.* New York: Putnam's, 2010.

Knox, Grace Louise, and Barbara B. Ferris, comps. *Connecticut Divorces: Superior Court Records for the Counties of New London, Tolland, and Windham, 1719–1910.* Bowie, Md.: Heritage Books, 1987.

Kornfeld, Eve, ed. *Creating an American Culture, 1775–1800: A Brief History with Documents.* Boston: Bedford/St. Martin's, 2001.

Kornhauser, Elizabeth Mankin. "Ralph Earl: The Face of the Young Republic." In Elizabeth Mankin Kornhauser, with Richard L. Bushman, Stephen H. Kornhauser, and Aileen Ribeiro, *Ralph Earl: The Face of the Young Republic,* 4–67, 92–99. New Haven, Conn.: Yale University Press, 1991.

Kornhauser, Elizabeth Mankin, with Aileen Ribeiro. "Catalogue." In Elizabeth Mankin Kornhauser, with Richard L. Bushman, Stephen H. Kornhauser, and Aileen Ribeiro, *Ralph Earl: The Face of the Young Republic,* 101–252. New Haven, Conn.: Yale University Press, 1991.

Kornhauser, Elizabeth M., and Christine S. Schloss. "Paintings and Other Pictorial Arts." In *The Great River: Art and Society of the Connecticut Valley, 1635–
1820*, edited by Gerald R. W. Ward and William N. Hosley, Jr., 135–83.
Hartford: Wadsworth Atheneum, 1985.

*The Lady's Assistant for Regulating and Supplying Her Table . . . Published from the Man-
uscript Collection of Mrs. Charlotte Mason.* 3rd edition. London: J. Walter, 1777.

Landau, Aaron. "Eating Abroad and at Home: English Identity and Native Food
in the Rio de la Plata, 1806–1862." In *Transnational England: Home and
Abroad, 1780–1860*, edited by Monika Class and Terry F. Robinson, 168–84.
Newcastle upon Tyne, Eng.: Cambridge Scholars, 2009.

Larkin, Jack. "'Printing Is Something Every Village Has in It': Rural Printing and
Publishing." In *A History of the Book in America*, vol. 2, *An Extensive Republic: Print,
Culture and Society in the New Nation, 1790–1840*, edited by Robert A. Gross and
Mary Kelley, 145–60. Chapel Hill: University of North Carolina Press, 2010.

Lehmann, Gilly. *The British Housewife: Cookery Books, Cooking, and Society in
Eighteenth-Century Britain.* Totnes, Eng.: Prospect, 2003.

"Letters of Abijah Bigelow, Member of Congress, to His Wife, 1810–1815." *Proceedings of the American Antiquarian Society*, new ser., 40 (1930): 305–406.

Lewis, Sinclair. *Babbitt.* New York: Harcourt, Brace, 1922.

Lewis, Thomas H. "The Landscape and Environment of the Connecticut River
Valley." In *The Great River: Art and Society of the Connecticut Valley, 1635–1820*,
edited by Gerald R. W. Ward and William N. Hosley, Jr., 3–15. Hartford:
Wadsworth Atheneum, 1985.

Library of Congress. "Books That Shaped America." http://www.loc.gov/book
fest/books-that-shaped-america.

Lockridge, Kenneth. "Land, Population and the Evolution of New England Society, 1630–1790." *Past and Present*, 39 (April 1968): 62–80.

Loughran, Trish. *The Republic in Print: Print Culture in the Age of U.S. Nation Building, 1770–1870.* New York: Columbia University Press, 2007.

Love, William DeLoss. *The Colonial History of Hartford Gathered from the Original
Records.* Hartford, 1914.

McCusker, John J. *How Much Is That in Real Money? A Historical Commodity Price
Index for Use as a Deflator of Money Values in the Economy of the United States.*
Worcester, Mass.: American Antiquarian Society, 2001.

McKerrow, Ronald B. *An Introduction to Bibliography for Literary Students.* 1927.
Reprint, New Castle, Del.: Oak Knoll Press, 1994.

Magnuson, Carole, comp. *The Barbour Collection of Connecticut Town Vital Records:
Windham, 1692–1850.* Baltimore: Genealogical Publishing, 2002.

Main, Gloria L. "Gender, Work, and Wages in Colonial New England." *William and Mary Quarterly*, 3rd ser., 51 (1994): 39–66.

———. "Naming Children in Early New England." *Journal of Interdisciplinary History* 27 (1996): 1–27.

———. *Peoples of a Spacious Land: Families and Cultures in Colonial New England.* Cambridge, Mass.: Harvard University Press, 2001.

———. "The Standard of Living in Southern New England, 1640–1773." *William and Mary Quarterly*, 3rd ser., 45 (1988): 124–34.

Main, Gloria L., and Jackson T. Main. "Economic Growth and the Standard of Living in Southern New England, 1640–1774." *Journal of Economic History* 48 (1988): 27–46.

Main, Jackson Turner. *Connecticut Society in the Era of the American Revolution.* Hartford: American Revolution Bicentennial Commission of Connecticut, 1977.

———. *The Social Structure of Revolutionary America.* Princeton, N.J.: Princeton University Press, 1965.

———. *Society and Economy in Colonial Connecticut.* Princeton, N.J.: Princeton University Press, 1985.

Markham, Gervase. *The English Housewife.* Edited by Michael R. Best. 1986. Reprint, Kingston, Ont.: McGill-Queen's University Press, 1994.

Mathews, Lois Kimball. *The Expansion of New England: The Spread of New England Settlement and Institutions to the Mississippi River, 1620–1865.* Boston: Houghton Mifflin, 1909.

"Memoir of the Life and Writings of John Trumbull, LL. D." In John Trumbull, *The Poetical Works of John Trumbull, LL. D.,* 1:7–22. Hartford: Lincoln and Stone, 1820.

Mennell, Stephen. *All Manners of Food: Eating and Taste in England and France from the Middle Ages to the Present.* 2nd edition. Urbana: University of Illinois Press, 1996.

Mohanty, Gail Fowler. *Labor and Laborers of the Loom: Mechanization and Handloom Weavers, 1780–1840.* New York: Routledge, 2006.

Monaghan, E. Jennifer. *A Common Heritage: Noah Webster's Blue-Back Speller.* Hamden, Conn.: Archon Books, 1983.

———. "Literacy Instruction and Gender in Colonial New England." In *Reading in America: Literature and Social History,* edited by Cathy N. Davidson, 53–80. Baltimore: Johns Hopkins University Press, 1989.

Morse, Jedidiah. *The American Geography; or, A View of the Present Situation of the United States of America.* Elizabethtown, N.J.: Shepard Kollock, 1789.

Mott, Frank Luther. *A History of American Magazines, 1741–1850.* Cambridge, Mass.: Harvard University Press, 1930.

Moxon, Elizabeth. *English Housewifry Exemplified in above Four Hundred and Fifty Receipts*. 9th edition. Leeds: Griffith Wright, 1764.

Moynihan, Ruth Barnes. "With 'Unshaken Heroism and Fortitude': Connecticut Women's Life and Work Two Hundred Years Ago." In *Voices of the New Republic: Connecticut Towns, 1800–1832*, vol. 2, *What We Think*, edited by Howard R. Lamar, 85–94, 274–75. New Haven: Connecticut Academy of Arts and Sciences, 2003.

Munsell, Joel. "Memoir of Charles R. Webster, the Father of Printing in Albany." In *The Annals of Albany*, 5:230–40. Albany, N.Y.: J. Munsell, 1854.

Neen, Johann N. "Creating Social Capital in the Early American Republic: The View from Connecticut." *Journal of Interdisciplinary History* 39 (2009): 471–95.

Neuberg, Victor. "Chapbooks in America: Reconstructing the Popular Reading of Early America." In *Reading in America: Literature and Social History*, edited by Cathy N. Davidson, 81–113. Baltimore: Johns Hopkins University Press, 1989.

New American Cookery; or, Female Companion . . . by an American Lady. New York: T. B. Jansen, 1805.

Nixon, Cheryl L. *The Orphan in Eighteenth-Century Law and Literature: Estate, Blood, and Body*. Burlington, Vt.: Ashgate, 2011.

Northumberland, Elizabeth Seymour Percy, Duchess of. *A Short Tour Made in the Year One Thousand Seven Hundred and Seventy One*. London, 1775.

Noyes, Harriette Eliza, comp. *A Memorial of the Town of Hampstead, New Hampshire*. Boston: George B. Reed, 1899.

Officer, Lawrence H., and Samuel H. Williamson. "The Annual Consumer Price Index for the United States, 1774–2015." Measuring Worth. https://www.measuringworth.com/uscpi/.

Opal, J. M. *Beyond the Farm: National Ambitions in Rural New England*. Philadelphia: University of Pennsylvania Press, 2008.

Ott, Cindy. *Pumpkin: The Curious History of an American Icon*. Seattle: University of Washington Press, 2012.

Oxford English Dictionary. Online. Oxford University Press.

Pasley, Jeffrey L. *"The Tyranny of Printers": Newspaper Politics in the Early American Republic*. Charlottesville: University Press of Virginia, 2001.

Pease, Theodore Calvin. *The Frontier State, 1818–1848*. 1918. Reprint, Urbana: University of Illinois Press, 1987.

Perlmann, Joel, and Dennis Shirley. "When Did New England Women Acquire Literacy?" *William and Mary Quarterly*, 3rd ser., 48 (1991): 50–67.

Perlmann, Joel, Silvana R. Siddall, and Keith Whitescarver. "Literacy, Schooling, and Teaching among New England Women, 1730–1820." *History of Education Quarterly* 37 (1997): 117–39.

Perry, Arthur Latham. *Williamstown and Williams College: A History*. 3rd edition. Norwood, Mass.: Norwood Press, 1904.

Peters, Richard, ed. *The Public Statutes at Large of the United States of America from the Organization of the Government in 1789, to March 3, 1845*. Vol. 1. Boston: Charles C. Little and James Brown, 1845.

Peterson, William N. "Ships and Shipping in Connecticut, 1790–1811." In *Voices of the New Republic: Connecticut Towns, 1800–1832, vol. 2, What We Think*, edited by Howard R. Lamar, 133–40, 281–82. New Haven: Connecticut Academy of Arts and Sciences, 2003.

Philbrick, Nathaniel. *Mayflower: A Story of Courage, Community, and War*. New York: Viking, 2006.

Purcell, Richard J. *Connecticut in Transition, 1775–1818*. Washington, D.C.: American Historical Association, 1918.

Putnam, Eben. *A History of the Putnam Family in England and America*. Salem, Mass.: Salem Press, 1891.

Raffald, Elizabeth. *The Experienced English Housekeeper*. 1769. Reprint, Lewes, Eng.: Southover Press, 1997.

Reed, Jacob Whittemore. *History of the Reed Family in Europe and America*. Boston: John Wilson, 1861.

Reilly, Elizabeth Carroll, and David D. Hall. "Customers and the Market for Books." In *A History of the Book in America, vol. 1, The Colonial Book in the Atlantic World*, edited by Hugh Amory and David D. Hall, 387–99. Cambridge: Cambridge University Press, 2000.

Rhoades, James. *The Georgics of Virgil Translated into English Verse*. London: C. Kegan Paul, 1881.

Ridley, Glynis. "The First American Cookbook." *Eighteenth-Century Life* 23, no. 2 (1999): 114–23.

Ridley, Matt. "What about August 1714? 300 Years since the Hanoverian Accession." *The Spectator*, August 1, 2014.

Risjord, Norman K. *The Representative Americans: The Romantics*. Lanham, Md.: Rowman and Littlefield, 2001.

Roberts, Matt T., and Don Etherington. *Bookbinding and the Conservation of Books: A Dictionary of Descriptive Terminology*. Washington, D.C.: Library of Congress, 1982.

Rohrer, James R. *Keepers of the Covenant: Frontier Missions and the Decline of Congregationalism, 1774–1818*. New York: Oxford University Press, 1995.

Romaine, Lawrence B. "Richard Alsop and His Universal Receipt Book." *Connecticut Historical Society Bulletin* 18 (1953): 18–24.

Root, Grace Cogswell, ed. *Father and Daughter: A Collection of Cogswell Family Letters and Diaries, 1772–1830*. West Hartford, Conn.: American School for the Deaf, 1924.

Roth, David M., and Freeman Meyer. *From Revolution to Constitution: Connecticut, 1763 to 1818*. Chester, Conn.: Pequot Press, 1975.

Roth, Randolph A. *The Democratic Dilemma: Religion, Reform, and the Social Order in the Connecticut River Valley of Vermont, 1791–1850*. Cambridge: Cambridge University Press, 1987.

Russell, Polly. "The History Cook: Le Cuisinier François, by La Varenne." *Financial Times*, September 19, 2015.

The Sentiments of an American Woman. Philadelphia: Dunlap, 1780.

Sewall, Samuel. *The Diary of Samuel Sewall, 1674–1729*. Edited by M. Halsey Thomas. 2 vols. New York: Farrar, Straus, and Giroux, 1973.

Shannon, R. *A Practical Treatise on Brewing, Distilling, and Rectification*. London: Robert Scholey, 1805.

Shields, David S. *Civil Tongues and Polite Letters in British America*. Chapel Hill: University of North Carolina Press, 1997.

Shiels, Richard D. "The Second Great Awakening in Connecticut: Critique of the Traditional Interpretation." *Church History* 49 (1980): 401–15.

Siegel, Andrew. "'Steady Habits' under Siege: The Defense of Federalism in Jeffersonian Connecticut." In *Federalists Reconsidered*, edited by Doron Ben-Atar and Barbara B. Oberg, 199–224. Charlottesville: University Press of Virginia, 1998.

Siegel, Nancy. "Cooking up American Politics." *Gastronomica* 8, no. 3 (Summer 2008): 53–61.

Sigourney, Lydia Huntley. *Sketch of Connecticut, Forty Years Since*. Hartford: Oliver D. Cooke, 1824.

Simmons, Amelia. *American Cookery*. Hartford: Hudson and Goodwin, 1796. Reprint with an introduction by Mary Tolford Wilson, New York: Oxford University Press, 1958.

———. *American Cookery*. 2nd edition. Albany, N.Y.: Charles R. and George Webster, 1796. Reprint with an introduction by Karen Hess, Bedford, Mass.: Applewood Books, 1996.

———. *American Cookery*. Hartford: Simeon Butler, 1798.

———. *American Cookery*. 3rd edition. Salem, N.Y.: Dodd and Rumsey, 1804.

———. *American Cookery*. Troy, N.Y.: Wright, Goodenow, and Stockwill, 1808.

——. *American Cookery*. 4th edition. Zanesville, Ohio: Putnam and Clark, 1816.

Sklar, Kathryn Kish. *Catharine Beecher: A Study in American Domesticity*. New Haven, Conn.: Yale University Press, 1973.

——. "The Schooling of Girls and Changing Community Values in Massachusetts Towns, 1750–1820." *History of Education Quarterly* 33 (1993): 511–42.

Slack, Paul. *The Invention of Improvement: Information and Material Progress in Seventeenth-Century England*. Oxford: Oxford University Press, 2015.

Sloat, Caroline F. "Connecticut's Home Dairies, c. 1800: 'Of Too Great Utility to Be Passed over in Silence.'" In *Voices of the New Republic: Connecticut Towns, 1800–1832*, vol. 2, *What We Think*, edited by Howard R. Lamar, 75–84, 272–74. New Haven: Connecticut Academy of Arts and Sciences, 2003.

Smith, Andrew F. "In Praise of Maize: The Rise and Fall of Corny Poetry." In *Food in the Arts*, edited by Harlan Walker, 194–205. Devon, Eng.: Prospect, 1999.

Smith, E. *The Compleat Housewife; or, Accomplish'd Gentlewoman's Companion*. 1753, 1773. Reprint, London: Literary Services and Production, 1968.

Smith, Elihu Hubbard. "Original Communications." *Monthly Magazine and British Register* 6, no. 37 (October 1798): 250–51.

Smith, J. Eugene. *One Hundred Years of Hartford's Courant: From Colonial Times through the Civil War*. New Haven, Conn.: Yale University Press, 1949.

Spiller, Elizabeth. "Introductory Note." In *Seventeenth-Century English Recipe Books; Cooking, Physic and Chirugery in the Works of Elizabeth Talbot Grey and Aletheia Talbot Howard*, edited by Elizabeth Spiller, ix–li. Burlington, Vt.: Ashgate, 2008.

Sprackling, Helen. *Customs on the Table Top: How New England Housewives Set out Their Tables*. Sturbridge, Mass.: Old Sturbridge Village, 1958.

Stavely, Keith W. F. *Puritan Legacies: Paradise Lost and the New England Tradition, 1630–1890*. Ithaca, N.Y.: Cornell University Press, 1987.

——. "The World All before Them: Milton and the Rising Glory of America." *Studies in Eighteenth-Century Culture* 20 (1990): 147–64.

Stavely, Keith, and Kathleen Fitzgerald. *America's Founding Food: The Story of New England Cooking*. Chapel Hill: University of North Carolina Press, 2004.

——. *Northern Hospitality: Cooking by the Book in New England*. Amherst: University of Massachusetts Press, 2011.

Stephen, Leslie, and Sidney Lee, eds. *Dictionary of National Biography*. 22 vols. London: Smith, Elder, 1908–9.

St. George, Robert Blair. "Artifacts of Regional Consciousness in the Connecticut River Valley, 1700–1780." In *Material Life in America, 1600–1860*, edited by Robert Blair St. George, 335–56. Boston: Northeastern University Press, 1988.

Stokes, Melvyn. "Introduction." In *The Market Revolution in America: Social, Politi-*

cal, and Religious Expressions, 1800–1880, edited by Melvyn Stokes and Stephen Conway, 1–20. Charlottesville: University Press of Virginia, 1996.

Sweeney, Kevin M. "From Wilderness to Arcadian Vale: Material Life in the Connecticut River Valley, 1635–1760." In *The Great River: Art and Society of the Connecticut Valley, 1635–1820,* edited by Gerald R. W. Ward and William N. Hosley, Jr., 17–27. Hartford: Wadsworth Atheneum, 1985.

———. "Furniture and the Domestic Environment in Wethersfield, Connecticut, 1639–1800." In *Material Life in America, 1600–1860,* edited by Robert Blair St. George, 261–90. Boston: Northeastern University Press, 1988.

Taylor, Alan. *William Cooper's Town: Power and Persuasion on the Frontier of the Early American Republic.* New York: Vintage, 1995.

Taylor, Theodora. "Amelia Simmons: An American Orphan." *Atlantic Monthly* 104 (1909): 425–28.

Theophano, Janet. *"Eat My Words": Reading Women's Lives through the Cookbooks They Wrote.* New York: Palgrave, 2002.

Thomas, Isaiah. *The History of Printing in America, with a Biography of Printers.* 2nd edition. Vol. 1. Albany, 1874. Reprint, New York: Burt Franklin, [1964?].

———. *The History of Printing in America, with a Biography of Printers.* Vol. 2. Worcester, Mass.: Isaiah Thomas, 1810.

Thomas and Andrews's Catalogue of Books, for Sale, . . . at Their Book and Stationary Store . . . Boston. Boston: Thomas and Andrews, 1793.

Thompson, E. P. *The Making of the English Working Class.* New York: Vintage, 1966.

Thornton, Tamara Plakins. *Cultivating Gentlemen: The Meaning of Country Life among the Boston Elite, 1785–1860.* New Haven, Conn.: Yale University Press, 1989.

———. *Handwriting in America: A Cultural History.* New Haven, Conn.: Yale University Press, 1996.

Towner, Lawrence W. "The Indentures of Boston's Poor Apprentices, 1734–1805." In *Past Imperfect: Essays on History, Libraries, and the Humanities,* edited by Robert W. Karrow, Jr., and Alfred F. Young, 36–55. Chicago: University of Chicago Press, 1993.

Tracy, Joseph. *The Great Awakening: A History of the Revival of Religion in the Time of Edwards and Whitefield.* Boston: Tappan and Dennet, 1842.

Trebay, Guy. "At Donohue's, a Nightly Steak, a Life Gone By." *New York Times,* May 29, 2015.

Trumbull, J. Hammond, ed. *The Memorial History of Hartford County Connecticut, 1633–1884.* 2 vols. Boston: Edward L. Osgood, 1886.

Trumbull, John, *M'Fingal: A Modern Epic Poem, in Four Cantos.* Hartford: Hudson and Goodwin, 1782.

Tyler, Bennet, comp. *New England Revivals as They Existed at the Close of the Eighteenth and the Beginning of the Nineteenth Centuries, Compiled Principally from Narratives First Published in the Connecticut Evangelical Magazine.* 1846. Reprint, Wheaton, Ill.: Richard Owen Roberts, 1980.

Ulrich, Laurel Thatcher. *The Age of Homespun: Objects and Stories in the Creation of an American Myth.* New York: Knopf, 2001.

Unger, Harlow Giles. *Noah Webster: The Life and Times of an American Patriot.* New York: Wiley, 1998.

Vanderpoel, Emily Noyes. *Chronicles of a Pioneer School from 1792 to 1833, Being the History of Miss Sarah Pierce and Her Litchfield School.* Edited by Elizabeth C. Barney Buel. Cambridge, Mass.: University Press, 1903.

Vester, Katharina. *A Taste of Power: Food and American Identities.* Oakland: University of California Press, 2015.

Vickers, Daniel. "Fisheries." In *Voices of the New Republic: Connecticut Towns, 1800–1832*, vol. 2, *What We Think*, edited by Howard R. Lamar, 127–31, 280–81. New Haven: Connecticut Academy of Arts and Sciences, 2003.

Vinton, John Adams. "Parsons Cooke." *Congregational Quarterly* 14 (1872): 219–45.

Waggoner, Paul E. "Fertile Farms among the Stones." In *Voices of the New Republic: Connecticut Towns, 1800–1832*, vol. 2, *What We Think*, edited by Howard R. Lamar, 45–57, 269–71. New Haven: Connecticut Academy of Arts and Sciences, 2003.

Wall, Wendy. *Recipes for Thought: Knowledge and Taste in the Early Modern English Kitchen.* Philadelphia: University of Pennsylvania Press, 2016.

Wansey, Henry. *An Excursion to the United States of North America in the Summer of 1794.* 2nd edition. Salisbury, Eng.: J. Easton, 1798.

Ward, Barbara McLean. "Metalwares." In *The Great River: Art and Society of the Connecticut Valley, 1635–1820*, edited by Gerald R. W. Ward and William N. Hosley, Jr., 273–339. Hartford: Wadsworth Atheneum, 1985.

Warner, Michael. *The Letters of the Republic: Publication and the Public Sphere in Eighteenth-Century America.* Cambridge, Mass.: Harvard University Press, 1990.

Washington, George. *The Diaries of George Washington.* Edited by Donald Jackson and Dorothy Twohig. 6 vols. Charlottesville: University Press of Virginia, 1976–79.

Wass, Ann Buermann, and Michelle Webb Fandrich. *Clothing through American History: The Federal Era through Antebellum, 1786–1860.* Santa Barbara, Cal.: Greenwood Press, 2010.

Watts, Steven. "Ministers, Misanthropes, and Mandarins: The Federalists and the Culture of Capitalism." In *Federalists Reconsidered*, edited by Doron Ben-Atar and Barbara B. Oberg, 157–75. Charlottesville: University Press of Virginia, 1998.

Weaver, William L. *History of Ancient Windham, Ct.: Genealogy.* Willimantic, Conn.: Weaver and Curtiss, 1864.

Weber, Bruce. "Robert H. Ellsworth Is Dead at 85 after a Life Devoted to Chinese Art." *New York Times,* August 7, 2014.

Webster, Noah. *The American Spelling Book; Containing, the Rudiments of the English Language for the Use of Schools in the United States.* 19th edition. Philadelphia: Johnson and Warner, 1816.

——. *Sketches of American Policy.* Hartford: Hudson and Goodwin, 1785.

——. *Ten Letters to Dr. Joseph Priestly [sic].* New Haven, Conn.: Read and Morse, 1800.

Weyler, Karen A. *Empowering Words: Outsiders and Authorship in Early America.* Athens: University of Georgia Press, 2013.

Wheaton, Barbara Ketcham. *Savoring the Past: The French Kitchen and Table from 1300 to 1789.* Philadelphia: University of Pennsylvania Press, 1983.

White, Lisa. "The Impact of Historic Lighting." In *Interior Finishes and Fittings for Historic Building Conservation,* edited by Michael Forsyth and Lisa White, 143–62. Oxford: Wiley-Blackwell, 2012.

Whiting, Harriet. *Domestic Cookery.* Boston, 1819.

The Whole Duty of a Woman. London: T. Read, 1737.

Willan, Anne, with Mark Cherniavsky and Kyri Claflin. *The Cookbook Library: Four Centuries of the Cooks, Writers, and Recipes That Made the Modern Cookbook.* Berkeley: University of California Press, 2012.

Wilson, C. Anne. *Food and Drink in Britain: From the Stone Age to the Nineteenth Century.* Chicago: Academy Chicago, 1991.

Wilson, Lisa. *Ye Heart of a Man: The Domestic Life of Men in Colonial New England.* New Haven, Conn.: Yale University Press, 1999.

Wilson, Mary Tolford. "Amelia Simmons Fills a Need: *American Cookery,* 1796." *William and Mary Quarterly,* 3rd ser., 14 (1957): 16–30.

Winthrop, Robert C. *Life and Letters of John Winthrop.* 2 vols. Boston: Little, Brown, 1869.

Wolf, Stephanie Grauman. *As Various as Their Land: The Everyday Lives of Eighteenth-Century Americans.* New York: HarperCollins, 1993.

Women Invited to War; or, A Friendly Address to the Honourable Women of the United States. By a Daughter of America. Boston: Edes and Son, 1787.

Wood, Gordon S. "Conspiracy and the Paranoid Style: Causality and Deceit in the Eighteenth Century." *William and Mary Quarterly,* 3rd ser., 39 (1982): 401–41.

——. *Empire of Liberty: A History of the Early Republic, 1789–1815.* Oxford: Oxford University Press, 2009.

Woodward, P. H. *One Hundred Years of the Hartford Bank Now the Hartford National Bank of Hartford, Conn.* Hartford: Case, Lockwood, and Brainard, 1892.

Wordsworth, William. *The Poetical Works of Wordsworth.* Edited by Thomas Hutchinson and Ernest de Selincourt. 1904. Reprint, London: Oxford University Press, 1936.

Yokota, Kariann Akemi. *Unbecoming British: How Revolutionary America Became a Postcolonial Nation.* Oxford: Oxford University Press, 2011.

Zagarri, Rosemarie. "Gender and the First Party System." In *Federalists Reconsidered,* edited by Doron Ben-Atar and Barbara B. Oberg, 118–34. Charlottesville: University Press of Virginia, 1998.

Zakim, Michael. *Ready-Made Democracy: A History of Men's Dress in the American Republic, 1760–1860.* Chicago: University of Chicago Press, 2003.

Zboray, Ronald J., and Mary Saracino Zboray. *Voices without Votes: Women and Politics in Antebellum New England.* Durham: University of New Hampshire Press, 2010.

Zea, Philip. "Furniture." In *The Great River: Art and Society of the Connecticut Valley, 1635–1820,* edited by Gerald R. W. Ward and William N. Hosley, Jr., 185–271. Hartford: Wadsworth Atheneum, 1985.

———. *Useful Improvements, Innumerable Temptations: Pursuing Refinement in Rural New England.* Deerfield, Mass.: Historic Deerfield, 1998.

Ziff, Larzer. *Puritanism in America: New Culture in a New World.* New York: Viking, 1973.

Index

Gardiner, Anne Gibbons, 29, 46–47, 49, 215
gentility. *See* refinement
Georgics (Virgil), 102, 175
Gere family: Isaac, 87, Jemima Kingsley, 87
Glasse, Hannah
—*The Art of Cookery Made Plain and Easy*:
 about, 43; *American Cookery* and, 197,
 205–6; authorship 39–40; dishes in, 190,
 197; English foodways and, 42; French
 dimension of, 37; in North America,
 29, 46, 212–13, 216; plagiarism and, 47;
 price, 16, 259, 290n12; social structure
 and, 189–90; title, 198
—career, 42–43
—*The Compleat Confectioner*, 43
—*The Servant's Directory*, 43
Glasse, John, 43
Glover, Joseph, 52–53
Goodrich, Samuel, 164
Goodrich, Samuel ("Peter Parley"), 58
Goodwin family
—Daniel, 116, 299n3
—Daniel (son of Daniel), 115–16
—George: about, 112; authorship of *American
 Cookery* and, 225, 241–42; career, 56–58,
 77, 221; social position, 27, 93–95
—Mary Edwards, 95, 116
—Samuel, 94–95
—See also *Connecticut Courant*; Hudson &
 Goodwin
*Grammatical Institute of the English Language,
 A. See* Webster, Noah: Webster's Blue
 Back Speller
Great Awakening, 24, 55, 314n33
Green family: S., 12, 59; Samuel, 53;
 Thomas, 56–57, 59; Timothy, 54
Greenleaf, Thomas, 63, 145, 295n30,
 312n74
Guthrie, William, 69

Hale, David, 261
Hale, Sarah Josepha, 16
Hall, Elizabeth, 118
Hamilton, Alexander, 101
handwriting, 238–39
Hanover, House of, 37–38
Hapless Orphan, The: advertisements,
 311n35; *American Cookery* and, 230, 240;
 plot, 229, 234; setting, 229–30
Harris, Daniel, 136
Harrison, Henry, 50
Harrison, Sarah, 46, 212–13
Harrop, Joseph, 43, 240

Hart, Levi, 261
Haswell, Anthony, 68
Henrietta Maria (wife of Charles I), 33,
 292n13
Hitchcock, Enos, 311n38
Hogarth, William, 7
Holt, John, 55
Hooker, Thomas, 264
Hopkins, J., 53
Howard, Henry, 37, 49
Hudson family
—Barzillai: about, 112; career, 57–58; social
 position, 27, 94–96
—Barzillai (grandson of Barzillai), 94
—Hannah Bunce Watson, 57–58, 95–96, 225
—Henry, 93–94
—See also *Connecticut Courant*; Hudson &
 Goodwin
Hudson & Goodwin: *American Cookery*
 and, 11–12, 26, 72, 112, 197, 220,
 308n45; Charles R. & George Webster
 and, 56, 77–79, 221, 242; Connecticut
 Wits and, 26, 101, 225, 240; employees,
 26, 68, 77, 221; enterprises, 11, 58,
 65–67, 130; insurance industry and, 94;
 political attitudes, 58, 65, 78, 101, 243;
 pseudonymous authorship and, 241–42;
 publications, 58, 61–62, 70–71, 74–76,
 100, 111, 117, 204, 223, 225, 313n8
humors, Galenic theory of, 34
Humphreys, David: *The Anarchiad*, 101;
 career, 27; Connecticut Academy of
 Arts and Sciences and, 109; *Poem on the
 Happiness of America*, 25, 102
Huntington, Samuel, 170
Hutchinson, Anne, 54

Illinois: College, 266; New England
 settlement and, 266
Indiana, Indianapolis, 139
influence, of *American Cookery*, 14–17
Ingersoll, Jared, 98, 251

Jackson, Sarah, 42
Jeffersonians, 26, 101–2, 173, 242–43, 265,
 312n74, 316n14
Johnson, Mary, 41, 46
Johnson, Samuel, 39
Johnston, Martha, 134

Kalm, Pehr, 253
Kane, Anne Eliza Clark, 128
Kane, Oliver, 128

KEITH STAVELY and KATHLEEN FITZGERALD are the authors of two previous books together, *America's Founding Food* (2004) and *Northern Hospitality* (University of Massachusetts Press, 2011), which have become standard works in the field of food studies. They have contributed to the *Proceedings* of the *Oxford Symposium on Food and Cookery* and *The Oxford Companion to Sugar and Sweets,* and have frequently spoken on New England and American foodways at historical societies, museums, libraries, and conferences, both here and abroad.

Stavely is a retired library director and an award-winning scholar of transatlantic Puritanism. Fitzgerald is director of the Willett Free Library in Saunderstown, Rhode Island. They live in Jamestown, Rhode Island.